interpretive simulations

Instructions for Students

To register and pay individually to access the required ebook and simulation for your course, please follow these steps:

1 **Watch for your Carpenter/Sanders StratSim access information email.** You will receive the following Carpenter Sanders StratSim access information in an email from Interpretive Simulations:

- User ID
- Password
- Site URL **http://www.interpretive.com/carpenter**

2 **Register and pay for Carpenter/Sanders StratSim.** Once you have your access information go to **www.interpretive.com/carpenter** to register by entering your User ID and Password where prompted to do so. After logging in, pay your individual license fee to access the ebook and simulation. You may also choose to purchase a printed version of the textbook.

3 **Access Carpenter Sanders/StratSim.** After paying the license fee, you will be able to access the ebook, simulation, and resources. Early payment and registration is recommended as all students in a team must have registered and paid before that team can participate in the simulation.

Need help? Go to

www.interpretive.com/carpenter

W9-BYK-411

Dynamic Perspectives on Strategy

What is it?

Dynamic perspectives on strategy give students a means of connecting the dots between internal resources and capabilities, ever- and increasingly rapid-changing external conditions, and firm and industry survival and profitability. Main concepts and tools related to dynamic strategy are put into action through student engagement in the integrated StratSim simulation.

Why is it important?

Taking a dynamic perspective on strategy allows students to see that change is inevitable in strategy, but it can occur rapidly or slowly. StratSim lets students experience this dynamism, and see how change is a function of their strategic choices and competitors' countermoves.

Where do I find it?

1. Chapter 6, *Crafting Business Strategy for Dynamic Contexts*, speaks directly to dynamic approaches to strategy and translates recent path-breaking research on dynamic perspectives into concepts and models students can use.

2. Using the "Strategy Diamond," which is introduced in Chapter 1 (Exhibit 1.5) on pages 12–16, students are taught to seek internal coherence and consistency in changing external environments.

3. Throughout the experience with the StratSim simulation.

Strategic Leadership

What is it?

Strategic Leadership is the role that top- and middle-managers play in strategy formulation and implementation. Students are the leadership, individually and in teams, in StratSim.

Why is it important?

Strategic Leadership is important in regards to dynamic strategy because managers are often the key sources of dynamic capabilities that allow firms to compete in turbulent and rapidly changing competitive environments. The benefits are three-fold:

1. Students can better see how the strategic tone is set at the top but that successful implementation is dependent on individuals like themselves.

2. The instructor has an opportunity to talk about the personalities of the executives involved in the cases they use, and how those personalities may play out in strategy formulation and implementation.

3. Beyond concepts, just as we see the effect of top managers on the strategies of real firms, students can see their personalities and capabilities, and those of competing teams, play out in their StratSim choices.

Where do I find it?

Strategic Leadership is first introduced in Chapter 1 (*Introducing Strategic Management*) on page 7, and then it is more fully developed in Chapter 2 (*Leading Strategically Through Effective Vision and Mission*). All chapters also include discussions of leaders in action.

The Interdependence of Formulation and Implementation

What is it?

Students will walk away from this material, and the StratSim experience, with a clear understanding that formulation and implementation are interdependent, and that effective formulation takes implementation details into account early in the strategy process.

Why is it important?

Executives often say, "I would rather have a mediocre strategy with great implementation than a great strategy with mediocre implementation."

Where do I find it?

The interdependence of formulation and implementation is most clearly illustrated through the StratSim experience. In the text, students see this interdependence in the "How Would *You* Do That?" feature. This pedagogic tool is located in every chapter, and is supported with end-of-chapter activities and material in the *Instructor Manual*. Examples of this feature can be found in Chapter 1 on pages 18–19 (JetBlue), Chapter 2 on pages 54–55 (Tritec), and in Chapter 6 on pages 184–185 ([yellow tail]).

Mason Carpenter

Professor Carpenter has a B.S. in Business Administration from California State University (Humboldt) and University of Copenhagen, Denmark, and an M.B.A. from California State University (Bakersfield). He also completed graduate studies in enology at the University of Bordeaux, France. Before obtaining his Ph.D. in strategy at the University of Texas, Austin, he worked in banking, management consulting, and software development. His research concerns corporate governance, top management teams, and the strategic management of global firms, and is published in *Strategic Management Journal, Academy of Management Journal, Academy of Management Review, Academy of Management Executive,* and *Human Resource Management.* He serves on the editorial boards of the *Academy of Management Journal, Academy of Management Review, Journal of Strategic Management Education,* and *Organization Science.* He was also voted Professor of the Year by M.B.A. students, and identified as one of the most popular professors in the *BusinessWeek* M.B.A. poll. He recently received the Larson Excellence in Teaching award from the School of Business, and the University of Wisconsin's Emil H. Steiger Distinguished Teaching Award.

Gerry Sanders

Professor Sanders is an associate professor and the Department Chair in Organizational Leadership and Strategy at the Marriott School of Management at Brigham Young University. He earned a Ph.D. in strategic management from the University of Texas at Austin. In 1996, Professor Sanders joined the faculty at BYU, where he teaches strategic management. He has also been a visiting professor at Penn State University. His research is in the area of corporate governance and its affects on firm strategy and performance. He has published extensively in the *Academy of Management Journal, Strategic Management Journal, Journal of Management, Human Resource Management,* among other outlets. His work on the effects of stock option pay has been featured in such outlets as the *New York Times,* the *Economist, BusinessWeek, CFO,* and on National Public Radio's Marketplace. Professor Sanders is on the Editorial Board of the *Academy of Management Journal* and the *Academy of Management Review.* In 2001 he received the Marriott School's J. Earl Garrett Fellowship and in 2003 he was designated a University Young Scholar. Prior to entering graduate school, Dr. Sanders spent twelve years in industry managing the acquisitions and financing of large portfolios of commercial real estate.

A Dynamic Difference

The version of **Strategic Management: A Dynamic Perspective,** and the *Integrated StratSim Experience,* is the product of an exciting new partnership that is designed to give you and your students an indepth and enduring understanding of Strategic Management. *StratSim* lets your students live and learn our fresh approach to strategy. This novel approach takes a dynamic perspective of competitive environments and firms. allowing for an integrated view of internal and external drivers of competitive advantage, a tight link between strategy formulation and implementation, and an explicit integration of the role of strategic leadership (at many levels of management) in formulating and implementing strategy.

StratSim is a competitive business strategy simulation that covers all the functional areas of managing a business. Teams compete directly against each other in this capstone simulation, within the environment of the fast-paced automobile industry. You control the difficulty level of the simulation by customizing the simulation with the many available options, in order to make the experience appropriate for undergraduate or graduate applications. Because *StratSim* is customized and fully integrated with *Strategic Management: A Dynamic Perspective,* its overarching theme is strategic management. It is at the core of all decisions made in *StratSim Management.* Students must determine their firms' resources and capabilities, and, as in the real world, even start the simulation with different resource positions across firms. They must analyze these in the context of their industry environment. Students then articulate their vision and mission for their organization and begin to formulate a strategy. The real learning comes when students then implement their strategies and must continually monitor their progress, make adjustments as needed, adapt to changing industry dynamics and evolving patterns of competition. Unlike most other simulations, *StratSim* incorporates many of the economic drivers of competitive advantage, such as economies of scale and scope. Thus, the integration of the text and simulation provides a powerful learning experience.

Our treatment of the process of strategic management—managing the firm's strategy formulation and implementation over time—allows us to bring *management* back into strategy. By returning strategic leadership into the teaching of strategy, and putting the students in hands-on leadership and strategic decision making roles through *StratSim,* students at all levels will experience and more readily see themselves as instrumental in the strategic management process.

Mason Carpenter   Wm. Gerard Sanders

Reviewers

Many people were involved in reviewing the manuscript, the book design, and our teaching package. All deserve special thanks.

Yusaf Akbar, *Southern New Hampshire University*

Peter Antoniou, *California State University at San Marcos*

Ram Baliga, *Wake Forest University*

Kunal Banerji, *Florida Atlantic University*

Pamela Barr, *Georgia State University*

Tim Blumentritt, *Marquette University*

Ingvild Brown, *George Mason University*

F. William Brown, *Montana State University*

Patricia Buhler, *Goldey-Beacom College*

Aruna Chandra, *Indiana State University*

Jim Combs, *Florida State University*

Joseph Coombs, *University of Richmond*

Kevin Cooper, *Cal Poly at San Luis Obispo*

Wade Danis, *Georgia State University*

Ajay Das, *Baruch College*

James Davis, *University of Notre Dame*

Robert DeFillippi, *Suffolk University*

Scott Droege, *Mississippi State University*

David Dudek, *University of Hartford*

Jo Ann Duffy, *Sam Houston State University*

Linda Edelman, *Bentley College*

Teri Elkins, *University of Houston*

William Enser, *University of Tennessee*

Charles Fishel, *San Jose State University*

Michael Frew, *Oklahoma City University*

Marianne Gauss, *LaSalle University*

Nicholas Georgantzas, *Fordham University*

Drew Harris, *Longwood University*

Donald Hatfield, *Virginia Tech*

Bruce Heiman, *San Francisco State University*

Scott Henley, *Oklahoma City University*

Theodore Herbert, *Rollins College*

Glenn Hoetker, *University of Illinois*

R. Kabaliswaran, *New York University*

Hyungu Kang, *Central Michigan University*

Marios Katsioloudes, *Saint Joseph's University*

Edward Levitas, *University of Wisconsin at Milwaukee*

Scott Marshall, *Portland State University*

Robert McGowan, *University of Denver*

Gerry McNamara, *Michigan State University*

Arlyn Melcher, *Southern Illinois University at Carbondale*

John Mezias, *University of Miami*

Grant Miles, *University of North Texas*

Patricia Nemetz Mills, *Eastern Washington University*

Rex Mitchell, *California State University at Northridge*

Jeffrey Nystrom, *University of Colorado at Denver*

Clifford Perry, *Florida International University*

Joseph Peyrefitte, *University of Southern Mississippi*

Steven Phelan, *University of Nevada at Las Vegas*

Gerhard Plaschka, *DePaul University*

Douglas Polley, *Saint Cloud State University*

Annette Ranft, *Florida State University*

Violina Rindova, *University of Maryland*

David Robinson, *Texas Tech University*

Michael Russo, *University of Oregon*

James Schaap, *University of Nevada*

Joseph Schenk, *University of Dayton*

Anurag Sharma, *University of Massachusetts*

Roy Suddaby, *University of Iowa*

Gordon Walker, *Southern Methodist University*

Edward Ward, *Saint Cloud State University*

Marvin Washington, *Texas Tech University*

John Watson, *Saint Bonaventure University*

Gwendolyn Whitfield, *Pepperdine University*

Robert Wiggins, *University of Memphis*

Duane Windsor, *Rice University*

Robert Wiseman, *Michigan State University*

Diana Wong, *Eastern Michigan University*

Mary Zellmer-Bruhn, *University of Minnesota*

STRATEGIC MANAGEMENT
A Dynamic Perspective

INTEGRATED STRATSIM SIMULATION EXPERIENCE

Mason A. Carpenter

University of Wisconsin-Madison

Wm. Gerard Sanders

Brigham Young University

In collaboration with Stu James, Interpretive Simulations

PEARSON

Prentice Hall

Upper Saddle River, New Jersey 07458

Library of Congress Cataloging-in-Publication Data

Carpenter, Mason Andrew.
 Strategic management : a dynamic perspective—integrated StratSim
simulation experience / Mason A. Carpenter, Wm. Gerard Sanders.
  p. cm.
  ISBN-13: 978-0-13-614905-7 (alk. paper)
  ISBN-10: 0-13-614905-7 (alk. paper)
 1. Strategic planning. I. Sanders, William Gerard. II. Title.
  HD30.28.C3773 2008
  658.4'012—dc22   2007000500

Senior Acquisitions Editor: David Parker
VP/Editorial Director: Jeff Shelstad
Senior Development Editor: Ronald Librach
Development Editor: Gina Huck
Editorial Assistant: Denise Vaughn
Marketing Manager: Anne Howard
Associate Director, Production Editorial: Judy Leale
Production Editor: Kevin H. Holm
Permissions Coordinator: Charles Morris
Manufacturing Buyer: Diane Peirano
Creative Director: Maria Lange
Interior Design: Solid State Graphics
Cover Design: Solid State Graphics
Cover Photos: Dan Loh/AP World Wide Photos; FP Photo/Jeff Christensen/Newscom; Chris Hondros/Getty Images
Illustration (Interior): Matrix
Photo Development Editor: Amy Ray
Director, Image Resource Center: Melinda Reo
Manager, Rights and Permissions: Zina Arabia
Manager, Visual Research: Beth Brenzel
Manager, Cover Visual Research & Permissions: Karen Sanatar
Image Permission Coordinator: Nancy Seise
Photo Researcher: Diane Austin; Terry Stratford
Composition: Carlisle Publishing Services
Project Management: Carlisle Publishing Services
Printer/Binder: Courier–Kendallville
Typeface: Minion 10/12

Credits and acknowledgments borrowed from other sources and reproduced, with permission, in this textbook appear on appropriate page or on page 289.

Pearson Education LTD.
Pearson Education Singapore, Pte. Ltd
Pearson Education, Canada, Ltd
Pearson Education–Japan

Pearson Education Australia PTY, Limited
Pearson Education North Asia Ltd
Pearson Educación de Mexico, S.A. de C.V.
Pearson Education Malaysia, Pte. Ltd

10 9 8 7 6 5 4 3 2 1
ISBN-10:   0-13-614905-7
ISBN-13: 978-0-13-614905-7

DEDICATION

My work on this book is dedicated to my wife Lisa, and to our boys Wesley and Zachary.

—MAC

This book is dedicated to my family—my wife Kathy, and our children Ashley, Adam, and Noelle—for providing the patience and support necessary to complete this project.

—WGS

BRIEF CONTENTS

CONTENTS

PART TWO   THE INTERNAL AND EXTERNAL ENVIRONMENT OF STRATEGY

PART THREE   **BUSINESS, CORPORATE, AND GLOBAL STRATEGIES**

5 Creating Business Strategies   130

PART FOUR   **LEVERAGING STRATEGIES FOR SUCCESS**

Acknowledgments

We wrote this book to improve the student and faculty experience with learning and teaching about strategic management. As we take the perspective of practicing managers, it is fitting that we first acknowledge the students, faculty, and managers who were directly and indirectly engaged in developing *Strategic Management: A Dynamic Perspective*. This includes our own students and colleagues at the University of Wisconsin-Madison and Brigham Young University, the many executives and managers we have consulted with and brought into our classes, and those we worked with in our travels as we developed this book over the past 4 years.

Although we had a specific vision for the book, we can't take full credit for all the content that supports that vision. In particular, we want to acknowledge the contributions of the many researchers whose work helps managers understand and cope with the challenges of crafting and implementing strategies in changing times. You will see their work cited throughout the text, and we encourage you to read the original studies (including our own) upon which the content of this book is based. We also want to acknowledge the many managers whose views and daily challenges helped us develop a theoretically rigorous, yet practically relevant and readable approach to strategic management. At many points along the way these colleagues challenged us with observations like, "That's nice, but how would you do that?" and forced us to continually refine our writing to connect the dots—from concept to action—so to speak.

Out of this group of researchers and managers, one team deserves particular note. This would be Don Hambrick at Penn State University and Jim Fredrickson at the University of Texas at Austin. These talented and prolific researchers and award-winning teachers have been leading the bandwagon to put managers back into strategy, and have been exceptional mentors to both of us. You can see their imprint in our early research, in the managerial orientation of our textbook, and in the strategy diamond that ties all the chapters together. This strategy diamond will endure long after they are done writing; it will create a rich and relevant learning environment for students of strategy, and it will provide managers a tool for thinking through and answering in the affirmative, "Yes, I really have a strategy!"

Finally, we thank our team at Prentice Hall for making the book a reality. We wanted a publisher who shared and supported our vision and high aspirations for the next generation of undergraduate and MBA strategy textbooks. We determined that Prentice Hall was a leader in product development and, most important, in selling those products once developed and published. After all, that is the message of our book—the interdependence of strategy formulation and implementation in dynamic contexts. We both reflected on the quality of our interactions with our new publisher's representatives and it was clear that Prentice Hall's reps were the best we had seen on our respective campuses. This combination of editorial, marketing, and sales excellence sealed the deal for us.

1

Part One
Strategy and
Strategic
Leadership in
Dynamic
Times

Introducing Strategic Management

After studying this chapter, you should be able to:

1. Understand what a *strategy* is and identify the difference between business-level and corporate-level strategy.

2. Understand why we study *strategic management*.

3. Understand the relationship between *strategy formulation* and *implementation*.

4. Describe the determinants of *competitive advantage*.

5. Recognize the difference between the *fundamental* view and the *dynamic* view of *competitive advantage*.

6. Understand how the StratSim simulation will allow you to study strategic management in a dynamic, hands-on environment.

▶ **1962**
Wal-Mart's
first store opens in
Rogers, Arkansas.

▶ **1970–1971**
Wal-Mart goes public in 1970.
Its first stock split occurs the
following year
(market price: $47.00).

A TALE OF TWO STORES

Sears' Early Dominance

The Sears versus Wal-Mart saga provides a striking example of strategy in action.[1] Sears was started as a catalog business in 1891, and through a combination of marketing savvy and a broad array of product offerings, sales grew briskly. With a vision of bringing the manufactured wonders of the world to the common people, the Sears Roebuck catalog offered everything from "guaranteed cures for stupidity" to products once available only to the social elite. To exploit its rapid growth, Sears soon took control of the production and distribution of its product offerings by establishing a network of factories that it either owned or financed.

Sears applied its catalog retail model to on-premise retailing in 1924, and from that point on, Sears dominated the retail industry for more than 50 years. At about the same time, General Robert E. Wood

▶ **1990–1991**
Wal-Mart's stock splits for the ninth time (market price: $62.50). The company enters the international market for the first time with the opening of Club Aurrera in Mexico City.

1995   2000

left competitor Montgomery Ward to lead Sears, where he would put in place the structures, systems, processes, people, and culture that would guide—and bind—Sears' strategy and actions far into the future.

Wood came to Ward, and then to Sears, as a graduate of West Point (Class of 1900). He had been in charge of logistics and supply during the building of the Panama Canal and had served as quartermaster general of the U.S. army in World War I. Upon discharge from the service, he joined Montgomery Ward as vice president in charge of merchandising. Wood was fascinated with census data, and it was his interest in and understanding of demographic and economic statistics that gave him insights into the deep changes taking place in the structure of the U.S. and Latin American markets.

Under Wood's leadership, Sears set the standard for competition in retailing with a business model that combined large and varied inventories of goods, product-line breadth, and distribution through both large-scale catalog operations and mall-based retail outlets, all supplied by a vast network of company-owned or company-controlled factories. Key players, including also-ran competitors Montgomery Ward and JCPenney, believed that the Sears way was the only way to compete in the industry. "There is no better illustration of what a business is and what managing means," declared a leading management guru, and during the 1960s, *Fortune* dubbed Sears "the paragon of retailers. It is number one in the United States, and number two, three, four and five."

As sales approached 1 to 2 percent of the country's gross domestic product in the 1960s and 1970s, Sears sought to dig deeper into America's pocketbook by moving into other businesses, including banking (Discover credit cards), investment (Dean Witter), and real estate services (Coldwell Banker), and investing further in an insurance business (Allstate) established in 1931.

Wal-Mart's Entry In 1973, however, just as Sears was crowning its success (and the legacy of General Woods) with the opening of its new corporate headquarters in the world's tallest building, Chicago's Sears' Tower, an even longer shadow on the future of retailing was being cast by Sam Walton's much more modest building in Bentonville, Arkansas—now corporate headquarters of Wal-Mart Stores Inc.

Sam Walton opened the first Wal-Mart Discount City store in 1962, after having run a successful Ben Franklin retail franchise for 20 years. Walton had grown up in the Depression and viewed hard work and thrift as a way of life. In building Wal-Mart, Walton brought these values to the company's culture, along with his never-say-never attitude and his against-the-odds management mentality. Although Target and Kmart also started operations in 1962, it would be the Wal-Mart strategy, fueled by Walton's passion to keep prices lower than those of his competitors, that redrew the map of global retailing. By 1970, the Wal-Mart chain had expanded to 30 stores in Arkansas, Missouri, and Oklahoma. Early expansion plans targeted rural areas with populations between 5,000 and 25,000. "Our key strategy," explained Walton, "was to put good-sized stores into little one-horse towns which everybody else was ignoring."

On the downside, Walton's geographical strategy meant that Wal-Mart had to build its own warehousing, transportation, and delivery systems from scratch. But because real estate and labor were less expensive in Wal-Mart's targeted U.S. locations, these investments actually lowered purchasing and carrying costs, and Walton passed the savings on to his customers in the form of lower prices. Wal-Mart built large warehouses so that it could buy in bulk, and the company-owned trucking fleet, which carried inventory from suppliers to storage and from storage to stores, further cut costs by moving inventory quickly from supplier to customer. Faced with dizzying growth in the 1980s, Wal-Mart then invested nearly $500 million in a state-of-the-art computerized inventory-management system that permitted managers to treat inventory as if it were all stored in one giant virtual warehouse (think of this concept as a forerunner of Amazon.com). By extending the technology to vendors, Wal-Mart not only strengthened its supplier relationships, but also shifted some of its carrying and distribution costs to vendors.

The paths of Sears and Wal-Mart crossed in the mid-1980s. At Sears, management was finding it increasingly difficult to balance the complex and competing needs of its hodgepodge of nonretail businesses like Allstate Insurance. The focus on nonretail businesses caused management to neglect retail operations, burdening the company with many outdated and unprofitable stores. On the retail side, one symptom of this neglect was Sears' slowness in adopting new information technologies. Also, its large investments in wholly owned production operations had made the once mighty retailer a lumbering dinosaur. Increased competition and declining market share would soon cause some industry analysts to sound the death knell for Sears, and over the next two decades the company steadily divested itself of its nonretail operations. The last of these, Sears' gargantuan credit-card operation, was sold to CitiGroup in late 2003 for $32 billion, and the company was, once again, a "pure" retailer.

Meanwhile, as Sears struggled to become leaner and more focused, Wal-Mart was systematically perfecting and expanding its powerful and highly profitable retailing model, primarily through its original Wal-Mart stores and, later, through its Sam's Warehouse Clubs and aggressive international expansion. As you can see in Exhibits 1.1 and 1.2, Sears' struggles vis-à-vis Wal-Mart were clearly visible—ranging from simple measures of firm size to overall profitability and market capitalization. Today, Wal-Mart is the largest retailer in the world, and the Wal-Mart model has become the dominant business model in worldwide retailing. It is interesting to see, however, that Wal-Mart's expansion globally has not been uniformly successful. For instance, it trails Carrefour in France, Tesco in the United Kingdom, and ALDI in Germany.

Sears, meanwhile, has made several unsuccessful efforts to turn itself around, and retail-industry experts have suggested that its best hope may be to plow the proceeds from the sale of its credit-card division back into its outdated retailing operations. Perhaps the most recent irony in the Sears saga is its acquisition by Kmart in 2005—within one year of Kmart's emergence from bankruptcy.

Why are some firms incredibly successful while others are not? And why is it that once they're successful, so few can sustain a high level of success? Although Sears was clearly once a very successful firm, even a half century of unrivaled success couldn't prevent Wal-Mart from taking over its position as the world's number-one retailer. In this text, we'll introduce you to the concepts that you'll need to answer questions about gaining and sustaining success in the world of business competition. ■

Exhibit 1.1 Two Retailers at a Glance

	Sears	**Wal-Mart**
Year founded	1891	1962
Stores, 1980	864	600
Stores, 2004	2,026	5,289
Revenues, 1980	$25,194 million	$1,643 million
Revenues, 2004	$36,100 million	$285,222 million
Net profits, 1980	$606 million (2.4% return on sales)	$55 million (3.3% return on sales)
Net profits, 2004	($507) million (−1.4% return on sales)	$10,267 million (3.6% return on sales)
Market capitalization, 1980	$4.8 billion	$1 billion
Market capitalization, 2004	$12.2 billion	$200.2 billion

Sources: "Sears, Roebuck & Co.," Hoover's (accessed August 4, 2005); "Wal-Mart Stores Inc.," Hoover's (accessed August 4, 2005); Wal-Mart Stores Inc., 2004 Annual Report (accessed August 4, 2005).

Exhibit 1.2 Sears and
Wal-Mart: A Financial
Comparison

*Source: Authors' analysis of data
compiled from Compustat.*

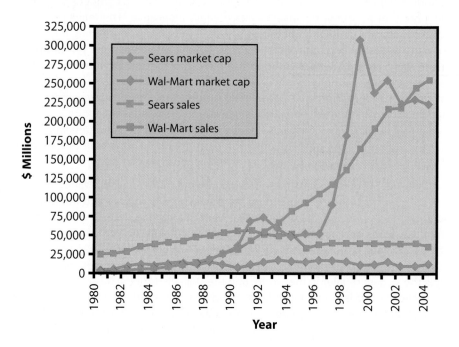

THREE OVERARCHING THEMES

As you've probably gathered from the topic of this book—*strategic management*—a firm's performance is directly related to the quality of its strategy and its competency in implementing it. You also need to understand that concerns about strategy preoccupy the minds of many top executives. Their responsibility is to see that the firm's whole is ultimately greater than the sum of its parts—whether these parts are distinct business units, such as Sears' retail operation and Allstate Insurance, or simply the functional areas that contribute to the performance of one particular business, such as Wal-Mart's massive distribution centers and retail operations. Good strategies are affected by and affect all of the functional areas of the firm, including marketing, finance, accounting, and operations. Thus, we'll also introduce you to the concepts and tools that you'll need to analyze the conditions of a firm and its industry, to formulate appropriate strategies, and to determine how to go about implementing a chosen strategy.

Three themes that run throughout this book are critical to developing competency in the field of strategic management:

1. ***Firms and industries are* dynamic *in nature.*** In recent years, theories and research have emerged on issues regarding dynamic markets and the importance of developing dynamic capabilities to create value. Our first theme, then, is the dynamic nature of both firms and their competitive environments. It's easy, for instance, to look at a financial snapshot of Wal-Mart and understand the competitive position that it commands in its industry. But we need to see Wal-Mart not as a snapshot but as an ongoing movie. Wal-Mart's current position wasn't the result of a single strategic decision but rather the product of many decisions made over time. Wal-Mart's current stock of resources and capabilities weren't always available to the firm; they had to be developed dynamically. For instance, its choice of remote locations required it to develop exceptional capabilities in logistics and supply-chain management. And as tempting as it is to use hindsight to see some of Wal-Mart's competitors as inept, they didn't sit idly by while Wal-Mart ascended to the top of the *Fortune* 500. For pedagogical simplicity, we first introduce some basic concepts in strategic management and then move on to discuss the concepts and tools that managers use to think of strategy in dynamic terms.

2. ***To succeed, the* formulation *of a good strategy and its* implementation *should be inextricably connected.*** Unfortunately, many managers tend to focus on formulating a plan of attack and give too little thought to implementing it until it's too late. Likewise, they may similarly give short shrift to the importance of strategic leadership in effectively bridging strategy formulation and implementation. In fact, research suggests that, on average, managers are better at formulating strategies

than they are at implementing them. This problem has been described as a "knowing–doing gap."[2] Effective managers realize that successfully implementing a good idea is at least as important as generating one. To implement strategies, the organization's leaders have numerous levers at their disposal. Levers such as organization structure, systems and processes, and people and rewards are tools that help strategists test for alignment—that is, the need for all of the firm's activities to complement each other and support the strategy.

3. ***Strategic leadership is essential if a firm is to both formulate and implement strategies that create value.*** Strategic leaders are those responsible for formulating firms' strategies—as a consequence of their hierarchical status in management this is their responsibility. In addition, strategic leadership plays two critical roles in successful strategy implementation, and it's important to highlight them here so that you can incorporate them into your own assessment of a strategy's feasibility as well as ensure that you include these roles in your implementation plans. Specifically, strategic leadership is responsible for (1) making substantive implementation-lever and resource-allocation decisions and (2) developing support for the strategy from key stakeholders.

The Role of the StratSim Simulation

SimConnect

StratSim provides an environment to experience these three overarching themes first-hand as managers of a large automobile manufacturer. Not only will you "watch" the on-going movie that is dynamic industry evolution, but you and your classmates also will become active participants or "actors" in that movie. Student teams will take over a uniquely positioned firm within the StratSim industry, with the challenge of formulating and implementing a successful business strategy. In effect, you will become the strategic leaders for your StratSim firm. However, because StratSim is a team-oriented experience, you will also have to develop support within your team for different strategic directions, and decide on the best organizational structure for managing and implementing your team's vision. Describing strategy formulation is one thing, but implementing a successful strategy in a dynamic setting is quite another, which is precisely the purpose of integrating the experiential nature of the simulation with the theory of this textbook. Therefore, with StratSim, you will be asked to go beyond gathering knowledge and on to experiencing and understanding at a more fundamental level through active learning. That will be your challenge in StratSim. We think you'll ultimately enjoy this challenge and enhance your understanding through this active approach to learning.

WHAT IS STRATEGIC MANAGEMENT?

Strategic management is the process by which a firm manages the formulation and implementation of its strategy. But we still need to ask ourselves: What is the *goal* of strategic management? What does "having a *strategy*" mean? Even if we're pretty sure that we have a strategy and a goal for it, how do we know whether we have a good strategy or a bad one?

strategic management Process by which a firm incorporates the tools and frameworks for developing and implementing a strategy

The Strategic Leader's Perspective

In the hit 2002 movie *My Big Fat Greek Wedding*, a proud Greek father (and businessman) challenges anyone who'll listen: "Say any word, and I'll tell you how the root of that word is Greek."[3] He's right about the word *strategy*, which is derived from the Greek *strategos*. Roughly translated, it means "the general's view," and thinking about military ranks and responsibilities is a good way to focus on the difference between the general's view and that of some lower-level officer. The primary responsibility of a lower-level officer might be supply logistics, infantry, or heavy armored vehicles. Thus, lower-level officers may not be too concerned with the overall plan because of their attention to detail in specific areas of responsibility. The general, however, must not only understand how *all* of the constituent parts interrelate, but must use that understanding to draw up a plan that will lead to victory—a strategy. In the business context, the idea of strategy, therefore, suggests a big-picture perspective on the firm and its context. We call this holistic view of the organization the *strategic leader's perspective*.

The success of a military strategy depends not only on the quality of the general's planning and the vision behind it, but also on the execution of the strategy by the forces under the general's command. In business settings, likewise, a strategy is of little use if it is not well executed. In addition, the quality of a strategy is often dependent on the leader's soliciting and utilizing the advice of other senior and mid-level leaders. In other words, a good leader can't afford to devise a strategy in isolation from the lower-level leaders who are responsible for executing it.

The ideas of strategy need not focus exclusively on military analogies just because the root of the word is from this context. You can see ideas analogous to the difference between the general's view and the lower-level officer's view in sports, education, personal life, and business. The important thing about the Greek derivation of the word *strategy* is that the big-picture perspective is fundamentally different from the detail of operational tactics.

In business, strategy requires a big-picture perspective. Up to this point, most of your business courses have probably focused on important but limited aspects of business. Indeed, most business-education classes are devoted to specialized areas of study on specific functional areas, such as finance or marketing. In strategic management, however, we're concerned with an overall, holistic view of the firm and its environment and the ways in which such a view determines the competitive decisions that businesspeople have to make. For this reason, when studying strategic management we generally take the perspective of the strategic leader. Recognize, however, that strategies often emerge from bottom-up processes and from fortuitous circumstances that the leader could not have anticipated. The strategic leader's perspective does not mean to suggest that plans are formulated in some linear fashion by a single leader. Rather, the strategic leader's perspective is the holistic consideration of the business and its environment rather than the myopic focus on a single functional area.

Why Study Strategy?

You may wonder why it is important to study strategy when your career is unlikely to begin at the level of strategic leadership. By the end of the chapter, the answer to this question should be obvious. But, by way of overview, it is important to understand that top executives are not lone wolves when it comes to devising and implementing strategy. They rely on lower-level managers to collect and analyze data regarding competition and commercial opportunities. Likewise, the better employees understand the firm's strategy, the better they'll be able to make choices that are consistent with it. It's critical, therefore, that managers at every level understand the firm's strategy and work toward implementing its strategic initiatives.

What Is Strategy?

The idea of "strategy" means different things to different people (and a lot of these ideas aren't particularly accurate).[4] In fact, experts in the field have formulated various definitions of *strategy*. We've adopted the simple and direct definition offered by Donald C. Hambrick and James W. Fredrickson, who define **strategy** as the central, integrated, externally oriented concept of how a firm will achieve its objectives.[5] A strategy thus encompasses the pattern of actions that have been taken and those that are to be taken by an organization in pursuing its objectives.[6]

strategy Central, integrated, externally focused concept of how the firm will achieve its objectives

Because firms are attempting to sell products or services to potential customers, an implication of strategy in this context is that the firm is attempting to gain an advantage over other potential providers of those products and services. Virtually all firms face some level of competition. A strategy helps a firm accomplish its objectives in the face of competition. Strategy is not, however, necessarily a zero-sum game in which one firm wins and one loses. In many instances, firms cooperate in some aspects of business and compete in others.

Exhibit 1.3 outlines the strategic management process that you will be exploring and applying throughout this textbook. From the exhibit, you can see how vision, goals and objectives, internal and external analysis, and implementation levers can be used to help formulate and implement strategy. Strategy outlines the means by which a firm intends to

Exhibit 1.3 The Strategic Management Process

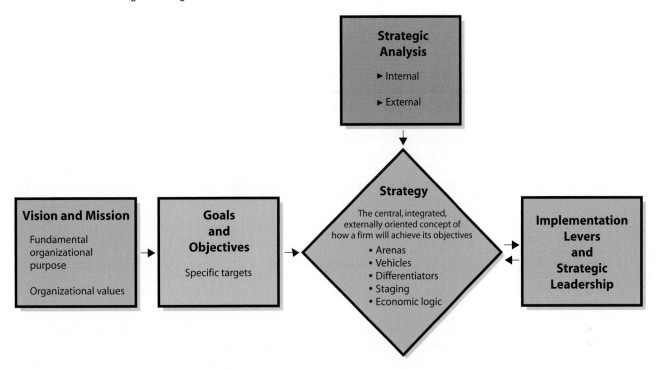

Source: Adapted from D. C. Hambrick and J. W. Fredrickson, "Are You Sure You Have a Strategy?" Academy of Management Executive *15:4 (2001), 48–59.*

create unique value for customers and other important stakeholders.[7] This definition of strategy is important because, as you will see later, it forces managers to think holistically and dynamically about what the firm does and why those activities consistently lead customers to prefer the firm's products and services over those of its competitors.

Business Strategy Versus Corporate Strategy

In studying strategy, you'll find it useful to distinguish between strategic issues at the *business level* and those at the *corporate level. StratSim* is primarily concerned with issues of business strategy. Some firms are focused sharply on their *business* strategy: They compete in only one or very few industries. Other firms compete in many industries. The opening vignette on Sears and Wal-Mart paints a picture of two firms that have similar core businesses (retailing) but have pursued vastly different corporate strategies—Wal-Mart has stuck with retailing, whereas Sears diversified into many unrelated industries, including insurance and stock brokerage services, before later divesting itself of these unrelated businesses. Some firms, such as General Electric (GE) or Vivendi, are called *conglomerates* because they're so diversified that it's difficult to pigeonhole them into any specific industry.

Consider the two largest competitors in the aircraft-engine industry. The largest is GE, with $11 billion in aircraft-engine sales; the second largest is Rolls-Royce PLC, with approximately $6.6 billion in total sales. Rolls-Royce gets most of its revenue—approximately 72 percent—from this industry. (The firm no longer makes luxury cars; the operation was parceled off to BMW and Volkswagen in 1998.) In contrast, GE is involved in hundreds of businesses, including such diverse enterprises as manufacturing light bulbs, medical devices, and commercial jet engines; providing home mortgages; broadcasting (it owns NBC); and operating self-storage facilities. It derives less than 10 percent of its revenue from aircraft engines. Within this industry, of course, both GE and Rolls-Royce face the same competitive pressures, such as determining how to compete against such rivals as Pratt & Whitney (the third-largest firm in the industry). In managing its portfolio of businesses, GE faces strategic issues that are less relevant to Rolls-Royce.

business strategy Strategy for competing against rivals within a particular industry

Business Strategy What sort of issues are these? **Business strategy** refers to the ways a firm goes about achieving its objectives within *a particular business*. In other words, one of GE's business strategies would be how it pursues its objectives within the jet engine business. This strategy may encompass such things as how it competes against Rolls-Royce for contracts from Boeing and Airbus, how it cooperates with other suppliers of technology it uses in designing its engines, and the decision to ramp up scale in an effort to reduce its costs. When Wal-Mart managers decide how to compete with Sears for consumer dollars, they, too, are engaged in business strategy. Business strategy, therefore, focuses on *achieving a firm's objectives within a particular business line*.

Increasingly, business strategy also takes into account the changing competitive landscape in which a firm is located. Two critical questions that business strategy must address are (1) how the firm will achieve its objectives *today*, when other companies may be competing to satisfy the same customers' needs, and (2) how the firm plans to compete *in the future*. In later chapters, we'll focus specifically on issues related to business strategy.

corporate strategy Strategy for guiding a firm's entry and exit from different businesses, for determining how a parent company adds value to and manages its portfolio of businesses, and for creating value through diversification

Corporate Strategy **Corporate strategy** addresses issues related to three fundamental questions:

1. *In what businesses will we compete?* In the 1970s and 1980s, for instance, Sears chose to branch out of retailing into credit cards, stock brokerage, and real estate, whereas Wal-Mart remained focused on the retail business. GE managers address corporate-strategy questions when deciding whether the firm should enter a new business. AT&T's past attempts to reorganize itself as distinct divisions with separate ownership—which is the same thing as deciding that the corporate parent should *not* compete simultaneously in all of these businesses—is a matter of corporate strategy.

2. *How can we, as a corporate parent, add value to our various lines of business?* At GE, for instance, senior management might be able to orchestrate synergies and learning across its commercial- and consumer-finance groups. Sears once thought that it could provide one-stop shopping at retail outlets for everything from tools to life insurance. Thus, corporate strategy also deals with *finding ways to create value by having two or more owned businesses cooperate and share resources*.

3. *How will diversification or our entry into a new industry help us to compete in our other industries?* Sears managers thought that one-stop shopping would benefit all of its ventures by increasing the number of customers inside its retail stores. More recently, Wal-Mart has found that diversification into the grocery business segment of retailing has increased retail foot traffic and boosted sales of nongrocery retail products.

STRATEGY FORMULATION AND IMPLEMENTATION

strategy formulation Process of developing a strategy

strategy implementation Process of executing a strategy

Earlier we defined *strategy* as the central, integrated, externally oriented concept of how a firm will achieve its objectives. **Strategy formulation** is the process of *deciding what to do*; **strategy implementation** is the process of performing all the activities necessary *to do what has been planned*.[8] Because neither can succeed without the other, the two processes are iterative and interdependent from the standpoint that implementation should provide information that is used to periodically modify business and corporate strategy. Our opening vignette demonstrates the nature of this interdependence. Wal-Mart formulated an initial strategy that called for it to compete as a discount retailer in rural markets. As the company grew, it found that in order to implement this strategy, it had to invest heavily in organizational structure, systems, and processes. Ironically, these early steps in strategy implementation enabled Wal-Mart to reformulate and execute the strategy that has propelled the company to its dominant position as the low-cost leader of its industry.

The Wal-Mart example also shows how good strategies represent solutions to complex problems. They help to solve problems *external* to the firm by enabling the production of goods or services that both beat the competition and have a ready market. They solve problems *internal* to the firm by providing all employees, including top executives, with clear guidelines as to what the firm should and should not be doing.

You might be more familiar with Rolls-Royce's automobiles than its jet engines. The fact is, however, that Rolls-Royce PLC no longer even makes luxury automobiles. The company's core business is now jet engines. Jet engines generate 72 percent of its revenues.

Strategy Formulation

So now we know that strategy formulation means deciding what to do. Some strategies result from rational and methodical planning processes based on analyses of both internal resources and capabilities and the external environment. Others emerge over time and are adopted only after an unplanned pattern of decisions or actions suggests that an unfolding idea may unexpectedly lead to an effective strategy. Sometimes the recognition of a strategically good idea is accidental, but corporate innovation and renewal are increasingly the products of controlled experiments and the opportunistic exploitation of surprise.[9]

During its early years, for instance, the chipmaker Intel was consciously focused on the design and manufacture of dynamic, random-access memory chips (DRAMs), and through the 1970s and early 1980s virtually all of the firm's revenue came from DRAMs. Intel's participation in the DRAM market was intentional and planned virtually from the moment of its founding. By 1984, however, 95 percent of the company's revenue came from the microprocessor segment of the industry. Ironically, Intel's participation in this segment of the industry was not planned by senior management. Rather, it evolved from an experimental venture to make processors for Busicom, a Japanese maker of calculators.[10] Unbeknownst and unforeseen by top management was the fact that market demand was shifting dramatically from DRAMs to microprocessors. Only through the Busicom experiment—and Intel's willingness to follow the signals this experiment sent them in terms of market-demand shifts—was the firm able to dramatically change its business strategy. To this day, Intel officials give credit for the firm's dominance in the microprocessor market to a strategy that emerged originally from a lower-level management initiative—one that, at the time, wasn't greeted with unanimous enthusiasm by senior management.[11]

Since their lucky foray into the microprocessor market, Intel managers have obviously focused on effective strategies for maintaining the firm's advantages in the segment while at the same time promoting experiments and exploiting surprises like Busicom to keep abreast of significant underlying market-demand shifts.

StratSim Demonstrates the Difference Between Strategy Formulation and Implementation

SimConnect

Strategy Formulation   In Exhibit 1.4, Firm D (Driven Motor Co.) set their strategy to be the leading low-cost provider of automobiles in the high-volume family and

Exhibit 1.4 StratSim Financial Summary

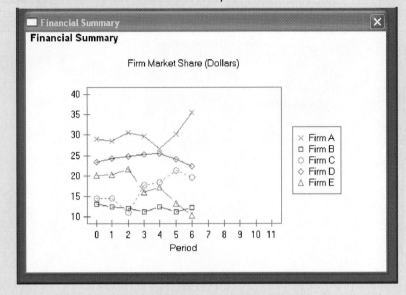

economy vehicle classes. Their strategic assumption was that by obtaining a leading market share position, this would ultimately reward them with lower costs due to economies of scale and experience effects.

Strategy Implementation   Though Firm D's strategy was based on sound theory and assumptions, their implementation ultimately failed. Why was this? Through year 4, by cutting price, they were able to gain share relative to Firm A as shown in Exhibit 1.4. However, because Firm D focused on price as their only source of competitive advantage and never achieved sufficient volume to gain a sustainable low-cost advantage relative to their competition, they ultimately left themselves vulnerable. Firm A was able to cut additional costs from their products through re-engineering while simultaneously improving their vehicle offerings in ways that were of value to their customers. This ultimately led Firm A to a better cost position and created a sustainable advantage relative to Firm D and the results are reflected in periods 5 and 6 as shown in Exhibit 1.4.

This example also underscores the fluid nature of strategy formulation and implementation. For several years, Firm D's strategy appeared to be working, but Firm A was able to negate the early price advantage through alternative cost reduction methods and providing other features that were of value to the market. In other words, price was ultimately only a temporary advantage without a corresponding cost advantage (internal) and value advantage (external).

The Strategy Diamond and the Five Elements of Strategy   Good strategy formulation means refining the elements of the strategy.[12] Remember, first of all, not to confuse *part* of a strategy—for example, being a low-cost provider or first mover in an industry—for strategy itself. Being a low-cost provider or first mover may be part of a strategy, but it's not a complete strategy.

As we noted earlier, a strategy is an integrated and externally oriented concept of how a firm will achieve its objectives—how it will compete against its rivals. Thus, a strategy consists of an *integrated set of choices*. These choices can be categorized as five related elements of strategy based on decisions that managers make regarding *arenas*, *vehicles*, *differentiators*, *staging*, and *economic logic*. We refer to this constellation of elements, which are central to the strategic management process outlined in Exhibit 1.3, as the *strategy diamond*. Most strategic plans focus on one or two such elements, often leaving large gaps in the overall strategy. Only when you have answers to your questions about *each of these five elements* can you determine whether your strategy is an integrated whole; you'll also have

Exhibit 1.5 The Business Strategy Diamond

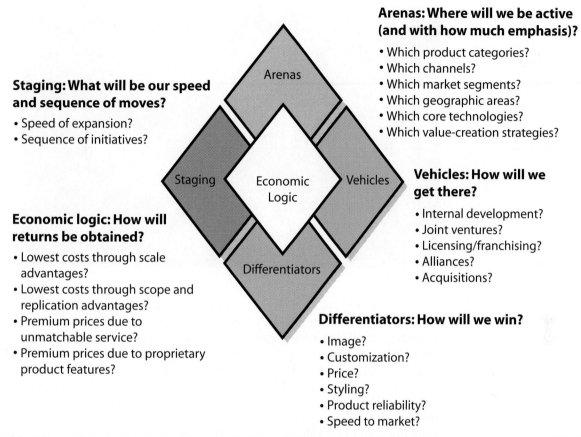

Staging: What will be our speed and sequence of moves?

- Speed of expansion?
- Sequence of initiatives?

Economic logic: How will returns be obtained?

- Lowest costs through scale advantages?
- Lowest costs through scope and replication advantages?
- Premium prices due to unmatchable service?
- Premium prices due to proprietary product features?

Arenas: Where will we be active (and with how much emphasis)?

- Which product categories?
- Which channels?
- Which market segments?
- Which geographic areas?
- Which core technologies?
- Which value-creation strategies?

Vehicles: How will we get there?

- Internal development?
- Joint ventures?
- Licensing/franchising?
- Alliances?
- Acquisitions?

Differentiators: How will we win?

- Image?
- Customization?
- Price?
- Styling?
- Product reliability?
- Speed to market?

Source: Adapted from D. C. Hambrick and J. W. Fredrickson, "Are You Sure You Have a Strategy?" Academy of Management Executive 15:4 (2001), 48–59.

a better idea of the areas in which your strategy needs to be revised or overhauled. As Exhibit 1.5 shows, a good strategy diamond considers five key elements in order to arrive at specific answers to five questions:

1. *Arenas:* Where will we be active?
2. *Vehicles:* How will we get there?
3. *Differentiators:* How will we win in the marketplace?
4. *Staging:* What will be our speed and sequence of moves?
5. *Economic logic:* How will we obtain our returns?

Let's take a closer look at each of these elements.

Arenas By **arenas**, we mean areas in which a firm will be active. Decisions about a firm's arenas may encompass its products, services, distribution channels, market segments, geographic areas, technologies, and even stages of the value-creation process. Unlike vision statements, which tend to be fairly general, the identification of arenas must be very specific: It will clearly tell managers what the firm should and should not do. In addition, because firms can contract with outside parties for everything from employees to manufacturing services, the choice of arenas can be fairly narrowly defined for some firms.

For example, as the largest U.S. bicycle distributor, Pacific Cycle owns the Schwinn, Mongoose, and GT brands and sells its bikes through big-box retail outlets and independent dealers, as well as through independent agents in foreign markets. In addition to these arena choices, Pacific Cycle has entirely outsourced the production of its products to Asian manufacturers. In outsourcing shoes and apparel lines, Nike follows a similar strategy in terms of arenas. One key difference, however, is that Nike, through its Nike Town retail outlets, has also chosen a direct retail presence in addition to its use of traditional retail distribution channels.

arena Area (product, service, distribution channel, geographic markets, technology, etc.) in which a firm participates

Pacific Cycle, based in Madison, Wisconsin, has carefully chosen the arenas in which it does business. The company designs and markets 10 different brands of bicycles, which it sells to big-box retailers and independent bike dealers around the world. Pacific Cycle does not actually manufacture any of the bikes itself, however. It outsources all of this work to companies in China and Taiwan instead.

vehicle Means for entering new arenas (e.g., through acquisitions, alliances, internal development, etc.)

Vehicles Vehicles are the means for participating in targeted arenas. For instance, a firm that wants to go international can achieve that objective in different ways. In a recent drive to enter certain international markets (such as Argentina), Wal-Mart has opened new stores and grown organically—meaning that it developed all the stores internally as opposed to by acquisition. Elsewhere (namely, in England and Germany), Wal-Mart has purchased existing retailers and is in the process of transferring its unique way of doing business to the acquired companies. Likewise, a firm that requires a new technology could develop it through investments in R&D. Or, it could opt to form an alliance with a competitor or supplier who already possesses the technology, thereby accelerating the integration of the missing piece into its set of resources and capabilities. Finally, it could simply buy another firm that owns the technology. In this case, then, the possible vehicles for entering a new arena include acquisitions, alliances, and organic investment and growth.

differentiator Feature or attribute of a company's product or service (e.g., image, customization, technical superiority, price, quality and reliability) that helps it beat its competitors in the marketplace

Differentiators Differentiators are features and attributes of a company's product or service that help it beat its competitors in the marketplace. Firms can be successful in the marketplace along a number of common dimensions, including *image*, *customization*, *technical superiority*, *price*, and *quality and reliability*. Toyota and Honda have done very well by providing effective combinations of differentiators. They sell both inexpensive cars and cars with high-end, high-quality features, and many consumers find the value that they provide hard to match. However, even though the best strategies often combine differentiators, history has shown that firms often perform poorly when they try to be all things to all consumers. It's difficult to imagine, for instance, a single product that boasts both state-of-the-art technology and the lowest price on the market. Part of the problem is perceptual—consumers often associate low quality with low price. Part of it is practical—leading-edge technologies cost money to develop and command higher prices because of their uniqueness or quality.

There are two critical factors in selecting differentiators:

- ■ ***These decisions must be made early.*** Key differentiators rarely materialize without significant up-front decisions, and without valuable differentiators, firms tend to lose marketplace battles.

- ■ ***Identifying and executing successful differentiators means making tough choices— tradeoffs.*** Managers who can't make tough decisions about tradeoffs often end up trying to satisfy too broad a spectrum of customer needs; as a result, they make too many strategic compromises and execute poorly on most dimensions.

Audi provides an example of a company that has aligned these two factors successfully. In the early 1990s, Audi management realized that its cars were perceived as low-quality, high-priced German automobiles—obviously a poor position from which to compete. The firm decided that it had to move one way or another—up market or down market. It had to do one of two things: (1) lower its costs so that its pricing was consistent with customers' perceptions of product quality or (2) improve quality sufficiently to justify premium pricing. Given limited resources, the firm could not go in both directions—that is, produce cars in both the low-price and high-quality strata. Audi made a decision to invest heavily in quality and image; it invested significantly in quality programs and in refining its marketing efforts. Ten years later, the quality of Audi cars has increased significantly, and customer perception has moved them much closer to the level of BMW and Mercedes. Audi has reaped the benefits of premium pricing and improved profitability, but the decisions behind the strategic up-market move entailed significant tradeoffs.[13]

Differentiators are what drive potential customers to choose one firm's offerings over those of competitors. The earlier and more consistent the firm is at defining and driving these differentiators, the greater the likelihood that customers will recognize them.

Staging **Staging** refers to the timing and pace of strategic moves. Staging choices typically reflect available resources, including cash, human capital, and knowledge. At what point, for example, should Wal-Mart have added international markets to its strategy? Perhaps if the company had pursued global opportunities earlier, it would have been able to develop a better sense of foreign-market conditions and even spread the costs of entry over a longer period of time. However, by delaying its international moves, the company was able to focus on dominating the U.S. market, which is, after all, the largest retail market in the world. Despite mixed results overseas, Wal-Mart is the undisputed leader in global retailing and has recently increased its emphasis on international markets as the basis for future growth.[14]

staging Timing and pace of strategic moves

Staging decisions should be driven by several factors: resources, urgency, credibility, and the need for early wins. Because few firms have the resources to do everything they'd like to do immediately, they usually have to match opportunities with available resources. In addition, not all opportunities to enter new arenas are permanent; some have only brief windows. In such cases, early wins and the credibility of certain key stakeholders may be necessary to implement a strategy.

Consider the case of the 2002 Winter Olympic Games. In June 1995, the International Olympic Committee (IOC) awarded the 2002 Winter Olympic Games to Salt Lake City, Utah. Complications arose, however, when reports surfaced in late 1998 that some individuals associated with the Salt Lake Olympic Committee (SLOC), the group responsible for securing the winning bid and managing the event, had bribed IOC members in order to bring the Games to their community. The Justice Department alleged that prior to the selection of Salt Lake City, two top members of SLOC had paid $1 million in cash and gifts to members of the IOC to secure the designation. Some of these payments allegedly went toward the funding of U.S. college educations for IOC delegates' children. Other funds paid for their first-class travel or lavish gifts. The scandal forced the ouster or resignation of several IOC officials and led to reforms that included a new international ethics code. It also resulted in a complete restructuring of the SLOC management team.

In 1999, Mitt Romney, a partner with Bain Capital (and now governor of Massachusetts), was hired to save the Winter Olympics. He reports that one of the first things his management team discovered upon agreeing to take over was that there was a $379-million deficit on an original budget of $1.5 billion (by comparison, the previous Winter Olympics in Nagano, Japan, spent $2.8 billion to stage the Games). One source of budget woes was that most major sponsors had reneged on their pledges of support. For instance, the CEO of one perennially strong sponsor of the Olympics reportedly quipped that "any CEO who signs up to sponsor these Winter Games should be fired." Romney realized that without major advertisers, the project was doomed to failure, and unfortunately, the previous management of SLOC had forfeited all credibility with potential advertisers. To reestablish credibility, Romney's team set out to rack up some key early wins. To achieve this goal, they determined to do three things: cut operating expenses, install a new management team, and land their first new advertising commitment. Once those three objectives had been accomplished, the new SLOC gained significant credibility with large advertisers and eventually succeeded in implementing its turnaround strategy. In fact, when the games were over and all the bills were paid, SLOC finished with a $100-million surplus. And the IOC, which only a few years earlier was threatening to move the games away from Salt Lake City, praised the leadership of SLOC and their efforts by noting, "The Salt Lake City Games were undoubtedly great Games . . . [that] left a wonderful legacy for the city and were financially a huge success."[15]

economic logic Means by which a firm will earn a profit by implementing a strategy

Economic Logic   **Economic logic** refers to how the firm will earn a profit—that is, how the firm will generate positive returns over and above its cost of capital. Economic logic is the "fulcrum" for profit creation. Earning normal profits, of course, requires a firm to meet all of its fixed, variable, and financing costs, and achieving desired returns over the firm's cost of capital is a tall order for any organization. In analyzing a firm's economic logic, think of both costs and revenues. Sometimes economic logic resides primarily on the *cost* side of the equation. Southwest Airlines, for example, can fly passengers for significantly lower costs per passenger mile than any major competitor. At other times, economic logic may rest on the firm's ability to increase the customer's willingness to pay premium prices for products (in other words, prices that significantly exceed the costs of providing enhanced products).

When the five elements of strategy are aligned and mutually reinforcing, the firm is generally in a position to perform well. The SimConnect Exhibit 1.6 shows you how the five facets of strategy are incorporated into the StratSim simulation. "How Would You Do That? 1.1" demonstrates how you would apply the strategy diamond to the highly successful airline JetBlue. High performance levels, however, ultimately mean that a strategy is also being executed well, and we now turn to strategy implementation.

Strategy Implementation Levers

Whatever the origin of a strategic idea, whether it was carefully planned from the outset or evolved over time by means of luck or experimentation, successful strategies are dependent on effective implementation. As discussed earlier in the chapter, *strategy implementation* is the process of executing the strategy—of taking the actions that put the strategy into effect and ensure that organizational decisions are consistent with it.[16] The process of implementation also encompasses the refinement, or change, of a strategy as more information is made available through early implementation efforts. The goal of implementation is twofold:

- To make sure that strategy formulation is comprehensive and well informed

- To translate good ideas into actions that can be executed (and sometimes to use execution to generate or identify good ideas)

In sports, a coach's play-calling is only as good as the excellence with which the players execute it. Likewise in business: The value of a firm's strategy is determined by its ability to carry it out. "Any strategy," says Michael Porter, one of the preeminent writers on the subject, ". . . is only as good as its execution."[17] Adds Peter Drucker, one of our most prolific writers on management: "The important decisions, the decisions that really matter, are strategic. . . . [But] more important and more difficult is to make effective the course of action decided upon."[18]

Strategy implementation is studied in college courses, and it's the subject of hundreds of books in business school libraries. We don't intend to supplant the results of all of this study, but we do want you to focus on the implications of a very basic fact: *The processes of strategy formulation and strategy implementation are inextricably linked.* The five elements of strategy, for instance, are related to both formulation and implementation. Good implementation means that an organization coordinates resources and capabilities and uses structure, systems, processes, and strategic leadership to translate an intended strategy to bottom-line results. Throughout the text we help you to see the relationship between formulation and implementation. Chapter 2 introduces you to the role of strategic leadership. At this point, and in order to help you consider the complexity of implementing a strategy, we introduce you to just the basic ideas of strategic leadership and implementation.

Exhibit 1.6   The Business Strategy Diamond Applied to StratSim   **Sim**Connect

Arenas: Where will we be active (and with how much emphasis)?
▸ Which vehicle classes?
▸ Which segments / customers?
▸ Which domestic regions to emphasize?
▸ B2B / International?
▸ Which technologies to emphasize?

Vehicles: How will we get there?
▸ Internal Development?
▸ Licensing / Joint Venture?
▸ Alliances?

Differentiators: How will we win?
▸ Image?
▸ Price?
▸ Service?
▸ Product Quality?
▸ Speed to Market?

Economic Logic: How will returns be obtained?
▸ Lowest costs through scale advantages?
▸ Lowest costs through scope and replication advantages?
▸ Lowest costs through design and process improvements?
▸ Premium prices due to unmatchable service?
▸ Premium prices due to proprietary product features?

Staging: What will be our speed and sequence of moves?
▸ Speed of expansion of product development centers, productive
  capacity, dealerships, new product introductions
▸ Sequencing of these expansion decisions. What needs to happen
  first? When do I need to expand capacity in order to meet demand
  for a new product initiative?

Source: StratSim

The Five Elements of Strategy at JetBlue

To experience how you might apply the strategy diamond, let's consider a recent entrepreneurial success story. The major U.S. airlines lost over $7 billion between 1998 and 2002. David Neeleman, however, confounded the experts when he decided that despite the industry's horrendous performance, the time was right to step down from his executive position at Southwest Airlines to launch a new airline. JetBlue took off on February 11, 2000, with an inaugural flight between New York City's John F. Kennedy International Airport and Fort Lauderdale, Florida. Today, the airline serves 20 cities around the country and intends to expand further. As you can see from the two graphs in Exhibit 1.7, JetBlue has obviously done something right. It is second only to Southwest Airlines in profitability and its market capitalization means that investors have high expectations for JetBlue's financial prospects.

To begin applying the strategy diamond to JetBlue, let's quickly review JetBlue's vision, which is to "bring humanity back to air travel" through product innovation and excellent service. It intends to be a low-fare, low-cost passenger airline that provides high-quality customer service. Using the strategy diamond, and public documents posted at www.jetblue.com, we can determine what strategy JetBlue has pursued in order to meet its stated objective.

- *In what* arenas *does JetBlue compete?* Management states that the company competes as a low-fare commercial air carrier, and caters to underserved but overpriced U.S. cities. Its main base of operations is John F. Kennedy airport in New York City, which serves the largest travel market in the country.

Exhibit 1.7 JetBlue and Its Industry

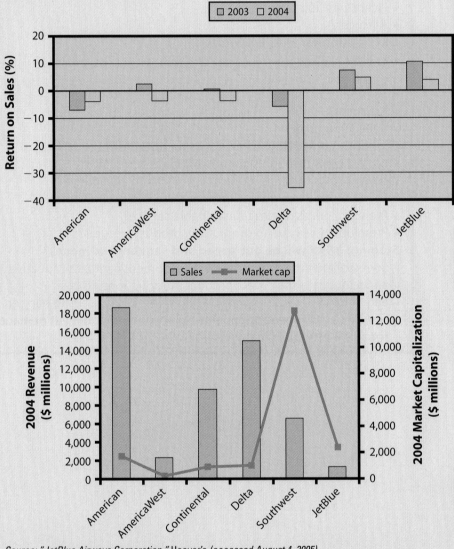

Source: "JetBlue Airways Corporation," Hoover's (accessed August 4, 2005).

»

- *What* vehicles *does JetBlue use to enter the arenas in which it competes?* JetBlue started from scratch and has achieved all of its growth in flights per day through internal growth. The firm could have grown by purchasing regional airlines, but chose not to.

- *What are its* differentiators? Price is a big part of JetBlue's strategy for winning new customers, but it also wants to develop the image that it is a low-fare airline with high-quality service. Although it offers only one class of service, the level of service is rather high for a low-fare airline. For instance, offering leather seating and individual in-seat live satellite TV.

- *How does JetBlue's* staging—*the speed of its expansion and the sequence of its growth initiatives—reflect its timetable for achieving its objectives?* JetBlue has grown from 1 route between 2 cities to routes serving 20 cities in just 3 years. At first, it limited itself to the East Coast (between its JFK home base and destinations in Florida and upstate New York), but it soon proceeded westward, establishing locations in Long Beach, California (to serve the Los Angeles area), Denver, Seattle, and most recently, San Diego. JetBlue has targeted more cities for future expansion.

- *What's the* economic logic *of JetBlue's strategy?* JetBlue's income statements show that its costs are significantly lower than

When former Southwest Airlines employee and JetBlue founder David Neeleman (shown vacuuming a plane) announced that he was launching a new airline company, people were aghast. Although the airline industry as a whole is undergoing dismal financial profits, JetBlue has found a way to prosper by effectively aligning the five elements of its strategy that is both internally consistent, and externally generates great market demand. The strategy includes low-fare but upscale service, complete with leather seats and satellite TV.

industry averages. These cost advantages appear to come from an *ability to perform key tasks in ways that are fundamentally less expensive* than those of competitors. By flying only one make of aircraft that is relatively fuel efficient, JetBlue also keeps maintenance and training costs down. By securing a home base at JFK at a time when the New York Port Authority was anxious to attract more air traffic, JetBlue secured lower airport fees. Locating in secondary locations (Long Beach instead of Los Angeles International Airport, Fort Lauderdale instead of Miami) also means lower-than-average airport fees. On the revenue side, although JetBlue offers very low fares, it wins customers from com-

petitors and uses its low cost incentive as a means to convert non-fliers to JetBlue customers. It has also attracted customers by concentrating on underserved, high-priced routes. As a result, it now boasts the highest load factor of any major airline.

Walking through the JetBlue's strategy diamond helps illustrate its strategy. The plan looks sound, but what is required to implement such a plan? The next sections of this chapter provide an overview of this critical issue.

Sources: JetBlue Airways Corp., *2002 Annual Report on Form 10-K,* including on the "Investor Relations" link on JetBlue's Web page; JetBlue Airways Corp., *2003 Annual Report on Form 10-K,* JetBlue Airways Corp., *2004 Annual Report on Form 10-K.*

Exhibit 1.8 Implementation Framework

Source: Adapted from D. Hambrick and A. Cannella, "Strategy Implementation as Substance and Selling," Academy of Management Executive *3:4 (1989), 278–285.*

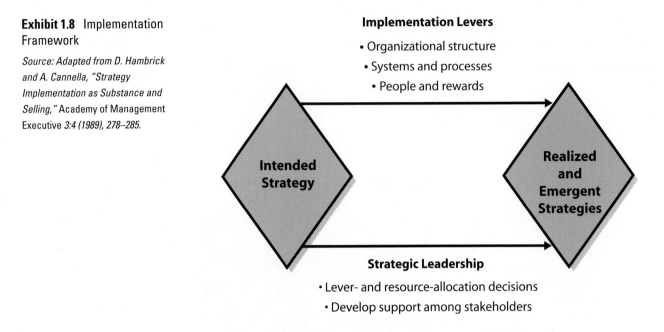

Implementation Levers

- Organizational structure
- Systems and processes
- People and rewards

Intended Strategy

Realized and Emergent Strategies

Strategic Leadership

- Lever- and resource-allocation decisions
- Develop support among stakeholders

To implement strategies, organization leaders have numerous levers at their disposal. The framework summarizing these levers is shown in Exhibit 1.8. We categorize these levers into three broad categories: (1) *organization structure*, (2) *systems and processes*, and (3) *people and rewards*. The strategist uses these tools to test for alignment, which is the need for all of the firm's activities to complement each other and support the strategy.

In addition, strategic leadership engages in a few activities related to implementing the strategy that are unique to their positional authority. As the exhibit suggests, implementation includes the activities carried out by the organization that are aimed at executing a particular strategy. Often, the strategy that is realized through these implementation efforts is somewhat different from the original plan. These deviations from the original plan are a result of explicit alterations of the strategy that result from feedback during early implementation efforts as well as from the exploitation of serendipitous opportunities that were not anticipated when the strategy was formulated.

Organization Structure *Structure* is the manner in which responsibilities, tasks, and people are organized. It includes the organization's authority, hierarchy, units, divisions, and coordinating mechanisms. At this point, we just need to remind ourselves of a few key questions that managers must consider when implementing a strategy:

- Is the current structure appropriate for the intended strategy?

- Are reporting relationships and the delegation of authority set up to execute the strategic plan?

- Is the organization too centralized (or decentralized) for the strategy?

Systems and Processes *Systems* are all the organizational processes and procedures used in daily operations. Obviously, these include control and incentive systems, resource-allocation procedures, information systems, budgeting, distribution, and so forth.

People and Rewards The *people and rewards* lever of the model underscores the importance of using all of the organization's members to implement a strategy. Regardless of your strategy, at the end of the day, it's your people who will have implemented it. Competitive advantage is generally tied to your human resources.[19] Successful implementation depends on having the right people and then developing and training them in ways that support the firm's strategy. In addition, rewards—how you pay your people—can accelerate the implementation of your strategy or undermine it. We have all seen instances in which unintended consequences happen because a manager rewards "A" while hoping for "B."[20]

Strategic Leadership

Strategic leadership plays two critical roles in successful strategy implementation, and it is important to highlight them here so that you can incorporate them into your own assessment of a strategy's feasibility as well as ensure that you include these roles in your implementation plans. Specifically, strategic leadership is responsible for (1) making substantive implementation lever and resource-allocation decisions and (2) developing support for the strategy from key stakeholders. Although a successful strategy is not generally formulated by a single person or a small group of leaders, successful strategy implementation requires active leadership to ensure that what emerges and what is realized are desirable.

SimConnect

Strategic Leadership and Implementation Levers in StratSim

In StratSim, how you organize and manage your team is a key element of success. There is no right way to organize and set your "corporate culture." Part of what you will need to decide is how best to delegate responsibilities to different members of your corporate team. Will you be functional or product managers? How will you incorporate competitive analysis? How will you allocate resources across different investment alternatives? Will you have a CEO or will decisions be made by consensus? All of these issues will be resolved through an intended as well as an emergent process. The exact way this process will evolve is ultimately up to your group, but realize that the simulation experience itself will also have an impact on your analysis and decision process. Time pressure will come into play. Unexpected competitor moves will challenge your initial game plan. New opportunities may require rethinking your organizational structure so as to not overlook them while managing today's businesses. Many groups will struggle with competing strategic visions among individuals within the team and, not surprisingly, members of your group may argue over resource-allocation decisions. These are the tensions inherent in any strategic organization. StratSim allows you to experience these strategic alternatives in a low-risk environment.

WHAT IS COMPETITIVE ADVANTAGE?

Earlier we defined *strategy* as the central, integrated, externally oriented concept of how a firm will achieve its objectives. We noted that within a firm's business operations, its objectives will generally encompass some notion of being successful at selling products or services to customers. Because virtually all firms face competition when trying to serve these customers, to achieve its objectives, a firm will have to be perceived by at least some customers as superior to its competition. Thus, the concept of strategy suggests a relationship between strategy on the one hand and performance and competitive advantage on the other. Specifically, we explained that a strategy encompasses the pattern of actions taken by a firm to achieve its objectives. These premises lead us to a logical conclusion: The activities of strategic management are based on the assumption that *firms attempt to achieve a position of competitive advantage over their rivals when serving target customers.*[21] Or, to put it another way: Firms prefer to be winners in their respective industries rather than subpar or even average performers. This leads us to define **competitive advantage** as a firm's ability to create *value* in a way that its rivals cannot.

Performance itself, however, is not competitive advantage; it's merely a result of it. A firm may achieve relatively high short-term performance levels without gaining any substantial advantage over its rivals. Maybe the company just had an unusually good year or

competitive advantage A firm's ability to create *value* in a way that its rivals cannot

took drastic measures to cut costs (perhaps to unsustainably low levels). By the same token, a firm may enjoy significant competitive advantage in some lines of business but still perform more poorly than its competitors because of other underperforming business units.

The question that we now want to answer is: *Why are some firms able to achieve greater advantages over rivals than other firms?* All firms are not alike. Dell, for example, seems to have some capabilities that other computer manufactures, such as Hewlett-Packard and IBM, haven't been able to duplicate. Toyota enjoys a similar advantage in the automotive industry. In fact, many industries (including pharmaceuticals, soft drinks, and retailing) are *not* characterized by perfect competition, and many companies earn more than "normal" income for many years. In addition, some firms appear to outperform competitors consistently, which is likely an indication that they have some form of competitive advantage over their rivals. As we will see, however, it's become increasingly difficult for any one firm to sustain a competitive advantage over a long period of time.[22]

Sim**Connect**

Competitive Advantage in StratSim

Just as in the real world, developing a unique source of competitive advantage is what separates the successful StratSim firm from the rest of the pack. At the beginning of the simulation, each firm starts with a unique set of strengths and weaknesses. You may choose to build on these, develop new competencies, and/or exploit the weaknesses of your competitors. You may also find that changes in the environment or competition present completely new dimensions that could provide a source of competitive advantage for your firm. Some sources of competitive advantage may be more sustainable than others.

There are a number of different ways that your firm can create competitive advantage within StratSim. However, because of the dynamic nature of the simulation, what works in one "industry" (a group of teams that directly compete) may not work in another. Context is important. In addition, as has already been discussed, recognizing a potential source of competitive advantage (formulation) is quite different from actually achieving that advantage (implementation). It will be important to develop systems and an organizational structure that will give your strategy an opportunity to work.

Determinants of Competitive Advantage

The field of strategic management focuses on explanations of competitive advantage—on the reasons why companies experience above- and below-normal rates of returns and on the ways that firms can exploit the limits of perfect competition. Generally speaking, there are two primary perspectives on this issue (perspectives that, as we shall see, reflect contrasting but complementary points of view):

- The *internal perspective* focuses on firms and potential internal sources of uniqueness.

- The *external perspective* focuses on the structure of industries and the ways in which firms can position themselves within them for competitive advantage.

Bridging these two fundamental perspectives is a third view called *dynamic strategy*, which seeks to explain why competitive advantage does not typically last over long periods of time. Let's examine each of these perspectives, or theories, more closely.

The Internal Perspective The internal perspective on competitive advantage is often called the *resource-based view of the firm*. It holds that firms are heterogeneous bundles of resources and capabilities. Proponents of this theory argue that firms are not "clones" of each other in terms of the resources that they own or to which they have access and that they have varying degrees of capability in performing different economic tasks. As a result, firms with superior resources and capabilities enjoy competitive advantage over other firms.[23] This advantage makes it relatively easier for these firms to achieve consistently higher levels of performance than competitors. Competitive advantage, therefore, arises when a company's resources allow its products, services, or businesses to compete successfully against rival firms in the same industries. The resource-based view also holds that a firm's bundle of resources may either hinder or help its entry into new businesses—an idea that we'll explore further in later chapters.[24]

The External Perspective   The external perspective on competitive advantage contends that variations in a firm's competitive advantage and performance are primarily a function of industry attractiveness. The external perspective suggests that competitive advantage comes from a firm's positioning within the competitive business environment.

The seminal work supporting this approach is Michael Porter's work on competitive strategy.[25] Porter's theory—sometimes called *industrial organization economics* (I/O economics)—suggests that firms should do one of two things: (1) position themselves to compete in attractive industries or (2) adopt strategies that will make their current industries more attractive. In some countries, for instance, carmakers lobby for import tariffs in order to make their domestic markets more attractive. When the strategy works, the access of foreign manufacturers to the market is limited, and the cost of participating in it is higher. (In later chapters, we'll explore in more detail the theoretical models and tools that help managers analyze, understand, and shape a firm's competitive environments.)

Fundamental Versus Dynamic Perspectives

Researchers have also realized that, in addition to internal and external determinants of competitive advantage, some industries or market segments are less stable than others. Not surprisingly, competitive advantage is more likely to endure in stable markets than in unstable ones. Conversely, the competitive advantage held by one firm over another tends to change very slowly in stable markets but more quickly in unstable ones.

The Fundamental Perspective   The global chocolate industry, for example, is relatively stable because a few firms—notably, M&M/Mars, Nestlé, and Hershey—dominate it in terms of both size and brands. In addition, demand for chocolate is relatively stable, growing with population growth. To stimulate growth, large companies try to formulate new candy bars. However, this type of growth is rather incremental and predictable. Smaller companies carve out niches in which to offer differentiated products, but this generally does not result in any significant upheaval of market dynamics. In such stable contexts, fundamental theories of competitive advantage usually explain most economic facts. The external (or positional) view of strategy tends to dominate questions of strategy formulation and implementation. Why? Because a firm's current market position, as gauged by market share or some other criterion, may be a good indicator of competitive advantage and provides a relatively accurate predictor of future performance. This view also tends to assume that industries are clearly defined, that competition is predictable, and that the future doesn't hold many surprises.

The Dynamic Perspective   But what about industries—such as computer chips or laser printers or medical products—in which it seems that competitive advantage can shift in a matter of months or even days simply because of a new product release or some other technological breakthrough?[26] A so-called *dynamic perspective* on competitive advantage has become increasingly important in explaining the economic facts in such industries in which markets converge, technologies rapidly change competitive conditions, capital markets become increasingly impatient, firms compete in multiple markets and multiple industries against common rivals, and the costs of establishing a competitive position soar (and so increase dramatically the cost of failure). The dynamic perspective suggests that a firm's current market position is *not* an accurate predictor of future performance or sustainable competitive advantage. Why not? Because current market position itself is not a competitive advantage but rather an outcome of past competitive activities. From the dynamic perspective, we look to the past for clues about how the firm arrived at its current position and to the future in an effort to predict the look of the new competitive landscape.

The External Dimension of the Dynamic Perspective Of course, the dynamic strategy perspective has both external and internal dimensions as well. On the external side, it's useful in analyzing "high-velocity" markets—markets that are changing rapidly and unpredictably.[27] Often, such changes result from technology, but as we noted earlier, there are usually several contributing factors. The dynamic perspective is also a good tool for examining industries characterized by *multimarket competition*—those in which firms tend to encounter the same rivals in multiple markets.[28] Goodyear, Michelin, and Bridgestone, for instance, compete head-to-head in tire markets around the world. Another form of multimarket competition is illustrated by Nestlé and Mars; these companies battle it out in global industries ranging from pet foods to snack foods and will often use resources from one industry to bolster competitive position in another—say, by offering retailer discounts on pet food in exchange for shelf space for snack foods. For instance, Proctor & Gamble's entry into Vietnam appears to be less driven by the profit motive (P&G tends to lose money on Vietnamese soap sales) than by a determination to keep rival Unilever in check. If P&G had not entered the Vietnamese market, Unilever could have reaped monopoly-like profits and proceeded to use the windfall to pay for competitive efforts against P&G in other markets. By competing with Unilever in a market in which it has no competitive advantage (and may not even seek one), P&G's strategy reduces Unilever's ability to wage war on other fronts.

The Internal Dimension of the Dynamic Perspective The dynamic perspective can also help us to focus on a firm's resources and capabilities, particularly those that lead to a *continuous flow* of advantages in resources or market position and those that strengthen the firm's ability to embrace (and even foster) continuous and sometimes disruptive *change*. Risk taking, experimentation, improvisation, and continuous learning are—at least from the dynamic perspective—key features of successful firms. Later in the text, we will explore several relevant analytical tools for shaping strategy formulation and implementation, including capabilities assessment, strategic options, technology roadmaps, and game-theory modeling. You'll also learn how to combine your analysis of an industry's cumulative technological development with your assessment of whether a firm can exploit an innovative product or disruptive technology through its entire life cycle or whether it must instead leap from product to product at strategically defined crossover points.

Finally—and by way of bringing this chapter full-circle to our opening vignette on Sears and Wal-Mart—note that the dynamic perspective also provides valuable insight into the formulation and implementation of strategies at firms competing in ostensibly stable markets and industries. In its early years, for example, few observers would have predicted that Sears would eventually be vulnerable against a tiny rural upstart like Wal-Mart. Given its own constraints, however, Wal-Mart had to develop highly efficient inventory-management systems if it wanted to earn the same profits as Sears. In other words, Wal-Mart's strategy for competitive advantage differed from that of Sears: Instead of trying to fight Sears according to Sears' own rules of retail-industry competition, Wal-Mart executed a dynamic strategy that called for a radical change in the way that retail business was done (namely, competing in rural locations through the use of highly sophisticated and proprietary logistics capabilities). To keep costs low in serving its far-flung network of rural retail stores, Wal-Mart needed to develop a more efficient way to manage inventory and distribution. By the time Wal-Mart appeared on Sears' radar, it was too late for the once-dominant retailer to protect its market share. We would find the same theme in stories about Amazon.com versus Barnes & Noble and U.S. mini-mills versus major steel producers.[29]

SUMMARY

1. Understand what *strategy* is and identify the difference between business-level and corporate-level strategy. *Strategic management* is the process by which a firm manages the formulation and implementation of its strategy. A *strategy* is the central, integrated, externally oriented concept of how a firm will achieve its objectives. Strategies typically take one of two forms: business strategy or corporate strategy. The objective of a business strategy is to spell out how the firm plans to compete. This plan integrates choices regarding arenas (where the firm will be active), vehicles (how it will get there), differentiators (how it will win), staging (the speed and sequence of its moves), and economic logic (how it obtains its returns). The objective of corporate strategy is to spell out which businesses a firm will compete in, how ownership by the corporate parent adds value to the business, and how this particular diversification approach helps each business compete in its respective markets.

2. Understand why we study *strategic management*. It should be clear to you by now that strategic management is concerned with firm performance. Strategic management holds clues as to why firms survive when performance suffers. Strategy helps you to understand which activities are important and why and how a plan, absent good execution, is perhaps only as valuable as the paper it's printed on.

3. Understand the relationship between *strategy formulation* and *implementation*. *Strategy formulation* is the determination of what the firm is going to do; strategy implementation is how the firm goes about doing it. These two facets of strategy are linked and interdependent. This interdependence is made strikingly clear by the strategy formulation model you are introduced to in this chapter, examples throughout the text.

4. Describe the determinants of competitive advantage. Competitive advantage is realized when one firm creates value in ways that its competitors cannot, such that the firm clearly performs better than its competitors. Advantage is not simply higher relative performance; rather superior performance signals the ability of a firm to do things

in ways its direct competitors cannot. The two primary views of competitive advantage—internal and external—are complementary and together are used to help formulate effective strategies. The internal view portrays competitive advantage to be a function of unique, firm-specific resources and capabilities. The external view holds that a firm's performance is largely a function of its position in a particular industry or industry segment given the overall structure of the industry. Profitable industries are considered attractive, and therefore, high firm performance is attributed to a firm's position in the industry relative to the characteristics of the industry or industry segment.

5. Recognize the difference between the *fundamental view* and the *dynamic view of competitive advantage*. Regardless of whether the firm takes an internal or external perspective toward competitive advantage, research shows that few firms persist in their dominance over competitors over prolonged periods of time. For most firms, therefore, competitive advantage is considered to be temporary. The dynamic perspective assumes that a firm's current market position is not an accurate predictor of future performance because position itself is not a competitive advantage. Instead, the dynamic perspective looks at the past for clues about how the firm arrived at its present position and to the future to divine what the new competitive landscape might look like. It also holds that it's possible for the firm to influence the future state of the competitive landscape.

6. Understand how the StratSim simulation will allow you to study strategic management in a dynamic, hands-on environment. StratSim provides you with an intense, but rich, learning-by-doing experience. You will be crafting your firm's strategy and then be challenged with executing it in the face of sometimes brutal competition. Because each firm starts with a unique set of resources and capabilities, including your management team, you will be immediately living in the dynamic strategy environment that most firms must contend with. Fortunately, the costs of making mistakes in StratSim are much less painful than in the real world, even though you gain all the benefits, which is another reason your StratSim experience will give you a competitive advantage long after having completed the course.

KEY TERMS

arena, 13
business strategy, 10
competitive advantage, 21

corporate strategy, 10
differentiator, 14
economic logic, 16

staging, 15
strategic management, 7
strategy, 8

strategy formulation, 10
strategy implementation, 10
vehicle, 14

REVIEW QUESTIONS

1. What is strategic management?

2. What are the key components of the strategic management process?

3. How does business strategy differ from corporate strategy?

4. What is the relationship between strategy formulation and strategy implementation?

5. What five elements comprise the strategy formulation diamond?

6. What are the internal and external perspectives of competitive advantage?

7. What are the fundamental and dynamic perspectives of competitive advantage?

8. Why should you study strategic management?

How Would **you** Do That?

1. Go to Warren Buffet's *Letter to Shareholder's* page at www.berkshirehathaway.com/letters/letters.html and read the most recent letter. How many of the strategy topics covered in this chapter can you find references to in the letter? Pick one of the businesses owned by Berkshire Hathaway and draft a strategy formulation diamond for it similar to the one outlined in the JetBlue example in the box entitled "How Would You Do That? 1.1."

2. Go back to the discussion of JetBlue in the box entitled "How Would You Do That? 1.1." Use the strategy implementation model in Exhibit 1.6 to identify what would be necessary to successfully implement JetBlue's strategy. How would the implementation levers be different for JetBlue than for some of the major airlines?

3. Review the StratSim case provided in the StratSim documentation on-line. Which firm do you believe to be the best positioned for success within the StratSim industry? What is your basis for this choice? How did you define success?

GROUP ACTIVITIES

1. Identify the characteristics of a firm that the members of your group would like to work for and try to identify an example of this type of firm. What's the difference between business and corporate strategy at this firm? How might that affect your experiences and opportunities in that organization? Use your knowledge of the firm's strategy to construct a high-impact job application cover letter to apply for a job with this firm.

2. How is international expansion related to business and corporate strategy? Identify a firm that may be thinking of expanding into new international markets. Apply the staging element of the strategy diamond to the firm's international expansion opportunities or plans. Which markets should it target first and why?

ENDNOTES

1. C. Hoge, *The First Hundred Years Are the Toughest: What We Can Learn from the Century of Competition Between Sears and Wards* (Berkeley, CA: Ten Speed Press, 1988); G. Weil, *Sears, Roebuck, U.S.A.: The Great American Catalog Store and How It Grew* (Briarcliff Manor, NY: Stein and Day, 1977); S. Walton with J. Huey, *Made in America: My Story* (New York: Bantam Books, 1992); A. Merrick and J. Hallinan, "Sears Pegs Its Revival on the Sale of Its Credit Card Unit," *Wall Street Journal* (Eastern edition), March 27, 2003, B4; K. R. Andrews, *The Concept of Corporate Strategy* 3rd ed. (Homewood, IL: Dow Jones/Irwin, 1987); C. W. Hofer and D. Schendel, *Strategy Formulation: Analytic Concepts* (St. Paul, MN: West, 1987); C. M. Christensen, "Making Strategy: Learning by Doing," *Harvard Business Review* 75:6 (1997), 141–156; V. Marsh, "Attributes: Strong Strategy Tops the List," *Financial Times*, November 30, 1998, p. 7; A. Grove, *Only the Paranoid*

Survive: How to Exploit the Crises Points That Challenge Every Company and Career (New York: Currency Doubleday, 1999).

2. J. Pfeffer and R. I. Sutton, *The Knowing–Doing Gap: How Smart Companies Turn Knowledge into Action* (Boston: Harvard Business School Press, 2000).

3. *My Big Fat Greek Wedding* (HBO Video, 2003).

4. M. Porter, "What Is Strategy?" *Harvard Business Review* 74:6 (1996), 61–78.

5. D. C. Hambrick and J. W. Fredrickson, "Are You Sure You Have a Strategy?" *Academy of Management Executive,* 15:4 (2001), 48–59.

6. K. R. Andrews, *The Concept of Corporate Strategy* 3rd ed. (Homewood, IL: Irwin, 1987).

7. R. H. Waterman, T. J. Peters, and J. R. Phillips, "Structure Is Not Organization," *Business Horizons* 23:3 (1980), 14–26.

8. Andrews, *The Concept of Corporate Strategy* 3rd ed. (Homewood, IL: Irwin, 1987).

9. S. Brown and K. Eisenhardt, *Competing on the Edge* (Boston: Harvard Business School Press, 1998); R. A. Burgelman and L. Sayles, *Inside Corporate Innovation* (New York: Free Press, 1986).

10. R. A. Burgelman, "Fading Memories: A Process Theory of Strategic Business Exit in Dynamic Environments," *Administrative Science Quarterly* 39 (1993): 24–56.

11. Burgelman, "Fading Memories"; Grove, *Only the Paranoid Survive.*

12. This section draws extensively from Hambrick and Fredrickson, "Are You Sure You Have a Strategy?"

13. Personal interviews with company executives.

14. T. Carl, "After Growing on Small Towns, Wal-Mart Looks to World for More Expansion," Associated Press Newswires, March 26, 2003.

15. L. R. Roche, "IOC Praises Magic, Financial Success of S.L. Games," *Deseret News*, November 27, 2002, B6. Some of the details of this section come from personal interviews with Frasier Bullock, Chief Operating Officer and Chief Financial Officer of SLOC.

16. *The Strategy Execution Imperative: Leading Practices for Implementing Strategic Initiative* (Washington, D.C.: Corporate Executive Board, 2001); Christensen, "Making Strategy."

17. M. F. Porter, "Know Your Place: How to Assess the Attractiveness of Your Industry and Your Company's Position in It," *Inc.,* September 1991, 90.

18. P. F. Drucker, *The Practice of Management* (New York: HarperCollins, 1954), 352–353.

19. See J. B. Barney and P. M. Wright, "On Becoming a Strategic Partner: The Role of Human Resources in Gaining Competitive Advantage," *Human Resource Management* 37:1 (1998), 31–46; J. Pfeffer, *Competitive Advantage Through People* (Boston: HBS Press, 1994).

20. S. Kerr, "On the Folly of Rewarding A, While Hoping for B," *Academy of Management Journal* 18:4 (1975), 769–783.

21. J. B. Barney, "Firm Resources and Sustained Competitive Advantage," *Journal of Management* 17:1 (1991), 99–121; M. A. Peteraf, "The Cornerstones of Competitive Advantage: A Resource-Based View," *Strategic Management Journal* 14:3 (1993), 179–191.

22. R. R. Wiggins and T. W. Ruefli, "Sustained Competitive Advantage: Temporal Dynamics and the Incidence and Persistence of Superior Economic Performance," *Organization Science* 13:1 (2002), 82–105.

23. Barney, "Firm Resources and Sustained Competitive Advantage"; Peteraf, "The Cornerstones of Competitive Advantage"; B. Wernerfelt, "A Resource Based View of the Firm," *Strategic Management Journal* 5:2 (1984), 171–180.

24. Peteraf, "The Cornerstones of Competitive Advantage"; C. A. Montgomery and S. Hariharan, "Diversified Expansion by Large Established Firms," *Journal of Economic Behavior* 15:1 (1991), 71–99.

25. M. Porter, *Competitive Strategy* (New York: Free Press, 1980).

26. C. M. Christensen, *The Innovator's Dilemma: When New Technologies Cause Great Firms to Fail* (Boston: Harvard Business School Press, 1997).

27. Brown and Eisenhardt, *Competing on the Edge.*

28. J. Gimeno and C. Woo, "Multimarket Contact, Economies of Scope, and Firm Performance," *Academy of Management Journal* 42:3 (1999), 239–259.

29. Christensen, *The Innovator's Dilemma.*

After studying this chapter, you should be able to:

1. Explain how strategic leadership is essential to strategy formulation and implementation.

2. Understand the relationships among vision, mission, values, and strategy.

3. Understand the roles of vision and mission in determining strategic purpose and strategic coherence.

4. Identify a firm's stakeholders and explain why such identification is critical to effective strategy formulation and implementation.

5. Explain how ethics and biases may affect strategic decision making.

6. Create a vision and mission statement for your StratSim firm based on the goals of your StratSim executive team.

▶ **David T. Kearns, 1982-1990**
Diversify Xerox's businesses; improve quality and efficiency to ward off foreign competition.
Stock high: $13.29
Stock low: $5.88

▶ **Paul A. Allaire, 1990-1999**
Shed unprofitable, noncore businesses; add cutting-edge products to Xerox's product lineup.
Stock high: $59.81
Stock low: $3.75

1980   1985

HOW TO PULL A $15-BILLION COW OUT OF A DITCH

From an outsider's perspective, there was very little in Anne Mulcahy's background at Xerox to suggest that she'd be prepared for the kind of crisis management that awaited her.[1] Most recently, she'd been vice president for human resources and chief staff officer to former chief executive officer (CEO) Paul A. Allaire. The Xerox board promoted Mulcahy to president in May 2000, ousting G. Richard Thoman after a mere 13 months and reinstalling Chairman Allaire as CEO. When Allaire stepped down on August 1, 2001, Mulcahy became the first female CEO in Xerox history.

The Fall from the Nifty 50 The Xerox story is pretty well known. Introduced in 1959, the Xerox 914 copier transformed office work and installed Xerox as a charter member of the so-called "Nifty 50"—the 50 stocks most favored by institutional investors. Since the 1970s,

▶ G. Richard Thoman,
1999-2000
Reinvent and restructure Xerox to better compete in alternative markets; cut costs and bring in "new blood."
Stock high: $64.00
Stock low: $19.00

▶ Paul A. Allaire,
2000-2001
Restore profitability and investor confidence.
Stock high: $29.31
Stock low: $4.44

▶ Anne M. Mulcahy,
2001-present
Rescue Xerox from bankruptcy and reignite growth.
Stock high: $17.24
Stock low: $4.42

1995   2000

however, Xerox has been crippled by competition (mostly Japanese), repeated failures to capitalize on innovations coming out of its own Palo Alto Research Center (PARC), and tardiness in embracing digital imaging. After years of weak sales, the company was foundering, and employees were as disgruntled as customers. Then things went from bad to worse. In October 2001, Xerox reported its first quarterly loss in 16 years, and as debt piled up, the Securities and Exchange Commission began investigating the company's accounting practices.

Although the move from senior executive to CEO was a huge jump, Mulcahy was given the chance because she'd instilled confidence in the board. "She has the strategic mind and toughness to serve as CEO," said board member (and Johnson & Johnson CEO) Ralph Larsen.

Mulcahy was a popular manager with years of experience in dealing with customers. Granted, she'd never been involved in product development and didn't boast Allaire's financial expertise, but she'd demonstrated smart decision-making skills as head of the company's $6-billion division for small-office equipment. She'd also put together one of its biggest acquisitions—the $925-million purchase from Tektronix Inc. of a color-printing division that's now a source of fast-growing revenues (in large part because Mulcahy had preserved the division's autonomy and many of its business practices).

Running the Gamut from Enthusiasm to Pragmatism   If there was ever any uncertainty about her qualifications as a CEO, they were soon dispelled. Mulcahy refined the Xerox vision and went out of her way to remind Xerox employees that the core values embedded in the company's mission statement had always been part of the firm's deep culture. More important, she moved decisively to align the firm's operations with its refined statement of mission and values.

On the less philosophical side, she sold Xerox's China and Hong Kong operations, and in March 2001 she raised $1.3 billion by selling half of its stake in a joint venture with Fuji. Mulcahy also proved willing to make other tough decisions. In June 2001, she closed down the unit that made desktop inkjet printers in Rochester, New York—a business that she'd once supported. Soon after taking the reins, she eliminated the company's stock dividend and announced that PARC would be spun off as a separate company.

Internally, she spread her message with a regular memo called "Turnaround Talk," which alternates between enthusiasm ("Together We Can Do It!") and pragmatism ("When we shut off the bottled water, it's not because we want to be mean-spirited. It's because all these little expenses . . . can spell the difference between losing money and turning a profit"). By 2002, stressing fidelity to the Xerox mission and long-term vision, she'd cut annual expenses by $1.7 billion, sold $2.3 billion worth of noncore assets, and reduced long-term debt to $9.2 billion, down from a high of $15.6 billion in 2000. Xerox returned to full-year profitability in 2002, generating $1.9 billion in operating-cash flow and $91 million in net income on $15.8 billion in sales.

The Next Chapter   In July 2003, with Xerox gaining market share in important segments with new-product introductions, Mulcahy announced that the current chapter in the Xerox "turnaround story" had been closed. Her new challenge would be reigniting growth. Even during weak sales years, she'd invested $1 billion annually in research and development, and she's betting big on growth through such service businesses as document-management flow and computer networking.

The task of turning Xerox around has taken its toll on Mulcahy's personal life. Friends say that she laughs when asked about hobbies and executive-suite privileges like golf. Nowadays, reports *Business Week,* Mulcahy "only has time for work and her family, including her two teenage sons." But that, concludes the article, is "the kind of effort it takes to pull a $15-billion cow out of a ditch—and then try to make it run." ■

Xerox Values
Since our inception, we have operated under the guidance of six core values:
- *We succeed through satisfied customers.*
- *We deliver quality and excellence in all we do.*
- *We require premium return on assets.*
- *We use technology to develop market leadership.*
- *We value our employees.*
- *We behave responsibly as a corporate citizen.*

STRATEGIC LEADERSHIP

Imagine starting a new job and then finding out that your job description includes the following items:

- You'll be personally responsible for the entire company's performance—success, or failure.
- You'll be relatively powerless to control most of what goes on in the organization.
- You'll have more authority than any other employee, but in using that authority, you'll make some people so unhappy that they'll harbor personal grudges against you.[2]

Congratulations: You're a CEO.

The basic responsibility of a CEO—*strategic leadership*—is so important that you'll find chapters on it in every management and organizational behavior book you pick up. Stories about leaders and leadership regularly command the covers and fill the pages of major business publications around the world. Some business leaders become celebrities.

What do these leaders do when they're on the job? *Leadership* is the task of exerting influence on other people's pursuit of goals in an organizational context. **Strategic leadership** is the task of managing an overall enterprise and influencing key organizational outcomes, such as company-wide performance, competitive superiority, innovation, strategic change, and survival. As the process of communicating the vision and mission that top executives espouse and model through their own actions, strategic leadership also sets the stage for strategy creation and implementation. Strategic leadership is often associated with individuals like Anne Mulcahy, but increasingly it's being exercised by teams of top executives. Given the complexity and speed of competitive change and uncertainty facing most firms today, this shift shouldn't be surprising.

strategic leadership Task of managing an overall enterprise and influencing key organizational outcomes

What This Chapter Is About

Most of this section explains why top executives, through their decisions and behavior, have both a symbolic and a substantive impact on the outcomes that concern a firm's key stakeholders. Thus we start by introducing the roles filled by top individual managers and management teams as they exercise strategic leadership. We'll discuss the functions of individuals and executive teams, as well as the conditions under which strategic-leadership efforts may flourish or founder. We will then discuss the ways in which vision, mission, values, and strategy relate to one another, and we'll show how vision and mission are reflected in the properties of strategy that we call *purpose* and *coherence.* Next, we'll introduce the principles of stakeholder analysis and explain why the best strategic leaders consider stakeholder interests when developing organizational vision and mission and strategies for realizing them. We conclude by showing how unethical and biased judgments can undermine even the best-laid strategic-leadership plans.

The Roles Leaders Fill

What do senior managers do? What occupies their days and nights and fills up their personal digital assistants (PDAs)? As our opening vignette suggests, their jobs are complex and multifaceted, and we can understand the CEO's job only by analyzing it in some detail.[3] Let's start by dividing executive activities into the three basic roles illustrated in Exhibit 2.1: *interpersonal, informational,* and *decisional.*

Interpersonal Roles   Some executive tasks derive from the status and formal authority that come with the job. They're often interpersonal in nature and have a degree of symbolic value. Many of these roles may seem to have little to do with the practical exigencies of running a company, but they frequently occupy a great of deal of a CEO's time in all firms, from the smallest to the very largest.

Figurehead and Liaison   As *figureheads,* top executives perform various ceremonial tasks, such as breaking ground at new facilities, hosting retirement dinners, and even fielding calls from irate stakeholders. As *liaisons,* they maintain relationships with external stakeholders, thus strengthening the company's links with its external environment. In this role,

Exhibit 2.1 The Roles That Leaders Play

Source: H. Mintzberg, The Nature of Managerial Work (New York: Harper and Row, 1973).

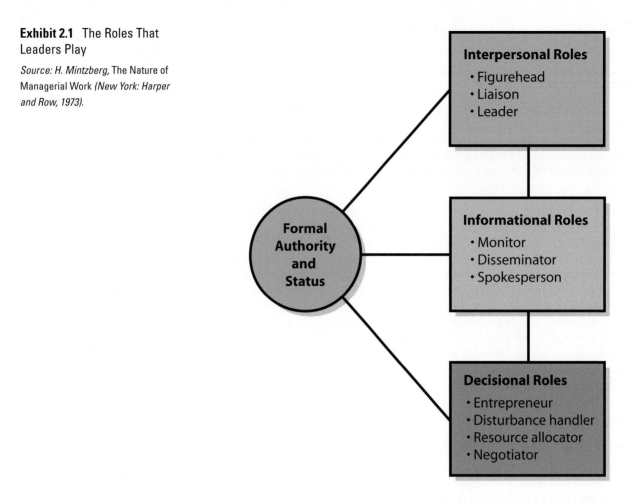

they serve on the boards of other companies, meet with suppliers and customers, and participate in charities and civic organizations.

Leader Whereas the role of liaison is horizontal in nature, leadership is a vertical relationship: Top executives are *leaders* because employees and other stakeholders who don't possess their authority look to them for motivation and direction. In this chapter, we'll focus on senior-leadership responsibilities, such as providing vision, purpose, and direction.

Informational Roles Informational roles include those of monitor, disseminator, and spokesperson. As *monitor,* the executive taps into a larger network of contacts, colleagues, and employees to collect and collate the information needed to understand the organization and its environment. An effective monitor, says strategic-leadership expert Henry Mintzberg, "seeks information in order to detect changes, to identify problems and opportunities, to build up knowledge about his milieu, to be informed when information must be disseminated and decisions made."[4]

Sharing Information: Disseminator and Spokesperson Not surprisingly, information is never in short supply; in fact, information overload is a common condition of executive life. Top managers are bombarded with reports, analyses, and projections and information about both internal operations and external events. Obviously, the good monitor must know what to do with all of this information. Much of it, of course, is passed on to people both inside and outside the firm who can put it to use. In passing information to internal stakeholders, executives are *disseminators;* in passing it to external stakeholders, they're *spokespersons.*

As disseminators, CEOs communicate not only factual information, such as data received from bankers and consultants, but also what's often called *value-based information.* In leading Xerox through a period of change, for example, Anne Mulcahy spent much of her time communicating value statements to both internal and external stakeholders.

CEO Richard Notebaert (center) of Qwest Communications fields a question during an employee meeting. The firm's 40,000 employees are internal stakeholders. In communicating with them, Notebaert is playing the role of disseminator. CEOs often become the "face" people for their companies.

As spokespersons, CEOs perform such communications tasks as lobbying, public relations, and formal reporting. CEOs communicate with both boards of directors, to whom they report, and the general public. Needless to say, being an effective spokesperson means focusing on the most current, accurate, and relevant information.

Decisional Roles   Perhaps the most obvious—some will say the most important—role of top managers is making key decisions about the company's strategy and future. In developing and implementing strategy, top executives may play any or all of four decisional roles: *entrepreneur, disturbance handler, resource allocator,* and *negotiator.*

The Entrepreneur   As entrepreneur, the CEO designs the firm's strategy. Clearly, many people are involved in the process, but the CEO must ultimately authorize major strategic initiatives and supervise their implementation.

The Disturbance Handler   Whereas the entrepreneurial role focuses on voluntary and proactive initiatives, disturbance handling deals with unforeseen situations or those in which the firm is involved involuntarily. Any number of "disturbances" can threaten the successful implementation of a strategy, including both internal and external conflicts. Internal conflicts, such as infighting by divisions or managers over responsibilities and authority, often require the CEO's arbitration. Likewise, the CEO will probably have to take action to smooth out conflicts in the distribution channel (a key supplier's announcement, for example, that it will no longer deal with the company on an exclusive basis).

The Resource Allocator   The role of resource allocator is crucial both to the task of formulating strategy and to the task of executing it successfully. If resources aren't effectively allocated, even a well-formulated strategy has little chance of success. With authority over the organization's financial, material, and human resources, the CEO is the only person who can manage the tradeoffs among competing strategic projects.

The Negotiator   As a negotiator, the CEO is usually concerned with nonroutine transactions involving other organizations. Such decisions as whether to acquire or merge with another firm, to sell a major division, or to renegotiate a labor contract require significant participation from the CEO.

The Surprised CEO   Obviously, then, being a CEO isn't easy.[5] What's astonishing, however, is the result of recent research showing that many new CEOs are quite surprised by many aspects of their jobs. Some report, for instance, that they're surprised at having to work with limited information and insufficient time to accomplish what they're expected to do.

Others are surprised that being a CEO means that they can no longer run day-to-day operations the way they once did. As heads of divisions or small companies, managers are much more deeply involved in nuts-and-bolts operations, but when they move into the executive suite of a large organization, they no longer have the time for hands-on management.

Yet other new CEOs learn the hard way that being the most powerful person in the organization doesn't mean that you can use power as liberally as you please; power is a privilege best indulged in moderation. Conversely, many CEOs reach the top rung on the organizational ladder only to be reminded—sometimes rudely—that they still have to answer to a board of directors. Finally, new CEOs are often surprised at how hard they have to work to make their brilliant strategies understood and get them accepted by a broad range of stakeholders.

In addition, as demonstrated by Anne Mulcahy's situation, many who rise to senior leadership positions in large organizations often pay a price—sacrificing their personal and family lives in order to meet their managerial responsibilities. Roger Deromedi, the recently appointed CEO of Kraft Foods, notes that "I travel about 40 percent of the time, so life is a balancing act. People often don't make time with their spouse that's separate from time with their kids. I prioritize my wife and family, which means I don't have as much time for outside interests."[6]

The Skill Set of the Effective Strategic Leader: The Level 5 Hierarchy

Level 5 Hierarchy Model of leadership skills calling for a wide range of abilities, some of which are hierarchical in nature

What does it take to be an effective organizational leader? Obviously, neither all leaders nor leadership challenges are created equal. A diverse set of skills, therefore, can come in handy. In this section, we'll discuss the development of leadership skill sets in terms of a model called the **Level 5 Hierarchy**, which was popularized by management researcher Jim Collins in the book *From Good to Great*.[7] The key to this framework is the idea that leadership requires a wide range of abilities, some of which are hierarchical in nature—in other words, that before mastering certain higher-level abilities, one must first master certain lower-level skills.[8] Collins proposes the five levels of leadership skills summarized in Exhibit 2.2.

- *Level 1.* Before becoming an effective leader, you must prove highly competent in your work. On the first level of leadership, therefore, productive contributions of your talent, knowledge, hard work, and skills must be made.

- *Level 2.* Senior management is often a team endeavor, and CEOs must be able to delegate major responsibilities to teams of senior executives. At level 2, therefore, you must also show the ability to work effectively as a member of a team.

- *Level 3.* After teamwork abilities have been demonstrated, you need to show the ability to manage other people—the ability to organize people and marshal resources to achieve specific objectives.

- *Level 4.* Next, you must prove capable of leading a larger organization by generating broad commitment to a clear vision of the organization's future. At level 4, you need to show the ability to lead a group to superior levels of performance. Anne Mulcahy, for example, didn't reverse Xerox's fortunes by herself. She assembled a team with diverse backgrounds and capabilities and drew upon their collective abilities.

- *Level 5.* Level-5 leadership tends to feature an unusual, even paradoxical, combination of skills. Level-5 leaders not only express an unwavering resolve, or *professional will*, to achieve higher goals but demonstrate a surprising degree of *professional modesty*. Let's take a closer look at these two managerial attributes.

Professional Will   Carrying out bold strategy moves requires commitment across the entire organization. A level-5 leader can translate strategic intent into the resolve needed to pursue a strategy—and usually to make hard choices—over a period of time.

Here's a good illustration. Walgreen Company was founded in 1901 by Chicago pharmacist Charles Walgreen. Eight years later, Walgreen began serving lunch at a new soda fountain, where, by the 1920s, he was doing his part to popularize the milk shake. Although food services remained a key part of Walgreen's business, the company realized during the 1960s that its classic soda-fountain operations were draining profits from the modern self-service retail operations that generated far greater sales per square foot. Now, to many people, soda fountains were a Walgreen hallmark, and because its history of food service

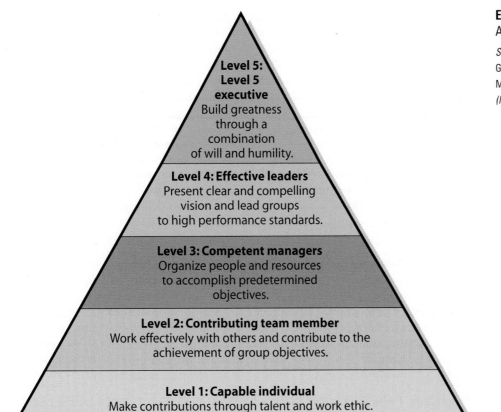

Exhibit 2.2 Level-5 Leaders:
A Hierarchy of Capabilities

Source: Adapted from J. Collins,
Good to Great: Why Some Companies
Make the Leap . . . and Others Don't
(New York: HarperBusiness, 2001).

Level 5:
Level 5
executive
Build greatness
through a
combination
of will and humility.

Level 4: Effective leaders
Present clear and compelling
vision and lead groups
to high performance standards.

Level 3: Competent managers
Organize people and resources
to accomplish predetermined
objectives.

Level 2: Contributing team member
Work effectively with others and contribute to the
achievement of group objectives.

Level 1: Capable individual
Make contributions through talent and work ethic.

was part of the firm's identity, there was considerable internal resistance to the idea of closing down the soda-fountain operations. In fact, CEO Charles Walgreen III found that phasing out food-service operations was more easily said than done; simply announcing his plan by no means ensured organization-wide cooperation. Ultimately, Walgreen set a deadline of five years, admonishing senior executives that "the clock is ticking." When reminded six months later that management had only five years to get out of the restaurant business, Walgreen reasserted his resolve to stick to the schedule: "Four and a half years," he replied.[9] In the final analysis, it was largely Walgreen's resolve that transformed the old model of the drugstore chain into a new (and more profitable) retail model.

Professional Modesty   Oddly, level-5 leaders also tend to be modest people—a fairly rare trait among people with upward career trajectories. Most research suggests that hubris is much more common than humility in the upper echelons of Corporate America, and given the drive that's needed to found or lead a successful firm, that fact shouldn't be surprising. And although examples abound of successful leaders who would not be described as modest, Collins' research suggests that companies that improve from average profitability and then beat the market over the long haul tend to be led by people who prefer to share credit rather than hog it. They tend to shun public attention, act with calm determination, and exercise their ambitions on the company's behalf rather than their own. They're also concerned about the future welfare of the company as well as its performance record during their own tenures.

What Does It Take to Be a CEO?

Having established the fact that senior executives influence the formation and implementation of strategy through both judgment and behavior, we know that it's worthwhile to understand what makes them think and act the way they do. We'll start by focusing on the characteristics of individual executives and the roles that they play in shaping strategic-leadership abilities.

Are you CEO material? Just what does it take? Charisma? Integrity? An Ivy League MBA? International management experience? Not surprisingly, there's no single answer to these seemingly simple questions. Although some answers involve such personality differences as charisma and emotional intelligence, others point to such demographic characteristics as gender, race, education, or work experience. There's little consensus on the issue of whether personality or background counts more, but understanding their actions is important if you want to understand successful leaders. With this fact in mind, let's take a closer look at all three perspectives on leadership characteristics: *personality differences, background and demographic differences,* and *differences in competence and actions.*

Personality Differences   Largely because psychological traits can be measured through surveys and other quantitative approaches, a large amount of research has been done on the personality or psychological determinants of strategic leadership. Many of these studies focus on four personality characteristics: *locus of control, need for achievement, tolerance for risk or ambiguity,* and *charisma and emotional intelligence.*[10]

What's Your Tolerance for Ambiguity?   Analyzing all of these characteristics goes beyond the purpose of this chapter, but you may find it instructive to investigate how you measure up on one key personality attribute—tolerance for ambiguity—compared to typical executives. *Tolerance for ambiguity* means that one tends to perceive situations as promising rather than threatening. If you are intolerant of ambiguity, then uncertainty or a lack of information, for example, would make you uncomfortable. Ambiguity arises from three main sources: novelty, complexity, and insolubility. You can use the ambiguity scale in Exhibit 2.3 to see how you measure up in terms of tolerance for ambiguity.

Personality Traits Versus Leadership Abilities   If there is indeed a correspondence between certain personality characteristics and leadership abilities, then (at least in theory) boards of directors could sift through applicant pools and choose CEOs on psychological grounds. Unfortunately, the jury is still out on the question of whether "natural" leaders can be classified according to personality differences or identified through psychological test instruments. In fact, some researchers warn against placing undue importance on trendy personality screens. In short, personality characteristics may be important in some respects, but defining and isolating effective leadership abilities is a complex task.

Background and Demographic Differences   *Background* differences typically refer to such factors as work experience and education, whereas *demographics* refers to such factors as gender, nationality, race, religion, network ties, and so forth.[11] Obviously, many factors of both kinds will figure prominently on your résumé.

Historically, the profile of the typical *Fortune*-500 top executive was a white male between the ages of 45 and 60 with a law, finance, or accounting degree from an Ivy League school.[12] Sociologists explain this pattern by pointing out that, for a long time, a large portion of the educated population—and thus of the managerial talent pool—consisted of white males. Moreover, white males were favored by certain structural features of the executive-employment market, including the usual prejudice of people to show favoritism toward people who are like them (in this case, white males).

Changes in demographics of business school students, as well as legal and social influence from lawsuits and legislation, have helped to diversify management ranks. Although there are significantly more female and minority managers at the start of the twenty-first century than there were just 20 years ago, few women and minorities have ascended to the level of CEO at the largest American companies. For instance, as of 2005 there were only 9 female CEOs among the 500 largest U.S. companies (1.8%), but this is double the number of just 9 years earlier. In addition, 16 percent of the corporate officers of these same companies are female, suggesting that change is happening, even if only gradually. It is interesting to note that the diversity of CEOs among privately owned smaller companies is much more reflective of the U.S. population. Although the diversity of large public companies has been slow to change, the diversity of leadership in smaller companies is much greater and growing.

Exhibit 2.3 Can You Tolerate Ambiguity?

You may have taken this survey earlier in the semester in preparation for this course. By definition, ambiguity characterizes strategic management and the study of strategy through cases. Your response to the case method itself is a function of your own attitude toward ambiguity. Take the following survey and tabulate your score to find out your tolerance for ambiguous situations.

Please respond to the following statements by indicating the extent to which you agree or disagree with them. Fill in the blanks with the number from the rating scale that best represents your evaluation of the item. There's a scoring key at the end of the survey.

1	Strongly disagree	5	Slightly agree
2	Moderately disagree	6	Moderately agree
3	Slightly disagree	7	Strongly agree
4	Neither agree nor disagree		

_____ 1.   An expert who doesn't come up with a definite answer probably doesn't know too much.

_____ 2.   I would like to live in a foreign country for a while.

_____ 3.   There is really no such thing as a problem that can't be solved.

_____ 4.   People who fit their lives to a schedule probably miss most of the joy of living.

_____ 5.   A good job is one where what is to be done and how it is to be done are always clear.

_____ 6.   It is more fun to tackle a complicated problem than to solve a simple one.

_____ 7.   In the long run it is possible to get more done by tackling small, simple problems rather than large and complicated ones.

_____ 8.   Often the most interesting and stimulating people are those who don't mind being different and original.

_____ 9.   What we are used to is always preferable to what is unfamiliar.

_____ 10. People who insist upon a yes or no answer just don't know how complicated things really are.

_____ 11. A person who leads an even, regular life in which few surprises or unexpected happenings arise really has a lot to be grateful for.

_____ 12. Many of our most important decisions are based on insufficient information.

_____ 13. I like parties where I know most of the people more than ones where all or most people are complete strangers.

_____ 14. Teachers or supervisors who hand out vague assignments give one a chance to show initiative and originality.

_____ 15. The sooner we all acquire similar values and ideals the better.

_____ 16. A good teacher is one who makes you wonder about your way of looking at things.

To score the instrument, **the even-numbered items must be reverse scored**. That is, the 7s become 1s, 6s become 2s, 5s become 3s, and 4s remain the same. After reversing the even-numbered items, sum the scores for all 16 items to get your total score. High scores indicate a greater *intolerance* for ambiguity. Use the comparison scores provided below to benchmark your own score, and read the following paragraphs to interpret the results.

Total Score

Subscores (follow same even/odd reverse scoring)

(N) Novelty score (sum 2, 9, 11, 13)   _____

(C) Complexity score (sum 4, 5, 6, 7, 8, 10, 14, 15, 16)   _____

(I) Insolubility score (sum 1, 3, 12)   _____

Being intolerant of ambiguity (relatively high score) means that an individual tends to perceive situations as threatening rather than promising. Lack of information or uncertainty, for example, would make such a person uncomfortable. Ambiguity arises from three main sources: *novelty*, *complexity*, and *insolubility*. These three subscales exist within the instrument you just completed.
Comparison total scores: Senior executives 44–48, MBAs 55–60.

Source: S. Budner, "Intolerance of Ambiguity as a Personality Variable," *Journal of Personality 30 (1982),* 29–50.

Although there are still a lot of white males with Ivy League degrees in the upper echelons of American business, we're now finding much greater diversity among top-management teams. Again, however, we need to remember that boards don't rely on any single criterion when choosing a CEO. In fact, our opening vignette features a CEO who came up not by following the usual accounting or finance track but rather through strategic human resource management.

Beside the fact that it's unethical (and, in many countries, illegal) to discriminate in hiring and promotion, a number of practical explanations account for the increasing diversity in the ranks of top managers, both in the United States and elsewhere:

- Although an advanced degree remains a typical prerequisite for promotion, college education is now available to more people than ever before. All around the world, schools compete for the best and brightest regardless of race, gender, or religion, and employers reap the benefits of more diverse talent pools.

- Groups tend to make better decisions when they can draw on heterogeneous perspectives, especially when facing turbulent or uncertain environments. When uncertainty makes it difficult to predict the future, top-management teams make better strategic decisions when they get input from diverse sources.[13]

- Companies today need top managers with strong international skills gained through work experience abroad. Because these skills are still fairly rare, even among college graduates, firms must look harder and farther to find them.[14]

- Firms increasingly seek competitive advantage through the quality of their human capital—the people who work for them. Because human capabilities are color, gender, and ethnicity blind, people with greater background and demographic diversity are rising to the ranks of upper management. Indeed, any form of bias that prevents talented employees from being promoted will put a firm at a distinct competitive disadvantage, particularly in terms of its ability to attract and retain talented people.

Competence and Actions Do actions speak louder than words (or perhaps even louder than personality, background, or demographic differences)? Among the main reasons that Anne Mulcahy rose to the top at Xerox was her experience as vice president and staff officer for customer operations in South and Central America, Europe, Asia, Africa, and China. Increasingly, the consensus on what it takes to make it to the top-executive ranks goes beyond skin color, gender, and even line items on a résumé. More companies are placing value on substantive work experience—looking as much for the knowledge gleaned from mistakes as for the successes accumulated along the way.

Mulcahy had already demonstrated courage and toughness when it came to making and sticking to decisions, and although such toughness may be a product of experience, many experts argue that superior executives are distinguished by a talent for strategic thinking. Mulcahy was promoted because of her proven strength as a business strategist as well as her decision-making toughness. What, exactly, does a "talent for strategic thinking" add to "toughness"? By *toughness*, we mean a willingness and ability to change an organization's strategic course even when that change represents a significant departure from its traditional way of doing business. Whereas the average manager emphasizes the efficient execution of a given plan, the strategic leader works not only to develop the plan in the first place, but to empower the organization to realize the vision behind it.

Strategists and nonstrategists differ in how they think about problems. Like personality differences, these differences are too broad to review in detail in this chapter. However, a few of these dimensions of strategic thinking are reviewed in the "Are You a Strategist?" exercise in Exhibit 2.4. Test yourself on a few dimensions of strategic leadership by taking the survey. As you can see, strategists are characterized by having a spirit of entrepreneurship and an eye to the future.

What Makes an Effective Executive Team?

In reality, of course, organizations need good managers as well as great leaders, just as armies need hard-working soldiers and inspirational generals. Ironically, one hallmark of great leadership is knowing when and how to follow the lead of others. In this section, we'll discuss the ways in which the interaction of members of a top-management team can

Answer each question with "Yes," "Mostly Yes," "Mostly No," or "No." Tally up the percentage of answers in each category.	Yes	Mostly Yes	Mostly No	No
1. Do you like to be entrepreneurial and come up with new ideas or plans but are also comfortable having others execute them? _____	☐	☐	☐	☐
2. Do you have clear guiding values for your actions (i.e., strategic intent and coherence)? _____	☐	☐	☐	☐
3. Do you think about your strengths and weaknesses before making major life choices? _____	☐	☐	☐	☐
4. Do you engage in activities that are in concert with your vision of the future and personal guiding values? _____	☐	☐	☐	☐
5. When you work with others, do you try to foster a climate where your colleagues can act freely in the interests of the objective you are seeking to achieve? _____	☐	☐	☐	☐
6. When you are working with others to achieve a certain objective, do you actively and regularly involve them in formulating the strategy to achieve that objective? _____	☐	☐	☐	☐
7. When working with others to achieve an objective do you seek harmony in matching your group's culture with your strategy? _____	☐	☐	☐	☐
8. Do you point out new directions and take novel approaches? _____	☐	☐	☐	☐
9. Have you been lucky so far (strategic leadership includes the ability to place oneself in positions that favor being lucky)? _____	☐	☐	☐	☐
10. Do you make a contribution to society and yourself (strategic leaders leave a legacy)? _____	☐	☐	☐	☐

If you answered "Yes" or "Mostly Yes" to these questions, congratulations—you have the makings of a strategic leader!

Exhibit 2.4 Are You a Strategist?

Source: Adapted from H. Hinterhuber and W. Popp, "Are You a Strategist or Just a Manager?" Harvard Business Review 70:1 (January–February 1992), 105–113.

influence—for better or for worse—the contributions of a strategic leader. At the very least, the team has the advantage of a division of labor, and in any case, no single person, regardless of talent and ability, can single-handedly attend to all the details encountered at the top of today's complex organizations.

The Executive Team in StratSim

SimConnect

StratSim provides a unique opportunity for you to experience being part of an executive team, and may well be your first experience doing so. Typically, you will be part of a team of 3 to 6 students whose objective is to effectively manage an organization for up to 10 simulated years. This time horizon is long enough to find out how well your team can work together to create and implement an effective strategy. It is essential that you recognize that your teamwork may be the most critical predictive element of your future success. Your StratSim team must respond to a complex and changing environment while managing the needs of interdependent, but often diverse, functional areas.

What exactly does this mean? Let's start with a very simple example in which three individuals are responsible for different arenas—one is focused on competition, another on marketing, and a third on manufacturing—but their team is responsible for managing decisions for the Euro utility vehicle. The person focused on competition has recognized that company D is about to launch a new utility vehicle, the marketing manager has just finished running some test markets that indicate a price change could have a significant impact on sales, and the manufacturing manager is concerned about minimizing retooling costs due to changes in production levels. Clearly, even this simple example demonstrates the complexity of decision making in a changing environment (competitive vehicle launch, potential impact of price changes, and how production scheduling impacts retooling costs). If these three teammates do not take the time and effort to share information and ideas, and listen to the potential impact of different decisions on each other's functional area, they will surely hurt their probability of making an informed and integrated decision.

This leads us to recall that one of the important traits of an effective manager (and management team) is having a tolerance for ambiguity. Again, this simple scenario illustrates how difficult it is to predict the actual outcomes of decisions as (for example) the team won't know the details of the competitive product launch, nor will they fully be able to predict the impact of price changes on sales volume. However, if they listen to the insights that each team member brings to the table, they will have a better chance of (a) improving their ability to estimate the actual outcome, (b) becoming more comfortable with the potential impact of different outcomes, (c) minimizing the damaging consequences of the different outcomes, and (d) adjusting their own strategies earlier in the process to improve their own odds for success. Because individuals vary in their tolerance for ambiguity, as you can test in the survey in Exhibit 2.3, it is important that the team be aware of these differences and take them into account in their decision making.

Teamwork and Diversity What does effective teamwork mean if the team consists of top-management personnel? Basically, effective teamwork requires three criteria:

1. The team responds to a complex and changing environment.

2. The team can manage the needs of interdependent but often diverse units, **arenas**, or functional areas.

3. The team is able to develop a coherent plan for executive succession.

There's a common key to satisfying the first two criteria: A team can accommodate diverse input while acting as an integrated unit. In other words, the team is composed of people who have diverse backgrounds in terms of demographics and experience but who can nevertheless work well together as a network and take advantage of the resources and knowledge they have access to by virtue of each team member's personal and professional networks. Large firms typically can afford, and often have, larger top-management teams than do smaller firms, which also means that executives in larger firms have access to broader personal and professional networks.

Succession Planning The third area, succession planning, has received increased attention in recent years as turnover among upper-echelon executives has increased. This is the case even among small firms, although the process is often made more complex by the fact that potential successors may include family members, in addition to current executives and outsiders hired from other companies. As a practical matter, succession planning has become more important because the rate of CEO dismissals by relatively large public firms

conceptlink

In Chapter 1, we define **arenas** as the element of strategy that specifies the areas in which a firm will be active.

has increased by 170 percent from 1995 to 2003 (from 30 out of 2,500 to 75). Globally, CEO job security is declining, with average tenure decreasing by 23 percent between 1995 and 2003, to a low of 7.6 years. Twenty-eight percent of the 238 CEOs who departed in 2003 were outsiders—the highest proportion in any year since 1995.[15]

Experts agree that a well-planned and executed succession process is essential for a successful transition. **Succession planning** is typically overseen by the board, often with an outside consulting firm, and usually involves the current CEO. In most cases, succession is typically considered final only when the new CEO is in place and the old one has departed. Why? Given the power that sitting CEOs may command, it's often better that a long-term CEO leave the company entirely. Boards, says Jeffrey Sonnenfeld, an expert on CEO succession, "should recognize that creators have a strong tendency to act like monarchs or generals, and both kinds have trouble giving things up."[16]

> **succession planning** Process of managing a well-planned and well-executed transition from one CEO to the next with positive outcomes for all key stakeholders

Even with CEO succession planning becoming more established and accepted in corporations around the world, its practice is a science tempered by a strong dose of art. The box entitled "How Would You Do That? 2.1" discusses the characteristics that a board might look for in a new CEO. The science part involves the development of a methodical approach to identifying desirable CEO characteristics and then drawing out a short list of candidates from a broad field of wanna-be CEOs. As you can see, the hard part comes into play when making the difficult judgments about who should make the short list and then ranking those candidates realistically in terms of their ability to meet the firm's strategic needs.

When the succession process founders, it can destroy the CEO's legacy—not to mention the company's health—by undermining investor confidence, depressing the stock price, creating dissension on the board, disrupting the continuity of ongoing initiatives, and even crippling the organization for years. Conversely, when the process goes well, a smooth transition fosters positive outcomes for the company and its stakeholders. General Electric, for example, conducted a meticulous search over several years before appointing Jeffrey Immelt, who ran the company's medical-systems division, to succeed CEO Jack Welch. By the time a final decision was made, according to insiders, Immelt had in effect been running the company for most of a year—planning acquisitions, attending employee reviews, and overseeing management team meetings. Similarly, when the founder and CEO of Boston auto-wash chain ScrubaDub sought to turn the leadership of the business over to his two sons, he did so only after they had thoroughly hashed out their respective roles and titles, the company's vision and mission, and their respective compensation and stock ownership packages. One brother now serves as CEO, responsible for R&D and operations, and the other serves as president, responsible for training, sales, and marketing.[17]

Sometimes, of course, the timing of a transition can't be predicted. In such cases, an even higher premium is placed on good managerial bench strength and prior planning. At McDonald's, for example, the promotion of Charlie Bell only hours after the sudden death of CEO Jim Cantalupo reassured employees and investors that the firm was under competent leadership. The smooth transition was possible only because the plan for Bell's succession was already in place, and a year later, when Bell himself resigned because of illness, the board already had Jim Skinner waiting in the wings. "The worst-case scenario planning of most companies," points out Jeffrey Sonnenfeld, "is only a Band-Aid transitional solution, not a strategic solution. McDonald's directors, by immediately naming a battle-tested insider, showed the wisdom of having a succession plan in place."[18]

StratSim Group Dynamics

SimConnect

If you are using StratSim in a classroom setting, you will likely be asked by your instructor to work in groups. Each group will pool its skills and resources to manage collectively the various roles and responsibilities in the simulation. Thus, the specific decisions your group will make depend on the responsibilities you are assigned.

Group work is the way business is most often conducted today. It can be rewarding and frustrating. It is critical that you learn how to make every group experience a success.

The Strategy for Finding the Right CEO

Well-run boards do not assume that CEOs are superhuman or have mystical powers to change a firm's fortunes overnight. However, as the opening vignette on Xerox highlights, the right CEO can make a huge difference in terms of substantive strategic decisions, symbolic actions, and figurehead activities. As a three-time CEO and a director on a number of boards, Betsy Atkins can attest that directors have learned a lot in recent years about hiring chief executives. From 1980 to 2000, the percentage of outside candidates selected for new CEO positions soared from 7 to 50 percent; however, firms found that outsiders were not the cure-all they had hoped for. As a result, boards are trying harder to promote from within rather than hiring charismatic, but untested, CEOs from the outside.

MAPPING STRATEGY: IDENTIFYING IMPLEMENTATION LEVERS AND VALUE-CREATING ACTIVITIES

Regardless of whether the search is internal or external, the board must build a consensus on what it is seeking in a CEO. Going into a search, the board must have a shared view of leadership, and directors must agree on the firm's strategic needs and how much strategic change they want; a search can be crippled from the start if some directors fear the new leader will change things too drastically or if they delude themselves into believing that the next CEO will be their corporate savior. Directors need to be able to assess internal or external candidates' passions and strength of convictions, as well as their ability to lead. One way to start the search and selection process is to simply map the firm's strategy onto specific tactical and longer-term operating needs. Good boards view succession planning as a way of systematically reflecting upon the specific levers that the CEO and other top managers can and should pull to effect organizational change. CEOs, although only one component in the organizational machinery, obviously affect the way in which value-creating activities are performed, monitored, and rewarded. Which value-creating activities a firm chooses to focus on and how they are implemented is, in turn, the cornerstone of competitive advantage. Yet because large companies perform literally hundreds of interrelated, value-creating activities, it can be difficult for even the most responsible boards—especially ones with several outside, "independent" directors—to understand clearly the way in which these many activities create value and, more to the point, how a new CEO can affect the success with which they are carried out.

To do this, board members must dig deep and ask tough questions. Boards must also develop better means for systematically obtaining relevant, specific information about how the company creates value. Recent comprehensive studies convincingly argue that a full 40 percent of directors do not have a sufficient understanding of their firms' value-creation process. This is the critical roadblock for good corporate governance, as companies adjust from legally mandated board compliance to strategically focused board empowerment. The lack of understanding is hardly surprising, given the way in which information generally flows from senior management to the board. In

»

many firms, for example, thick binders of market data and analysts' reports are compiled and distributed to directors by the chief financial officer (CFO) two weeks before the board convenes. How many directors have the time or inclination to comb through these binders? How do such masses of ill-digested information help them understand the value-creation process?

To remedy the gaps in board members' knowledge of their firms, many leading board-governance experts argue that boards should "map" the company's strategy at a high level so that they can visualize why and how performing certain activities helps to achieve objectives and goals along several critical dimensions—financial, customer, operational, and developmental. A strategy can illustrate the correlation—or set of cause-and-effect linkages and pathways—among employee retention, deeper understanding of customer needs, enhanced customer loyalty, bigger margins, and enhanced profitability.

Balancing Quantitative and Qualitative Factors

Although numerous quantitative measurements are available, such as stock price history or background experience, the attributes that may have the greatest impact on a candidate's potential success are softer, qualitative ones. Atkins acknowledges that

directors need to be able to assess passion and strength of convictions as well as ability to lead. Atkins admits to her personal experience in this regard related to her brief tenure on the board of HealthSouth, a national chain of surgery and rehabilitation clinics. CEO Richard Scrushy, she recalls, was "impressive and forceful, [but] there was something about him that raised my antennae." She was right: Since 2003, 14 former HealthSouth employees, including all 5 of its former CFOs, have pleaded guilty to federal fraud charges. Scrushy is charged with 85 counts, including fraud, conspiracy, and money laundering. From that experience, Atkins learned that "the charismatic 'star' CEO leadership style is inconsistent with developing an open environment and an empowered management team."

Atkins did a better job at Lucent Technologies, where the board recruited CEO Pat Russo. Acknowledging that Lucent was going through significant upheaval and needed an inspiring, high-integrity team builder to stabilize and rebuild the company, the board set out to find someone with these qualitative attributes of leadership. That's how they settled on Russo.

Wiser for these experiences, Atkins is convinced that in evaluating candidates board members must assess their social interactions with the company's

directors. "It's a mistake," she says, to hire a CEO solely on the basis of formal presentations and discussions. Personal conversations often yield unexpected insight into a candidate's personality. An attentive interviewer, says Atkins, can detect the nuances in pregnant pauses that aren't always apparent in a preference write-up. After all, leadership is a collection of personal behaviors, political and people skills and judgment—and much of that is typically suppressed in formal settings. In social interactions, it's easier to ask open-ended questions, such as "What are you proudest of in your career?" or "What was the most difficult challenge you ever faced?" A director with a well-trained ear can then discover whether the candidate thinks in terms of building teams to accomplish objectives or is a lone ranger. "There's no way to analyze those qualities on a spreadsheet."

Atkins also thinks it's crucial for directors to do some background checking of their own rather than relying entirely on others. It's not that she doesn't trust executive-search firms. "It's just that they obviously have an incentive to close the transaction through a hiring decision, rather than prolong the debate."

Source: R. Fulmer & J. Conger, *Growing Your Company's Leaders* (New York: Amacom, 2004).

One of the most frequent complaints with group work is the amount of time wasted in trying to get organized and make decisions. There are also complaints that individual members are not "pulling their weight." To reduce these problems, your group should answer the following questions in your first meeting:

1. When, where, and how often should we meet?
2. How should we efficiently and effectively conduct our meetings?
3. Should we choose a CEO? What authority should this person have?
4. How should we divide the tasks among group members?
5. How do we resolve issues and make final decisions?
6. How do we encourage and maintain a high quality of contribution?
7. How will we deal with personal conflicts among group members?

Over time, the group should assess whether it is functioning efficiently and effectively. The group may have to reorganize to best meet the current needs of the business as your product portfolio changes, new competitive situations arise, and more information becomes available.

THE IMPRINT OF STRATEGIC LEADERSHIP: VISION AND MISSION

Top executives provide the context for strategy formulation and implementation through the vision and mission that they not only espouse, but that they also model through their own actions. Sometimes, they're the originators of the vision and mission; at other times, they're caretakers or agents who work to sharpen employees' shared understanding of the vision and mission. In any case, the vision and mission remain central, and that's why the overarching model of strategy management that we introduced in Chapter 1 starts with vision and mission.

Defining *Vision* and *Mission*

vision Simple statement or understanding of what the firm will be in the future

mission Declaration of what a firm is and what it stands for—its fundamental values and purpose

We define **vision** as a simple statement or understanding of what the firm will be in the future. A statement of vision is forward looking and identifies the firm's desired long-term status. In contrast, a **mission** is a declaration of what a firm is and stands for—its fundamental values and purpose. Because it's difficult to execute a strategy if it can't be described or understood, firms with clearly and widely understood visions and missions find it easier to make strategic decisions entailing difficult tradeoffs.

Thus, as you can see in Exhibit 2.5, vision and mission influence strategy formulation and implementation. Sometimes this influence is exercised when leaders focus explicitly on defining or refining a firm's vision, as was the case with Mulcahy at Xerox. More often, however, an organization's vision and mission are well established and functional. In these cases, leaders work to formulate the firm's strategy in a manner that's consistent with the fundamental values and purpose expressed in its statements of core beliefs. A shared understanding of the firm's direction and values helps guide both executives and employees in their daily decisions and actions. Vision and mission, therefore, reinforce and support strategy; conversely, strategy provides a coherent plan for realizing vision and mission.

Once you've finished this and the next section, you should be able to identify a firm's vision and mission and understand their roles in more complex organizational activities. You'll understand how vision and mission are translated into strategic action, and you'll be able to make recommendations for improving organizational performance or competitive position. You'll see how vision and mission contribute to the organizational functions that we call *strategic purpose* and *strategic coherence*. Because strategy can be successful only to the extent that key stakeholders (customers, suppliers, government, and employees) facilitate its implementation, you'll also learn how to use the tool that we call *stakeholder analysis*.

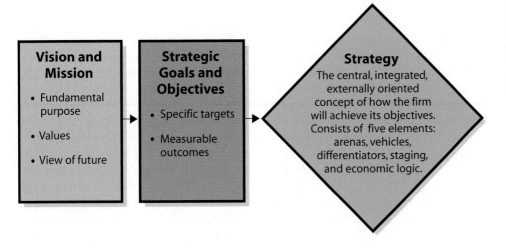

Exhibit 2.5 Vision, Mission, and Strategy

Adapted by *D. C. Hambrick and J. W. Fredrickson, "Are You Sure You Have a Strategy?" Academy of Management Executive 15:4 (2001), 48–59.*

What Should Vision and Mission Statements Encompass?

A study by the consulting firm Bain and Company reports that 90 percent of 500 firms surveyed issue some form of vision and mission statements.[19] Toward what end? Together, vision and mission statements not only express a firm's identity and describe its work but inform both managers and employees of the firm's direction. They're not strategies in and of themselves, but they convey organizational identity and purpose to critical stakeholders both inside and outside the firm.

Vision: The Uses of Ambition and Ambiguity In the early 1950s, Sony stated its vision of "becoming the company that most changes the worldwide image of Japanese products as being of poor quality." Back in 1915, CitiBank (now CitiGroup) announced its grandiose vision of becoming "the most powerful, the most serviceable, the most far-reaching world financial institution the world has ever seen."[20] As these two examples suggest, vision statements generally express long-term action horizons, and they're ambitious by design, because ambition forces the firm to stretch both by challenging external competitors and by questioning the internal status quo. Because they're often ambiguous, they don't inhibit the firm from reaching for the stars (or at least aspiring to reach for the stars). Ambiguity also enables flexibility for changing strategy or implementation tactics when it looks as if business as usual isn't going to realize the expressed vision.

Mission: The Uses of Core Values A firm will use its mission statement to identify certain core concepts, such as its purpose, or *raison d'être;* values and beliefs; standards of behavior; or corporate-level aims.[21] All employees are supposed to internalize core ideals and call upon them to guide their decisions and actions. At 3M, for example, a core value is the innovative solution of problems. Merck wants employees to preserve and improve human life, and Wal-Mart wants them to devote themselves to selling ordinary folks the same things that affluent people buy.[22]

Why Vision and Mission Statements Are Not Substitutes for Strategy

It should be obvious by now that clearly articulated, coherent, and widely understood vision and mission statements are not substitutes for strategy. Nevertheless, we need to spend a little time on this point.

In 1993, when outsider Lou Gerstner was hired as CEO and charged with the daunting task of saving IBM from potential ruin, he announced that "the last thing IBM needs (right now) is a vision." The statement was widely circulated (although press reports usually edited out the words "right now"),[23] as was Gerstner's charge that IBM's vision was nothing but a litany of platitudes, like those of firms who declare commitment to "total quality" or "customer service." Having discovered that some divisions at IBM were busier squabbling over the distribution of revenue than responding to customer needs, Gerstner was more interested in consistent and tangible managerial action.

Likewise, vision statements don't help much if managers view them as cure-alls for organization ailments or if they paint pictures of a future that's clearly unattainable. Sometimes, a vision is so irrelevant to organizational reality that employees and customers simply reject it. Small firms, in particular, need a clear vision and mission to provide them with focus, but they also need a concrete strategy to translate concepts and resource constraints into profitable action. In the case of IBM, an enormous firm, Gerstner wanted to send a strong message to all employees that serious changes were needed if the company was to survive—changes that would extend far beyond any revamped statement of vision.

Vision and mission can be powerful tools, but because they're general and ambiguous by design, they must be realized through carefully crafted and executed strategy. Firms undergoing strategic change are especially susceptible to serious discrepancies between a new vision statement that's crafted on high and the organizational processes designed to realize it on the factory floor. As you can see from Exhibit 2.6, Gerstner did in fact have a clear vision for IBM (namely, to get it back to the top spot in its industry), but he first set out to anchor this vision in specific goals and objectives derived from a focused and clearly articulated strategy. IBM's prospects were gloomy back in 1993, but thanks to Gerstner's clear-headed understanding of the relationship between strategy and vision (and his talent for leadership), IBM is once again one of America's most admired companies.

Goals and Objectives

goals and objectives Combination of a broad indication of organizational intentions (*goals*) and specific, measurable steps (*objectives*) for reaching them

superordinate goal Overarching reference point for a host of hierarchical subgoals

To be effective, then, visions and missions must be spelled out in terms of specific quantitative or qualitative **goals and objectives** for directing strategic actions. Often firms will also state a **superordinate goal** to serve as an overarching reference point for other goals and objectives. Wal-Mart's annual report, for example, states that the company will grow sales and profits by 20 percent per year; Ryanair says that it will be Europe's largest airline in seven years; Matsushita intends to become a "Super Manufacturing Company." Ultimately, the strength with which a firm's vision and mission are anchored in relevant goals and objectives will determine which ones walk the talk and which ones just talk the talk.

If talk of visions and superordinate goals conjures up images of crystal balls and astrology, don't be too surprised. Some executives treat vision and mission statements as symbolic pronouncements, and in many organizations they exist on a different plane than actual strategy and strategic actions. Such discrepancies are symptomatic of various condi-

Exhibit 2.6 Key Elements of Gerstner's 1993 Vision for IBM

Source: D. Kirkpatrick, "Gerstner's New Vision for IBM," Fortune, November 15, 1993, 119–124.

- IBM will not be split up and its many parts will be even more closely coordinated.

- IBM will reassert its identity as customers' primary computing resource.

- The company will be the dominant supplier of technology in the industry.

- PowerPC, a new microprocessor design, will be IBM's centerpiece. Built into many future computers, it will run a wide range of standard industry software. And it will steeply cut manufacturing costs.

- Mainframes are no longer central to the strategy, but IBM will still make them, now with microprocessors.

- IBM is its own worst enemy. Employees must waste fewer opportunities, minimize bureaucracy, and put the good of the company before their division's.

tions. Perhaps the firm is floundering from a lack of clear or unique strategic direction; perhaps its strategy is too complex; maybe management has lost sight of the competitive realities facing the company.

Research suggests that the best-performing firms boast clear visions and missions.[24] Effective strategic leaders craft these statements for a variety of reasons:

- To crystallize and disseminate the firm's strategy among employees
- To provide a shared logic for the firm's view of its internal and external environments and its treatment of stakeholders
- To galvanize concerted strategic action
- To link strategy formulation to implementation by tying vision and mission to specific and measurable goals and objectives

At many companies, managers are responsible for tracking strategic progress with a tool called a **balanced scorecard,** which is a system for translating vision and strategy into tangible performance measured by such criteria as return on sales, sales growth, and customer retention.

Finally, well-articulated and frequently shared vision and mission statements provide an impetus and rationale for ongoing strategic change, helping managers resolve the continuing tension between the static and dynamic facets of competitive situations.

concept link

In Chapter 8, we describe the *balanced scorecard* as a strategic support system devised to help managers translate vision and strategy into business-level and operating-unit-level performance along several critical dimensions.

STRATEGIC PURPOSE AND STRATEGIC COHERENCE

An overview of the examples presented in this chapter should tell you that it's relatively easy to compose a snappy vision statement. You should also have gathered by now that having vision and mission statements doesn't guarantee higher levels of performance. For one thing, some statements are more effective than others. How so? Research suggests the importance of the process used to develop and articulate statements. Performance, for example, is positively correlated with the integration of internal stakeholders—in other words, manager and employee satisfaction with the statement-development process.[25] This is yet one more reason why we'll focus on the stakeholder-analysis tool in the next section and why we stress the importance of considering stakeholders in the practice of strategic leadership. First, however, let's focus on the two most critical aspects of effective vision and mission statements: *strategic purpose* and *strategic coherence*.

Strategic Purpose

Vision and mission statements are actually statements of organizational identity and purpose that can guide executives in making corporate decisions. After all, one individual—even a group of individuals—can cope with only so much complexity in a problem. Vision and mission statements provide all employees with **strategic purpose**: a simplified, widely shared model of the organization and its future, including anticipated changes in its environment.

strategic purpose Simplified, widely shared mental model of the organization and its future, including anticipated changes in its environment

Tradeoffs, Options, and Other Decisions
Most major strategic decisions require tradeoffs—deciding on one course of action may necessarily eliminate other options. In addition, although some courses of action may satisfy the needs of some stakeholders, they may adversely affect others.

The consumer-products companies Mars Inc. and SC Johnson, for example, remain private corporations. When you visit either firm's Web site, you'll see that independence is a core value for both. Moreover, private ownership means greater flexibility in strategic choices: Because neither firm must cater to the stock market as a stakeholder, each can choose to make costly investments in the kinds of socially responsible programs that often draw fire from the shareholders of public companies. And the tradeoffs? The growth potential of each firm is limited, and it's more difficult to arrange for employee ownership, whether through direct share ownership or stock options.

Newman's Own, founded by actor Paul Newman and a partner in 1982, makes and sells salad dressing, lemonade, popcorn, salsa, steak sauce, and other food items through major grocery chains in the United States and abroad. In 2003, McDonald's announced that it would use Newman's Own dressings exclusively in its new Premium Salad line. Newman expects this alliance to increase profits by 25 percent. The firm's success derives from two policies anchored in its vision: (1) It insists on top-quality products with no artificial ingredients or preservatives. (2) It donates all after-tax profits to educational and charitable organizations, including UNICEF, Habitat for Humanity, and the Hole in the Wall Gang Camp for seriously ill children. The determination to combine commerce with philanthropy underlies a fairly unique vision, but it's guided the company's strategy for more than two decades. The tradeoff? Although adhering to a strongly held corporate philosophy helps managers choose certain courses of action over others, the decision to use more expensive natural ingredients means sacrificing higher short-term profitability.

Even a company with a more traditional profit orientation can be guided by a fairly simple vision. Michael Dell founded Dell Computers in 1984 on an investment of $1,000. His vision was to sell computer systems directly to customers. The company now has more than 55,000 employees and boasted revenues in excess of $49 billion in 2005.[26] Such rapid growth, however, means that the great majority of Dell employees are relative newcomers to the corporate family, which puts pressure on the company to preserve the values that guided it in its early years. Dell training, therefore, strives to imbue all employees with the "Soul of Dell"—the set of values that guides all of the firm's business practices.

As you can see in Exhibit 2.7, Matsushita Electric, the Japanese parent company of Panasonic, is preparing to stretch by comparing what the company does today with what it will have to do to become a "Super Manufacturing Company" in the future. Such a company, explains Matsushita CEO Kunio Nakamura, "must in essence be 'light and speedy.' Now when the nature of business is changing, emphasis will be placed on the maintenance, broadening and strengthening of IT, on R&D and marketing. Moreover, Matsushita at present is like a heavy lead ball loaded with assets. In the future we need to cast off superfluous assets and become a company that can move lightly like a soccer ball."[27]

The Challenge of Closing the Gap   The challenge posed by a strategic purpose is to close the gap between the firm's aspirations and its current capabilities and market positions. All strategies, for example, address the tradeoff between efficiency and effectiveness, and a firm can easily fall into the trap of adhering to its current strategy (say, becoming more efficient) even though customers no longer value its products (in other words, becoming less effective). Like long-term personal goals, the forward-looking aspect of strategic purpose means more than merely setting long-term goals that require stretch. Rather, an effective strategic purpose must be tied to a coherent set of activities, near-term goals, and objectives anchored in *measurable strategic outcomes*—that is, *strategic coherence.*

Strategic Coherence

An effective strategy is coherent. As we saw in Chapter 1, a firm's strategy entails an integrated set of choices regarding the five elements of the *strategy diamond.* **Strategic coherence**

strategic coherence Symmetric coalignment of the five elements of the firm's strategy, the congruence of functional-area policies with these elements, and the overarching fit of various businesses under the corporate umbrella

Exhibit 2.7 Creating Strategic Purpose at Matsushita

Source: "In the Pursuit of a Super Manufacturing Company," Panasonic *(accessed July 18, 2005), at matsushita.co.jp/corp/vision/president/interview2/en/index.html.*

Matsushita's Goal: To Become a 21st-Century "Super Manufacturing Company"		
	Today: A Conventional Manufacturing Company	**Tomorrow: A 21st-Century Super Manufacturing Company**
Role	Providing goods	Providing solutions
Investment	Principally capital investment	Expansion of R&D, marketing, and IT investment
Information	From the company	Interactive/direct contact with customers
Organization	Pyramid	Flat and web

(versus *incoherence*) is the symmetrical coalignment of the five elements of the firm's strategy, the congruence of policies in such functional areas as finance, production, and marketing with these elements, and the overarching fit of various businesses under the corporate umbrella. Successful firms depend on dozens of critical elements operating in concert and in balance. These elements are integrated so that everyone from design to manufacturing to marketing to accounting understands them in the same way.

conceptlink

In Chapter 1, we identify the five elements of the *strategy diamond* as vehicles, differentiators, staging, arenas, and economic logic.

In practice, some firms suffer from incoherent and fragmented strategies. For instance, a firm's decision to grow rapidly through acquisitions may be out of sync with its attempts to differentiate its products on the basis of strong brand equity. Some firms lack coherence because functional areas are treated like independent domains, as if they were silos of business activity that don't need orchestrated cooperation. Finally, some firms lack a coherent strategy because they move in and out of new businesses, as AT&T has done over the past two decades.

Applying the Strategy Diamond   How can firms achieve strategic coherence? The answer seems to be serious commitment to, and widespread communication of, well-understood and shared organizational vision and values. The strategy diamond framework is useful in testing the coherence of the elements of a strategy. We reintroduce it here because it's useful in testing for strategy coherence. From an internal perspective, a coherent strategy aligns all of the strategy's strategic, tactical, and design elements. From an external perspective, coherence is an alignment of the strategy with the industry environment and the vision of where and how the firm will be positioned in that environment in the future. Incoherence tends to plague firms that allocate resources primarily in response to competitors' strategies. As a result, it will appear as if their actions and functions are about average for the industry. In reality, of course, there's nothing distinctive about such a firm because it has in effect allowed its competitors to determine its strategy.

The Clear and Compelling Vision Statement   In many ways, strong vision statements function as guidelines for clear and compelling strategies that distinguish a firm from its competitors. What do we mean by "compelling"? Namely, that the underlying strategy is not only coherent but is accepted as truthful and useful by employees, customers, and other key stakeholders.[28] A clear vision of what the organization wants to achieve, coupled with an unambiguous understanding of its mission, helps managers make coherent strategic decisions.

STAKEHOLDERS AND STAKEHOLDER ANALYSIS

Stakeholders are individuals or groups who have an interest in an organization's ability to deliver intended results and maintain the viability of its products and services. We've already stressed the importance of stakeholders to a firm's vision and mission. We've also explained that firms are usually accountable to a broad range of stakeholders, including shareholders, who can make it either more difficult or easier to execute a strategy. This is the main reason why strategy formulators must consider stakeholders' interests, needs, and preferences. Considering these factors in the development of a firm's vision and mission is a good place to start, but first, of course, you must identify critical stakeholders, get a handle on their short- and long-term interests, calculate their potential influence on your strategy, and take into consideration how the firm's strategy might impact stakeholders (beneficially or adversely).

stakeholder Individual or group with an interest in an organization's ability to deliver intended results and maintain the viability of its products and services

As we've already seen, for instance, one key stakeholder group is composed of the CEO and the members of the top-management team. This group is important for at least three reasons:

1. Its influence as either originator or steward of the organization's vision and mission

2. Its responsibility for formulating a strategy that realizes the vision and mission

3. Its ultimate role in strategy implementation

Typically, stakeholder evaluation of both quantitative and qualitative performance outcomes will determine whether or not strategic leadership is effective. We summarize some relevant performance outcomes in Exhibit 2.8. Different stakeholders may place more

Exhibit 2.8 Some Financial and Nonfinancial Performance Metrics

Financial Performance Metrics	Nonfinancial Performance Metrics
► Return on sales	► Customer retention
► Return on assets	► Customer satisfaction
► Return on equity	► Customer complaints
► Sales per employee	► Employee turnover
► Sales growth	► Product returns
► Inventory turn	► Product quality
► Accounts receivable turn	► Patents
► Debt ratio	► New products released
► Current ratio	► Product development speed
► Cost reduction	► Reputation
	► Web traffic

emphasis on some outcomes than other stakeholders who have other priorities.

Stakeholders and Strategy

Managers perform stakeholder analysis in order to gain a better understanding of the range and variety of groups and individuals who not only have a vested interest in the formulation and implementation of a firm's strategy but who also have some influence on firm performance. Strategists thus develop vision and mission statements not only to clarify the organization's larger purpose but to meet or exceed the needs of its key stakeholders.

Stakeholder analysis may also enable managers to identify other parties that might derail otherwise well-formulated strategies, such as local, state, national, or foreign governmental bodies. Finally, stakeholder analysis enables organizations to better formulate, implement, and monitor their strategies, and this is why stakeholder analysis is a critical factor in the ultimate implementation of a strategy.

Identifying Stakeholders

The first step in stakeholder analysis is identifying major stakeholder groups. As you can imagine, the groups of stakeholders who will be affected either directly or indirectly by or have an effect on a firm's strategy and its execution can run the gamut from employees to customers to competitors to governments.

Let's pause for a moment to consider the important constituencies charted on our stakeholder map. Before we start, however, we need to remind ourselves that stakeholders can be individuals or groups—communities, social or political organizations, and so forth. In addition, we can break groups down demographically, geographically, by level and branch of government, or according to other relevant criteria. In so doing, we're more likely to identify important groups that we might otherwise overlook.

With these facts in mind, you can see that, externally, a map of stakeholders will include such diverse groups as governmental bodies, community-based organizations, social and political action groups, trade unions and guilds, and even journalists. National and regional governments and international regulatory bodies will probably be key stakeholders for global firms or those whose strategy calls for greater international presence. Internally, key stakeholders include shareholders, business units, employees, and managers.

Steps in Identifying Stakeholders Identifying all of a firm's stakeholders can be a daunting task. In fact, as we will note again shortly, a list of stakeholders that is too long actually may reduce the effectiveness of this important tool by overwhelming decision makers with too much information. To simplify the process, we suggest that you start by identifying groups that fall into one of four categories: *organizational, capital market, product market,* and *social.* Let's take a closer look at this step.

Step 1: Determining Influences on Strategy Formulation   One way to analyze the importance and roles of the individuals who comprise a stakeholder group is to identify the people and teams who should be consulted as strategy is developed or who will play some part in its eventual implementation. These are *organizational stakeholders,* and they include both high-level managers and frontline workers. *Capital-market stakeholders* are groups that affect the availability or cost of capital—shareholders, venture capitalists, banks, and other financial intermediaries. *Product-market stakeholders* include parties with whom the firm shares its industry, including suppliers and customers. *Social stakeholders* consist broadly of external groups and organizations that may be affected by or exercise influence over firm strategy and performance, such as unions, governments, and activists groups. The next two steps are to determine how various stakeholders are impacted by the firm's strategic decisions and the degree of power that various stakeholders wield over the firm's ability to choose a course of action.

Step 2: Determining the Effects of Strategic Decisions on the Stakeholder   Step 2 in stakeholder analysis is to determine the nature of the effect of the firm's strategic decisions on the list of relevant stakeholders. Not all stakeholders are impacted equally by strategic decisions. Some effects may be rather mild, and any positive or negative effects may be secondary and of minimal impact. At the other end of the spectrum, some stakeholders bear the brunt of firm decisions, good or bad.

In performing step 1, companies often develop overly broad and unwieldy lists of stakeholders. At this stage, it's critical to determine the stakeholders who are most important based on how the firm's strategy impacts the stakeholders. You must determine which of the groups still on your list have direct or indirect material claims on firm performance or which are potentially adversely impacted. For instance, it is easy to see how shareholders are affected by firm strategies—their wealth either increases or decreases in correspondence with firm actions. Other parties have economic interests in the firm as well, such as parties the firm interacts with in the marketplace, such as suppliers and customers. The effects on other parties may be much more indirect. For instance, governments have an economic interest in firms doing well—they collect tax revenue from them. However, in cities that are well diversified with many employers, a single firm has minimal economic impact on what the government collects. Alternatively, in other areas individual firms represent a significant contribution to local employment and tax revenue. In those situations, the impact of firm actions on the government would be much greater.

Step 3: Determining Stakeholders' Power and Influence over Decisions   The third step of a stakeholder analysis is to determine the degree to which a stakeholder group can exercise power and influence over the decisions the firm makes. Does the group have direct control over what is decided, veto power over decisions, nuisance influence, or no influence? Recognize that although the degree to which stakeholders are affected by firm decisions (i.e., step 2) is sometimes highly correlated with their power and influence over the decision, this is often not the case. For instance, in some companies frontline employees may be directly affected by firm decisions but have no say in what those decisions are. Power can take the form of formal voting power (boards of directors and owners), economic power (suppliers, financial institutions, and unions), or political power (dissident stockholders, political action groups, and governmental bodies). Sometimes the parties that exercise significant power over firm decisions don't register as having a significant stake in the firm (step 2). In recent years, for example, Wal-Mart has encountered significant resistance in some communities by well-organized groups who oppose the entry of the megaretailer. Wal-Mart executives now have to anticipate whether a vocal and politically powerful community group will oppose its new stores or aim to reduce their size, which decreases Wal-Mart's per-store profitability. Indeed, in many markets, such groups have been effective at blocking new stores, reducing their size, or changing building specifications.

Once you've determined who has a stake in the outcomes of the firm's decisions as well as who has power over these decisions, you'll have a basis on which to allocate prominence in the strategy-formulation and strategy-implementation processes. The framework in Exhibit 2.9 will also help you categorize stakeholders according to their influence in determining strategy versus their importance to strategy execution. For one thing, this distinction may help you identify major omissions in strategy formulation and implementation.

Exhibit 2.9 Mapping Stakeholder Influence and Importance

Source: Adapted from R. E. Freeman, Strategic Management: A Stakeholder Approach (Boston, MA: Pitman, 1984).

		Power of the Stakeholder over Strategic Decisions			
		Unknown	Little/no power	Moderate degree of power	Significant power
Effect of Strategy on the Stakeholder	Unknown				
	Little/no effect				
	Moderate effect				
	Significant effect				

Having identified stakeholder groups and differentiated them by how they are affected by firm decisions and the power they have to influence decisions, you'll want to ask yourself some additional questions:

■ Have I identified any vulnerable points in either the strategy or its potential implementation?

■ Which groups are mobilized and active in promoting their interests?

■ Have I identified supporters and opponents of the strategy?

■ Which groups will benefit from successful execution of the strategy and which may be adversely affected?

■ Where are various groups located? Who belongs to them? Who represents them?

Although the stakeholder-analysis framework summarized in Exhibit 2.9 is a good starting point, you'll find that many of the strategic-analysis tools that we introduce in succeeding chapters will also help you determine which stakeholders may be most critical to the success of your chosen strategy (and why). Ultimately, because vision and mission are necessarily long-term in orientation, identifying important stakeholder groups will help you to understand which constituencies stand to gain or lose the most if they're realized. The effective application of stakeholder analysis for a newly appointed manager is described in the box entitled "How Would You Do That? 2.2". From this example, you can see why stakeholder analysis should be an important input into both strategy formulation and implementation and how the roles of certain stakeholders create important interdependencies between formulation and implementation.

ETHICS, BIASES, AND STRATEGIC DECISION MAKING

Because the stakes are so high when executives make strategic decisions, they must do everything they can to make sure that those decisions are sound. You should thus weigh two additional factors before committing yourself to a major strategic endeavor: (1) whether the decision is ethical and (2) whether any potential biases have clouded your strategic decision-making process.

It should be obvious by now that our conception of strategy is that it is a means to accomplish organizational goals. The fact that we see numerous examples in the media of corporate scandals suggests the unfortunate observation that some people justify any means to accomplish a desired goal. Although it would be unfair to suggest that most cor-

In February 2004, former Enron CEO Jeffrey Skilling (handcuffed) appeared in federal court in Houston, Texas, where he was charged with 35 counts of conspiracy, securities fraud, wire fraud, and insider trading. According to the government, Skilling presided over accounting schemes to inflate the energy-trading company's earnings, leading to its collapse (and the loss of thousands of jobs) in 2001. Some say Enron's flawed incentive system was to blame. Employees were lavishly rewarded for making the company look good, whether their actions were legal or not.

porations engage in deliberate acts of malfeasance to accomplish their goals, and that all executives are crooks, it would likewise be unwise to ignore such potential problems and the safeguards that can help firms avoid unethical behavior. Although there's no reason why a sound strategy has to have any hint of unethical motives or tactics, managers must take precautions to ensure that their firms don't figure in the next headline trumpeting the ethical bankruptcy of Corporate America.

In addition to ethical lapses, strategic decision making can be subject to a number of common decision-making biases. When executives fail to recognize and account for them, they may unwittingly pursue a course of action that they'd otherwise avoid. In this section, we'll review some of the ethics- and bias-related issues that may arise in the course of strategic decision making.

Ethics and Strategy

A quick survey of business history and recent business news will give you a good idea of the disastrous effects that questionable strategies can have on shareholders, clients, and even decision makers themselves. Enron is the most notorious recent example, but it's certainly not the only—nor even the most egregious—case. In early 2004, for example, Royal Dutch/Shell Group announced that executives had knowingly overstated oil and gas reserves by 4.5 million barrels, or 23 percent. In October of that year, Shell announced that it would have to "restate" its reserves by another million barrels. Investors were naturally unhappy at being misled about the firm's key assets, and its management ranks soon underwent a major shakeup.[29] Executives at other companies—notably Adelphia, a telecommunications provider, and Tyco, a diversified manufacturer and services provider— have been indicted (and some convicted) for diverting firm resources to private use. In other instances, misbehavior has taken the form of fraud; at the hospital chain HealthSouth, for example, no fewer than five onetime CFOs have been convicted in a $2.5-billion case of accounting fraud.[30]

Why Organizations Are Vulnerable to Ethics Violations In some of these cases, a few key executives were responsible for the violations of legal and ethical standards. In others, the misdeeds required a larger cast of characters. So why shouldn't organizations just be careful to hire principled people? For one thing, companies are often vulnerable because of organization-level conditions. In this section, we'll review two of these

Driving Stakeholder Analysis at Tritec Motors

Two of the challenges of performing stakeholder analysis are determining how stakeholders are affected by a firm's decisions and how much influence they have over the implementation of the decisions that are made. Not all stakeholders are affected in the same way, and not all stakeholders have the same level of influence in determining what a firm does. When stakeholder analysis is executed well, as you will see from the following example of the Tritec joint venture in Curitiba, Brazil, the resulting strategy has a better chance of succeeding, because the entities you might rely on in the implementation phase also helped to formulate the strategy.

THE STALLED MOTOR MAKER

Formed in 2001, the Tritec joint venture between Daimler-Chrysler and BMW represented a $400-million state-of-the-art engine manufacturing facility in Curitiba, Brazil. From the start, however, production problems with the new motors were wreaking havoc with BMW's newly minted line of wildly successful Mini Coopers. On the Chrysler side, Daimler's acquisition of the U.S. firm resulted in the triage of the main line of vehicles that would receive engines from the Curitiba plant. In sum, the Curitiba plant was producing poor-quality engines for BMW, and Daimler was paying for half of a factory that it was not even using.

In stepped Bob Harbin, a 25-year employee of Chrysler. Bob was given 90 days to come up with a plan to fix Tritec's problems. This was a make-or-break assignment for Harbin. Fortunately, Harbin knew how to apply stakeholder analysis, and he knew that the key players he involved in designing the turnaround strategy would likely be instrumental in executing it as well. In some cases, even if they did not have a role in implementation, certain stakeholders, such as the Brazilian government, could actually hurt Tritec's turnaround chances.

THE DISCOVERY PROCESS

Harbin spent the first five days of his assignment meeting with top executives at Daimler and BMW, both to gain an understanding of their needs and expectations and to determine how much discretion they would afford him if drastic changes were needed. After all, the corporate partners were essentially Tritec's financial backers and its only customers. Next, he spent two weeks in Curitiba meeting with everyone from the shop-floor employees to his future management team. He also spent time with key local parts suppliers as well as members of the newly installed Brazilian government. The government was particularly important because of the tax incentives and export credits that it had put into place to entice Tritec to Brazil; however, the change in government meant that those credits were in danger of being annulled. Throughout this discovery process, Harbin reiterated a common vision: "If we can't produce quality engines and get them to BMW on time, then the plant will likely be closed. No job, no tax revenues, no engines. Period." Not only did this quickly gain each stakeholder's attention, it also fostered cooperation and a sense of urgency among all the key players.

SENDING MESSAGES AND IMPLEMENTING A PLAN

After the first 30 days, Harbin assembled his leadership team based on impressions gained during his early interviews. Most of his team were Brazilians, which sent a strong message of confidence to the Brazilian workforce as well as to the Brazilian government. Together, Harbin and his team put together a rescue plan for the engine-manufacturing ⟫

process; he then took this plan back to Germany for endorsement by both BMW and Daimler. With the key pieces of the plan in place and the most important stakeholders squarely behind the plan—the alliance partners, the Brazilian government, Tritec's employees, and the new Tritec management team—Harbin began the steady process of turning around Tritec.

Although there were some minor setbacks along the way, within one year the factory was a world benchmark plant in many areas for both Daimler and BMW. By 2005, Tritec's production quality and efficiency were so high that even Toyota executives considered it one of the world's best-run auto-engine plants.

PLOTTING ROLES

Although every firm has multiple stakeholders, in this particular case the major stakeholders can be identified as BMW, Daimler-Chrysler, local employees, suppliers, the Brazilian government, and the leadership team. What roles did these stakeholders play in the tough decisions faced by Harbin? Let's take each stakeholder individually and plot them on the stakeholder-analysis grid (see Exhibit 2.A).

What role does BMW play in this situation? BMW is an owner/investor in the Tritec joint venture; thus on the power dimension BMW would be plotted in the far-right column, because it has voting and veto rights over all major decisions. However, BMW plays another role as well; it is the customer buying

		Power of the Stakeholder over Strategic Decisions			
		Unknown	Little/no power	Moderate degree of power	Significant power
Effect of Strategy on the Stakeholder	Unknown				
	Little/no effect		Brazilian government		
	Moderate effect			BMW suppliers	Leadership team
	Significant effect		Employees		BMW Daimler-Chrysler

Exhibit 2.A Stakeholder-Analysis Grid

the engines made in this factory. Thus, BMW simultaneously has an economic interest apart from its ownership stake. Consequently, BMW is located in two places on the stakeholder analysis grid.

Daimler's position is a bit more straightforward; it is an equity investor in the plant—thus it has an equity interest—and it has voting rights over all major decisions.

What position do the suppliers have? In terms of interests, they have a nonownership economic interest in the health of the plant. If the plant were to close, they would lose a major buyer. What influence/power do they have over decisions? They do not have major decisional power, but they do wield economic power.

What about employees? Employees do not directly influence factory decisions, but they do have an economic, nonequity stake in the factory. What about the Brazilian government? The government clearly has a stake in ensuring that local businesses are prosperous. However, that stake is not as direct or significant as an equity stake or employees' or suppliers' economic interest.

What does this analysis suggest? It suggests that if BMW does not get on board, all bets are off. Moreover, although the government is a critical stakeholder, at this stage of the game it is not as critical as making sure suppliers, employees, and management implement a plan that keeps BMW and Daimler-Chrysler satisfied.

conditions—*authority structures* and *incentive systems*—and show how avoiding certain pitfalls can reduce a firm's risk.

Authority Structures   Whereas some organizational characteristics foster potential opportunities for exploiting the system, others discourage potential whistle-blowers from alerting the proper authorities.[31] For example, because responsibility is distributed throughout an organization and tasks are specialized, there's a tendency for people to assume that someone else will blow the whistle on suspicious activity. The phenomenon, of course, can also be observed in society at large, as in cases in which bystanders will ignore an accident or criminal activity on the assumption that someone else will intervene.

The authority structure of modern organizations also inhibits lower-level employees from disclosing questionable practices. People who are relatively obedient tend to follow the directions of legitimate authorities even when they know that what they're doing is dubious.[32] And, of course, whistle-blowing is not an attractive option when those who are engaged in the questionable behavior occupy positions of authority.

Incentive Systems   The larger the potential reward, the more some people are willing to compromise their standards. Research shows, for instance, that business-unit managers are more likely to defer income to subsequent accounting periods when earnings targets in their bonus plans won't be met or when they've already reached maximum payouts.[33]

More recently, some analysts have questioned whether stock-option pay induces executives to make decisions designed to improve near-term stock prices rather than to enhance the firm's long-term competitive position. Because of the potential effect that financial incentives can have on managerial behavior, firms must take stronger measures to ensure that they're not "rewarding A, while hoping for B."[34]

The Role of Corporate Governance   *Corporate governance*—the roles of owners, directors, and managers in making corporate decisions—can reduce the risk of unethical and illegal activities. Because many unethical deeds are the work of individuals acting alone, even good governance can't guarantee ethical behavior. However, *poor* corporate governance provides a breeding ground for *un*ethical behavior. More and more firms are thus using governance mechanisms to discourage undesirable activities.

Threats to Rational Strategic Decision Making

When managers aren't fully aware of the biases influencing their judgment and strategic decision making, the quality of strategic decision making is bound to suffer. In this section, we'll sort potential biases into three sets of theories that we may hold about the conditions under which we make decisions: *theories about ourselves, theories about other people,* and *theories about our world*.[35]

Theories About Ourselves   It shouldn't come as any surprise to hear that your self-perceptions influence your judgment and decisions. For instance, because strategic decision making is characterized by uncertainty and ambiguity, you'd expect that most senior executives are confident in their ability to make judgments under such conditions.

illusion of favorability Decision-making bias under which people tend to give themselves more credit for their successes and take less responsibility for their failures

illusion of optimism Decision-making bias that leads people to underestimate the prospect of negative future events while overestimating the prospect of positive outcomes

illusion of control Decision-making bias under which people believe that they're in greater control of a situation than rational analysis would support

Some Common Illusions   When self-confidence, however, borders on the belief in one's own superiority, rational decision making may be impaired. Confidence, for example, is sometimes associated with an **illusion of favorability**, under which people tend to give themselves more credit for their successes and take less responsibility for their failures. A related bias, **illusion of optimism**, leads people to underestimate the prospect of negative future events while overestimating the prospect of positive outcomes.

Potentially compounding these biases is the **illusion of control**—a person's belief that he or she is in greater control of a situation than rational analysis would support. Research, for example, shows that when people are allowed to touch a playing card before it's been reshuffled into the deck, they're more likely to believe that they can find it again on a random draw than if they hadn't touched it. In reality, of course, their odds are the same under both circumstances.

Escalation of Commitment   These three illusions also contribute to a decision-making bias called **escalation of commitment**—the willingness to commit additional resources to a failing course of action. Obviously, this particular bias might well influence an executive's decision to change a strategy, to pursue an acquisition even though the bidding has reached astronomical levels, or to continue or discontinue a particular project related to current strategy.

Similarly, research shows that a manager who initiates a project is less likely to perceive that it's failing, more likely to remain committed to it, and more likely to continue funding it than the manager who comes on board after the project is underway. People also tend toward increased commitment to innovative products than to less innovative products. Such findings suggest that simply giving managers better information won't necessarily lead to better decisions. They also indicate that escalation of commitment is a more serious problem during new-product development than after a product has been rolled out.[36] In short, escalation of commitment seems to be a particularly dangerous decision-making bias, especially when we consider the ambiguity and uncertainty inherently involved in most strategic decisions.

Self-Serving Fairness Bias   According to some researchers, executives believe that they are fair people and want to act in ways that are perceived as fair and just. Like most people, however, they usually do a better job of tracking their own contributions to a project and thus tend to take more credit for good outcomes than they give. As a result of this tendency, which is called a **self-serving fairness bias**, executives may rationalize lavish pay and perks on the grounds that they earned them because they contributed more than others.

Overconfidence Bias   Finally, there's the pitfall of the **overconfidence bias**—people's tendency to place erroneously high levels of confidence in their own knowledge or abilities. This bias is compounded by the fact that people generally seek confirmatory evidence of their beliefs while discounting contradictory evidence. The combination of self-serving and overconfidence biases means that executives are quite likely to hold themselves and their organizations in high esteem. Research shows that executives who hold themselves in particularly high esteem are most likely to overpay seriously for acquisitions.[37]

The Consequences of Bias   So, what are the potential ethical consequences of strategic decision-making biases? The worst-case upshot of confidence-related biases is that some executives believe that they aren't subject to the same rules as everyone else. Top managers may delude themselves that they can get away with unethical or even felonious behavior because they believe either that they won't be caught or that, if they are, their status will protect them from the consequences.

If they succumb to self-serving fairness bias, the parties to an alliance or merger negotiation may proceed according to highly differing perspectives on what's fair and appropriate. Conceivably, such misperception can sabotage a deal that's good for the stakeholders whose assets have been entrusted to a company's negotiators. Overconfidence, then, can lead both to faulty judgments (and even ethical errors) based on misperception and to faulty judgments of fact.

Theories About Other People   In many ways, our theories about other people reflect our theories about ourselves:

- We give ourselves more credit than we deserve and others less.
- We expect more credit and reward and expect others to accept less.
- We view positive future outcomes as more likely than negative outcomes but believe that the outcomes achieved by others are more likely to fail.
- We think that we're better than others at judging uncertain futures and so give more credence to our plans than to those of others.
- We believe that although we're acting on the best knowledge of present and future conditions, others are acting on imperfect knowledge.

escalation of commitment Decision-making bias under which people are willing to commit additional resources to a failing course of action

self-serving fairness bias Decision-making bias under which people believe that they're fair and want to act in ways that are perceived as fair and just

overconfidence bias Decision-making bias under which people tend to place erroneously high levels of confidence in their own knowledge or abilities

The combination of biases about ourselves and biases about others can be tied to such far-reaching negative outcomes as industry overexpansion, which often occurs because each industry incumbent assumes that the others won't take competitive action when in fact every firm almost certainly will. As a result, because each player acts on the assumption that it knows something that the others don't, an industry that can support only 10 production facilities becomes glutted with 20.[38]

Ethnocentrism and Stereotyping   In addition to these obvious biases, our theories about other people also encompass both *ethnocentrism* and *stereotyping*. **Ethnocentrism** is a belief in the superiority of one's own ethnic group, but it can be interpreted more broadly as the conviction that one's own national, group, or cultural characteristics are "normal" and ordinary. That belief, of course, renders everyone else foreign, strange, and perhaps dangerous.

In fact, we're all ethnocentric to some degree. Your ethnocentrism accounts for your opinion of foreigners' speech patterns and favored cuisines. Being ethnocentric, then, doesn't necessarily mean that you're hostile toward other groups, but it does mean that you probably regard your group as superior. Ethnocentrism is dangerous because it's automatic and often subtle.

In part, the illusion of superiority stems from the belief that one's own group has multiple dimensions, whereas other groups can be characterized according to one relatively homogeneous characteristic—say, nationality, gender, or ethnicity. When you've reached this stage, you're engaged in **stereotyping**—relying on a conventional or formulaic conception of another group based on some common characteristic. The fallacy of ethnocentrism, then, is the belief in your own group's superiority; the fallacy of stereotyping lies in ascribing limiting characteristics to an entire set of people.

The Consequences of Ethnocentrism and Stereotyping   In terms of strategic and ethical decision making, ethnocentrism and stereotyping can have disastrous results. U.S. automakers, for example, ignored the Japanese competitive threat for decades because of a twofold mistaken belief: (1) that American car manufacturers were the best in the world and (2) that Japanese automakers could never produce high-quality vehicles. Thus ethnocentrism and stereotypes combined to blind U.S. (and European) carmakers to the emergence of extremely formidable rivals.

Stereotyping puts executives at risk of making unethical, unfair, and sometimes illegal decisions because it limits their evaluations of other people to group affiliation while ignoring individual qualities. Ethnocentrism exposes businesspeople to rationally and ethically unsound decisions because it exaggerates the differences between us and them.

Theories About the World   Today's top executives must be able to understand global events—or at least know where to get the information they need. Otherwise, it's too easy to misjudge the risks and consequences of an action with international ramifications. The trick, of course, is knowing what you don't know. Granted, it's often impossible to foresee all the possible consequences of a strategic choice, but a good starting point is the premise that "you can never do just one thing."[39] All actions, in other words, have multiple consequences, some intended, some unintended.

For example, the management of Levi Straus & Co. (LS&CO.) has a firm commitment to its corporate values. LS&CO. quickly stepped in to enforce a policy of not using contractors who employ child labor. Upon finding that a subcontractor in Bangladesh was employing children younger than 14, LS&CO. made the factory rectify the situation. Levi's decision to demonstrate its commitment to ethical practices and global social responsibility by discouraging child labor had an unintended consequence: Because factory jobs were no longer available, poor families that depended on their daughters' incomes resorted to pushing them into prostitution. Where did Levi Straus go wrong?

ethnocentrism Belief in the superiority of one's own ethnic group or, more broadly, the conviction that one's own national, group, or cultural characteristics are "normal"

stereotyping Relying on a conventional or formulaic conception of another group based on some common characteristic

Arguably, a few fallacious theories about the world resulted in a faulty perception of certain stakeholders: Levi's looked initially only at the situation of the girls and inadvertently ignored the needs of their families. Once discovering the complication, LS&CO. decided to pay for the underage children to go to school and guarantee jobs in the factory once they were of age.

Similarly, imperfect theories about the world may lead executives to discount low-probability events or to underestimate the probability of certain activities becoming public. The effects of such poor judgment can snowball into strategic and ethical blunders. In the early 1970s, for example, internal safety tests on the Ford Pinto revealed that under rare rear-impact conditions the gas tank could explode. The defect could be remedied with a $10 part, but Ford opted for a less costly response and, what's worse, covered up its own test results when the fatal rear-end crash turned out to be more common and more deadly than the company had figured.[40] The more recent example of how Ford proactively responded to tire problems from its chief supplier Bridgestone/Firestone, which caused some SUVs to roll when experiencing a flat, suggests that Ford may have learned its lesson.

Related to these imperfections in strategic decision making is the fact that we tend to discount the future and to place lower values on collective outcomes. In other words, we often focus on today's problems because we believe them to be more important than those that may be encountered down the road. Similarly, because we're prone to underestimate the consequences of our actions on large groups, we tend to ignore collective outcomes. Ford's behavior in the Pinto case, for example, contributed to public perception that the auto industry couldn't, or wouldn't, police itself on the issue of safety—a reaction that, in turn, led to an unprecedented raft of auto-safety regulations.

Risk and Cause-and-Effect Assessment As we've already suggested, uncertainty and risk are inescapable facets of executive life. A far-reaching decision may involve risks to jobs, worker or public safety, the environment, or corporate survival. Interestingly, research shows that we tend to perceive risks entailing potential losses differently than risks entailing potential gains: We tend to be *risk-seeking* when the outcome of an action is perceived as a gain but *risk-averse* when it's perceived as a loss—even when rational analysis would show that both outcomes are equally probable.[41]

What's more, even when we can rationally evaluate the probability of risks, we tend to overestimate our ability to control them by assessing cause-and-effect relationships. Many people know, for instance, that daily fluctuations in the stock market are random, but they still lend credence to theories about daily stock-price movements espoused by financial analysts. Moreover, we tend to overestimate the role of people in "causing" events. Why? Primarily because we find it easy to imagine people doing something different to prevent or correct an undesirable event. This tendency is unfortunate for CEOs and members of their executive teams because boards often replace them in order to demonstrate that they're dealing with the cause of failed strategies and recurring losses.

So, what do these decision-making biases mean for strategic and ethical decision making? The Ford Pinto example shows how both strategic and ethical decision making can be impaired by faulty theories about actions and events and the ways in which people respond to them. In many ways, it also shows how one set of risk perceptions could have led to different outcomes. Ford's behavior, for instance, may have been different if executives had framed the question facing them in some other way, such as "Would you pay $10 a Pinto to avoid passenger death and additional regulatory costs?"

A much broader issue, at least in terms of ethics, relates to our tendency to discount the future. Some analysts point to short-term thinking in order to explain decaying urban infrastructure, national budget deficits, the collapse of the world's lake and ocean fisheries, global warming, and environmental destruction.[42]

SUMMARY

1. Explain how strategic leadership is essential to strategy formulation and implementation. **Strategic leadership** is concerned with the management of an overall enterprise and the ways in which top executives influence key organizational outcomes, such as performance, competitive superiority, innovation, strategic change, and survival. Leaders typically play three critical roles—interpersonal, informational, and decisional—all of which support the firm's vision and mission and the implementation of its strategy. The **Level 5 Hierarchy** is a model of leadership skills that calls for a wide range of abilities, some of which are hierarchical in nature. Leaders can be distinguished by personality and demographic differences, and strategic leadership can be exercised either by individuals or groups.

2. Understand the relationships among vision, mission, values, and strategy. An organizational **vision** is a simple forward-looking statement or understanding of what the firm will be in the future. A **mission** is a declaration of what a firm is and what it stands for—its fundamental values and purpose. Together, mission and vision statements express the identity and describe the work of a firm. They also state the firm's direction. Vision and mission statements support strategy, which provides a coherent plan for realizing the firm's vision and mission.

3. Understand the roles of vision and mission in determining strategic purpose and strategic coherence. Guidance in making decisions is important because there's only so much complexity in a given problem with which any individual or group can reasonably cope. Vision and mission statements are thus useful because they inform all employees of the firm's **strategic purpose**—a simplified, widely shared model of the organization and its future, including anticipated changes in its environment. The challenge posed by a defined strategic purpose is closing the gap between aspirations on the one hand and current capabilities and market positions on the other. **Strategic coherence** refers to the symmetrical coalignment of the five elements of the firm's strategy, the congruence of functional-area policies with these elements, and the overarching fit of various businesses under the corporate umbrella.

4. Identify a firm's stakeholders and explain why such identification is critical to effective strategy formulation and implementation. Stakeholder analysis improves the understanding of the range and variety of parties who have a vested interest in the formulation and implementation of a firm's strategy or some influence on firm performance. The first step in stakeholder analysis is identifying stakeholder groups that are affected by or that may affect the firm's strategy. The second step calls for identifying those stakeholders who are important for strategy formulation and implementation, those for whom the strategy will be important, and those who are influential in determining the strategy. The third step involves categorizing stakeholders according to their influence in determining strategy versus their importance in its execution. Stakeholder analysis also helps expose any major omissions in strategy formulation and implementation.

5. Explain how ethics and biases may affect strategic decision making. Strategic leadership and strategic decision making have much in common. Indeed, strategic leadership can be characterized by strategic decision making and the actions in which it results. The effectiveness of strategic decision making is threatened when managers act unethically or without being fully aware of the biases influencing their judgment. Ethical lapses may reflect an individual shortcoming, but they can often be traced to a lack of clear organizational mechanisms for making individuals accountable for their actions. Decision-making biases, or threats to rational decision making in general, result from theories about oneself, theories about other people, and theories about one's world. They may impair both rational and ethical decision making and even an organization's ability to realize its vision and mission.

6. Create a vision and mission statement for your StratSim firm based on the goals of your StratSim executive team. Since you now have a good understanding of what a vision and mission statement look like, you should be able to try your hand at crafting them. This is an important building block in your StratSim experience, because it clarifies the objectives of your team and provides guidance to your strategic decisions going forward.

KEY TERMS

REVIEW QUESTIONS

1. Why is strategic leadership important for effective strategy formulation and implementation?

2. How do the characteristics of strategic leadership differ between individuals and teams?

3. What is a vision? A mission?

4. How are vision and mission related to strategy? What roles does strategic leadership play in realizing vision and mission?

5. How does strategy differ from vision and mission?

6. What is strategic purpose?

7. What is strategic coherence?

8. Who are a firm's stakeholders? Why are they important?

9. What tools can you use to identify the impact of various stakeholders on the firm and the impact of the firm on various stakeholders?

10. Why are ethics and biases relevant to strategic decision making and strategic leadership?

How Would you Do That?

1. Building on the CEO-successor selection process described in the box entitled "How Would You Do That? 2.1," devise a succession plan for the dean of your business school. Be sure to include the following in your succession-planning process: (a) Translate your school's strategy into actual operating needs and key activities; (b) identify the skills needed for these operating needs and activities; (c) outline an internal and external candidate search process; and (d) develop a list of goals and milestones and a compensation structure that ties actions to the strategic drivers of success at your school.

2. Based on the framework applied to Tritec Motors in the box entitled "How Would You Do That? 2.2," use the opening vignette on Anne Mulcahy at Xerox to map out the key stakeholders in her turnaround effort. Which stakeholders would you expect to be most resistant? Most supportive? Create a 90-day action plan for Mulcahy, following the example laid out by Bob Harbin in "How Would You Do That? 2.2."

3. Design a vision and mission statement for your StratSim firm. This is not your firm's strategy, but instead two key documents that will convey your organizational identity and purpose. The vision statement should be somewhat ambiguous, and provide an ambitious statement that everyone on your team can point to as the simulation progresses for directional guidance. The mission statement should address your team's core values and beliefs that help define your company's purpose. Your instructor may ask you to turn in these documents as an assignment, but even if not, your team should refer to these documents as guideposts as you develop and reassess your strategy in StratSim.

4. What are the specific goals and objectives for your StratSim firm? These should be clearly measurable so that your whole team can determine if you are successfully meeting these goals. You may want to think of these goals and objectives in the context of a balanced scorecard. In other words, you may have multiple performance measures, some financial such as year-over-year growth in net income, while others may be nonfinancial, such as firm preference or implementation of innovation. Your instructor may ask you to turn in these documents as an assignment, but even if not, your team should refer to these documents as guideposts as you develop and reassess your strategy in StratSim.

GROUP ACTIVITIES

1. (a) Craft a vision and mission statement for your business school and then for your college or university as a whole. How are these statements related? How are they similar? How do they differ? How are they similar or different from those that you might draw up for a for-profit organization? (b) Using the vision and mission you crafted, develop a list of key stakeholders for your school and their relative power and stake in the school. Which of these stakeholder groups is accounted for in your vision and mission statement, and which ones are left out? Did you identify any stakeholder groups that could negatively affect your realization of this vision and mission?

2. What roles should strategic leadership play in the realization of the vision and mission statements that you articulated in the previous question? Whom have you identified as strategic leaders?

ENDNOTES

1. W. M. Bulkeley and J. S. Lublin, "Xerox Appoints Insider Mulcahy to Execute Turnaround as CEO," *Wall Street Journal* (Eastern edition), July 27, 2001, A3; P. Moore, "Anne Mulcahy: She's Here to Fix Xerox," *Business Week,* August 6, 2001, 47; A. Klein, "Xerox to Expand Color-Printing Business," *Wall Street Journal* (Eastern edition), September 23, 1999, B12; J. Bandler, "Xerox Profit Falls, but CEO Sees a 'Breakthrough,'" *Wall Street Journal* (Eastern edition), July 29, 2003, A3; J. Bandler, "Xerox Corp.: CEO Sees Improving Finances, Broadening Product Offering," *Wall Street Journal* (Eastern edition), May 16, 2003, B6; O. Kharif, "Anne Mulcahy Has Xerox by the Horns," *Business Week Online,* May 29, 2003 (accessed June 21, 2005), at www.businessweek.com/technology/content/may2003/tc20030529_1642_tc111.htm.

2. M. Porter, J. Lorsch, and N. Nohria, "Seven Surprises for New CEOs," *Harvard Business Review* 82:10 (2004), 62–72.

3. This discussion of the nature of CEO job responsibilities draws heavily from the seminal work of H. Mintzberg, *The Nature of Managerial Work* (New York: Harper and Row, 1973).

4. Mintzberg, *The Nature of Managerial Work,* 67.

5. Information in this paragraph is based on Porter, Lorsch, and Nohria, "Seven Surprises for New CEOs," 62–72.

6. Stanford Graduate School of Business Alumni Profiles (accessed July 12, 2005), at www.gsb.stanford.edu/news/profiles/deromedi.shtml.

7. J. Collins, *Good to Great: Why Some Companies Make the Leap . . . and Others Don't* (New York: HarperBusiness, 2001).

8. Collins, "Level 5 Leadership: The Triumph of Humility and Fierce Resolve," *Harvard Business Review* 79:1 (2001), 67–76.

9. Collins, "Level 5 Leadership," 73.

10. For a review of this material, see D. Whetten and K. Cameron, *Developing Management Skills,* 5th ed. (Upper Saddle River, NJ: Prentice Hall, 2002).

11. For a comprehensive review of this literature, see M. A. Carpenter, W. G. Sanders, and M. A. Geletkanycz, "The Upper Echelons Revisited: The Antecedents, Elements, and Consequences of TMT Composition," *Journal of Management* 30 (2004), 749–778.

12. M. Useem and J. Karabel, "Pathways to Corporate Management," *American Sociological Review* 51 (1986), 184–200.

13. S. L. Keck, "Top Management Team Structure: Differential Effects by Environmental Context," *Organization Science* 8 (1997), 143–156.

14. M. A. Carpenter, W. G. Sanders, and H. B. Gregersen, "International Experience at the Top Makes a Bottom-Line Difference," *Human Resource Management* 39:2/3 (2000), 277–285; Carpenter, Sanders, and Gregersen, "Bundling Human Capital with Organizational Context: The Impact of International Experience on Multinational Firm Performance and CEO Pay," *Academy of Management Journal* 44 (2001), 493–512.

15. C. Lucier, R. Schuyt, and J. Handa, "CEO Succession 2003: The Perils of 'Good' Governance" (accessed June 21, 2005), at www.boozallenhamilton.com.

16. S. Hamm, "Former CEOs Should Just Fade Away," *Business Week,* April 12, 2004 (Online Extra) (accessed July 12, 2005), at www.businessweek.com/magazine/content/04_15/b3878092_mz063.htm; J. Sonnenfeld, *The Hero's Farewell: What Happens when CEOs Retire* (New York: Oxford University Press, 1991).

17. P. Estess, "Twos Company," entrepreneur.com, May 1997 (accessed June 22, 2005), at www.entrepreneur.com/article/0,4621,227207,00.html.

18. C. Hymowitz and J. S. Lublin, "McDonald's CEO Tragedy Holds Lessons," *Wall Street Journal,* April 20, 2004, B1.

19. C. K. Bart and M. C. Baetz, "The Relationship Between Mission Statements and Firm Performance: An Exploratory Study," *Journal of Management Studies* 35 (1998), 823–853.

20. J. C. Collins and J. I. Porras, *Build to Last* (New York: Harper Business, 1997).

21. Bart and Baetz, "The Relationship Between Mission Statements and Firm Performance"; A. Campbell and S. Yeung, "Creating a Sense of Mission," *Long Range Planning* 24:4 (1991), 10–20; P. Drucker, *Management: Tasks, Responsibilities, and Practices* (New York: Harper and Row, 1974); R. D. Ireland and M. A. Hitt, "Mission Statements: Importance, Challenge and Recommendations for Development," *Business Horizons* 35:3 (1992), 34–42.

22. Collins and Porras, *Build to Last.*

23. D. Kirkpatrick, "Gerstner's New Vision for IBM," *Fortune,* November 15, 1993, 119–124.

24. J. Collins and J. Porras, "Building a Visionary Company," *California Management Review* 37 (1995), 80–100; W. Kim and R. Mauborgne, "Charting Your Company's Future," *Harvard Business Review* 80:6 (2002), 5–11.

25. Bart and Baetz, "The Relationship Between Mission Statements and Firm Performance."

26. "Company Background: The History and Overview of Dell" (accessed July 12, 2005), at www1.us.dell.com/content/topics/global.aspx/corp/background/en/index?c=us&l=en&s=corp.

27. About Panasonic: Vision (accessed January 11, 2005) at panasonic.co.jp/global/about/vision/index.html.

28. Kim and Mauborgne, "Charting Your Company's Future."

29. M. Curtin, "THE SKEPTIC: Thorough Shell Revamp, But Where's the Oil?" *Dow Jones International News,* October 28, 2004.

30. B. Berkrot, "First HealthSouth Sentencing Set for Wednesday," Reuters, November 11, 2003.

31. This discussion draws heavily on R. Gandossy and J. Sonnenfeld, "I See Nothing, I Hear Nothing: Culture, Corruption, and Apathy," in Gandossy and Sonnenfeld (eds.), *Leadership and Governance from the Inside Out* (Hoboken, NJ: Wiley, 2004), 3–26.

32. S. Milgram, *Obedience to Authority* (New York: Harper, 1974).

33. P. M. Healy and J. M. Wahlen, "A Review of the Earnings Management Literature and Its Implications for Standard Setting," *Accounting Horizons* 13 (1999), 365–383.

34. S. Kerr, "On the Folly of Rewarding A, While Hoping for B," *Academy of Management Journal* 18 (1975), 769–783.

35. This material draws from behavioral decision theory. Excellent references are D. Kahneman, P. Slovic, and A. Tversky, *Judgment Under Uncertainty* (Cambridge: Cambridge University Press, 1982); M. Bazerman, *Judgment in Managerial Decision Making* (New York: John Wiley, 1994); J. Janis, *Groupthink* (Boston: Houghton-Mifflin, 1982).

36. J. Schmidt and R. Calantone, "Escalation of Commitment During New Product Development," *Journal of the Academy of Marketing Science* 30:2 (2002), 103–118.

37. M. Hayward and D. C. Hambrick, "Explaining the Premiums Paid for Large Acquisitions: Evidence of CEO Hubris," *Administrative Science Quarterly* 42 (1997), 103–127.

38. E. Zajac and M. Bazerman, "Blindspots in Industry and Competitor Analysis: Implications of Interfirm (Mis)perceptions," *Strategic Management Journal* 16 (1991), 37–57.

39. G. Hardin, *Filters Against Folly* (New York: Penguin Books, 1985).

40. R. Nader, *Unsafe at Any Speed* (New York: Grossman, 1965).

41. This material draws from behavioral decision theory. Excellent references are D. Kahneman, P. Slovic, and A. Tversky, *Judgment Under Uncertainty* (Cambridge: Cambridge University Press, 1982); M. Bazerman, *Judgment in Managerial Decision Making* (New York: John Wiley, 1994); J. Janis, *Groupthink* (Boston: Houghton-Mifflin, 1982).

42. D. M. Messick and A. Tenbrunsel, *Behavioral Research and Business Ethics* (New York: Sage, 1996).

Examining the Internal Environment: Resources, Capabilities, and Activities

After studying this chapter, you should be able to:

1. Explain the *internal context of strategy*.

2. Identify a firm's resources and capabilities and explain their role in firm performance.

3. Define *dynamic capabilities* and explain their role in both strategic change and firm performance.

4. Explain how value-chain activities are related to firm performance and competitive advantage.

5. Explain the role of managers with respect to resources, capabilities, and value-chain activities.

6. Understand your StratSim firm's internal resources, capabilities, and activities using the VRINE framework and analyze the value chain for your firm.

► **1968**
Driven by the desire to make better products in a better way, engineers Bob Noyce and Gordon Moore found the Silicon Valley startup Intel. Intel develops its first product, the 3101, a 68-bit memory chip (shown) the following year.

► **1971**
Empowered by Noyce and Moore, Intel employees press for and develop the world's first commercial microprocessor, the 4004 (shown). IBM agrees to use a subsequent version of the microprocessor in 1981— a major sales victory for Intel.

STRATEGY INSIDE INTEL

In 1968, three engineers—Robert Noyce, Gordon Moore, and Andy Grove—left secure jobs at Fairchild Semiconductor to create a new company in Mountain View, California, called Intel.[1] Their goal: to build a company that would develop technology for silicon-based semiconductor chips.

Processing Competitive Threats   Initially, Intel (the name is a contraction of "*int*egrated *el*ectronics") made read-only memory chips for computers and experienced early success in the industry. Before long, however, Asian competitors stepped up their competitive practices, using low-cost capital financing, large advantages in economies of scale, and aggressive pricing to dominate global market share. In addition, technological improvements in new generations of memory chips continued at lightning speed. These forces

► **1986**
Intel develops its next chip design, the 286, and licenses it to other semiconductor manufacturers. The revenues are used to expand Intel's manufacturing capabilities and to build larger "fabs," or fabricators.

► **2005**
The "Intel Inside" campaign, initially launched in 1991, continues to make Intel the best-known semiconductor manufacturer across the globe.

1995   2000

converged to create an extremely volatile market. As a result, Intel and other U.S. memory-chip companies suffered financially.

Fortunately for Intel, just when competition was intensifying in the memory-chip business, a new microprocessor technology that Intel had developed earlier was paying off and picking up some of the slack. In 1971, Intel introduced the world's first commercial microprocessor, the 4004. When a subsequent generation of the chip (the 8088) was chosen for the IBM PC in 1981, Intel secured its place as the standard setter in the microprocessor business.

A Few Knowledgeable Workers Go a Long Way   Intel's transition from a memory-chip company to the leading manufacturer of microprocessors was not planned. In fact, the official corporate strategy was to compete primarily in the memory-chip market, not the microprocessor market, based on Intel's senior executives' views that the firm's historic success in memory chips could be carried into the future. Rather, the company's production managers started shifting manufacturing capacity from memory chips to microprocessors because the yields per wafer square inch were higher. They followed a rather simple managerial rule—allocate production capacity based on a "margin-per-wafer-start." Margins on memory wafers were declining and margins for microprocessor wafers were increasing. In light of this change, Intel production managers shifted production capacity toward microprocessors, and they did so rapidly, because Intel's incentive and accountability systems rewarded plant managers based on wafer yields. Moreover, the chairman and CEO of Intel had successfully nurtured a strong internal culture that encouraged open debate about strategic initiatives and discouraged the use of hierarchy or position over the power of knowledge to make key decisions. The confluence of these factors—Intel's experiment with microprocessors, IBM's selection of the Intel chip, the excessive price competition in the memory market, and Intel's organizational processes that enabled plant managers to make these changes without explicit approval from senior management—enabled Intel to change rapidly from a memory-chip company to a microprocessor company.

Taking Strategic License   An important benefit of the change to microprocessors was the evolution of Intel's capabilities beyond narrow technical design to the implementation of complex design architectures in logic products, which gave Intel a much larger market domain. As the standard setter and chief supplier for the world's largest PC maker, Intel became a formidable player in the microprocessor industry. IBM, however, was reluctant to allow a small company be the sole supplier of such a key technology. Consequently, Intel chose to license the technology to other companies to satisfy IBM's concern. It licensed its next chip design, the 286, to other semiconductor firms, such as Advanced Micro Devices (AMD). Licensing reinforced Intel's status as an industry technology architecture leader, and it also enabled the company to supplement profits from its own sales with the healthy fees paid by licensees.

With a patent on the microprocessor design that had become the industry standard, Intel controlled a valuable intellectual property. The licensing fees paid by other firms were substantial; nevertheless, Intel moved to ease its dependence on outside manufacturers by adopting a three-pronged approach to improving its competitive position:

- The company used revenues from licensing agreements and profits from chip sales to fund the expansion of its manufacturing capacity and manufacturing-processing capabilities. Intel realized that if it could improve the manufacturing process, it would not only control the technology that semiconductor firms used to make processors, but it might also be able to generate cost savings. With a superior manufacturing process in hand, Intel then increased manufacturing capacity by building larger fabrication plants (called "fabs"), which also resulted in superior economies of scale.

- At the same time that Intel was building both innovation and manufacturing capability for microprocessors, the PC industry was expanding and credible threats to IBM were emerging. Compaq decided to adopt the 486 chip design after IBM decided to delay adoption of the chip, and other small PC companies soon followed Compaq's lead. The new chip proved to be a success with consumers. Because Intel had been investing in additional capacity in its fabs, it was able to exploit these new dynamics in the PC industry. Intel started revoking licensing agreements from other semiconductor companies for future generations of the Intel microprocessor. This move allowed Intel to capture a larger market share and boosted profits because canceling licenses eliminated competitors and the number of PC makers was increasing dramatically.

■ Intel set out to brand its product in order to make it the microprocessor of choice among end users, even if similar products entered the market. PC manufacturers, of course, preferred to source their technology from multiple suppliers. Thus, Intel still faced the threat that AMD or some other upstart would begin to compete aggressively and weaken its market share. Intel responded by advertising its product to end users—the individual consumers who purchase PCs from computer makers. The campaign was so successful that consumers turned out to be willing to pay higher prices for PCs with "Intel Inside." ■

INTERNAL DRIVERS OF STRATEGY AND COMPETITIVE ADVANTAGE

In this chapter, we'll introduce theories and models that explain why some firms outperform their rivals and others lag behind. You have probably been introduced to a very simple tool in other classes (such as marketing) called *SWOT analysis*. Recall that SWOT is an acronym for *s*trengths, *w*eaknesses, *o*pportunities, and *t*hreats. This chapter deals primarily with firms' strengths and weaknesses, or the resource-based inputs into the strategy process. These are internal characteristics of firms. Firms within an industry generally have different strengths and weaknesses, and those differences often have a strong bearing on which firms win competitive interactions. We will introduce you to more rigorous models that help managers diagnose their strengths and weaknesses and prescribe future actions to exploit their strengths or remedy their weaknesses. Of course, a complete understanding of a firm's strengths and weaknesses requires an understanding of competitors. Chapter 4 will introduce the basic tools for analyzing competitors, thereby enabling you to evaluate firms relative to their competitors.

This chapter focuses on firms' resources and capabilities, the choices managers make when configuring the activities they chose to perform internally (versus outsourcing), and the role of managers in allocating, reconfiguring, and exploiting firm resources and capabilities. All firms, of course, must consider the external context when formulating and implementing strategy, but focusing on the internal perspective reminds us that firms differ in terms of resources and capabilities. We'll examine several models and analytical tools that will help you analyze and formulate competitive strategies.

Our opening vignette has already given us some insight into the internal sources of competitive advantage. Although the microprocessor industry is extremely competitive, Intel has been able to maintain its competitive advantage over most of its rivals for an extended period of time. This fact suggests that Intel has access to internal resources and capabilities that other firms do not. Many firms in the industry, for example, are capable of making innovations in chip design. Intel, however, has always been able to get new products to market faster than its competitors and get them there in the volume necessary to achieve significant cost advantages. This advantage in speed to market results, in part, from Intel's ability to convince computer makers to use its products and from its ability to move new products into production in a timely manner.

However, as we also noted in the opening vignette, at one point Intel was forced to license its technology to other manufacturers because its chief customer demanded multiple sourcing options. Being forced to license the technology to other firms meant that Intel didn't have the immediate in-house capacity to manufacture chips fast enough and in large enough quantities to satisfy market demand. The firm addressed this problem by investing heavily to improve its manufacturing processes. The related judgment and willingness of management to undertake such a risk—new semiconductor plants cost over $1 billion to build and take several years to complete—may be considered another of Intel's internal strengths. This combination of speed to market and manufacturing-process capability means that Intel can charge significant price premiums during the first months following a new-product release. Competitors who get to market later must settle for lower profits because prices have fallen.

concept link

In Chapter 1, we explain that the field of strategic management focuses on explanations of **competitive advantage,** which we define as a firm's ability to create value in a way that its rivals can't.

As our description of Intel's history, strategy, and performance suggests, the firm's advantage is due, in part, to its use of engineering expertise to create valuable technologies, operational efficiencies to make its new products proprietary standards in the industry, and marketing skills to exploit its ability to speed products to market. Not surprisingly, its competitive advantage translates into higher levels of performance.

Firms in many other industries have also managed to do what Intel has done—namely, to outperform major competitors for extended periods of time. As you can see in Exhibit 3.1, such firms can be found in industries ranging from microprocessors to retail grocers to automobile makers. Notice that the average profitability (return on sales and return on assets) for firms within these very different industries varies significantly across firms over long periods of time. Intel's average return on assets (ROA) and return on sales (ROS), which are measures of financial performance that gauge profits as a percentage of total sales and total assets, respectively, dwarf those of its nearest competitor, Texas Instruments. In the exhibit, note that these figures are higher than competitors' in each year, as well as on average across all 10 years. Whether we look at high-tech industries, such as semiconductors, traditional heavy industry, such as automobile manufacturing, or a retail business, such as grocery stores, within industries some firms perform much better than others over time. For instance, Publix and Safeway have been superior performers in the grocery business.

One of the primary purposes of this chapter is to help you understand how such differences in profitability materialize and what firms can do to improve their performance relative to firms in their industry.

Models of Competitive Advantage

This chapter presents the two dominant models that help to explain how and why some firms perform better than others. These two models both suggest that differences in long-term-performance outcomes across firms within the same industry are derived largely from different levels of competitive advantage. However, the source of competitive advantage differs between these perspectives. The first explanation as to why some firms perform better than others attributes this success to fundamental differences in what firms own and what they can do. The most basic part of this model deals with the roles played by a firm's *resources* and *capabilities*. A more advanced version of this model is necessary to understand how these differences evolve over time. The second model for why firms differ within industries focuses not on resources, but on *what activities firms choose to engage in*. This activity perspective, treated toward the end of this chapter, relies heavily on the value chain and the advantages firms might gain by configuring value-chain activities in ways to add more value to their products or services than competitors. We'll explain how these two models help to determine which firms are able to develop a competitive advantage and potentially perform above industry averages and which ones suffer from liabilities and struggle to keep up.

Management

Finally, whether we trace a firm's competitive advantage to its resources and capabilities or to the organization of its value-chain activities, we must always consider the role played by its managers. Senior and mid-level managers make key decisions about how to acquire, allocate, and discard resources, and they're also in charge of organizing a firm's value-chain activities. This is why we include managers' strategic decision-making capabilities as a potentially valuable internal input into strategy. Exhibit 3.2, on page 70, provides an overview of how resources, capabilities, and managerial decision making are interdependent; all are necessary to understand how and why firms perform differently within similar industry environments. As we'll explain in more detail later, notice how the role of management is both to use the resources and capabilities to devise strategies and to make decisions about reconfiguring resources and capabilities. Indeed, managers play the unique role of being both resources and capabilities and making choices about the stewardship and deployment of other resources and capabilities (our opening vignette on Intel is a case in point here).

U.S. Semiconductor Industry

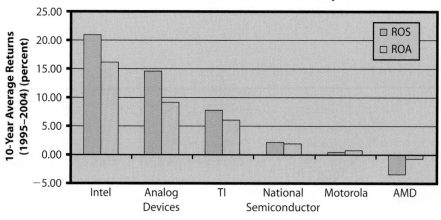

Exhibit 3.1 Comparative Performance in Selected Industries

Global Auto Industry

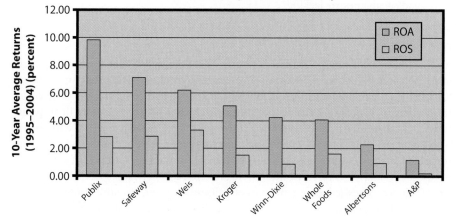

U.S. Grocery Store Industry

Exhibit 3.2 Resources, Capabilities, and Managerial Decisions

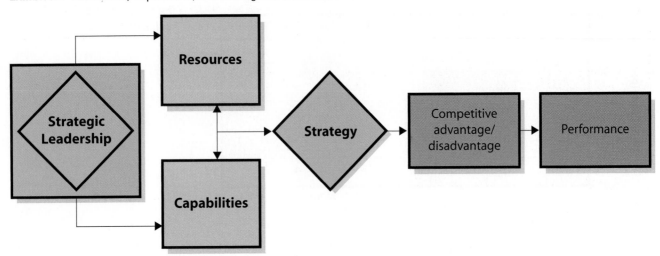

RESOURCES AND CAPABILITIES

concept link

In Chapter 1, we explain that the *internal perspective on competitive advantage* is often called the *resource-based view* of the firm because it holds that firms are heterogeneous bundles of resources and capabilities.

Resources and capabilities are the fundamental building blocks of a firm's strategy. The choices made by firms' managers relative to the five elements of a strategy, as organized by the strategy diamond, require resources and capabilities. For instance, if a firm wants to enter new arenas, it will need appropriate resources and capabilities in order to compete there. In addition, no matter how a firm plans to differentiate its products—whether on quality, image, or price—it needs the right resources and capabilities to make the differentiation real. Likewise, when a firm is deciding on the best way to enter a new market— whether by means of acquisition, alliance, or internal development—it has to consider its available resources and capabilities. Sometimes a firm uses a vehicle such as an acquisition or an alliance specifically for the purpose of acquiring resources or capabilities that it does not currently own.[2] Not surprisingly, successful strategies exploit the resources and capabilities that a firm enjoys and put the firm on a path to acquire missing resources and capabilities and upgrade existing ones, whereas unsuccessful strategies often reflect the fact that critical resources and capabilities are lacking.

Resources

resources Inputs used by firms to create products and services

What, exactly, do we mean by *resources*? **Resources** are the inputs that firms use to create goods or services. Some resources are rather undifferentiated inputs that any firm can acquire. For instance, land, unskilled labor, debt financing, and commodity-like inventory are inputs that are generally available to most firms. Other resources are more firm specific in nature.[3] They are difficult to purchase through normal supply chain channels. For instance, managerial judgment, intellectual property, trade secrets, and brand equity are resources that are not easily purchased or transferred. From this description, it is clear that some resources have physical attributes; these are referred to as *tangible* resources. Other resources, such as knowledge, organizational culture, location, patents, trademarks, and reputation are *intangible* in nature. Some resources have both tangible and intangible characteristics. Land, for instance, has physical properties and satisfies certain functional needs. At the same time, some properties may have value as a resource by virtue of their location, which is an intangible benefit arising from unique proximity to customers or suppliers due to preferences or relative location.

Because tangible resources are easier to identify and value, they may be less likely to be a source of competitive advantage than intangible resources. This is because their tangible nature gives competitors a head start on imitation or substitution. But some tangible resources are quite instrumental in helping firms achieve favorable competitive positions, partly because of their intangible benefits. Wal-Mart, for example, enjoys near-monopoly status in many rural locations. As the first large retailer in a rural market, Wal-Mart has locked out potential competitors who won't build facilities in locations that can't support two stores. Thus, one reason for Wal-Mart's formidable competitive position in rural markets is its tangible real estate. Similarly, Union Pacific Railroad's control of key rail property gives it a competitive advantage in the transportation of certain materials, such as hazardous chemicals.

Likewise, McDonald's controls much more than a valuable brand name (an intangible resource that does in fact convey a significant advantage). Like Wal-Mart, it also controls a great deal of valuable real estate by virtue of its location near high-traffic centers. Indeed, without its prime real-estate locations, McDonald's would have a less valuable brand name. Obviously, the pace at which McDonald's grew required a certain capability in finding the needed real estate.

Capabilities

Capabilities refer to a firm's skill in using its resources (both tangible and intangible) to create goods and services. A synonym that is often used to describe the same concept is *competences*. For simplicity, we use the term *capabilities*. Capabilities may be possessed by individuals or embedded in company-wide rules and routines.[4] In essence, they are the combination of procedures and expertise that the firm relies on to engage in distinct activities in the process of producing goods and services. Several examples of companies and their capabilities are listed in Exhibit 3.3. For instance, Wal-Mart is widely regarded as having excellent capabilities related to the management of logistics, which it uses to exploit resources such as large stores, store locations, its trucking fleet, and massive distribution centers.

Capabilities span from the rather simple tasks that firms must perform to accomplish their daily business, such as taking and fulfilling orders, to more complex tasks, such as designing sophisticated systems, creative marketing, and manufacturing processes. Collectively, these capabilities are the activities that constitute a firm's **value chain**. Not all capabilities are of equal value to the firm—a fact that has, in turn, given rise to the rapid growth of **outsourcing**. Outsourcing is contracting with external suppliers to perform certain parts of a company's normal value chain of activities. Later in the chapter, you will be introduced to a special class of capabilities known as *dynamic capabilities*.

Two other special classes of capabilities with which you should be familiar, if for no other reason than that they are part of the generally used business vocabulary, are *distinctive competences* and *core competences*. **Distinctive competences** (or *distinctive capabilities*) are

capabilities A firm's skill at using its resources to create goods and services; combination of procedures and expertise on which a firm relies to produce goods and services

value chain Total of primary and support value-adding activities by which a firm produces, distributes, and markets a product

outsourcing Activity performed for a company by people other than its full-time employees

distinctive competence Capability that sets a firm apart from other firms; something that a firm can do which competitors cannot

Company	Capability	Result
Wal-Mart	Logistics—distributing vast amounts of goods quickly and efficiently to remote locations.	200,000-percent return to shareholders during first 30 years since IPO.
The Vanguard Group	Extraordinarily frugal system using both technological leadership and economies of scale for delivering the lowest cost structure in the mutual-fund industry.	25,000-percent return to shareholders during the 30-plus year tenure of CEO John Connelly. Shareholders in Vanguard equity funds pay, on average, $30 per $10,000 versus a $159 industry average. With bond funds, the bite is just $17 per $10,000.
3M	Generating new ideas and turning them into innovative and profitable products.	30 percent of revenue from products introduced within the past four years.

Exhibit 3.3 A Few Extraordinary Capabilities

Sources: G. Stalk, P. Evans, and L. E. Shulman, "Competing on Capabilities: The New Rules of Corporate Strategy," Harvard Business Review *70:2 (1992), 54–65; R. Makadok, "Doing the Right Thing and Knowing the Right Thing to Do: Why the Whole Is Greater Than the Sum of the Parts,"* Strategic Management Journal *24:10 (2003), 1043–1054.*

core competence Capability which is central to a firm's main business operations and which allow it to generate new products and services

the capabilities that set a firm apart from other firms. **Core competences** (or *core capabilities*) are those capabilities that are central to the main business operations of the firm; they are the capabilities that are common to the principle businesses of the firm and that enable the firm to generate new products and services in these businesses.

The relationship between resources and capabilities can be further illustrated by a few more examples. Intel's manufacturing capacity (i.e., its plants, equipment, and production engineers), its patented microprocessor designs, and its well-established brand name are among its key resources. Intel has also demonstrated the organizational capability to design new generations of leading-edge microprocessors and to do so rapidly. In addition, Intel has demonstrated marketing adroitness by creating the "Intel Inside" campaign, which stimulated greater demand and higher switching costs among end users—the customers of Intel's customers. This clearly suggests a marketing capability. The combination of Intel's resources and capabilities enables its managers to execute a value-creating strategy and achieve a formidable competitive advantage in the microprocessor industry.

In the oil industry, too, we can see that resources and capabilities aren't uniformly developed by all competitors. Some firms, for example, are highly integrated. These integrated firms are involved in every stage of the value chain, including risky and time-consuming oil exploration and extraction activities. BP, ChevronTexaco, ExxonMobil, and Royal Dutch/Shell all possess significant capabilities in exploration and extraction, refining, distribution, and marketing. As a result, they also own rights to significant petroleum deposits around the world, and these reserves are potentially valuable tangible resources. In contrast, other oil companies are involved primarily in "downstream activities." These companies gear their capabilities to refining, distribution, and marketing. Valero Energy and Sunoco, for instance, are the largest independent U.S. oil refiners and distributors. Neither, however, is active in exploration. Their resources include refineries, pipelines, distribution networks, and equipment, but both buy crude oil from other companies.

The important complementary relationship between one of McDonald's tangible resources (real estate) and one of its capabilities (its site-location skills) are highlighted in the following example. For instance, few people go out for the sole purpose of buying a hamburger or a taco. Most fast-food purchases are impulse buys, and this fact points to just one reason why site location is so important in the fast-food industry. Like magazines and candies strategically placed at supermarket checkout counters, fast-food outlets are situated by design. At one time, McDonald's used helicopters to assess the growth of residential areas: Basically, planners looked for cheap land alongside thoroughfares that would one day run through well-populated suburbs.

Today, the site-location process is even more high-tech. In the 1980s, McDonald's turned to satellite photography to predict urban sprawl. The company has developed a software package called *Quintillion*, which integrates information from satellite images, detailed maps, demographic information, CAD drawings, and sales data from existing stores. With all of this information at its disposal, McDonald's has taken the strategy of site location to new heights. Prime locations, of course, command prime dollars: The difference between the cost of a prime location and a mediocre site could be three times the price per square foot.[5]

SimConnect

Resources and Capabilities of Your StratSim Firm

In StratSim, each of the five firms starts with unique resources and capabilities. Perhaps more importantly, however, is that your team will have the ability to develop these important drivers of competitive advantage. For example, your firm may have an advantage in technology capabilities that allows your firm to develop vehicles with higher attributes than the competition. You might decide that these attributes are important for differentiating your vehicles in particular target markets. If this assumption is true, then technology is an important resource for your firm. The second consideration is to ask if the advantage is sustainable? In StratSim, the answer is yes, but only if (a) your firm continues to invest in and develop these technology capabilities, (b) your firm chooses to implement these capabilities in your vehicles through the product development process, and (c) your team continues to analyze your advantage relative to the competition. For example, if your competition does not choose to develop these capabilities, your original advantage may be maintained without additional investment. But, if instead, your competitor invests heavily in technology capabilities, you will at least need to match those investments to maintain your source of competitive advantage.

Another potential advantage might be lower production costs. When you analyze your firm, you may find that it has a cost advantage over the competition. Typically, cost advantages would be obtained through (a) higher volumes (experience and scale effects), (b) lowering costs through reengineering the product design, and/or (c) offering products that share common parts and design (in StratSim, vehicles that have the same specifications, same class, etc. drive lower costs either in product development or unit costs). However, your firm must decide how best to use this advantage and again, whether it is a key driver of competitive advantage. We should also add that your firm should always monitor competitive activity in any area that you consider a driver of competitive advantage.

These are two examples of resources and capabilities in StratSim, but there are many others including probably the most important one—your management team. Your ability to analyze information and make informed decisions that are consistent with your strategy and based on solid strategic principles will be your ultimate advantage. Yes, all teams do start in different positions, but all have the opportunity to improve their position, meet objectives, and ultimately "win" in their industry. It is up to your team to find the most effective means to do so!

The VRINE Model

In a given industry, then, all competitors do not have access to the same resources and capabilities—a fact that should have significant implications for the strategies that they develop. In addition, one firm's resources or capabilities aren't necessarily as effective as another's in helping it develop or sustain a competitive advantage. Why do some resources and capabilities enable some firms to develop a competitive advantage? Exhibit 3.4 summarizes five basic characteristics that determine whether a resource or capability can help a firm compete and, indeed, achieve superior performance: (1) value, (2) rarity, (3) inimitability, (4) nonsubstitutability, and (5) exploitability.

According to the **VRINE model** (for *v*alue, *r*arity, *i*nimitability, *n*onsubstitutability, and *e*xploitability), resources and capabilities contribute to competitive advantage to the extent that they satisfy the five components of the model. VRINE analysis helps managers systematically test the importance of particular resources and capabilities and the desirability of acquiring new resources and capabilities. In the following sections, we'll explain and provide examples of each VRINE characteristic.

VRINE model Analytical framework suggesting that a firm with resources and capabilities which are valuable, rare, inimitable, nonsubstitutable, and exploitable will gain a competitive advantage

Value A resource or capability is *valuable* if it enables a firm to take advantage of opportunities or to fend off threats in its environment.[6] Union Pacific (UP) Railroad, for example, maintains an extensive network of rail-line property and equipment on the U.S. Gulf Coast. It operates in the western two-thirds of the United States, serving 23 states, linking every major West Coast and Gulf Coast port and reaching east through major gateways in Chicago, St. Louis, Memphis, and New Orleans. UP also operates in key north-south corridors (see Exhibit 3.5). It's the only U.S. railroad to serve all six gateways to Mexico, and it interchanges traffic with Canadian rail systems.

Its rail system is a tangible resource that enables UP to compete with other carriers in the long-haul transportation of a variety of goods. UP is, for example, the nation's largest hauler of chemicals, much of which traffic originates along the Gulf Coast near Houston, Texas. The company enjoys this advantage because it owns the physical resources necessary to compete in this market—the railway right of way through strategic areas—and because it has the specialized capability to transport chemicals safely and cost effectively. Government

Exhibit 3.4 Applying the VRINE Model

	The Test	The Competitive Implication	The Performance Implication
Is it Valuable?	Does the resource or capability allow the firm to meet a market demand or protect the firm from market uncertainties?	If so, it satisfies the value requirement. Valuable resources are needed to compete in an industry, but value by itself does not convey an advantage.	Valuable resources and capabilities have the *potential* to contribute to *normal profits* (profits that cover the cost of all inputs, including capital).
Is it Rare?	Assuming that the resource or capability is valuable, is it scarce relative to demand or is it widely possessed by competitors?	Valuable resources that are also rare contribute to a *competitive advantage*, but that advantage may be only temporary.	A *temporary competitive advantage* can contribute to *above-normal profits*, at least until the advantage is nullified by other firms.
Is it Inimitable and/or Nonsubstitutable?	Assuming that the resource is both valuable and rare, how difficult is it for competitors either to imitate it or substitute other resources and capabilities that yield similar benefits?	Valuable and rare resources and capabilities that are difficult to imitate or substitute can contribute to *sustained competitive advantage.*	A sustained competitive advantage can contribute to *above-normal profits for extended periods of time* (until competitors find ways to imitate or substitute or environmental changes nullify the advantage).
Is it Exploitable?	If the resource or capability satisfied any or all of the preceding VRINE criteria, can the firm actually exploit it?	Resources and capabilities that satisfy the VRINE criteria but that cannot be exploited can still contribute to significant opportunity costs in the sense that competitors may have to invest large sums to match them. If they can be exploited, a firm may realize its potential competitive and performance implications.	Firms that control but don't exploit VRINE resources and capabilities generally suffer from lower levels of financial performance and depressed market valuations *relative to what they would enjoy if they could in fact exploit them* (although they won't be in as bad a shape as competitors who don't control any VRINE-certified resources and capabilities).

Source: Adapted from J. B. Barney, "Looking Inside for Competitive Advantage," Academy of Management Executive *9:4 (1995), 49–61.*

studies indicate that railroads are very efficient compared to alternative forms of transportation (such as truck and air) for the transportation of chemicals. Thus, railroad assets are valuable because they enable the company to provide a cost-effective means of transporting chemicals. In addition, because the Gulf Coast is the source for most chemical production in the United States, this network permits UP to take advantage of a market opportunity.

Alternatively, UP owns many rights of ways that are no longer active. These resources would appear to convey no value to UP unless it can find a new use for these properties although UP's ownership of them is a deterrent to new railroad industry events. Consequently, UP frequently sells these abandoned railway rights of way to communities for such things as bike trails, and not to competing railroad operators.

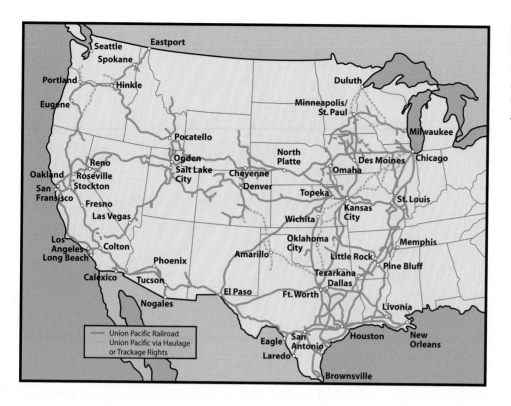

Exhibit 3.5 The Union Pacific Right-of-Way System

Source: Union Pacific, "System Map" (accessed August 4, 2005), at www.uprr.com/aboutup/maps/sysmap/index.shtml.

Finally, it is worthwhile to remember that some resources that can be sources of value can also be abused and consequently become sources of corporate overhead. For instance, consider a small fleet of business jets owned by a company. Occasionally, the company may need to be able to get top executives in and out of remote or congested locations quickly, which would make the jets a valuable resource. However, in other situations, the jets may be a costly convenience and an example of corporate excess that provide no real economic value.

If a firm cannot use a resource to minimize threats or take advantage of opportunities, then it probably doesn't enhance its competitive position. In fact, some experts suggest that owning resources that *don't* meet the VRINE criteria for value actually puts a firm at a competitive *disadvantage*. Why? Because the capital tied up in the resource could be put to better use,[7] the capital could be reinvested in other resources that do satisfy the value requirement of VRINE, or the capital could be redistributed to shareholders.

Rarity   *Rarity* is defined as scarcity relative to demand. An otherwise valuable resource that isn't rare won't necessarily contribute to competitive advantage: Valuable resources that are available to most competitors simply enable a firm to achieve parity with everyone else. Sometimes such resources may be called *table stakes,* as in poker, because they are required to compete in the first place. But when a firm controls a valuable resource that's also rare in its industry, it's in a position to gain a competitive advantage. Such resources, for example, may enable a company to exploit opportunities or fend off threats in ways that competitors cannot. When McDonald's signs an agreement to build a restaurant inside a Wal-Mart store, it has an intangible location advantage over Burger King and Wendy's that is not only valuable but also rare because it has an exclusive right to that geographic space.

How rare does a resource have to be in order to offer potential competitive advantage? It's a difficult question to answer with any certainty. At the two extremes, of course, *only one* firm has the resource or *every* firm has it, and the answer is fairly obvious. If only one firm possesses a given resource, it has a significant advantage. Monsanto, for instance, enjoyed an advantage for many years because it owned the patent to aspartame, the chemical compound in NutraSweet. As the only legal seller of aspartame, Monsanto dominated the artificial-sweetener market. Such is typically the case in the pharmaceutical industry for those who are first or second to patent and market a therapy for a particular disease.

Monsanto enjoyed a competitive advantage for many years because it owned the patent to aspartame, the chemical compound in NutraSweet. The patent on aspartame ran out in 1992, and in 2000 Monsanto sold NutraSweet to private investors. NutraSweet now faces fierce competition from other aspartame-containing products, and newer and more popular nonaspartame-based sweeteners.

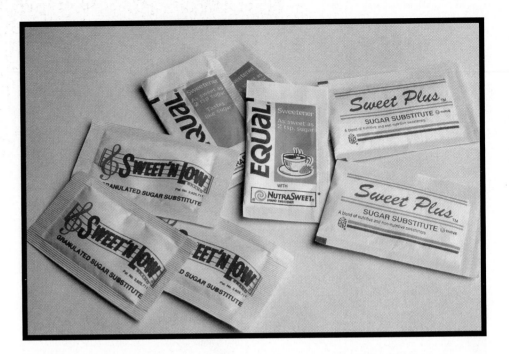

Satisfying the rarity condition, however, doesn't necessarily require *exclusive* ownership. When a resource is controlled by a handful of firms, those firms will have an advantage over the rest of the field. Pfizer was first to the market for a drug to treat erectile dysfunction with its Viagra product, but it was later joined by two other products offered by competitors (Levitra® and Cialis®). Pfizer no longer has a monopoly in the market to treat this condition, but the three firms collectively control resources that are scarce relative to demand. Thus, Pfizer's resource, the patent for Viagra, would still seem to satisfy both the value and the rarity requirements of VRINE. Consider an example from another context. Both Toyota and Honda, for example, can build high-quality cars at relatively low cost, and the products of both firms regularly beat those of rivals in both short-term and long-term quality ratings. The criterion of rarity requires only that a resource be scarce *relative to demand*. It also follows, of course, that the more exclusive the access to a valuable resource, the greater the benefit of having it.

A firm that controls a valuable and scarce resource or capability may create a competitive advantage, but there is no assurance that the advantage will persist. We now turn to the two criteria that must be satisfied if the advantage is to be sustained.

Inimitability and Nonsubstitutability   A valuable and rare resource or capability will grant an advantage only so long as competitors don't gain possession of it or find a close substitute. We review these two criteria jointly because they work in similar fashions. The criterion of *inimitability* is satisfied if competitors cannot acquire the valuable and rare resource quickly or if they face a cost disadvantage in doing so. The *nonsubstitutability* criterion is satisfied if a competitor cannot achieve the same benefit using different combinations of resources and capabilities. When a resource or capability is valuable and rare and contributes to a firm's advantage, one can assume that competitors will do all they can to get it. Of course, firms can acquire needed resources or capabilities in a number of different ways, including internal investment, acquisitions, and alliances. They can, for instance, form alliances in order to learn from and internalize a partner's capabilities.[8]

Some firms find alternative resources or capabilities that "mimic" the benefits of the original. For several years, for example, Barnes & Noble and Borders enjoyed formidable advantages in the retail-book industry. Their sheer size gave them an immense advantage over smaller players: Because they had access to more customers, they were able to take advantage of greater buying power. Eventually, however, Amazon.com's ability to substitute online for conventional retail marketing provided a feasible substitute for geographic accessibility to consumers. Generally speaking, then, valuable and rare resources can provide competitive advantage only as long as they're difficult to imitate or substitute.

The High Cost of Imitation and Substitution   Several factors can make resources and capabilities difficult to duplicate or substitute. A rival might, for instance, try to acquire a competitor or supplier that possesses the resource it needs.[9] But acquisitions of this kind often entail large premiums that result in a buyer's paying more for a resource than it cost competitors to develop the original.[10] In 1999, for example, when Cisco purchased Cerent in order to acquire fiber-optic data-transfer capabilities, it ended up paying $6.9 billion for a startup company with just $10 million in sales.[11] Cisco desperately wanted the capabilities of Cerent, but managers felt it would take too long to develop those capabilities internally. Absent Cisco's excellent capabilities in merger integration and new product distribution, therefore, the firm would be at a cost disadvantage relative to any competitor who could develop the same collective capabilities for less money.

Inimitability, Nonsubstitution, and Property Rights   Perhaps the most straightforward cause of resources and capabilities being difficult to imitate or substitute is property rights. Competitors can be prevented from copying resources if they are protected by ownership rights. For instance, patented items or processes cannot be directly copied during the term of the patent without the imitator's being subject to severe legal repercussions. Media companies own copyrights on titles in their libraries. Because of this, it is very difficult for competitors to substitute for Mickey Mouse. However, property rights alone do not protect all resources and capabilities from imitation or substitution.

Inimitability, Nonsubstitution, and Time   Another factor that can make resources and capabilities difficult to imitate or substitute is the unique historical conditions surrounding their development or the fact that their acquisition requires the passage of time.[12] Sometimes a firm's resources and capabilities are the result of unique historical events that converged to its benefit. For instance, in order to build troop moral during World War II, General Dwight D. Eisenhower requested that Coca-Cola be available to all American servicemen and servicewomen. To ensure that GIs could buy Coke for five cents a bottle, the government and Coca-Cola cooperated to build 64 bottling plants around the world. In the long term, Coke gained the competitive advantage of instant global presence, both in bottling capacity and brand recognition.[13] At war's end, Coke ramped up its overseas production and marketing and succeeded in penetrating new markets. In effect, Coke's market entry had been subsidized by the government, and rival Pepsi faced considerable cost disadvantages in competing with Coke's international presence. Coke's global advantage over Pepsi remains even today. Of Coke's $21.9 billion sales in 2004, fully 70 percent were from outside North America, whereas just 54 percent of PepsiCo's $18.2 billion in beverage sales were from outside North America.[14]

The simple passage of time creates inimitability and nonsubstitutability as well, typically because the original owner may have built up the value of the resource or capability through a process of gradual learning and improvement that can't be matched through catch-up programs. For instance, firms that invest a given rate of R&D spending over an extended time period appear to produce larger gains in knowledge and intellectual property than firms that invest at twice the same level over half the time.[15] Thus, we can say that a resource is difficult to imitate if shorter development time results in inferior imitations.

Causal Ambiguity   Another factor that makes imitation difficult is **causal ambiguity**. For a number of reasons, it may be difficult to *identify* or *understand* the causal factors of a resource or capability—the complex combination of factors that make it valuable.[16] A firm, for example, may enjoy a resource that resulted from a complex convergence of activities that the company itself doesn't fully understand.[17] For example, 3M enjoys an enviable capacity for innovation that, at least in part, is a function of company culture. A competitor may copy certain 3M policies—say, allowing employees to spend 10 percent of their time experimenting on potential new products—but it will be more difficult to imitate the complex culture of cooperation and rewards that facilitates innovation at 3M. The causal

causal ambiguity Condition whereby the difficulty of identifying or understanding a resource or capability makes it valuable, rare, and inimitable

Causal ambiguity makes 3M's products hard to imitate. The company has a long history of innovation. Its culture makes it a socially complex organization that competitors can't quite duplicate.

process, in other words, would be difficult to identify because it's *socially complex*. Products that are technologically complex are relatively easier to duplicate (say, by adopting such processes as reverse engineering) than are socially complex organizational phenomena.[18]

Exploitability   The fifth and final VRINE criterion reminds us that mere possession of or control over a resource or capability is necessary but not sufficient to gain a competitive advantage: A firm must have the organizational capability to *exploit* it; that is, the firm must be able to nurture and take advantage of the resources and capabilities that it possesses.

The question of exploitability is, of course, quite broad, but in this case, we're focusing on *a company's ability to get the value out of any resource or capability that it may generate.* Thus, the issue of an organization's exploitative capability incorporates all of the dimensions of a firm's value-adding processes. Although we may not deal directly with organizational processes until the final criterion in the VRINE model, bear in mind that, without this skill, a firm won't get much benefit from having met any of the first four VRINE criteria. A valuable resource or capability that is also possessed by many other competitors has the potential to give the firm competitive parity, but only if the firm also has the exploitative capabilities to implement a strategy that utilizes the resource or capability. Likewise, a firm that possesses a valuable and rare resource will not gain a competitive advantage unless it can actually put that resource to effective use.

In fact, many firms do have valuable and rare resources that they fail to exploit (in which case, by the way, their competitors aren't under much pressure to imitate them). For many years, for instance, Novell's core NetWare product gave it a significant advantage in the computer networking market. In high-tech industries, however, staying on top requires continuous innovation, and according to many observers, Novell's decline in the 1990s reflected an inability to innovate in order to meet the demands of changing markets and technology. But shortly after he was hired from Sun Microsystems to turn Novell around, new CEO Eric Schmidt arrived at a different conclusion: "I walk down Novell hallways," he reported, "and marvel at the incredible potential for innovation here. But Novell has had a difficult time in the past turning innovation into products in the marketplace."[19] The company, Schmidt confided to a few key executives, was suffering from "organizational constipation."[20] According to its new CEO, Novell had the resources and capabilities needed to innovate, but it lacked the exploitative capability (especially in its product-development and marketing processes) to get innovative products to market in a timely manner.

Xerox, too, went through a period when it was unable to exploit its resources to innovate products. At a dedicated facility in Palo Alto, California, Xerox had established a successful research team known as Xerox PARC. Scientists in this group invented an impressive list of innovative products, including laser printers, Ethernet, graphical-interface software, computers, and the computer mouse. All of these products were commercially successful, but, unfortunately for Xerox shareholders, they were commercial successes for other firms. Xerox couldn't get information about them to the right people in a timely fashion. Why? Largely because the company's bureaucracy tended to suffocate ideas before they had a chance to flow through the organization. Compensation policies ignored managers who fostered innovations and rewarded immediate profits over long-term success.[21]

The VRINE model can be used to assess any resource or capability in order to determine if it is a source or potential source of competitive advantage and, if so, whether that advantage is likely to be temporary or sustained. To illustrate how this is done, we use the VRINE model in the box entitled "How Would You Do That? 3.1" to analyze Pfizer's ownership of the patents for Zoloft as a possible source of competitive advantage.

Where Do Resources Come From? Our earlier definitions of *resources* and *capabilities* describe them as something the firm may own or possess. However, we have also suggested that many resources and capabilities cannot be easily purchased. Brand equity, for example, can't be readily purchased unless a company purchases an existing brand from another company. Otherwise, a brand will need to be developed, and that takes time. The brand equity of Coke, for example, has been developed through decades of marketing efforts with investments in the hundreds of millions per year. Toyota's reputation for quality automobiles has been developed through stringent quality-control methods; Intel's R&D capability is the result of years of investment. In other words, resources such as brand equity, reputation, and innovative capability result from policies and strategies that have been implemented over extended periods of time; they can't be acquired through one-time purchases.

DYNAMIC CAPABILITIES

Thus far, our discussion of resources and capabilities has portrayed a rather static view. However, the process of developing, accumulating, and losing resources and capabilities is inherently dynamic. We now introduce two concepts to demonstrate the dynamic aspects of resources and capabilities. The first deals with *stocks versus flows*; the second deals with a special class of capability referred to as a *dynamic capability*.

Resources as Stocks and Flows

Resources can be thought of as both stocks and flows. A firm's stock of resources and capabilities is what it possesses at any given point in time. However, that stock of resources and capabilities was created over time through a combination of initial endowment and accumulated investment. Consider the resource stock represented by a patent. To a large degree, the value of the patent depends on the level of innovation its original discovery represented, and that discovery was probably the result of years of investment and a process of trial and error. However, continual resource inflows may augment the value of the patent. For instance, additional R&D investments may lead to further discoveries that can be bundled with the original patent. Alternatively, investments in marketing efforts can spur demand, which leads to increased value. However, value also dissipates over time, as in the gradual expiration of the patent. The key point is that the value of resources and capabilities is a function of both the level (or stock) of resources and capabilities and the net effect of additional investment and depreciation.

This stock can be increased through development activities and sustained investment. It can be reduced through the divestiture of business units, loss of key personnel, and shifts in the competitive environment that alter the value of given resources. Remember, too, that strategic resources and capabilities are accumulated *over time*. Thus, the *process* of resource accumulation through dynamic capabilities is fundamentally different from the static possession of stocks of resources and capabilities.

How Do Drug Patents Stand Up to VRINE?

If you were studying Pfizer and the pharmaceutical industry using the VRINE model you would probably identify a number of resources and capabilities that may be the source of competitive advantage. You would probably identify patents, R&D capabilities, and marketing as key resources and capabilities. Let's walk through the VRINE model as applied to Pfizer's patents for Zoloft (sertraline HCl), an antidepressant known as a selective serotonin reuptake inhibitor (SSRI).

VALUE

Do Pfizer's two patents on Zoloft provide value? In any given year, about 7 percent of the U.S. population (approximately 20 million people) will express a depressive disorder. Approximately 16 percent of adults will experience depression at some point in their lives. Women are twice as likely as men to experience depression. Thus, it appears that having a patent for a treatment for depression would enable a pharmaceutical company to take advantage of a large market opportunity.

RARITY

Pfizer's patents on Zoloft give it the exclusive right to use the chemical compound sertraline HCl to treat depression (the patents are scheduled to expire in 2006). When the patents expire, generic drug makers will be able to sell copied versions of the drug. The patents for Zoloft are definitely rare during the term of the patents but will not be after they expire (assuming that several generic companies make the drug, its scarcity relative to demand will decline).

INIMITABILITY

Pfizer is certainly not the only large pharmaceutical company that desires to profit from therapies for depression. However, a patent makes direct imitation illegal until the patent expires.

NONSUBSTITUTABILITY

Competitors can and do attempt to find substitute compounds that have similar effects. Indeed, Zoloft itself was a Pfizer innovation in the face of Eli Lilly's patent for Prozac. Zoloft is not the only treatment for depression; other SSRIs include Prozac, Paxil, and others. The patents for Zoloft may convey temporary advantage, but Pfizer's value from them will probably erode over time as others invent substitute compounds and as the patents expires, resulting in direct imitation.

EXPLOITABILITY

To satisfy this VRINE criterion Pfizer needs to be able to move drugs from successful clinical trial to market distribution. Fortunately for Pfizer, distribution is one of its core competences. Indeed, Pfizer has more drug representatives than any other pharmaceutical company. Pfizer also has large cash reserves that can be used to bring sufficient quantities of the product quickly to market prior to the lapsing of the patents.

The verdict? As you may have guessed by now, Pfizer's patents on Zoloft stand up to the VRINE framework, suggesting that patents are a resource that can generate competitive advantage. Note, however, that Zoloft is such a resource because Pfizer also possesses the complementary resources and capabilities underlying its exploitability.

Sources: "Could Cymbalta Bring Cheer for Lilly?" *IMS Health.com*, August 23, 2004 (accessed August 4, 2005), at open. imshealth.com; C. Baysden, "Report: Blockbuster Drug Marketing Costs Average $239M," *Triangle Business Journal*, February 24, 2005 (accessed August 4, 2005), at triangle.bizjournals.com; "Medication for Depression: Antidepressant Medications," *Psychology Information Online* (accessed August 4, 2005), at www.psychologyinfo.com.

Rebundling Resources and Capabilities

Beyond making investments to augment the accumulation of resources and capabilities, firms can make decisions about how resources and capabilities are utilized and configured, and thereby change their fundamental value. And although a firm can't easily change its stock of resources and capabilities, it can reconfigure or integrate them in new ways. **Dynamic capabilities** are processes by which a firm integrates, reconfigures, acquires, or divests resources in order to achieve new configurations of resources and capabilities.[22] In fact, the term *dynamic* is added to the description of these special kinds of capabilities because it refers to a firm's ability to modify and revise its resources and capabilities to match a shifting environment. The ability to reconfigure firm resources and capabilities is especially critical in markets that move quickly, and it is typically seen in complex areas of the firm, such as its culture, knowledge base, and ability to learn.

Dynamic capabilities are manifest in several ways. The ability to integrate different resources and capabilities to create new revenue-producing products and services is a dynamic capability.[23] Disney, for instance, recently launched its "Princess Line," which brings together merchandise based on famous female Disney characters. The effort required that Disney integrate development and marketing campaigns geared toward groups of characters that had before been developed and marketed separately.[24] Reconfiguring or transferring resources and capabilities from one division to another is another form of a dynamic capability. Mail Boxes Etc. (MBE), the postal center that was recently purchased by UPS, illustrates this fact. By encoding its knowledge of how to start up a master-area franchise, MBE created "templates" for future franchisees. New master-area franchisees are required to duplicate the template exactly prior to making any adjustments to meet local market needs. This is because their internal research shows that master-area franchisees who duplicate the template significantly outperform those who first customize the model.[25] The opening vignette about Intel also illustrates how resource-allocation rules can result in a dynamic capability to reallocate resources to new uses.

The rebundling of resources and capabilities is also accomplished through alliances and acquisitions. Resources and capabilities can both be acquired and lost through these vehicles. Cisco has been able to launch many new products by strategically acquiring bits and pieces of network architecture through acquisitions.[26]

The dynamic view of resources and capabilities differs somewhat from the traditional view. It emphasizes the need to renew resources and capabilities, either in order to keep pace with a changing environment or to reconfigure the organization proactively (i.e., to change the environment). One or both of these capabilities—the ability to adapt to change or to initiate it—is particularly important in industries in which time to market is critical, technological change is rapid, and future competition is difficult to forecast.[27] When incumbent firms, even strong companies, don't have such capabilities, they're likely to be outmaneuvered by new competitors who are ready to introduce new industry standards.[28] Consequently, the value of a firm's portfolio of resources and capabilities is directly affected by its dynamic capability to reconfigure resources and capabilities to the evolving requirements of the competitive environment.

More complex forms of dynamic capabilities are typically associated with dynamic or turbulent environments. As we saw in our opening vignette, for example, Intel's internal organizational processes and organizational culture enabled it to make a dramatic change from one technological platform to another.[29] Specifically, the firm was able to shift scarce manufacturing resources from the memory-chip business to the emerging microprocessor business in a very brief period of time.

dynamic capabilities A firm's ability to modify, reconfigure, and upgrade resources and capabilities in order to strategically respond to or generate environmental changes

conceptlink

Among the three overarching themes of the book that we introduce in Chapter 1 is the principle that both firms and industries are *dynamic* in nature: Because their markets are dynamic, firms must develop dynamic capabilities to create value.

THE VALUE CHAIN

Earlier in the chapter, we demonstrated that firms in the same industry differ in their resources, capabilities, and dynamic capabilities and that these differences account for much of the variance in firm performance that we see within industries. Firms in the same industry may also differ in the scope and type of their value-chain activities. As we saw in our discussion of the *strategy diamond* model in Chapters 1 and 2, firms can make unique

concept link

In Chapter 1, we explain the *strategy diamond* as an integrated set of choices regarding arenas, vehicles, differentiators, staging, and economic logic. In Chapter 2, we define **strategic coherence** as the symmetrical co-alignment of these five elements of the firm's strategy and the congruence of functional-area policies with them.

decisions about the value-chain *arenas* in which they'll participate within a given industry. Consider the oil industry, which we discussed earlier. Valero and Sunoco make very different choices about which value-chain activities to engage in (e.g., refining and distribution but not exploration) relative to the major integrated oil companies. Even if two firms possess similar resources and capabilities, it is still possible for one firm to gain the upper hand and achieve a competitive advantage. One way this can be done is by having a different configuration of value-adding activities.[30]

Firms make products or provide services by engaging in many different activities. The basic structure of these activities is embodied in the firm's value chain. Value-chain activities are of two types: primary activities and support activities. *Primary activities* include inbound logistics, operations, outbound logistics, marketing and sales, and service. *Support activities* include human resources, accounting and finance operations, technology, and procurement. The term *support activities* may seem to minimize the importance of these operations, but bear in mind that all activities—primary and support—are potential sources of competitive advantage (or disadvantage).

Exhibit 3.6 depicts the value chain for a hypothetical Internet startup. Notice that the primary activities are located along the horizontal axis and represent the value-added activities that are necessary to sell a product. For instance, an Internet retailer would need to access a product (either by purchasing it from a supplier or manufacturing it) and store merchandise that it plans to sell to customers. The operations of an Internet company are primarily electronic (e.g., server operations, billing, collections), but analogous operations are performed in all businesses. To fulfill orders, the outbound logistics steps of the value chain would include matching the merchandise with the order and organizing the shipping to the customer. Marketing and service functions differ a bit with an Internet company compared to a conventional retailer, but in reality the same functional marketing tasks are completed, just in different ways.

Exhibit 3.6 The Value Chain for an Internet Startup

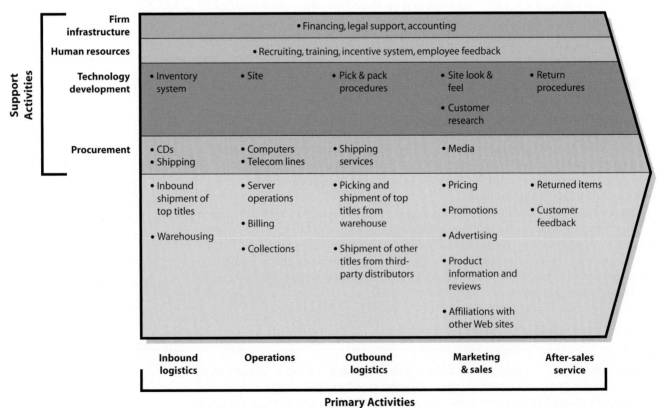

Source: The generic value chain model was developed by M. E. Porter, Competitive Advantage: Creating and Sustaining Superior Performance *(New York: The Free Press, 1985), p. 47.*

Support activities are represented on the top half of the vertical axis. Again, although these activities are generally portrayed as not being a part of the primary logistics involved in securing inputs, adding value, and fulfilling orders, when you see the types of activities performed by support functions, you begin to realize that any company would be hard-pressed to fulfill orders without these functions being performed.

Firms can use value-chain activities to create value by either finding *better* ways to perform the same activities or by finding *different* ways to perform them. However, any advantage obtained by doing the same activities but better than competitors may be short-lived. Best practices in activities are often rapidly diffused throughout industries. Eventually, rivals improve performance in activities that they once performed less efficiently than industry leaders. For instance, logistical tactics that prove efficient at one firm often show up at rival firms through consultants or as a result of outsourcing. Thus, performing the same activities better than rivals usually results in a temporary advantage. Alternatively, configuring value-chain activities in different ways than competitors makes it harder for rivals to imitate those activities. This is due to what is known as *tradeoff protection*.

Tradeoff Protection

By organizing their value-chain activities in unique and specific ways, firms may be able to make imitation quite difficult. Gaining advantage through value-chain configuration usually involves a rather complex system of activities. When a firm reconfigures the value chain, it exercises some tradeoffs. By adding or dropping certain activities, it may necessitate the elimination or addition of other activities. Rivals find it very difficult to imitate a system of interdependent activities because they have made some investments in their system of activities that may be irreversible. Generally, companies won't imitate activities if doing so would mean abandoning one or more activities that are essential to their own strategies.[31] In other words, they'll balk at the tradeoff.

To illustrate this point, let's consider some differences between the value-chain activities of Southwest Airlines and those of most other major U.S. airlines, which are summarized in Exhibits 3.7 and 3.8. Southwest has achieved unrivaled cost advantages among large airlines by radically pruning the number of activities that it performs and by undertaking others in nontraditional ways. As a result, the configuration of its value chain is fundamentally different from those of most other airlines. Southwest, for example, uses only one type of aircraft—a strategy that reduces maintenance and training costs. In addition, the chosen aircraft is efficient for the kind of shorter flights that comprise most of Southwest's schedule. Southwest has also cut many of the services normally provided by major carriers (such as baggage transfers, meals, and assigned seats).

conceptlink

In Chapter 1, we emphasize that the *strategic management process*, which outlines the means by which a firm intends to create value for customers, consists of activities designed to lead customers to prefer its products over those of its competitors.

conceptlink

In Chapter 2, we observe that most major strategic decisions involve *tradeoffs*—that deciding on one course of action generally eliminates other options.

	Southwest	Major Airlines
Technology and Design	• Single aircraft	• Multiple types of aircraft
Operations	• Short-segment flights • No meals • No seat assignments • Single class of service • No baggage transfers to other airlines • Smaller markets and secondary airports in major markets	• Hub-and-spoke system • Meals • Seat assignments • Multiple classes of service • Baggage transfers to other airlines • Larger markets and major airports, some smaller markets served, largely though alliances with regional carriers
Marketing	• Limited use of travel agents • Word of mouth	• Extensive use of travel agents

Exhibit 3.7 Value-Chain Activities in the U.S. Airline Industry

Sources: Transportation Workers Union, TWU Airline Industry Review, *2004 (accessed February 18, 2005), at www.twuatd.org; Bureau of Transportation,* TransStats Reports, *2004 (accessed August 4, 2005), at www.transtats.bts.gov.*

Exhibit 3.8 Comparative
Costs for U.S. Airlines

*Source: Comparative Airline Costs
Fourth Quarter 2004 TWU Airline
Industry Review, a publication of the
Transportation Workers Union,
accessed February 18, 2005
(accessed at www.twuatd.org);
Bureau of Transportation Statistics,
TransStats reports
(www.transtats.bts.gov).*

Airline	2004 Revenue ($ millions [U.S.])	2004 Cost of Available Seat Miles (CASM)
AirTran	279	8.42
Alaska	656	10.03
American	4,541	9.72
AmericaWest	579	7.81
Continental	2,397	9.49
Delta	3,641	10.23
JetBlue	334	6.03
Northwest	2,753	10.31
Southwest	1,655	7.77
United	3,988	10.16
USAir	1,660	11.34

As a result of its unique configuration of activities, Southwest operates at a significantly lower cost than its competitors. We can confirm this conclusion by taking a look at a factor known as *CASM* (cost of available seat miles), which is a common measure of costs in the airline industry. As you can see in Exhibit 3.8, Southwest's CASM is significantly lower than that of every major competitor. Why don't other major airlines imitate Southwest's value chain? Primarily because doing so would mean ceasing certain activities that are fundamental to their operations. Although many airlines have stopped serving meals to save costs, they can't stop transferring luggage, abandon the hub-and-spoke system, or convert exclusively to Boeing 737s. So many tradeoffs would mean changing their business model completely. Thus, Southwest has protected its advantage by configuring its value-chain activities in such a way that imitating them is not attractive to competitors.

Further analysis of Exhibit 3.8 reveals another important insight. The airline with the lowest CASM is actually JetBlue. This recent startup has been able to imitate much of Southwest's value chain and then even make a few modifications that have further lowered costs (e.g., newer, more fuel-efficient planes, low-cost labor). This illustrates that although it may be very difficult for an established competitor to imitate the successful value-chain configuration of a leading company, a new entrant has much more flexibility to do so. A new firm that hasn't already made irreversible commitments to another value-chain configuration may be in a better position to imitate a successful value-chain configuration and even make improvements upon that model.

Innovation and Integration in the Value Chain   IKEA, a Swedish furniture company, has built a hugely successful business by almost completely reconfiguring the value-chain activities of the furniture industry by transferring delivery and assembly to the customer. IKEA's stores double as warehouses. The furniture is shipped in flat-packed boxes. Customers shop among display models, but then take the unassembled furniture off the shelves and assemble it at home. This significantly lowers the costs of production and distribution.

Similarly, Dell's success is based on an innovative reconfiguration of sales, distribution, and customer-service activities in the personal-computer industry that exploits the growing base of knowledgeable PC consumers around the world. Dell PCs use components manufactured entirely by suppliers. In addition, its distribution and marketing operations rest on a direct-sales model that avoids retailers. This combination of strategies—outsourcing component manufacturing and distributing finished products directly—was a radical departure from the business models that prevailed in the industry.

Many competitors have tried to imitate this model, but at Dell the model supports—and is integrally linked to—a *chain* of value-adding activities. Large established PC firms have never been able to duplicate Dell's cost structure because they haven't been willing or able to make all of the tradeoffs that would be necessary to imitate its value-chain activities.

The message in each of these examples is pretty much the same: The key to the value-chain approach to competitive advantage is not only developing value-chain activities that differ from those of rivals but also configuring them so that they're integrally related and can't be imitated without significant tradeoffs. *Value-chain fit* is important, Michael Porter reminds us, because it locks out imitators by "creating a chain of activities that is as strong as its strongest link."[32]

Outsourcing and the Value Chain

Given that strategy is about making tradeoffs, one of the most fundamental tradeoffs managers make today is whether to outsource a historically integral value-chain activity. Indeed, the value chain forces managers to identify activities and capabilities the firm must possess itself and those that can be performed outside of the firm. Referring back to IKEA, one of IKEA's innovations was to outsource furniture assembly to the end consumer.

Outsourcing is not new; it is just that it has become so prevalent, and sometimes contentious, especially when it involves the loss of domestic jobs, that it may seem relatively new. Part of this prevalence is due to the broad number of choices managers have in terms of outsourcing; they are able to outsource nearly any activity that they please. Although outsourcing a value-chain activity may be feasible and lower a firm's direct costs and overhead, based on what you have learned about the resource and capability perspective, you should know that caution must be exercised. For instance, if a firm outsources its marketing or distribution function, it may lose access to the knowledge of customer preferences that inspired its early product breakthroughs in the first place. This perhaps explains why brand leaders such as Nike and Pacific Cycle (Schwinn brand) have outsourced functions such as manufacturing and have instead focused their efforts on activities surrounding product development, logistics, brand management, and customer retention and expansion.

conceptlink

In Chapter 1, we show how the decision to *outsource* certain functions reflects a choice of **arenas**—of areas in which a firm will be active as opposed to those in which it won't be active.

STRATEGIC LEADERSHIP: LINKING RESOURCES AND CAPABILITIES TO STRATEGY

The opening vignette in this chapter notes the central role of leaders in managing a firm's resources and capabilities. It is important to not lose sight of the fact that it is a firm's managers who scan its external and internal environments and consequently decide how to use resources and capabilities and how to configure value-chain activities based on their assessment of those sometimes rapidly changing environments. Indeed, the role of managers is so critical that some experts include managerial human capital among a firm's resources; others include management among a company's dynamic capabilities.[33] A recent McKinsey consulting report concluded that "companies that overlook the role of leadership in the early phases of strategic planning often find themselves scrambling when it's time to execute. No matter how thorough the plan, without the right leaders it is unlikely to succeed."[34] To incorporate these views, we regard managers as *decision agents*—the people who put into motion the processes that use the firm's resources and capabilities.

conceptlink

In Chapter 2, we define **strategic leadership** as the task of managing an overall enterprise and influencing key organizational outcomes.

Senior Managers

In addition to deciding how to use resources and capabilities and configuring a firm's value-chain activities, senior managers also set the context that determines how frontline and middle managers can add value. Recall from the opening vignette that senior managers did not change Intel's strategy from memory chips to microprocessors—at least not until frontline managers made that change a *fait accompli*.

Strategy research has shown that senior managers in the most effective firms around the globe view their organizations as portfolios of processes—specifically, entrepreneurial, capability-building, and renewal processes—and key people, such as those who comprise the firm's middle and frontline managerial ranks.[35] Collectively, these processes may be seen as part of a firm's culture.

The *entrepreneurial process* encourages middle managers to be externally oriented—to seek out opportunities and run their part of the business as if they owned it. Senior managers who foster this process are stepping back from the notion that they are the sole visionaries and saviors of the company and instead seek to share this responsibility with the managers on the front lines. The *capability-building process* also looks to middle managers to identify, grow, and protect new ways to create value for the organization and its key stakeholders. In many ways, this process is the internal side of the externally oriented entrepreneurial process. Finally, the *renewal process* is senior managers' way of shaking up the firm and challenging its historic ways of operating; however, this process is based on information learned through current business activities performed elsewhere in the firm.

We can see all three of these processes taking place in the opening vignette about Intel. Senior management had put into place processes and a culture that encouraged entrepreneurial activities. Similarly, middle management helped the firm to develop new capabilities to capitalize on the microprocessor opportunity. Finally, senior management stepped in to validate this major change in strategy, based on upgraded organizational resources and capabilities related to logic-device architecture. The only piece missing from the opening case is the role played by senior management in the selection, retention, and promotion of middle and frontline managers.

Of course, not all senior managers are equipped equally to act effectively. Obviously, basic managerial talent isn't bestowed equally on all managers, even if they have risen to the highest levels in the organization. Moreover, specific experiences and backgrounds will make some managers better qualified to work with a specific bundle of resources. Researchers have discovered, for instance, that multinational firms (those with operations in several countries) achieve higher levels of performance when their CEOs have had some experience in foreign operations.[36] In addition, entrepreneurial operations must often rely on few or no valuable or rare resources. Managers of these enterprises generally start with ideas and goals and not much more. In such situations, the positive influence of managers is even more important.[37] Likewise, in firms facing financial or competitive turmoil, the galvanizing and enabling effects of superior senior management are also more pronounced.

Southwest Airlines founder and former CEO Herb Kelleher created a value chain for his company unlike that of any of his competitors. Using a low-fare, no-frills, no-reserved-seating approach, Southwest has managed to earn a profit for 30 years straight—an astonishing feat in the airlines industry.

Middle Managers

From the discussion on senior managers, you should be able to see that middle managers play a key role in what the firm is doing and what it may be adept at doing in the future. The entrepreneurial, capability-building, and renewal processes all require the involvement, choices, and actions of middle and frontline managers. Executives must consider their leadership pool as they shape strategy and align their leadership-development programs with long-term aspirations. Particularly in large firms, the effect of senior executives on firm performance is a function of the choices they have made about the context in which frontline managers work and the appointment of particular managers themselves.

Strategic leadership researcher Quy Nguyen Huy has identified four areas where middle managers are better positioned to contribute to competitive advantage and corporate success than are senior executives:[38]

- **Entrepreneur.** Middle managers are close enough to the front lines to spot fires, yet far enough away to understand the bigger picture. Because middle management ranks are typically more diverse in terms of ethnicity, gender, experience, and geography, this group has the potential to contribute richer ideas than the senior-management team.
- **Communicator.** Middle managers are typically long tenured and have very broad social networks. This gives them great credibility with employees, and they are therefore better able to move change initiatives in nonthreatening ways. Their tenure also gives them deep knowledge about how to get things done in the organization.
- **Psychoanalyst.** Internal credibility also enables middle managers to be more effective in quelling alienation and chaos, as seen by high productivity among anxious employees during times of great change. Because they know their troops, frontline managers also know when and how to provide one-on-one support and problem solving.
- **Tightrope walker.** Particularly in the case of dynamic capabilities and dynamic environments, firms are faced with the need to balance continuity and radical change. Middle managers are well poised to accomplish this balancing act. With the right process in place courtesy of senior executives, middle managers can help the firm avoid inertia and too little change or slow change and also avoid the paralyzing chaos accompanying too much change too quickly.

In many ways, it's the central role of upper and middle management that distinguishes the internal perspective on strategy from the external perspective that we'll discuss in Chapter 4. After all, if competitive advantage results from the different characteristics of firms, then the key task in the role of management is to identify resources and capabilities, specify the resources that will create competitive advantage, locate an attractive industry in which to deploy them, and then select the strategy to get the most out of them. Finally, it's the job of managers to choose *when* to change a firm's mix of resources, capabilities, and targeted markets. As you learned in Chapter 2, the managements of smaller firms typically differ from those of larger firms in terms of their overall number, not the roles that they play. This means that in smaller firms senior leaders, often the owners or company founders, may wear many if not all of the middle and frontline manager hats described.

SUMMARY

1. Explain the *internal context of strategy*. Firms facing similar industry conditions achieve different levels of competitive advantage and performance based on their internal characteristics and managerial choices. Although firms must always take the external context into account when formulating and implementing strategy, the internal perspectives stress the differences among a firm in terms of the unique resources and capabilities that they own or control. These perspectives offer important models and analytical tools that will help you to analyze and formulate competitive strategies.

2. Identify a firm's resources and capabilities and explain their role in its performance.
Resources are either tangible or intangible. Resources and capabilities that help firms establish a competitive advantage and secure higher levels of performance are those that are valuable, rare, and costly to imitate. The VRINE model helps you analyze resources and capabilities. A resource or capability is said to be valuable if it enables the firm to exploit opportunities or negate threats in the environment. In addition, the firm must have complementary organizational capabilities to exploit resources and capabilities that meet these three conditions. Rare resources enable firms to exploit opportunities or negate threats in ways that those lacking the resource cannot. Competitors will try to find ways to imitate valuable and rare resources; a firm can generate an enduring competitive advantage if competitors face a *cost disadvantage* in acquiring or substituting the resource that is lacking. Unique historical conditions that have led to resource or capability development, time-compression diseconomies, and causal ambiguity all make imitation more difficult. Firms often use alliances, acquisitions, and substitution with less costly resources as mechanisms to gain access to difficult-to-imitate resources.

3. Define *dynamic capabilities* and explain their role in both strategic change and a firm's performance.
The process of development, accumulation, and possible loss of resources and capabilities is inherently dynamic. The resource-accumulation process and dynamic capabilities are fundamentally different from the static possession of a stock of resources and capabilities. Dynamic capabilities are processes that integrate, reconfigure, acquire, or divest resources in order to use the firms' stocks of resources and capabilities in new ways. The ability to adapt to changing conditions or to proactively initiate a change in the competitive environment is particularly important in industries in which time-to-market is critical, technological change is rapid, and future competition is difficult to forecast.

4. Explain how value-chain activities are related to firm performance and competitive advantage.
Firms produce products or offer services by engaging in many activities. The basic structure of firm activities is illustrated by the firm's value chain. The value chain is divided into primary and support activities. One way a company can outperform rivals is it can find ways to perform some value-chain activities better than its rivals or to find different ways to perform the activities altogether. Selective outsourcing of some value-chain activities is one way to perform activities differently. Competitive advantage through strategic configuration of value-chain activities only comes about if the firm can either deliver greater value than rivals or deliver comparable value at lower cost. The essence of the activity-based value-chain perspective of competitive advantage is to choose value-chain activities that are different from those of rivals and to configure these activities in a way that are internally consistent and that requires significant tradeoffs should a competitor want to imitate them.

5. Explain the role of managers with respect to resources, capabilities, and value-chain activities.
Managers make decisions about how to employ resources in the formulation and implementation of strategy. Managers are the decision agents that put into motion the use of all other firm resources and capabilities; they are key to the success of a firm's strategy. Managers with specific experiences and backgrounds may be more qualified to work with a specific bundle of resources owned by a firm. The influence of managers is more pronounced in contexts such as entrepreneurial phases, turnarounds, and competitive turmoil.

6. Understand your StratSim firm's internal resources, capabilities, and activities using the VRINE framework and analyze the value chain for your firm.
Obviously, your VRINE analysis will be a very important factor in how you compete in StratSim. Because each firm starts with different resources and capabilities, the teams managing those firms will likely make very different strategic choices. Similarly, since your strategy is the means by which you will realize your vision and mission, you will likely want to see your firm's unique resources, capabilities, and value-chain activities clearly reflected in vision, mission, and strategy.

KEY TERMS

capabilities, 71
causal ambiguity, 77
core competence, 72

distinctive competence, 71
dynamic capabilities, 81

outsourcing, 71
resources, 70

value chain, 71
VRINE model, 73

REVIEW QUESTIONS

1. What are resources? How do different types of resources differ?

2. What is a capability?

3. What are the five components of the VRINE model?

4. How do time and causal ambiguity relate to the value, rarity, and inimitability of a resource or capability?

5. What is the difference between a stock of resources and capabilities and a flow of resources and capabilities?

6. What are dynamic capabilities? How do they differ from general capabilities?

7. What is a firm's value chain? How does it figure into a firm's competitive advantage?

8. What is your role as a manager in linking resources and capabilities to strategy and competitive advantage?

How Would you Do That?

1. In the box entitled "How Would You Do That? 3.1," we walked through how to apply the VRINE model to evaluate the value of Pfizer's patents. Later in the chapter, we walked you through the concept of the value chain. Identify the value chain for another organization. Are there activities that this organization performs differently than its rivals? Start by looking at the firm's products, services, or target markets. Likewise, examine the programs of a few leading rivals. Do any of the rival firms' value-chain activities give them a competitive advantage? If so, why don't others imitate these activities?

2. What resources and capabilities does your focal organization possess? What are the resources and capabilities possessed by rivals? How do your focal organization's resources and capabilities fare relative to those of the rivals' when you apply the VRINE model to them?

3. Apply the VRINE model to your StratSim firm. By applying these concepts, you should uncover your firm's internal strengths. Furthermore, we encourage you to consider how you could better utilize these strengths.

Value—What resources or capabilities are particularly valuable for your StratSim firm?

Rarity—What resources or capabilities does your firm possess that are unique to your firm?

Inimitability and Nonsubstitutability—Are these rare resources or capabilities difficult for your competitors to obtain? What is required of your competition to match this competitive advantage?

Exploitability—How is your StratSim firm currently exploiting this advantage? How could you make better use of these advantages?

4. Map out the value-chain activities for your StratSim firm. Be sure to discuss them within the limits of the simulation. In other words, do not make assumptions that are not options in StratSim even if they might be possibilities. The constraints of the game exist to make it a manageable activity, and discussing issues that are not possibilities will not help your performance in the simulation. Focus on those activities that you can impact.

GROUP ACTIVITIES

1. What is the role of luck in gaining possession of a particular resource or capability? Can a firm manage luck? Give an example of a resource or capability that a firm garnered through luck and determine whether it was subsequently well managed.

2. Some firms' products are so well known that the entire category of products offered in the industry (including rivals' products) is often referred to by the leading firm's brand name (which is called an *eponym*). Identify one such product and discuss whether its brand recognition gives the leading firm a competitive advantage. Why or why not?

ENDNOTES

1. www.intel.com and Hoover's (accessed June 28, 2005); K. M. Eisenhardt and J. A. Martin, "Dynamic Capabilities: What Are They?" *Strategic Management Journal* 21 (2000), 1105–1121.

2. J. Haleblian and S. Finkelstein, "The Influence of Organizational Acquisition Experience on Acquisition Performance: A Behavioral Learning Perspective," *Administrative Science Quarterly* 44:1 (1999), 29–56; F. Vermeulen and H. Barkema, "Learning Through Acquisitions," *Academy of Management Journal* 44:3 (2001), 457–476.

3. D. J. Teece, G. Pisano, and A. Shuen, "Dynamic Capabilities and Strategic Management," *Strategic Management Journal* 18 (1997), 509–529.

4. R. R. Nelson and S. G. Winter, *An Evolutionary Theory of Economic Change* (Cambridge, MA: Belknap Press of Harvard University Press, 1982).

5. english.pravda.ru/usa/2001/11/03/20045.html and www.restaurantreport.com/qa/location.html (accessed June 28, 2005).

6. J. B. Barney, "Firm Resources and Sustained Competitive Advantage," *Journal of Management* 17:1 (1991), 99–120.

7. Barney, "Firm Resources and Sustained Competitive Advantage."

8. C. K. Prahalad and G. Hamel, "The Core Competence of the Corporation," *Harvard Business Review* 68:3 (1990), 79–92.

9. L. Capron and W. Mitchell, "The Role of Acquisitions in Reshaping Business Capabilities in the International Telecommunications Industry," *Industrial and Corporate Change* 7:4 (1998), 715–730.

10. P. R. Haunschild, "How Much Is That Company Worth? Interorganizational Relationships, Uncertainty, and Acquisition Premiums," *Administrative Science Quarterly* 39:3 (1994), 391–414.

11. B. Labaris, "Has Your Vendor Gone Buyout Crazy?" *Computerworld* 33:36 (1999), 34–35.

12. J. B. Barney, "Looking Inside for Competitive Advantage," *Academy of Management Executive* 9:4 (1995), 49–61; I. Dierickx and K. Cool, "Asset Stock Accumulation and Sustainability of Competitive Advantage," *Management Science* 35:12 (1989), 1504–1511.

13. M. Pendergrast, *For God, Country and Coca-Cola* (New York: Basic Books, 1993).

14. Coca-Cola, *2004 Annual Report*; PepsiCo, *2004 Annual Report*.

15. Dierickx and Cool, "Asset Stock Accumulation and Sustainability of Competitive Advantage."

16. Dierickx and Cool, "Asset Stock Accumulation and Sustainability of Competitive Advantage."

17. Nelson and Winter, *An Evolutionary Theory of Economic Change*.

18. Barney, "Looking Inside for Competitive Advantage"; Dierickx and Cool, "Asset Stock Accumulation and Sustainability of Competitive Advantage."

19. Author's personal communication with Margaret Haddox, Novell Corporate Librarian, October 2003.

20. Author's personal communication with former Novell executives, September 2003.

21. D. T. Kearns and D. A. Nadler, *Prophets in the Dark* (New York: HarperCollins, 1992); Barney, "Looking Inside for Competitive Advantage."

22. Eisenhardt and Martin, "Dynamic Capabilities."

23. Eisenhardt and Martin, "Dynamic Capabilities."

24. B. Orwall, "In Disney Row, an Aging Heir Who's Won Boardroom Bouts," *Wall Street Journal*, December 5, 2003, A1.

25. G. Szulanski and R. J. Jensen, "Overcoming Stickiness: An Empirical Investigation of the Role of the Template," *Managerial Decision Economics*, forthcoming.

26. Eisenhardt and Martin, "Dynamic Capabilities."

27. Teece, Pisano, and Shuen, "Dynamic Capabilities and Strategic Management."

28. C. Christensen, *The Innovator's Dilemma* (New York: Harper Business Press, 1997).

29. R. Burgelman, "Fading Memories: A Process Theory of Strategic Business Exit in Dynamic Environments," *Administrative Science Quarterly* 39:1 (1994), 24–56.

30. M. E. Porter, "What Is Strategy?" *Harvard Business Review* 74:6 (1996), 61–78.

31. Porter, "What Is Strategy?"

32. Porter, "What Is Strategy?"

33. Barney, "Firm Resources and Sustained Competitive Advantage."

34. T. Hseih and S. Yik, "Leadership as the Starting Point of Strategy," *McKinsey Quarterly* 1 (2005), 11–26.

35. S. Ghoshal and C. A. Bartlett, "Changing the Role of Top Management: Beyond Structure to Processes," *Harvard Business Review* 73:3 (1995), 86–96; C. A. Bartlett and S. Ghoshal, "Changing the Role of Top Management: Beyond Systems to People," *Harvard Business Review* 73:3 (1995), 132–134.

36. M. A. Carpenter, W. Sanders, and H. Gregersen, "Bundling Human Capital with Organizational Context: The Impact of International Assignment Experience on Multinational Firm Performance and CEO Pay," *Academy of Management Journal* 44:3 (2001), 493–512.

37. M. A. Carpenter, T. G. Pollock, and M. M. Leary, "Testing a Model of Reasoned Risk-Taking: Governance, the Experience of Principals and Agents, and Global Strategy in High-Technology IPO Firms," *Strategic Management Journal* 24:9 (2003), 803–820.

38. Q. Huy, "In Praise of Middle Managers," *Harvard Business Review* 79:8 (2001), 72–79.

After studying this chapter, you should be able to:

1. Explain the importance of the external context for strategy and firm performance.

2. Use PESTEL to identify the macro characteristics of the external context.

3. Identify the major features of an industry and the forces that affect industry profitability.

4. Understand the dynamic characteristics of the external context.

5. Show how industry dynamics may redefine industries.

6. Use scenario planning to predict the future structure of the external context.

7. Understand the external environment in your StratSim industry through PESTEL analysis and identify industry dynamics at play within your StratSim industry using the five forces model.

▶ **Roberto C. Goizueta, 1981-1997**
Strategy: Seek out profitable new business lines and "kick Pepsi's can" by taking over Coke's distribution services via the launch of the Coca-Cola Bottling Company.
Stock high: $125.50
Stock low: $30.25

▶ **Wayne Callaway, 1986–1996**
Strategy: Foster the entrepreneurial spirit of Pepsi's people in order to compete more effectively in the global environment and in different industries, such as the fast-food market.
Stock High: $98.25
Stock Low: $21.62

▶ **Roger Enrico, 1996–2001**
Strategy: Jettison some of Pepsi's slow-growing businesses and take the bloat out of others. Win the Cola War by concentrating on emerging overseas markets not already dominated by Coke.
Stock High: $69.12
Stock Low: $27.56

1980   1985

A CHRONICLE OF THE COLA WAR

The Cola Wars is a defining feature of the history of the soft-drink industry.[1] Its roots can be traced back to 1886, when a pharmacist in Atlanta, Georgia, concocted a headache tonic that he sold for five cents a glass. His bookkeeper named the remedy "Coca-Cola" and committed its secret formula to writing. About a decade later, and just a few hundred miles away in New Bern, North Carolina, another pharmacist created Pepsi Cola.

Over a century later, the stakes in the soft-drink industry are enormous. The average American consumes 53 gallons of carbonated beverages per year—about 29 percent of the total consumption of all liquids! Coke and Pepsi have battled for decades to conquer market share in what is regularly one of the most profitable mature industries in the world. Experts estimate that gross margins in soft-drink concentrate are approximately 83 percent and net margins about

▶ **Douglas N. Daft, 2000-2004**
Strategy: Repair Coke and restore a stock price deflated by saturated U.S. sales, failed acquisitions, and product contamination in Europe.
Stock high: $63.06
Stock low: $37.07

▶ **Steve Reinemund, 2001-present**
Strategy: Grow and diversify PepsiCo's businesses beyond the soft-drink market by motivating employees and providing superior leadership.
Stock high: $57.12
Stock low: $35.01

▶ **E. Neville Isdell, 2004-present**
Strategy: Promote Coke's 400 brands globally and diversify its product line to adapt to the changing beverage tastes of U.S. consumers.
Stock high: $51.16
Stock low: $38.41

1995   2000

35 percent. With such enormous profit potential at stake, it's no wonder that Coke and Pepsi go to great lengths to defend their turf.

Trading Punches Although Coke has long been dominant, Pepsi has worked hard to weaken its enemy's position. In 1950, for example, Pepsi recruited a former Coke marketing manager and proclaimed the battle cry "Beat Coke." In the 1960s, Pepsi launched its "Pepsi Generation" campaign to target younger buyers. In the mid-1970s, spurred by the success of blind taste tests in Texas, Pepsi launched a nationwide offensive called the "Pepsi Challenge." Coke, however, refused to retreat, countering with such tactics as retail-price cuts and aggressive advertising.

Coke's tactics intensified after Roberto Goizueta became CEO in 1981. Once in command, Goizueta more than doubled advertising, switched to lower-priced sweeteners, sold off noncarbonated-beverage businesses, and introduced new flavors and diet versions of existing brands. Coke's victories included Diet Coke, the most successful new product introduction of the 1980s. Then, however, Coke made a serious tactical error: It tried to reformulate the 100-year-old recipe for Coke. When consumers rebelled, Coke was forced to retreat to the original formula. Pepsi proclaimed the effort to reformulate Coke as an admission that Pepsi had a superior taste.

The value-chain activities that bring carbonated beverages to market are centered on four functions: production (producing concentrate), marketing (managing a portfolio of brands), packaging (bottling finished products), and distribution (distributing products for resale). Concentrate is the syrup that provides the distinctive flavor to soft drinks. Historically, the major beverage companies focused on the production of concentrate and marketing, and independent regional bottlers were tasked with packaging and distribution. Bottlers mixed the soft-drink concentrate with sweetener and carbonated water and then packaged and distributed the finished product in cans, bottles, or bulk (for restaurant and other on-premises sales). In the early years, both Coke and Pepsi expanded rapidly by granting franchises to independent bottlers around the country. This strategy avoided huge investments in capital-intensive bottling operations.

Bottling Operations However, as the industry matured, the economics of bottling operations changed. For one, older franchised bottling plants were proving to be inefficient. These plants were typically only large enough to serve the territory the bottler controlled through its franchise agreement. Although modern bottling technology made costs savings possible with larger plant sizes, local franchised bottlers had little incentive to invest in larger plants. Because franchise agreements typically limited bottlers to defined geographic markets, larger modern plants would often exceed their capacity requirements. Two trends resulted in a change in the bottling industry. First, a few bottling companies saw an opportunity to buy up local franchises in contiguous markets and restructure local operations by building large plants designed to serve multiple markets. As these bottling operations began to grow in size, they also grew in power relative to Coke and Pepsi, which posed a legitimate threat to Coke and Pepsi. This threat led to the second trend in the bottling industry. Even though bottling operations generated much less than half the operating margins of concentrate production, both Coke and Pepsi entered the bottling industry. They began buying up independent bottling operations, consolidating territories, and building newer, more efficient facilities.

Although entering the bottling industry could have diluted Coke's and Pepsi's earnings, they actually were able to use this move to improve their overall performance. They did this in two ways. First, by purchasing the bottling operations based on existing profitability, they were able to buy these strategic operations cheaply relative to their value once they restructured operations and made them more efficient. Second, both Coke and Pepsi later divested part of their holdings by spinning off bottling subsidiaries (based on higher profitability) but retaining significant holdings in these now partially owned subsidiaries. These ownership positions enabled them to counteract any power that these operations may have had in negotiations were they to be completely independently owned and operated.

A New Age   In recent years, competition has taken on some new dimensions. Historically, the soft-drink industry has been distinct from the noncarbonated, nonalcoholic beverage industries. However, the success of bottled water and tea has attracted Coke and Pepsi to the noncarbonated, nonalcoholic beverage industries, blurring the traditional boundaries between the soft-drink and noncarbonated, nonalcoholic industries. In addition, soft-drink industry participants have been creating new products in existing segments as well as creating entirely new segments. Recently, firms have been launching new diet drinks aimed at attracting customers who would normally shun anything labeled as a diet product.

An outside observer might think that such a fierce battle for market share would gradually erode the combatants' profitability. Since the mid-1960s, however, both Coke and Pepsi have increased market share by about 11 percent, and both enjoy healthy profits. Entry barriers created by large market shares, tremendous brand equity, and ownership or control of regional bottlers explain much of this profitability. Of course, that increased market share had to be captured from weaker rivals, although competitors like Cadbury Schweppes and private label suppliers are making up ground as well. Perhaps the only thing that is certain at this point is that the global hostilities between the two cola superpowers are far from over. ■

THE EXTERNAL CONTEXT OF STRATEGY

To formulate an effective strategy—one that has a good chance of helping you achieve your objectives—it is crucial that you understand the external environment. It is the external environment that provides the business opportunities to the firm. However, the external environment is also a source of threats—forces that may impede the successful implementation of a strategy. The external environment in which firms compete exerts a strong influence on firms' profitability.

As we noted at the start of Chapter 3, where we discussed some tools for identifying the internal determinants of a firm's strengths and weaknesses, you should think of the chapters on the internal and external contexts of strategy as related sections of a single unit: Individually, each discussion provides you with only half of the information you need to analyze a firm's strategy.

In this chapter, you'll learn how to identify the external opportunities and threats that affect every firm's strategy. Taken together, these two chapters provide the tools that will enable you to perform a rigorous analysis of the firm's competitive environment and its capabilities to implement a strategy. In previous coursework, you probably approached these issues with *SWOT analysis*, which is a relatively simple tool. The tools provided in Chapters 3 and 4 will help you systematically analyze what you could only do intuitively with the SWOT tool.

The long-term profitability of both Coke and Pepsi has probably been influenced by the structure of the soft-drink industry. Many enterprising entrepreneurs have seen this long-term propensity to make lots of money in the soft-drink industry and have desired to share in that wealth. Many small, profitable companies have emerged, yet, none has succeeded in becoming a major player alongside Coke and Pepsi. In this chapter, you will begin to understand why some industries are more profitable than others, why some industries are easier to enter than others, and what firms can do to influence these environmental factors in their favor.

Industry- and Firm-Specific Factors

Knowing what industry- and firm-specific factors affect a firm is critical to understanding its competitive position and determining what strategies are viable. We can examine the complementary roles of industry- and firm-specific factors on firm performance in many different industries. For instance, consider the venerable position of Coca-Cola in the soft-drink industry. Clearly, Coca-Cola has some firm-level advantages over its competitors.

Exhibit 4.1 Comparative Industrywide Levels of Profitability, 1995–2004

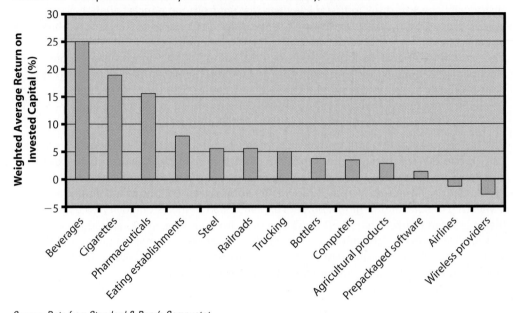

Source: Data from Standard & Poor's Compustat.

However, what happened when Coca-Cola entered the wine industry? The entry of Coca-Cola into the wine industry won't change at least two fundamental facts, namely, there is relatively little brand loyalty in wine, and the sale and distribution of the product is heavily regulated in most parts of the world. In 1977, Coke swallowed up industry giants Taylor Wine and Sterling Vineyard. As a beverage, wine is not entirely unrelated to Coke's core products, but unfortunately, Coke never mastered the complexities of a production and distribution process that's often as much an art as a science. After ringing up huge losses for a few years, Coke sold off its wine businesses—for much less than it initially paid for them. Evidently, some things don't go better with Coke.

As shown in Exhibit 4.1, profitability varies widely from industry to industry. Even without the analytical tools to which you'll be introduced in this chapter, you can see that there must be some things about the airline industry relative to the pharmaceutical industry that result in such drastic differences in profitability. Likewise, there are probably factors about the soft-drink industry that have helped Coke and Pepsi maintain such high profits over such an extended period of time. Why *are* some industries more profitable than others? For instance, why is the beverage industry (e.g., Coke, Pepsi, and their competitors) so much more profitable than the bottling industry?

What is needed to answer these questions are tools that allow you to systematically analyze a firm's external context. In the following sections you will be introduced to these tools. The proper use of these tools will help identify some of the major reasons industries differ so much in their long-term profitability.

We'll start this chapter by introducing methods for analyzing the macro environment and firms' industries. We then draw attention to the dynamic facets of the external environment.

Fundamental Characteristics of the External Context

concept link

In Chapter 2, we discuss the importance of *stakeholder analysis*, which we characterize as a series of steps for determining the nature and extent to which certain groups, both internal and external, have not only a vested interest in a firm's strategy, but also some influence on its decisions and performance.

Identifying the industry in which a firm competes is a logical starting point for analyzing its external context. By the fundamental characteristics of an industry, we mean those factors that are relevant to firm performance at a given point in time—the distinct features that you'd see if you could take an industry snapshot. Remember, too, that industry analysis will include many, but not all, of a firm's key external stakeholders. Thus, in order to avoid blind spots in an industry analysis, managers should always integrate their analysis of a firm's industry with a broader stakeholder analysis like that discussed in Chapter 2.

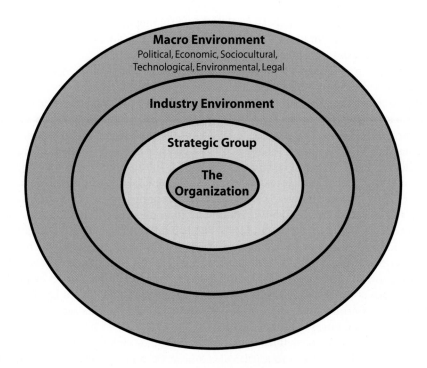

Exhibit 4.2 The External Environment of the Organization

Key Questions

Managers should ask the following questions when analyzing the firm's external context: "What macro environmental conditions will have a material effect on our ability to implement our strategy successfully?" "What is the firm's industry?" "What are the characteristics of the industry?" and "How stable are these characteristics?" By addressing such questions, managers can gain a better sense of a firm's strategic options and challenges. Managers must remain focused on the industry, not on a particular firm operating within it. Focusing on Coca-Cola alone will not provide much information on the general characteristics of the soft-drink industry, especially given the fact that Coke is far from average in terms of resources and capabilities. In addition, an industry analysis examines much more than simply the competitors in the industry. Our goal throughout this chapter is to present a deeper understanding of the external context in which *all* firms in an industry operate.

The external environment has two major components: the macro environment and the industry environment. The industry environment is composed of strategic groups—groupings of firms that seem to be more similar in certain ways than other members of the larger industry. The various levels of analysis necessary to examine a firm's external context are summarized in Exhibit 4.2. We will start with the macro environment most removed from the firm and work our way toward more micro analysis.

MACRO ENVIRONMENT

The macro environment refers to the larger political, economic, social, technical, environmental, and legal issues that confront the firm. To analyze the macro environment, we introduce the PESTEL model and present the determinants and consequences of globalization.

PESTEL Analysis

A simple but important and widely used tool that can be used to develop an understanding of the big picture of a firm's external environment is **PESTEL analysis**. PESTEL is an acronym for the *p*olitical, *e*conomic, *s*ociocultural, *t*echnological, *e*nvironmental, and *l*egal context(s) in which a firm operates. It provides a nonexhaustive list of potential influences of the environment on the organization. It helps managers gain a better understanding of the opportunities and threats they face and consequently aids them in building a better

PESTEL analysis Tool for assessing the political, economic, sociocultural, technological, environmental, and legal contexts in which a firm operates.

vision of the future business landscape and how the firm might compete profitably. PESTEL analysis is a useful tool for understanding market growth or decline. Its primary focus is on the future impact of macro environmental factors.

Firms need to understand the macro environment to ensure that their strategy is aligned with the powerful forces of change that are affecting their business landscape. When firms exploit changes in the environment, they are more likely to be successful than when they simply try to survive or oppose change. A good understanding of PESTEL also helps managers avoid strategies that may be doomed to failure for reasons beyond their control. Finally, understanding PESTEL is a good starting point for entering into a new country or region.

The fact that a strategy is congruent with PESTEL in the home environment gives no assurance that it will be so aligned in new geographic arenas. For example, when the online clothier Lands' End sought to expand its operations from the United States to Germany in 1996 it ran into local laws prohibiting Lands' End from offering unconditional guarantees on its products. In the United States, Lands' End had built its reputation for quality on its no-questions-asked money-back guarantee. However, this practice was considered illegal under Germany's regulations governing incentive offers and price discounts. The political skirmish between Lands' End and the German government finally came to an end in 2001, when the regulations were abolished. Although the regulations did not put Lands' End out of business in Germany, they did slow its growth there until the laws against advertising unconditional guarantees were abolished.

PESTEL analysis involves three steps. First, you should think through the relevance of each of the PESTEL factors to your particular context. Second, you identify and categorize the information that applies to these factors. Third, you analyze the data and draw conclusions. A mistake too many students make is to stop at the second step. A second common mistake is to assume that your initial analysis and conclusions are correct without testing your assumptions and investigating alternative scenarios.

The PESTEL analysis framework is presented in Exhibit 4.3. It has six sections, one for each of the PESTEL headings. The table includes sample questions or prompts, the answers to which will help you determine the nature of opportunities and threats in the macro environment. The questions are not meant to be exhaustive; rather, they are merely exemplars of the types of issues that you should be concerned about in the macro environment.

Political Factors   The political environment can have a significant influence on businesses as well as affect consumer confidence and consumer and business spending. Managers need to consider numerous types of political factors. For instance, the stability of the political environment is particularly important for companies entering new markets. In addition, government policies with respect to regulation and taxation vary from state to state and across national boundaries. Political considerations also encompass trade treaties, such as NAFTA, and regional trading blocks, such as ASEAN and the European Union (EU). Such treaties and trading blocks tend to favor trade among the member countries and to impose penalties or less favorable trade terms on nonmembers.

Economic Factors   Managers also need to consider the macroeconomic factors that will have near- and long-term effects on the success of their strategies. Factors such as inflation rates, interest rates, tariffs, the growth of the local and foreign national economies, and exchange rates are critical. Unemployment rates, the availability of critical labor, and the local labor costs also have a strong bearing on strategy, particularly as it relates to where to locate disparate business functions and facilities.

Sociocultural Factors   The social and cultural influences on business vary from country to country. Depending on the type of business the firm operates, factors such as the local languages, the dominant religions, leisure time, and age and lifespan demographics may be critical. Local sociocultural characteristics also vary on such things as attitudes toward consumerism, environmentalism, and the roles of men and women in local society. Making assumptions about local sociocultural norms derived from your experience in your home market is a common cause of early failure when entering new markets. However, even home-market norms can change over time, often caused by shifting demographics

conceptlink

In Chapter 1, we define **arenas** as the areas, ranging from products and technologies to market segments and geographic locations, in which a firm will be active.

Exhibit 4.3 The Dimensions of PESTEL Analysis

Political
- How stable is the political environment?
- What are local taxation policies and how do these affect your business?
- Is the government involved in trading agreements such as EU, NAFTA, ASEAN, or others?
- What are the foreign-trade regulations?
- What are the social-welfare policies?

Economic
- What are current and projected interest rates?
- What is the level of inflation, what is it projected to be, and how does this projection reflect the growth of your market?
- What are local employment levels per capita and how are they changing?
- What are the long-term prospects for gross domestic product (GDP) per capita and so on?
- What are exchange rates between critical markets and how will they affect production and distribution of your goods?

Sociocultural
- What are local lifestyle trends?
- What are the current demographics and how are they changing?
- What is the level and distribution of education and income?
- What are the dominant local religions and what influence do they have on consumer attitudes and opinions?
- What is the level of consumerism and what are popular attitudes toward it?
- What pending legislation affects corporate social policies (e.g., domestic-partner benefits, maternity/paternity leave)?
- What are the attitudes toward work and leisure?

Technological
- What is the level of research funding in government and industry and are those levels changing?
- What is the government and industry's level of interest and focus on technology?
- How mature is the technology?
- What is the status of intellectual-property issues in the local environment?
- Are potentially disruptive technologies in adjacent industries creeping in at the edges of the focal industry?

Environmental
- What are local environmental issues?
- Are there any pending ecological or environmental issues relevant to your industry?
- How do the activities of international pressure groups (e.g., Greenpeace, Earth First, PETA) affect your business?
- Are there environmental-protection laws?
- What are the regulations regarding waste disposal and energy consumption?

Legal
- What are the regulations regarding monopolies and private property?
- Does intellectual property have legal protections?
- Are there relevant consumer laws?
- What is the status of employment, health-and-safety, and product-safety laws?

due to immigration or aging populations. For example, Coca-Cola and Pepsi have grown in international markets due to increasing levels of consumerism outside of the United States.

Technological Factors The critical role of technology will be discussed in more detail later in the chapter. For now, suffice it to say that technological factors have a major bearing on the threats and opportunities firms encounter. Does technology enable products and services to be made more cheaply and to a better standard of quality? Do technologies provide the opportunity for more innovative products and services, such as online stock trading, reduction in communications costs, and increased remote working? How might distribution be affected by new technologies? All of these factors have the potential to change the face of the business landscape.

Environmental Factors   The environment has long been a factor in firm strategy, primarily from the standpoint of access to raw materials. Increasingly, however, this factor is best viewed as a direct- and indirect-operating cost for the firm, as well as from the lens of the footprint left by a firm on its respective environments in terms of waste, pollution, etc. For consumer-products companies such as Pepsi, for example, this can mean waste-management and organic-farming practices in the countries from which raw materials are obtained. Similarly, in consumer markets it may refer to the degree to which packaging is biodegradable or recyclable.

Legal Factors   Finally, legal factors reflect the laws and regulations relevant to the region and the organization. Legal factors may include whether the rule of law is well established and how easily or quickly laws and regulations may change. It may also include the costs of regulatory compliance. For instance, Coca-Cola's market share in Europe is greater than 50 percent, and as a result, regulators have asked that Coke give up shelf space to competitors' products in order to provide greater consumer choice.

As you can see, many of the PESTEL factors are interrelated. For instance, the legal environment is often related to the political environment in that laws and regulations will change only when politicians decide that such changes are needed.

Globalization

Over the past decade, as new markets have been opened to foreign competitors, whole industries have been deregulated; state-run enterprises have been privatized; and globalization has become a fact of life in almost every industry.[2] Because of this, the topic of globalization spans both the subjects of PESTEL analysis and industry analysis in both relatively stable and dynamic contexts. We define **globalization** as the evolution of distinct geographic product markets into a state of globally interdependent product markets.

Globalization entails much more than a company simply exporting products to another country. Some industries that aren't normally considered global do in fact have strictly domestic players, but they're often competing alongside firms with operations in many countries, and in many cases, both sets of firms are doing equally well. In contrast, in a truly global industry, the core product is standardized, the marketing approach is relatively uniform, and competitive strategies are integrated in different international markets.[3] In these industries, competitive advantage clearly belongs to the firms that can compete globally.

A number of factors reveal whether an industry has globalized or is in the process of globalizing. In Exhibit 4.4, we've grouped them into four categories: *market*, *cost*, *government*, and *competition*.[4]

Markets   The more similar markets in different regions are, the greater the pressure for an industry to globalize. Coke and Pepsi, for example, are fairly uniform around the world because the demand for soft drinks is largely the same in every country. The airframe-manufacturing industry, dominated by Boeing and Airbus, also has a highly uniform market for its products because airlines all over the world have the same needs when it comes to large commercial jets.

globalization Evolution of distinct geograhic markets into a state of globally interdependent product markets

Exhibit 4.4 Factors in Globalization

Sources: Adapted from M. E. Porter, Competition in Global Industries (Boston: Harvard Business School Press, 1986); G. Yip, "Global Strategy in a World of Nations," Sloan Management Review 31:1 (1989), 29–40.

Pressures Favoring Industry Globalization			
Markets	**Costs**	**Governments**	**Competition**
• Homogeneous customer needs • Global customer needs • Global channels • Transferable marketing approaches	• Large scale and scope economies • Learning and experience • Sourcing efficiencies • Favorable logistics • Arbitrage opportunities • High R&D costs	• Favorable trade policies • Common technological standards • Common manufacturing and marketing regulations	• Interdependent countries • Global competitors

Governments can have a huge impact on trade by setting industry-wide standards and regulations. In some parts of Western Europe, for example, people and freight can't travel easily from country to country without switching railroads. Because each country's rail standards and technology are different from its neighbors', rail lines are in some cases incompatible with one another.

Costs　In both the soft-drink and airframe-manufacturing industries, costs also favor globalization. Coke and Pepsi realize economies of scope and scale because they make such huge investments in marketing and promotion. Because they're promoting coherent images and brands, they can leverage their marketing dollars around the world. Similarly, Boeing and Airbus can invest millions in new-product R&D only because the global market for their products is so large.

Governments and Competition　Obviously, favorable trade policies encourage the globalization of markets and industries. Governments, however, can also play a critical role in globalization by determining and regulating technological standards. Railroad gauge—the distance between the two steel tracks—would seem to favor a simple technological standard. In Spain, however, the gauge is wider than in France. Why? Because back in the 1850s, when Spain and neighboring France were hostile to one another, the Spanish government decided that making Spanish railways incompatible with French railways would hinder a French invasion.

The cell-phone industry offers a more recent example. The EU has mobilized around one GSM standard, whereas most of the North American market adheres to another GSM standard or the CDMA standard that originally dominated most of the U.S. market. Although recent breakthroughs have made multistandard phones possible, these differences still create fragmented markets for cell-phone manufacturers, such as Motorola and Nokia. Moreover, the interdependence of the European and North American markets means that manufacturers must maintain a strong regional presence. Finally, recent entrants into the industry, including Samsung and NEC, already engage in other global operations. Thus, the problem of multiple standards and the entry of large global competitors both spur globalization in the industry.

Now that you understand how PESTEL analysis and an assessment of globalization can help you characterize the general conditions of the macro environment, you are prepared to delve deeply into industry analysis. The next section reviews critical information that will help you analyze the structure of an industry and better understand your competitors.

INDUSTRY ANALYSIS

In market economies where competition is encouraged and monopolies are not allowed, firms should be able to earn only "normal" profits—that is, enough return to cover the cost of production and the cost of capital. Why? Because of competition. When there is perfect competition, there are numerous sellers and buyers (no monopolies), perfect information, relatively homogenous products offered by different firms, and no barriers to entry or exit. What happens if firms earn greater-than-normal profits (as most managers and shareholders are trying hard to accomplish)? Competition will increase, usually through the entry of new firms into the industry, and profits will be driven back to normal levels. Conversely, if profits fall *below* normal levels, some firms will exit, easing competition and allowing profits to increase to normal levels. However, even a casual reexamination would suggest that many industries must not be held to the laws of perfect competition because we see some industries with long-run average profits far exceeding normal levels and others with profits way below such levels.

In this book, however, we have asserted more than once that the strategist's goal is to develop a *competitive advantage* over rivals. When one firm enjoys an inherent advantage over other firms in its industry, above-normal returns are possible (at least for the firm with the advantage) because competition under these conditions is not perfect. In contrast to the conditions of perfect competition, imperfect competition is characterized by relatively few competitors, numerous suppliers and buyers, asymmetric information, heterogeneous products, and barriers that make entry into an industry difficult. Industry analysis helps managers determine the nature of the competition, the possible sources of imperfect competition in the industry, and the possibility of the firm's earning above-normal returns.

I/O Economics and Key Success Factors

The insights that help managers analyze an industry originate in a discipline called *industrial organization (I/O) economics*. Fortunately, one does not need to be an economist to understand the basic tools of industry analysis. These tools enable managers to understand the business landscape in which the firm operates. These tools and the insights derived from their use should be used iteratively with the tools of internal analysis. However, for simplicity's sake we will hold constant the internal condition of the firm and focus on external conditions in this chapter.

One implication of industry analysis is that firms perform best when they select a strategy that fits the industry environment. Researchers often argue that the goal of managers should be to acquire the necessary skills and resources, often called the **key success factors (KSFs)**, to compete in their industry environment.[5] For example, KSFs in the soft-drink industry might include (1) the ability to meet competitive pricing; (2) extensive distribution capabilities, including ownership of vending machines and cold-storage cases; (3) marketing skills to raise consumer brand awareness in a highly crowded marketplace; (4) a broad mix of products, including diet and noncaffeinated beverages; (5) global presence; and (6) well-positioned bottlers and bottling capacity.

On the surface, this strategy-development process is similar to the process of strategy formulation and implementation that we discussed in Chapter 3, with one critical difference: According to the I/O approach, the appropriate strategy, key assets, and requisite skills are dictated by *industry* characteristics. Why do I/O researchers regard KSFs as a function of the industry? Simply because all firms in an industry must possess them in order to be viable. Thus, KSFs fit the definition of valuable resources as defined in Chapter 3 because they are like table stakes in a poker game: You need the money just to get a seat at the poker table. The soft-drink example shows that these stakes actually create barriers to entry because they are complex and costly to put in place. KSFs are resources and skills that would satisfy the *value* criteria from the VRINE model introduced in Chapter 3, though by definition they will not satisfy the *rareness* criterion. Thus, possessing KSFs will not grant a firm a competitive advantage over other key players in the industry, but it will permit it to compete against such firms.

I/O researchers also argue that the analyst should focus primarily on the industry as a whole, and not on a particular firm, because KSFs are easily transferred from one firm to another. Thanks to relatively efficient markets, firms can readily buy the KSFs they need. In summary, the I/O approach suggests that managers should study an industry in order to understand which strategies are rewarded most profitably and to acquire the industry-relevant KSFs required to implement them.

concept link

The tools for internal analysis that we discuss in Chapter 3 include the **VRINE model** for assessing a firm's resources and capabilities, **dynamic capabilities** as a measure of its ability to reconfigure its resources and capabilities, and the **value chain** as a measure of its ability to find better or different ways of performing its key activities.

key success factor (KSF) Key asset or requisite skill that all firms in an industry must possess in order to be a viable competitor

concept link

In Chapter 3, we describe the **VRINE model** as a five-pronged test for determining the extent to which a firm's **resources** and **capabilities** will contribute to competitive advantage: They're *valuable* if they allow a firm to take advantage of opportunities or fend off threats and *rare* if they're scarce relative to demand.

What Is an Industry?

Economists define an *industry* as a firm or group of firms that produce or sell the same or similar products to the same market. Is there such a thing as a one-firm industry? If a firm holds a *monopoly*—if it's the only seller in the market—then it's the only firm in the industry. Many utilities operate as monopolies (and are typically regulated or owned outright by government bodies).

Fragmentation and Concentration   In a *duopoly* or *oligopoly*, the market is dominated by only two or a few large firms, and the industry is characterized as concentrated. In our opening vignette on the Cola War, it is clear that the soft-drink industry is very concentrated. At the other end of the spectrum, industries in which there's no clear leader are characterized as fragmented.

How can we determine the extent to which an industry is concentrated or fragmented? One useful tool is the *concentration ratio*, which represents the combined revenues of the largest industry participants as a ratio of total industry sales. For manufacturing industries, the U.S. Department of Commerce calculates these ratios at different levels, according to the number of firms treated as the industry's largest—4, 8, 20, or 50. Thus, we refer to these ratios as C4, C8, C20, and C50, respectively. Industry concentration is one of several important factors in industry analysis, because concentration affects the intensity of competition in an industry. For instance, fragmented markets are believed to be more competitive than concentrated markets, whereas concentrated markets are more difficult to enter.

To determine what constitutes an industry, it is necessary to identify clear classifications of products or markets. In the case of Coke and Pepsi, for instance, the industry could be defined as the *beverage industry*. This industry would include every firm that manufactures beverages—Lipton (tea), Starbucks (coffee), Seagram's (liquor), Heineken (beer), Mondavi (wine), Ocean Spray (juice), Coke and Pepsi (soft drinks), and so on. However, such a broad definition makes analysis very difficult and probably obscures important micro-level structural features. Coke and Pepsi's industry could alternatively be defined as the *carbonated soft-drink* industry. There is no definitive rule as to where to draw the boundaries when analyzing an industry. The key is to not be so inclusive that important factors that differ across heterogeneous markets cannot be detected (e.g., Are there key differences between alcoholic-beverage markets and soft-drink markets?) nor so exclusive that important threats are missed (e.g., Does excluding bottled water from the carbonated soft-drink industry miss the main growth segments?).

Defining Industry Boundaries   Indeed, the answer to the question "What industry am I in?" is not as simple as it might seem, even if you're only thinking about something to drink. You'll probably be surprised by the implications of different answers that can be given to this deceptively simple question. This is because industries are typically composed of many segments with different structural characteristics. In the midst of the Cola War, both antagonists were looking for ways to grow. Hard-nosed head-to-head competition was one option, but a simpler strategy involved merely redefining what industry each company was in—say, *beverages* in general or, more particularly, *soft-drink beverages*. Toward this end, Coke bought Minute Maid in 1960, and since then Coke and Pepsi seem to have agreed that they're in the *nonalcoholic-beverage* industry, which includes not only soda but also juices and teas. Pepsi purchased Tropicana (juices) in 1999 and South Beach Beverage in 2000. Coke bought Odwalla (juices) in 2001.

Today, the hottest new-product area in the nonalcoholic-beverage business is water—bottled water, to be exact. Bottled water is a multibillion-dollar growth industry, and it's well on its way to becoming the most consumed beverage in America (except for soft drinks). With an active market consisting of nearly half of all Americans, bottled water is on track to surpass beer, milk, and coffee to become the second-best-selling beverage in the United States.

Exhibit 4.5 Concentration in Selected U.S. Industries

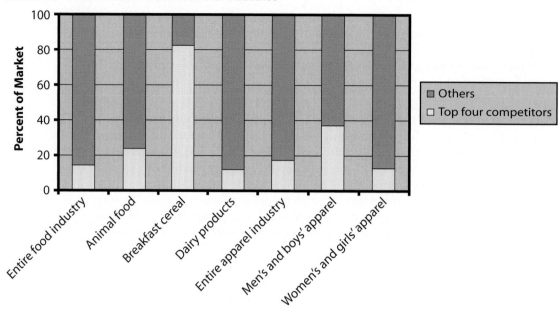

Source: U.S. Census Bureau, "Economic Census: Concentration Ratios," Economic Census 2002 (accessed July 15, 2005), www.census.gov/epcd/www/concentration.html.

Although Coke is big in soda, it comes in a distant third in the global bottled-water business.[6] With 70 brands in 160 countries, Nestlé, a Swiss company, controls nearly a third of the market, and its share is growing. In North America alone, Nestlé sells nine domestic brands, including Arrowhead, Poland Spring, and Deer Park, and five imported brands, including San Pellegrino and Perrier. Pepsi, with a nearly 10-percent share, comes in second with Aquafina, the top-selling single-serve bottled water in the United States. Coca-Cola is third (though not last) with Dasani, which has 8 percent of the market. Recently, however, Coke entered into a partnership with France's Groupe Danone that may vault it into second place once it begins producing, marketing, and distributing Danone's niche brands, which include Evian.

At least one thing should be clear by now: Before getting into an industry, the firm's managers must know the type of product and the geographic market that they're considering. Exhibit 4.5 underscores the importance of drawing industry boundaries in a way that enables managers to understand the dynamics of competition. As shown in Exhibit 4.5, concentration ratios vary dramatically among segments within the same broad industry group. In comparison to other industries, for example, the food industry is relatively fragmented: The four largest manufacturers account for only 14 percent of sales. Within this broad grouping, however, some areas are highly concentrated; the four largest competitors, for instance, account for a full 83 percent of breakfast-cereal sales. The apparel industry also consists of numerous segments. Concentration ratios in the men's and boys' segment are quite different from those in the women's and girls' segment: Sales are much more concentrated in the former. The differences in concentration ratios remind us that industry dynamics vary dramatically across various sectors of the same industry. As demonstrated by such differences in concentration ratios, the definition of an industry is critical to gaining an understanding of the competitive dynamics facing firms that operate in it and, ultimately, to the formulation of a strategy for competing in it.

A Model of Industry Structure

Once the boundaries of the industry to be analyzed have been identified, the next step is to examine the industry's fundamental characteristics and structure. The model shown in Exhibit 4.6 identifies five forces that determine the basic structure of an industry. These five forces were identified by Michael Porter as the industry **five-forces model**.[7] The horizontal axis is a stylized version of the industry value chain. An industry purchases inputs, or sup-

The **value chain** that we describe in Chapter 3 is the *organizational* value chain that consists of all the activities in which a firm engages in order to add more value than competitors and thus gain competitive advantage.

five-forces model Framework for evaluating industry structure according to the effects of rivalry, threat of entry, supplier power, buyer power, and the threat of substitutes

Exhibit 4.6 The Five Forces of Industry Structure

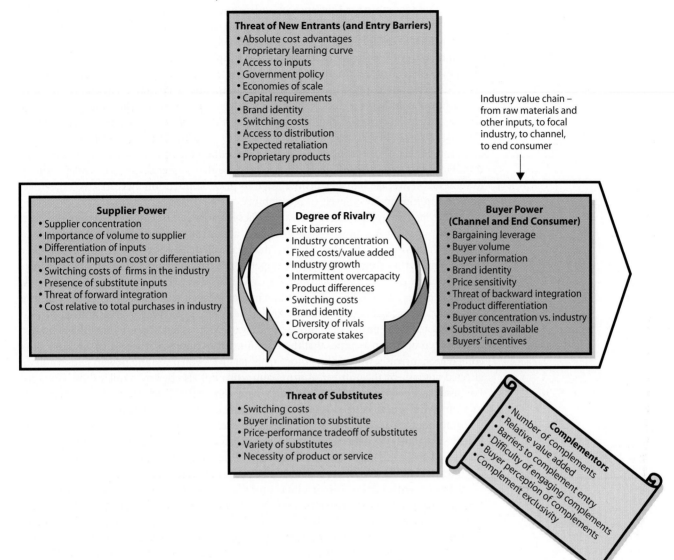

Source: Adapted from M. E. Porter, Competitive Strategy: Techniques for Analyzing Industries and Competitors *(New York: Free Press, 1980).*

plies, from other industries. Likewise, an industry sells its products or services to customers, which are often other businesses but may be retail consumers as well. In negotiations with suppliers and buyers, transactions are not always between parties of equal negotiating strength. The five-forces model draws attention to factors that systematically alter the negotiating strength in favor of suppliers, industry members, or buyers. Likewise, the model draws attention to threats posed by the possibility of new entrants (and conversely, the difficulty of exit) and possible substitute products from other industries or industry segments, either of which can pose threats to industry participants.

It's sometimes useful to think of these forces as countervailing sources of power all vying for a larger piece of the industry's total profits. Recall that when an industry is characterized by perfect competition, rivals in an industry will achieve normal levels of profitability—enough to pay for all factors of input, including the cost of capital. However, industries actually vary considerably in their average level of returns. A key reason for this variance in industry profitability is differences in the power of these five forces across different industries.

Rivalry Firms can compete in an industry in many ways. The intensity of competition is known as **rivalry**. The key questions to ask when analyzing the degree of rivalry in an

rivalry Intensity of competition within an industry

industry include: Who are the competitors? How do rival firms compete? Which firms will be identified as competitors? Because an understanding of the nature of rivalry is so important, we include a separate section on competitor analysis that details ways in which the future actions of competitors can be more accurately predicted.

At this stage of the analysis, it is important simply to come to a better sense of the overall nature of rivalry within an industry. The outcome associated with high degrees of rivalry is generally defined in terms of price competition. The most aggressive forms of competition include price wars. When firms are willing to sacrifice their margins through significantly lower prices, it can be assumed that the nature of the rivalry is very intense. This is not to say that competition isn't serious in industries in which price wars are not common. Rather, in those industries firms have found non-price-based forms of competition. From this definition of rivalry, it is easy to see that higher degrees of rivalry result in lower levels of average industry profitability: As price competition increases, average prices decline, resulting in lower levels of profitability.

What factors tend to increase rivalry? These factors can be categorized into attributes about firms within the industry and attributes about the products or markets themselves. First we will review the attributes of firms that make them likely to compete on prices. When there are numerous competitors, price competition is typically more intense than when there are only a few competitors. Consider the Cola War reviewed in the opening vignette. As intense as that rivalry has been, competition in most periods has focused on nonprice factors. Although advertising to build brand loyalty has been very expensive for Coke and Pepsi, it has been less harmful to profits than intense price wars. More generally, recall that the definition of perfect competition assumes that there are numerous buyers and sellers. In addition, price competition increases when competitors are of relatively equal size and power. Thus, rivalry is affected not only by the number of firms competing but also by how similar those firms are. For instance, the software industry includes many competitors, but Microsoft's size relative to most firms has the effect of marginalizing the threat of price competition.

Another firm-level factor that increases the threat of price competition is the degree to which the industry is strategically important to competitors. Recall that many firms are diversified and compete in multiple industries. Price competition tends to be fiercer when the industry is a key business for the major players in that industry.

Characteristics about the products and markets within an industry can also have a strong influence on the degree of price competition. Price competition tends to be fiercer in industries that are growing slowly. When a company's products are difficult to differentiate from those of competitors, they are forced to compete on price. Price competition is reduced when firms are able to create the impression that their products are different from those of competitors. Coke and Pepsi, for example, have spent billions of dollars to build brand equity and loyalty. Likewise, when there are very low costs for buyers to switch from one firm's offerings to another's, then competitors feel compelled to motivate buyer loyalty with aggressive pricing. Conversely, when customers face high switching costs, there is less pressure to keep prices low because a firm's buyers are somewhat locked in. Finally, industries characterized by high fixed costs, such as the airline industry, are more prone to price wars.

Threat of Entry and Exit Barriers   Not surprisingly, industries that boast relatively high average profitability attract the attention of firms operating elsewhere that are looking for promising new arenas in which to compete. Paradoxically, industries with consistently high average profitability also tend to be those that are the most difficult to enter. The degree to which new competitors may enter an industry and make rivalry more intense is known as the **threat of new entry**. Conditions that make it difficult to enter an industry are known as **barriers to entry**. Note that perfect competition is characterized by the absence of barriers to entry. Several industry characteristics contribute to such barriers, including strong brands, proprietary technologies, and other bases for product differentiation. Certain technologies, for instance, give their owners cost advantages that new entrants can't readily match or compensate for. In some industries, restricted access to investment capital or distribution channels constitutes barriers. Other industries, such as computer-chip manufacturing, require large incremental capital investments in specialized manufac-

threat of new entry Degree to which new competitors can enter an industry and intensify rivalry

barrier to entry Condition under which it is more difficult to join or compete in an industry

turing facilities. In others, the need for location-based or preferential access to distribution networks can hinder or block entry by new players.

Consider the case of the soft-drink industry. With such perennially high levels of profit experienced by Coke and Pepsi, one would expect the industry to attract envious firms and entrepreneurs. And to be certain, there have been many new entrants at the margins and in newer segments not yet dominated by Coke and Pepsi. However, there has yet to be a successful entrant to the cola segment that has been able to capture a significant share of the market. A number of brave companies have tried. For instance, Sir Richard Bransen's Virgin Group has tried twice to enter the soft-drink market. In 1998, the British billionaire rode into New York's Times Square atop a tank, promising a battle with Coke and Pepsi. Virgin tried extensive hard-edge advertising to gain market awareness. However, it found it nearly impossible to secure premium shelf space in traditional retail outlets. In addition to facing a considerable brand-awareness chasm, Virgin discovered that the cost and time required to secure equal footing in retail establishments was prohibitive. After pulling out of the United States for a period, Virgin is giving it another try in America. The strategy this time is to be a niche player, having secured a deal for distribution through 7-Eleven stores.[8] Thus, entry barriers in the soft-drink industry include both extreme levels of brand loyalty and virtual control of prime distribution channels. The only competitive space available for new entrants in the near term appears to be on the periphery of the market. Thus, new entry is most often seen with local brands, private-label offerings, and specialty drinks.

The greater the degree of difficulty that potential entrants face in accumulating the resources necessary to compete in an industry, the higher the barriers to entry, and high barriers to entry have the effect of reducing potential competition by limiting supply and reducing rivalry. This results in higher prices and higher levels of average profitability than in industries in which there are fewer barriers to entry. Conversely, firms may face high **exit barriers** when it is very costly to leave an industry or market, particularly given the opportunity set possessed by any given incumbent. Firms with high exit barriers are typically forced to compete aggressively. For instance, the exit barriers in the airline industry are very high because air carriers have few opportunities outside of air travel, and those firms that exit the industry are likely to do so only by selling off their business and otherwise dissolving the firm.

exit barriers Barriers that impose a high cost on the abandonment of a market or product

Indeed, a firm may remain in an industry due to high exit barriers even when the business is not profitable. As an example, Litton Industries was very successful in building ships for the U.S. Navy in the 1960s. However, when the Vietnam war ended and defense spending plummeted, Litton was so heavily invested in shipbuilding that it could not feasibly exit the industry, particularly given the high specialized investment in now-unattractive shipbuilding facilities. As a result, Litton was forced to stay in the shipbuilding market even though it was unattractive and declining.

Supplier Power   In transactions between industry participants and firms in supply industries, the relative power of each party affects both the pricing of transactions and the profitability of each industry. The degree to which firms in the supply industry are able to dictate favorable contract terms and thereby extract some of the profit that would otherwise be available to competitors in the focal industry is referred to as **supplier power**. When focal-industry participants have negotiating strength, suppliers have limited bargaining power, and the focal industry acts to reduce supplier industry performance rather than the other way around. Suppliers are powerful when they control such factors as prices, delivery lead times, minimum orders, post-purchase service, and payment terms.

supplier power Degree to which firms in the supply industry are able to dictate terms to contracts and thereby extract some of the profit that would otherwise go to competitors in the focal industry

Supplier power arises when the suppliers are relatively concentrated, control a scarce input, or are simply bigger than their customers. In some cases, firms in a focal industry need a unique product or service and have only a few alternative suppliers to which to turn. In these instances, of course, suppliers can demand higher prices.

For instance, from the opening vignette it is easy to see that the soft-drink industry is very consolidated and the two major players are very large. They purchase most of their inputs in commodity markets (e.g., sweeteners, food coloring). As a result, suppliers have no leverage over soft-drink manufacturers. In contrast, consider the situation from the point of view of the bottlers, who buy soft-drink concentrate from manufacturers like Coke and Pepsi and cans and bottles from canning companies. The bottling industry faces significant supplier-power problems because their concentrate suppliers are heavily consolidated. When a firm has a franchise to bottle Coke (or Pepsi), the contract is exclusive, meaning that it has agreed to let Coke or Pepsi be its supplier in perpetuity. By contract, the bottler cannot buy cola products from any other concentrate maker. Thus, soft-drink bottlers face a condition of considerable supplier power.

Likewise, the jewelry business requires access to diamonds. Because South Africa's DeBeers controls over 50 percent of the world's diamond supply, it is in the position to force jewelry makers to pay high prices for its diamonds.

Even when an industry is sourcing products that may be considered commodities, such as textiles or wood, suppliers can impose payment terms that implicitly raise the cost of the resource for the focal industry. Such is the case when the supplier industry is more consolidated than the focal industry. Because the furniture industry, for example, is highly fragmented, no single manufacturer has very much power when bargaining with the larger wood and fabric suppliers who provide the industry's primary raw materials. Suppliers of wood have many possible firms to which to sell.

Supplier power is also high when firms in the supply industry present a threat of forward integration—that is, if it's possible for them to manufacture finished products rather than just sell components to manufacturers. Coke and Pepsi, for example, could easily integrate forward into bottling instead of just supplying bottlers with concentrate. They have demonstrated this by purchasing bottlers in the past. This potential gives them significant power in negotiating prices with their bottling networks.

Finally, suppliers are powerful when firms in the focal industry face significant switching costs when changing suppliers. For instance, companies purchasing enterprise resource planning (ERP) software have several supplier choices, including SAP, Oracle, and PeopleSoft. However, once a firm purchases from one supplier and incurs the significant implementation costs associated with ERP, it will be very reluctant to switch to another supplier because the costs of doing so are significant. Because of the high costs involved in switching ERP systems, firms switch suppliers less frequently than one would expect in a market with many sellers.

In summary, in transactions between industry participants and firms in supply industries, the relative power of each party affects both the pricing and profitability of each industry. When focal-industry participants have negotiating strength, suppliers have lim-

South Africa's DeBeers controls half of the world's diamonds. As such, it wields a great deal of buyer and supplier power and controls the prices that it both pays and charges for diamonds.

ited bargaining power, and the focal industry acts to reduce the supplier-industry performance rather than the other way around.

Buyer Power   The reciprocal of supplier power, **buyer power** is the degree to which firms in the buyers' industry are able to dictate favorable terms on purchase agreements that extract some of the profit that would otherwise be available to competitors in the focal industry. When firms in the focal industry sell to their customers (i.e., buyers), those transactions are subject to the same bargaining forces just reviewed for supplier power. Buyers, for example, whether in a business-to-business or business-to-consumer relationship, compete with sellers by trying to force prices down.

Several factors lead to buyers having high degrees of relative power over their suppliers. A buyer group has greater power in the exchange relationship with its suppliers when the buyers are prestigious and when their purchases represent a significant portion of the sellers' sales. By the same token, if a product has little value for the buyer group, buyers are more powerful negotiating with firms in the industry. A buyer group is also powerful when it has numerous choices, such as when the products and prices of multiple competitors are easy to compare. Tire makers, for instance, have little power over carmakers because their product is standardized and there are many competitors in the industry. If a tire maker tried to raise prices, large automobile manufacturers would turn to one of several other firms that could fill their needs. Conversely, when buyers have few alternatives, their power is minimal, and industry prices increase, resulting in higher than average industry profitability.

Consider the extreme case of the Green Bay Packers of the National Football League. The Packers have maintained a waiting list for season tickets for the past 43 years; the average wait is 30 years. Because there are few other entertainment alternatives in Green Bay, Wisconsin, there is essentially one seller and many buyers for the opportunity for professional sports entertainment. The team is certainly under no pressure to discount prices.[9]

Information also provides buyers with power, particularly when they have choices, when the products are relatively inexpensive, or when products are not heavily regulated. New-car buyers, for example, are relatively powerful not only because there are numerous makes and models in every category, but because they can now use the Internet to compare products and prices online. In contrast, dealers don't have a corresponding advantage when negotiating with carmakers because operating agreements require them to sell certain manufacturers' products.

Finally, buyers are powerful to the extent that they pose a threat of backward integration. Large brewers, for instance, could conceivably make their own beer cans (in fact, some do). The implicit threat that these buyers of aluminum cans could move backward into a supplier's industry naturally diminishes the supplier's price-setting power.

What About Retail Consumers?   Let's make a final—and critical—point about the role of buyer power in any definition of an industry. Note that the industry is the unit that we're analyzing: The focal point of our assessment of rivalry in an industry is the industry segment that we've chosen to analyze. Consequently, when we talk about buyers, we don't mean end retail consumers (unless, of course, we're analyzing a retail-market segment—grocery stores, new-car dealers, department stores, etc.). Japan's Matsushita Electric Industrial, for example, markets many well-known electronics brands, including Panasonic, Quasar, and JVC. When Matsushita markets Panasonic TVs, its targeted customers are not household consumers but, rather, large retail chains and electronics wholesalers. Certainly, retail consumers are important, but they don't negotiate directly with manufacturers, and they don't wield any direct power in nonretail segments. Consumers affect industry profits indirectly when they exercise power as the last link in an industry value chain. An analysis of Panasonic's industry segment would examine the relative power of Matsushita and its rivals in negotiating with retailers, such as Best Buy and Circuit City, who carry their products.

Threat of Substitutes   Sometimes products in other industries can satisfy the same demand as the products of the focal industry. The degree to which this is the case is known as the **threat of substitutes**. Recall, for example, our earlier discussion of bottled water and soft drinks. These two different types of products may be substituted for one another in satisfying

buyer power Degree to which firms in the buying industry are able to dictate terms on purchase agreements which extract some of the profit that would otherwise go to competitors in the focal industry

threat of substitutes Degree to which products of one industry can satisfy the same demand as those of another

the demand of some customers. If we defined Coke and Pepsi's industry as soft drinks, then bottled water would be a substitute to which we'd have to pay attention. Consider the case of the movie-rental business. Blockbuster faces direct competition from Hollywood Video, Movie Gallery, Netflix, and other regional and local chains. What are substitutes for DVD and video rental services? Customers' options seem to be increasing. Cable and satellite TV would seem to be a separate industry from movie rentals. However, movie channels available through these outlets would seem to be clear substitutes for movie rentals. And, more recently, the availability of on-demand movie streaming through cable and satellite providers seems to provide an even closer substitute product. Thus, the prices that Blockbuster and other movie-rental businesses can charge is to some extent limited by the availability of viable substitutes.

Even when market segments aren't as closely related as cable and satellite TV are to the movie-rental industry, products may still be potential substitutes. In the broadest sense, a *substitute* is any product that satisfies a common interest. The desire for leisure, for instance, can be satisfied with both books and travel. Narrowing the classification scheme, consider substitute products between segments in the travel industry. At Southwest Airlines, for example, the primary competition for many shorter flights comes not from other airlines but, rather, from competitors in the automobile- and bus-transportation segments. Thus, within certain geographic limitations, automobiles and bus service are substitutes for airline travel.

It should be clear by now that the prevalence of viable substitute products from other industries places pressures on the prices that can be charged in the focal industry. When there are no viable substitutes, there is less pressure on price. Consequently, average industry profits tend to be lower when clear substitutes are available.

SimConnect

Five Forces as applied to StratSim

Threat of New Entrants. In StratSim, the threat of new entrants applies primarily to two aspects of the simulation. First, what are the barriers to entry for a firm entering a new product class that is new to them? The most obvious entry barrier is the product development time and cost. Entering a new class requires three years in a development center and a significant investment. However, there are other costs to enter a market such as advertising (building of awareness), economies of scale, and experience effects within a vehicle class (resulting in lower unit costs with higher market share).

Buyer Power. Each customer in StratSim has a different need structure and price sensitivity. Thus, buyers who are more price sensitive and who have more vehicles to choose from will exert this power and drive the market toward commoditization. Remember that customers will also consider alternative vehicles. For instance, although a consumer customer may prefer a minivan, a utility vehicle may satisfy many of the same needs such as passenger and storage capacity as a minivan.

Threat of Substitutes. As discussed previously, consumer customers are willing to substitute one product for another and face little switching costs to do so. Although not specifically addressed in the simulation, consumers are also considering alternatives such as used vehicles and substitute modes of transportation which impact overall demand as well as demand within particular segments.

Supplier Power. Depending on market conditions, the price of materials and labor may vary considerably. If raw materials or suppliers face heavy demand, inputs may rise significantly. However, the automobile manufacturers, due to their sheer size, do exert considerable pressure on supplier prices. Labor rates are negotiated with unions and also face some uncertainty. Unions may strike on manufacturers who pay below-market wages or who lay off workers more often than their competitors.

Degree of Rivalry. Ultimately, you and your classmates will determine the degree of rivalry in the simulation. Some industries are fairly stable with little change in the status quo. In this scenario, firms will typically compete in the vehicle classes and customer segments where they started and make incremental improvements to their corporate infrastructure and vehicle offerings. In other cases, industries will be highly competitive with firms making significant investments in technology and product development centers often resulting in a highly competitive, dynamic environment. The level of rivalry typically becomes apparent to all participants in three or four simulated years as competitors enter new spaces and investments in corporate infrastructure are revealed.

The Impact of Complementors As we noted at the beginning of this discussion, the five forces that we've just described comprise a model of industry structure proposed by Michael Porter. When these forces are strong, industry profitability tends to be reduced. More recently, some researchers have argued that the players outlined in the five-forces model do not always compete exclusively in zero-sum games. Sometimes these players work together to create value jointly rather than competing to divide the market. **Complementors** are players who provide complementary rather than competing products and services.[10]

The characteristics of complements are shown in Exhibit 4.6. Firms in the music and electronics industries, for example, sell products that must be used together. Each benefits from the other's presence. Likewise, when people buy hotdogs, an increase in sales of buns, condiments, and beverages is likely. These three products are marketed by complementary industry segments (which is why grocers can sell buns below cost to stimulate sales of higher-margin hot dogs). Sometimes firms in the same industry or suppliers and buyers simultaneously play the role of complementors. For instance, United and Delta compete fiercely in trying to attract customers to fill their seats. However, when upgrading their fleets to a newer plane, both airlines are probably better off when they jointly order a new model from Boeing or Airbus. Because both are in the market for new planes at the same time, aircraft manufacturers are able to achieve greater economies of scale with larger orders, thereby lowering the cost of new planes.

This example helps introduce a more formal definition of *complementor:* A complementor is any factor that makes it more attractive for suppliers to supply an industry on favorable terms or that makes it more attractive for buyers to purchase products or services from an industry at prices higher than it would pay absent the complementor. However, even though a firm or industry segment fulfills a complementor role, it may still compete with firms in the focal industry. A firm or industry segment may simultaneously play the roles of complementor and competitor (as in the Delta/United example). In addition, a complementor that results in increased focal-industry sales will not necessarily share equally in the increased bounty. These relationships still have elements of bargaining power akin to supplier and buyer relationships; one party to a complementor relationship may receive more of the benefit than the other even though both are better off.

Customers, then, are likely to put a higher value on the products of one industry segment when they already have or have access to complementary products from another segment.[11] The value of computer peripherals obviously increases as the number of personal computers increases. Likewise, the value of a commercial real-estate development is enhanced if there are neighboring amenities valued by business tenants, such as restaurants, entertainment venues, and transportation facilities. More new cars are sold when affordable financing is easier to get or dealers offer extended service warranties. Thus, financing and warranty arrangements can be regarded as complementors to the retail new-car market.

Finally, note one important difference between complementors and the other five forces in this model of industry analysis: Whereas the five forces typically work to *decrease* industry profitability, the presence of strong complementors may *increase* profits by increasing demand for an industry's products.

Using the Industry-Structure Model An understanding of the five industry forces and complementors can help managers evaluate the general attractiveness of an industry as well as the specific opportunities and threats facing firms in their focal segment. An industry is most attractive—that is, has the highest profit potential—when attractive complementors furnish positive externalities and when the effects of the other five forces are minimal. The pressure on operating margins will be significantly lower than in industries in

complementor Firm in one industry that provides products or services which tend to increase sales in another industry

which suppliers or buyers exercise high levels of power, in which entry barriers are low, and in which abundant substitute products are available.

How does industry analysis affect strategy formulation? A good industry analysis will enable an executive to answer a few basic questions with much greater certainty than could be done before the analysis. Some of these questions include the following: Does the firm's current strategy fit with current industry conditions? What changes in the industry may result in misalignment? Which elements of the firm's strategy will need to be altered to exploit future industry conditions?

When using the five-forces model to formulate strategy, remember that these forces are not static. The actions of various industry players keep industry conditions in an almost constant state of flux. Consequently, unattractive industry structure isn't necessarily an omen that profitability is destined to be marginal. Wise strategists use information gleaned from the study of industry structure to formulate strategies for dealing with threats highlighted by industry analysis.

Remember, too, that this type of analysis views industry forces from an overall industry perspective and not from that of any particular firm. The industry-wide effect of these forces will determine whether an industry is attractive or not. We walk through the use of Porter's five-forces analysis in the box entitled "How Would *You* Do That? 4.1."

Strategic Group and Competitor Analysis

One of the purposes of industry analysis is to develop a clear understanding of who the firm's competitors are and what their behaviors are likely to be in the future. Consequently, after completing a five-forces analysis, it is often helpful to investigate more deeply the strategies and behaviors of the firm's competitors. We briefly review two frameworks that managers find useful in gaining an understanding of their competitors: *strategic-group analysis* and *competitor analysis*.

Strategic Groups   By the time you've finished your industry analysis, you will probably have realized that rival firms, though often similar, are rarely identical. The U.S. airline industry, for instance, has several full-service carriers, such as United, American, and Delta, but there are also a number of discount airlines (Southwest and JetBlue) and regional carriers (Skywest and Midwest Express). The European airline industry has a similar structure. In the department-store industry, Wal-Mart and Nordstrom obviously take different approaches to strategy and rarely compete directly for the same customers. In the beer industry, Anheuser-Busch, SABMiller, and MolsonCoors have more in common with each other than any of them has in common with Sam Adams or Heineken.

A distinguishable cluster of competitors within an industry is called a strategic group. A **strategic group** is a subset of firms that, because they have similar strategies, resources, and capabilities, compete against each other more intensely than with other firms in the industry.[12] When groups of firms share strategies, resources, and capabilities that differ from those of other groups, they face different opportunities and threats, even though they operate within the same industry.[13] One way to recognize differences in opportunities and threats is to examine the different effects of the five forces on different strategic groups. Barriers to entry in the beer industry, for example, may vary significantly in the way they affect different strategic groups. Which is more likely to emerge, a local premium brand or a global midmarket brand? Obviously, it's the former. Why? Because barriers to entry, including the required capital investment, the power of established brands, and such incumbent advantages as retail slotting allowances, are too strong among the makers of widely distributed midmarket brands.

Mapping Strategic Groups   Mapping the strategic groups in an industry is a good exercise. Start by identifying the dimensions that most clearly differentiate firms. In Exhibit 4.7, for example, we differentiate groups in the bicycle industry according to pricing and distribution channel. In other cases, we may use firm size or geographic scope—any key factor that distinguishes the members of one strategic group from those of another. The best criteria are usually the same ones that would be used to segment a market.

Remember, however, that the objective is to identify *direct competitors*. Thus, the segmentation dimensions should reveal strategic groups characterized by the most intense

conceptlink

In Chapter 3, we define a firm's **resources** as the inputs that it uses to create goods or services and its **capabilities** as its skill in using its resources.

strategic group Subset of firms which, because of similar strategies, resources, and capabilities, compete against each other more intensely than with other firms in an industry

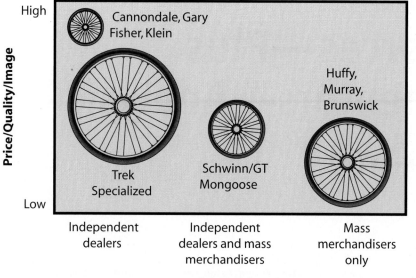

Exhibit 4.7 A Strategic Map of the U.S. Bicycle Industry

internal competition. The circles on the map in Exhibit 4.7 are placed in the space that best depicts the center spot of that particular strategic group. The size of the circles represents the relative size of the group. Notice that the size of the low-end mass-merchandizing segment is roughly equivalent to the size of the segment that focuses on higher-quality bikes sold through independent bike shops (e.g., Trek, Specialized). In this industry, some competitors attempt to sell through both major distribution channels, but in aggregate these make up a smaller portion of the market.

The fact that we can segment market competitors into their central locations in the business landscape doesn't mean, of course, that strategic groups don't also compete with other strategic groups. Relatively similar groups are more likely to be mutual threats than are groups with significantly different characteristics. For instance, Trek faces more competition from Cannondale brands than it does from Huffy. However, for its lower-end models, Trek does experience some competition with Schwinn. Similarly, luxury-hotel chains face a greater threat from high-quality business hotels than from the economy-hotel market. In addition, when firms first expand they often have less difficulty moving into strategic groups that have similar bases of operations than into more distantly related groups. Marriott, for example, moved into budget hotels (with its Fairfield Inn chain) only after it had successfully expanded into a midmarket space served by its Courtyard by Marriott chain.

We analyze strategic groups to get a more detailed look at the competitive environment in which firms operate. Through such an analysis, we can more readily identify a firm's closest competitors (something that most decision makers can usually do intuitively). More importantly, however, we can also better identify any probable *future competition* that we might otherwise ignore or underestimate. Likewise, analyzing strategic groups helps us identify growth opportunities because it makes us focus on potential competitive positions that are compatible with a firm's unique set of resources and capabilities.

SimConnect

Competition and Rivalry in StratSim

In StratSim, your "industry" is defined as those firms with whom you directly compete. Depending on the number of students in a course, a course may be made up of multiple industries, all of which start in the same competitive situation, face the same external environment, but evolve differently due to the competitive rivalry among firms and the investments firms make with regard to technology, product development, marketing, distribution, and firm infrastructure.

Within a StratSim "industry," there are multiple ways to define your competition. At the strategic group level, you may find that there are two or three competitors who

A Five-Forces—Plus Complementors—Analysis of the U.S. Airline Industry

Let's apply the five-forces model to the U.S. airline industry to illustrate how it is used in practice. The first step is to identify the industry—where to draw the boundaries to start the analysis. Examination of data maintained by the U.S. Department of Transportation reveals that the Department categorizes the airline industry into four groups: international, national, regional, and cargo. International carriers are characterized by firms with large planes that fly just about anywhere in the world. Companies in this segment typically have revenues in excess of $1 billion. National airlines have revenues between $100 million and $1 billion and fly domestically only. Regional airlines are smaller airlines with revenues below $100 million. Cargo airlines do not fly commercial passengers; they specialize in the transportation of goods. We could analyze all airlines, but cargo lines serve very different customers. In practice, we may iterate through a few boundary definitions, but for simplicity let's focus on national airlines (sales of at least $1 billion). Note that this will include all U.S. international airlines as well because they are also large national airlines.

RIVALRY

The next step would be to identify the key players in the national passenger-airline market. Who are the rivals? You could turn to numerous available data sources to identify the key players. Using hoovers.com, we identify the top-three competitors as United, American, and Delta; other competitors include AirTran, Alaska Air, America West, Continental Airlines, Hawaiian Air, JetBlue, Northwest Airlines, Southwest Airlines, and US Airways. These competitors are not all competing the same way, and you may want to sketch out how different groups compete (e.g., low cost, hub-and-spoke networks), but we leave that for another exercise. How competitive is this industry? Is competition based on price or nonprice competition? It would not take a lot of research to discover that this is a highly competitive industry. Most airlines make extremely low returns; indeed, many are currently losing money. The annals of airline history document many price wars, and airlines also compete with nonprice competitive tactics such as frequent-flier programs.

POWER OF SUPPLIERS

Who are the suppliers to national airlines? Most, such as caterers, airports, airplane manufacturers, and security firms, are oligopolies, meaning that the airlines are in a less advantageous position. Key suppliers include makers of aircraft, and two companies, Boeing and Airbus, dominate that market and are able to garner significant profits at the airlines' expense by virtue of their specialized positions and government subsidies. The other key supply for airlines is fuel. Due to macro environmental issues (e.g., oil shortages), the price of fuel is currently proving a very problematic issue for airlines. However, this is not a » function of supplier power but, rather, conditions in the oil market.

POWER OF BUYERS

To whom do national airlines sell their services? Buyers can be categorized into three primary groups: business travelers, leisure travelers, and buyers of large blocks of seats known as consolidators, who buy excess seat inventory at large discounts. What bargaining power do these customers have? Switching costs are very low, though airlines have increased them somewhat through frequent-flier programs. Buyers are price sensitive, but they have very little individual buyer power.

THREAT OF SUBSTITUTES

What is the likelihood that airline customers will use alternative means of transportation? When it comes to business travelers, this would seem minimal. However, communication technology has proven to be a viable substitute for some forms of business travel. For leisure travelers, the threat of substitutes is mainly for shorter flights. Thus, alternatives such as auto and bus transportation are more viable substitutes for regional airlines

and national airlines that specialize in shorter flights (e.g., Southwest).

THREAT OF NEW ENTRANTS

The capital intensity of the airline industry would appear to pose a formidable entry barrier. However, JetBlue, AirTran, and other entrants have proven that financing is available when there is a convincing business plan and when economic conditions are conducive to the business model proposed. Brand name and frequent-flier plans would also seem to be deterrents to entry. However, JetBlue's success demonstrates that customers are willing to switch airlines if the price is right.

THE ROLE OF COMPLEMENTORS

The primary complementors in the airline industry are vacation-industry participants, credit card companies, and rental-car agencies. Credit card companies have teamed up with airlines to augment frequent-flier programs. Vacation-industry firms team up with airlines to bundle services and stimulate demand in both industries. Rental-car companies team up with airlines to offer promotions and customer loyalty programs. Because

such loyalty marketing programs decrease price competition, they tend to be good for incumbent profitability.

In summary, it would appear that supplier power, buyer power, substitutes, and complementors do not pose ominous threats to the airline industry. The only two forces within the industry that could account for the poor performance of the industry would seem to be relatively low entry barriers and competitive rivalry.

The implications of this analysis vary depending on which competitor we are interested in. What Delta should do to better align itself with industry conditions is not at all what Southwest should consider. A quality industry analysis would be the same regardless of the company of interest, but the implications would vary.

Sources: J. E. Ellis, "The Law of Gravity Doesn't Apply: Inefficiency, Overcapacity, Huge Debt . . . What Keeps U.S. Carriers Up in the Air?" *BusinessWeek,* September 26, 2005, p. 49; H. Tully, "Airlines: Why the Big Boys Won't Come Back," *Fortune,* June 14, 2004, p. 101.

seem to be positioned similarly in the industry. As an example, they may compete in the "high end," have similar distribution structures, or technology capabilities. It is important to recognize this early and consider how these competitors may impact your strategy and performance. In addition to the strategy group level, you will also need to consider competition within particular segments and/or vehicle classes. Defining this competitive arena will be central to how your firm views the industry, competition, and customers—and will ultimately define the language you use to design your strategy. For instance, you may define competitors as those firms that have a significant share of (a) particular vehicle class (e.g. minivans), (b) a particular consumer segment (e.g., high income), or (c) a particular customer (e.g., high income buyers who prefer minivans).

Predicting Competitors' Behaviors   After identifying the firm's closest rivals, it is important to gain a better understanding of what their future behaviors are likely to be. The specific rivals that are most pertinent to the analysis are those in the firm's same strategic group, those likely to move into the group, and those operating in groups that the firm may enter in the future. In the opening vignette on the Cola War, it is clear that Coke and Pepsi care deeply about what the other is doing. Neither wants to be caught off guard by a move the other may make in the future. Likewise, as new strategic groups have emerged in the beverage industry, such as in the flavored ice teas or premium sodas, they have had to pay more attention to these upstarts.

Several goals can be achieved by closely analyzing the firm's closest competitors. For instance, you may gain a better understanding of what competitors' future strategies will be. Similarly, you may gain a better appreciation for how competitors will respond to your strategic initiatives. Finally, you may also conclude that your firm's actions may influence competitors' behaviors, and some of these reactions may be to your benefit (or detriment). Although the firm's strategy should not be *determined* by competitors' behaviors, it should be *influenced* by what you think your competitors' behaviors are likely to be.

Porter suggests a four-step approach for making predictions about competitors. The first step in predicting the behaviors of competitors is to understand their objectives. These objectives are often surprisingly easy to determine if the companies are publicly held firms, because they are usually communicated with regularity to shareholders through disclosure documents. The second step is to determine the competitors' current strategies. If you have already completed a strategic-group map, you probably have a good idea of what those strategies are. Further insight can be gained by using the strategy diamond and using public documents to see what competitors are doing in terms of arenas, vehicles, differentiators, staging, and economic logic. The third step is a bit more difficult, but it is critical to understanding the competitors' future behaviors: What assumptions does each competitor hold about the industry and about itself? People's behaviors are strongly influenced by the assumptions they make about themselves and the world. Again, communications between top executives and shareholders often hold insights into what these assumptions may be. Finally, the competitors' future behaviors will likely be related to the resources and capabilities they possess. What are the competitors' key strengths and weaknesses?

After addressing these four primary questions, you are in a position to make reasonable predictions about what your competitors are likely to do in the future. For instance, are they about to change their strategy? You may also gain insights into their likely reaction to any initiatives you are pondering.

conceptlink

In Chapter 1, we characterize the *strategy diamond* as the integrated set of choices that a firm makes about these five elements.

DYNAMIC CHARACTERISTICS OF THE EXTERNAL CONTEXT

The various models and analytical tools that we've discussed so far can provide an excellent snapshot of a firm's external context. In some industries, such a snapshot view gives a fairly accurate portrayal of what the business landscape will be like for the foreseeable future. In other cases, however, a snapshot captures little more than a first impression: The essential features of many industries are often undergoing gradual or rapid change. What's worse, snapshot views may give an overblown picture of a firm's competitive advantage: All we see may be a firm that's staked out a nice position in an attractive market, reaps enormous profits, and regularly makes large deposits in the bank. But if you'll recall our story about Sears and Wal-Mart at the beginning of Chapter 1, you know that competitive advantage doesn't always stand the test of time and that overconfidence in the strength of one's competitive position is often a prelude to organizational decline.

Research increasingly shows that the durability of competitive advantages varies by industry or market.[14] For instance, the structural characteristics of some industries, such as utilities and transportation, will shift very little in the absence of significant regulatory changes. Other industries or markets may be undergoing gradual changes that may evolve into the kind of dramatic changes that we described in our story about Sears and Wal-Mart, where the change in market structure was dramatic but evolved over a long period of time. This is typically the case in the consumer-products industry. As a rule, the relatively static analysis afforded by the five-forces model, plus the complementors dimension, applies best to industries such as these.

Industries in a third category, however, may be undergoing substantial change, whether because of the scale and scope of environmental changes, because of the rapid pace of such changes, or because of a combination of both. Dramatic change, for instance, can result from deregulation, which may bring about significant changes in key success factors and completely redesign the competitive playing field. Deregulation in the airline industry gave rise to discount carriers such as Southwest Airlines and JetBlue. Once a segment of niche players, the discount segment now poses a serious threat to the traditional hub-and-spoke segment dominated by American and United.

Dramatic changes in technology can dramatically change the business landscape and alter the nature of competitive advantage within an industry. In such cases, a relatively stable industry can be thrown into disarray until a new equilibrium is reached. Up until the mid-1980s, for example, the pineapple industry was relatively sleepy and fragmented. Then, Fresh Del Monte (a Cayman Island company separate from the U.S. Del Monte) introduced a new variety developed by scientists at the Pineapple Research Institute. This "Extra Sweet Gold" pineapple has a bright gold color, rather than the pale yellow of the traditional pineapple; it is sweeter, less acidic, and highly resistant to parasites and rotting. Early introductions into the U.S. market were limited to a few cities on the East Coast. The pineapple was so well received that Fresh Del Monte quickly raised prices and exported the pineapple to all major U.S. markets. Despite higher prices, the Extra Sweet Gold captured 70 percent of the market.

What propelled Fresh Del Monte to the top of the market and allowed it to maintain the lion's share of what one would normally consider to be a commodity market? Fresh Del Monte successfully exploited a technological development that other firms ignored. Once it proved successful, Fresh Del Monte claimed proprietary rights to this particular strain of pineapple and was able to forestall other producers from planting the same variety. Eventually, the courts ruled that Fresh Del Monte did not have exclusive legal rights to this strain of pineapple, and companies such as Chiquita and Dole are now converting much of their production to this particular strain. Once again, dominance in the pineapple industry is up for grabs.

In this part of the chapter, we'll describe some tools for analyzing industries and formulating strategy in a dynamic context. We start by reviewing the most fundamental reason why some industries are more dynamic than others—the fact that the five forces or essential complementors are changing, not static. We then discuss two macro-level drivers of industry change: the *industry life cycle* and *discontinuities*. Although globalization itself is a profoundly important driver of change, as you read earlier in the chapter, it often goes hand in hand with the changes that accompany industry evolution and technological discontinuities.

Drivers of Change: Making the Five-Forces Model Dynamic

While learning to apply the various facets of industry analysis, you probably observed that some of your conclusions about industry structure would have to be modified if a given factor, such as the competitive behavior of one or more firms, altered any one of the five forces. One way to focus on the dynamic nature of the external context is to stop thinking of your analysis in terms of an industry snapshot and start thinking of it in terms of a "storybook" that shows how an industry structure is changing or may change. Any of the five forces that we have described so far can change significantly, and when that happens, the industry's structure and balance of power will probably be upset. Again, remember that some industries are dynamic simply because of the *rapid pace* of change. Think about the almost daily releases of new products in such markets as cell-phone handsets, laser-jet printers, and digital cameras.

Exhibit 4.8 lists a few potential sources of change and their effects on industry structure and profitability. Entry barriers, for instance, may be weakened, perhaps because of changes in technology. The industry may be in its early stages, with many firms jockeying for position, many of whom will probably go out of business or be acquired as the industry matures. As the industry becomes more dynamic, such factors as substitutes and complementors may become more important. Finally, as an industry matures, buyers become more knowledge-

Exhibit 4.8 Dynamics of Industry Structure

Industry Rivalry
- *Increase in industry growth* → Reduced rivalry and less pressure on prices
- *Globalization of industry* → Increased rivalry as new foreign players enter the market, pressure for scale economies leading to consolidation, and market domination by fewer but larger competitors
- *Change in mix between fixed and variable costs* → Shift to greater fixed costs creating more pressure to maintain sales levels and leading to greater propensity to compete on price

Threat of New Entrants
- *Decline in scale necessary to compete effectively* → Increased rivalry because it's easier for start-ups to enter and effectively compete
- *Increases in customer heterogeneity* → Easier entry because some customer segments are likely to be underserved plus increased ability to protect those segments that the firm serves well
- *Increased customer concentration* → Reduces threat of new entry, leading to less pressure to compete on price

Bargaining Power of Suppliers
- *Increasing concentration of firms in supply industries* → Greater supplier power and likelihood of reduced profitability in focal industry
- *Forward-integration by some key suppliers* → Loss of power in focal industry because of reduction in number of viable suppliers
- *Emergence of substitute inputs that are good enough to satisfy basic needs* → Reduction of supplier power and increased profits for focal industry

Bargaining Power of Buyers
- *Increased fragmentation of buyers' industry* → Reduction in buyer power as the number of potential buyers increases and size of buyer industry declines relative to size of focal industry
- *Improvement in buyer information* → Increased buyer power because of ability to compare
- *Emergence of new distribution channels* → Reduction in buyer power because focal industry has more options

Threat of Substitutes
- *Emergence of a new substitute* → Reduced ability to maintain high prices due to more buyer alternatives
- *Decline in the relative price performance of a substitute* → Reduction in the threat of substitutes and pressure to maintain lower prices

Role of Complementors
- *Emergence of new complementors* → Increased demand and less pressure on prices in focal industry
- *Higher barriers to entry in complementor industry* → Greater complementor leverage and ability to profit from complementary relationship
- *Lower barriers to entry in complementor industry* → Reduction in leverage of individual complementors leading to net increase of possible firms who can serve as complementors and increased demand

---

Source: Adapted from M. E. Porter, Competitive Strategy: Techniques for Analyzing Industries and Competitors *(New York: Free Press, 1980).*

able about product features and costs. We'll start our discussion of industry-change drivers by examining the effects of changing industry life cycles.

Industry Life Cycle   Exhibit 4.9 illustrates the **industry life cycle**. An industry's life cycle is the pattern of evolution it follows from inception through to its current state and possible future states. You have probably learned of a similar concept in your studies of marketing relating to the product life cycle. It so happens that competitive dynamics often follow a similar evolution at the industry level—from the point at which an industry emerges to the point at which it matures or perhaps even stagnates. The industry life cycle is a powerful driver of industry dynamics because it's a phenomenon characterized by change.

Evolution and Commoditization   One common result of this evolution is that an industry tends to become characterized by price competition, partly because many or most of its incumbents acquire similar resources and capabilities and so offer fairly similar products. This trend is called **commoditization**—the process by which sales eventually come to depend less on unique product features and more on price.[15] Commoditization even affects technologically sophisticated products. Take the cell-phone industry for example. Although handset sales are booming thanks to the addition of cameras, music players, and fancy software, cell-phone voice services are fast becoming a basic commodity distinguished primarily by price. It is a pattern that other industries, from airlines to personal computers, have followed in recent decades as onetime technological breakthroughs became widely available.

Some cell-phone service providers are introducing new services, such as picture messaging and video downloads, but the revenue they generate is minuscule alongside the vast sums spent on voice calls, and their growth is expected to be slow. In Europe, there has been an influx of so-called no-frills service providers that basically use a model similar to that of low-cost airlines. Even the U.S. market, although still growing, has already become more

industry life cycle Pattern of evolution followed by an industry from inception to current and potential future states

commoditization Process during industry evolution by which sales eventually come to depend less on unique product features and more on price

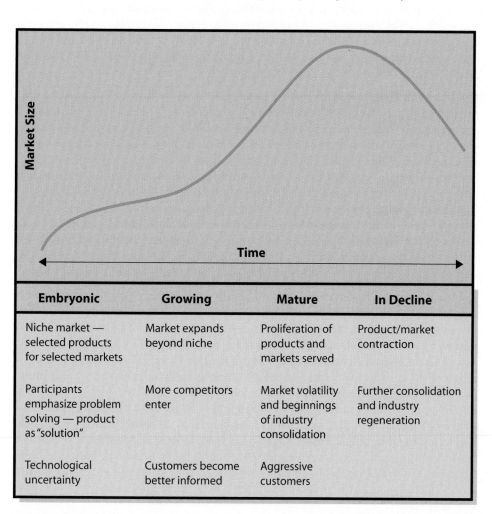

Exhibit 4.9 Industry Life Cycle Curve

Sources: Adapted from K. Rangan and G. Bowman, "Beating the Commodity Magnet," Industrial Marketing Management 21 (1992), 215–224; P. Kotler, "Managing Products Through Their Product Life Cycle," in Marketing Management: Planning, Implementation, and Control, 7th ed. (Upper Saddle River, NJ: Prentice Hall, 1991).

Embryonic	Growing	Mature	In Decline
Niche market — selected products for selected markets	Market expands beyond niche	Proliferation of products and markets served	Product/market contraction
Participants emphasize problem solving — product as "solution"	More competitors enter	Market volatility and beginnings of industry consolidation	Further consolidation and industry regeneration
Technological uncertainty	Customers become better informed	Aggressive customers	

commoditized, with prices plunging and companies locked in fierce competition for new customers. A marked slowdown in revenue growth could exacerbate the long-running price war in the United States, where competition has pushed the average per-minute cost of a call down more than 65 percent in the past four years, according to Yankee Group, a consulting firm.[16] One effect of the slowdown is increasing globalization and consolidation in the cell-phone industry, as some of Europe's big service providers look for revenue growth by expanding outside their home markets. Demand for cell-phone services is growing much faster than analysts had expected in Southeast Asia, Africa, Latin America, and other emerging markets, which tend to be dominated by a couple of local players.

Evolution and Reinvigoration   As some industries mature, however, certain segments may emerge to reinvigorate them, sometimes even restoring their status as growth industries (as a matter of fact, it's hard to imagine any industry that doesn't have at least one growth segment). The bicycle industry, for example, has existed for more than 200 years, and during that time, technological advances have periodically increased the product's popularity and given rise to growth segments in an otherwise stagnant industry. In the 1960s, for instance, the emergence of children's bike designs and the 10-speed accelerated sales. More recently, the mountain bike has not only spurred sales growth but has spawned many new specialized bike-manufacturing companies.

Evolution and Information   Although most of the factors involved in the evolution of an industry are fairly obvious, the role of information and customer learning has only recently begun to attract the attention of researchers.[17] We're beginning to see, for example, that the effects of learning, information, and competition can conspire to enable newer entrants to replace industry leaders, especially in the later stages of industry-wide change. The emergence of computer retailer Dell is an excellent example. Originally, because Dell targeted sophisticated buyers—buyers who were technologically savvy and who needed little education on the uses of a personal computer—it was able to invest less money in pre- and post-sales activities. Dell could sell leading-edge PCs at a relatively low price and still make a profit, and as the market matured and price competition became more intense, Dell was able to leapfrog IBM and other larger companies.

Evolution and Tactics   The effect of customer learning and information often isn't apparent until later in the life cycle. In the early stages, because there's usually a lack of knowledge and information about new products, customers tend to look to industry incumbents not only as a source of education but as a form of insurance in the way of more extensive product support. During the transition from introduction to growth, as once-new products establish themselves and become accepted, incumbents often add extra services, such as shipping, training, or extended warrantees at little or no cost in order to retain sales momentum through the growth phase. Taken together, these factors usually mean higher *average* margins in the early stages of growth because high and increasing operating costs are usually offset by relatively high prices. Again, such was the case in the early years of the PC market, when it was dominated by such players as IBM and Compaq. Discounters like Dell were considered fringe players back when they occupied a small, specialized market niche.

Technological Discontinuities   The link between technological discontinuities and industry change should be readily apparent from our discussion of industry evolution as a driver of change.[18] Moreover, technology is one of the key factors in the PESTEL framework you learned about earlier in the chapter: Discontinuities are a special, intensive case of technological change in action. Get in the habit of thinking broadly about the nature of the changes that create technological discontinuities. Technological discontinuities are much more extreme than mere incremental technological change.

To examine these extreme forms of change, it is important to understand first that technological discontinuities include both changes in science-based technologies (such as innovations) and business-process technologies (such as new business models). The two major forms of technology are *process technology* and *product technology*. Process technology refers to the devices, tools, and knowledge used to transform inputs into outputs. Product technology creates new products.[19] Needless to say, technological changes can have traumatic effects on industries and firms.[20] Indeed, major technological changes often alter firm environments and industry structures significantly. Of course, not all technological changes affect competitors and industries equally. Some, for example, work to the advantage of incumbents, others to that of new entrants.

Disruptive Product-Related Change Patterns of technological change often reflect gradual *incremental* evolutionary change. However, other forms of episodic change are also prone to punctuate industry evolution; we characterize these forms of change as *discontinuous* change.[21] Discontinuous technological change occurs when breakthrough technologies appear, sometimes sustaining the competencies of incumbent firms and sometimes destroying them. Competency-sustaining technologies are typically introduced by incumbents. Those that destroy incumbents' competencies are called **disruptive technologies**. In many instances, these disruptions have been introduced by new firms.[22]

For instance, of 116 major innovations introduced in the minicomputer industry (the precursor to the personal computer), 111 were incremental sustaining technological improvements and only 5 were disruptive. All 111 sustaining technologies were introduced by incumbents, whereas all 5 disruptive technologies were introduced by outsiders—firms specializing in new personal computers. In the disk-drive industry, virtually every new generation of technology has led to the demise of the market leader. The arrival of the personal computer, for example, heralded the downfall of every major competitor in the minicomputer industry.[23]

Disruptive Process-Related Change It's important to remember that disruptive technologies can be process related as well as product related. The development of total quality manufacturing (TQM) methods, for instance, eventually elevated the Japanese auto industry to world-class status. TQM programs such as six sigma are process innovations. No automaker in the world can now ignore the competitive threat posed by such firms as Toyota and Honda, and, in fact, many who once did are now struggling to emulate the TQM methods pioneered by these one-time fringe players.

More recently, when Southwest Airlines radically changed the business model that had long dominated the industry, established full-service airlines originally took little notice. Why? Because Southwest's new process couldn't help them meet the needs of their most profitable customers. In time, however, the number and length of Southwest's flights reached the point at which the services provided by its model could satisfy the demands of customers who normally used larger airlines.

Likewise, Wal-Mart's business model was originally of little threat to Sears because it focused on rural areas that Sears was happy to ignore. Eventually, Wal-Mart's model was transferable to larger markets, but it was too late for Sears to respond. A similar pattern unfolded in the U.S. steel industry. At first, large firms such as U.S. Steel ignored the emergence of so-called "mini-mills" because their unsophisticated technology was efficient only in turning out the least profitable products. But as the capabilities of mini-mill technology improved, so did the ability of the new firms to enter more profitable segments of the industry.

When Industries Divide

The industry life cycle model is too simplistic to describe the evolution of many industries. In some cases, one industry becomes two or more distinct but related industries. One cause of such a split is the decision by a firm to divest a once-core business that has been separated from the firm's original core because of industry changes. As a rule, the divestiture is prompted by the emergence of a new market.

Such was the case with 3Com Corporation and its Palm division. 3Com originally specialized in modems, which have both hardware and software components. In developing this interface, 3Com innovated a new product that linked the two components. It was called the Palm Pilot, and it soon defined the new personal data assistant (PDA) industry. Once convinced that the PDA industry was distinct from its core business in the modem industry, 3Com sold off its Palm division in a public stock offering. New entrants into the PDA industry began to specialize in either the software or hardware side of the business, with Sony, Compaq, and Dell making hardware and Palm and Microsoft selling software.

disruptive technology
Breakthrough product- or process-related technology that destroys the competencies of incumbent firms in an industry

Now Palm is weighing the idea of breaking up into two smaller firms—one that specializes in software and one that develops hardware. Remember: Before 3Com's original innovation, there was no such thing as a PDA industry—let alone any subindustries.

Finally, industries may divide when the market for a particular product becomes large enough that firms can economically justify dedicating a distribution channel to it. This type of division typically results in new industry *segments* or *subindustries* rather than in new industries. A good example is the emergence of so-called *category killers* in various retail industries—industry segments composed of large, highly specialized retail chains, such as PETsMART or Home Depot and Lowe's. They're called "category killers" because they aim to dominate whatever category they participate in by offering the broadest possible assortment of goods at the lowest possible prices. The Internet has spawned a number of such segments and some well-known firms, including Amazon.com and BarnesandNoble.com in books and Travelocity.com and Expedia.com in travel.

When Industries Collide

Although some changes lead to industry division, others result in new industry definitions that consolidate two or more separate industries into one. As you read this section of the chapter, note the distinction between industry *consolidation* and industry *concentration*. Whereas *concentration* results in an industry with fewer players, *consolidation* results in fewer industries. Ironically, changes in concentration can lead to either consolidation or division.[24]

Today, for example, both the global media and entertainment industries seem to be agglomerations of many once-distinct industries. The definition of the media industry now includes firms with a significant presence in both program distribution (they own or control television networks) and program content (they own or develop new shows). The largest incumbents are often called media and entertainment *conglomerates* (which suggests organizations composed of unrelated divisions), but in reality the dominant players, including Fox, Disney, Viacom, and VivendiUniversal, have consolidated a broad range of functions that were once performed by suppliers, substitutes, complementors, or even customers.

Industry division and convergence happens over time. Opportunities to create significant value tend to be greatest for firms that lead the charge in convergence and division of industries. However, when firms define their industries very broadly, performing external analysis becomes much more complicated. For instance, framing a printing company like Kinko's as a simple printer versus a marketing-communications firm connotes a broadly different set of industry conditions.

Now that you're familiar with a few key drivers of industry change, it is important that you understand the particular implications of technological and business-model breakthroughs for both the pace and extent of industry change. The *rate* of change may vary significantly from one industry to the next. The rate of change in the computing industry, for example, has been much faster than in the steel industry; nevertheless, changes in both industries has prompted complete reconfigurations of industry structure and the competitive positions of various players. The idea that all industries change over time and that business environments are in a state of constant flux is relatively intuitive. As a strategic decision maker, therefore, the question you need to keep asking yourself is, how accurately does current structure (which is relatively easy to identify) predict future industry conditions?

USING SCENARIOS TO PREDICT THE FUTURE

Strategic leaders use the information revealed by the application of industry analysis to uncover what the traditional SWOT framework calls *opportunities* and *threats*. You can use SWOT analysis to assess the implications of your industry analysis, both for your focal firm and for an industry in general. However, SWOT analysis works best with one situation or scenario and provides little direction when you're uncertain about potential changes to critical features of the scenario. Scenario planning can help in these cases.

Scenario Planning

Scenario planning helps leaders develop detailed, internally consistent pictures of a range of plausible outcomes as an industry evolves over time. The results of scenario planning can also be incorporated into strategy formulation and implementation, particularly through the staging component of the strategy diamond. An understanding of the PESTEL conditions; the level, pace, and drivers of industry globalization; and the dynamic five-forces model will also provide insight into the outcomes of certain scenarios.

The purpose of scenario planning, however, is to provide a bigger picture—one that displays specific trends and uncertainties. Developed in the 1950s at the global petroleum giant Royal Dutch/Shell, the technique is now regarded as a valuable tool for integrating changes and uncertainties in the external context into overall strategy.[25] Unlike forecasts, scenarios are not straight-line, one-factor projections from present to future. Think of them as complex, dynamic, interactive stories told from a future perspective. To develop useful scenarios, executives need a rich understanding of their industry along with broad knowledge of the diverse PESTEL and global conditions that are most likely to affect them. Exhibit 4.10 details the six basic steps in scenario planning.

conceptlink

In Chapter 1, we define **staging** as the timing and pace of strategic moves and indicate that, as a process of matching opportunities with available resources, it entails the assessment of possible outcomes.

Exhibit 4.10 Six Steps in Scenario Planning

Step 1: Define target issue, time frame, and scope for scenarios. The scope will depend on your level of analysis (i.e., industry, subindustry, or strategic group), the stage of planning, the nature and degree of uncertainty, and the rate of change. Generally, four scenarios are developed—summarized in a grid—to reflect extremes of possible worlds. To fully capture critical possibilities and contingencies, it may be desirable to develop a series of scenario sets.

Step 2: Brainstorm a set of key drivers, decision factors, and possible scenario departure or divergence points. These could include social unrest, shifts in power, regulatory change, market or competitive change, and technology or infrastructure change. Other significant changes in external contexts, such as natural disasters, might also be considered.

Step 3: Develop the framework by defining two specific axes. These axes should represent two dimensions which provide the greatest uncertainty for the industry. In the box titled "How Would You Do That 4.2," for instance, the example on the credit-union industry identifies changes in the playing field and technology as the two greatest areas of uncertainty up through the year 2005.

Step 4: Flesh out the pictures. Show in detail how the four worlds would look in each scenario. It's often useful to develop a catchy name for each world as a way to further develop its distinctive character. One of the worlds will probably represent a slightly future version of the status quo, whereas the others will be significant departures from it. In our credit-union scenarios, *Chameleon* describes a world in which both the competitive playing field and technology undergo radical change, whereas *Wallet Wars* describes an environment of intense competition but milder technological change; in *Technocracy*, the radical changes are in technology, whereas in *Credit-Union Power*, credit unions encounter only minor change on both fronts.

Step 5: Specify indicators that can signal which scenario is unfolding. These can be either trigger points that signal that the change is taking place or milestones that mean that the change is more likely (e.g., if a particular but little known technological standard is adopted by a large industry supplier, such as Microsoft, or customer, such as CitiGroup).

Step 6: Assess the strategic implications of each scenario. Micro-scenarios may be developed to highlight and address business-unit- or industry-segment-specific issues. Consider needed variations in strategy, key success factors, and the development of a flexible, robust strategy that might work across several scenarios.

Sources: Adapted from P. J. H. Schoemaker, "When and How to Use Scenario Planning," Journal of Forecasting 10 (1991), 549–564; Schoemaker and C. A. J. M. van der Heijden, "Integrating Scenarios into Strategic Planning at Royal Dutch/Shell," Planning Review 20:3 (1992), 41–46; P. J. H. Schoemaker, "Multiple Scenario Development: Its Conceptual and Behavioral Foundation," Strategic Management Journal 14 (1993), 193–213.

How Would *You* Do That? 4.2

Develop Scenarios for Credit Unions

Based on a PESTEL analysis, experts in the credit-union industry would identify two significant macroeconomic factors: (1) regulatory—affecting both the types of businesses that credit unions can compete in and the entry of new players and consolidation of existing ones; and (2) technological—the speed with which new technologies related to banking are both developed and adopted by consumers. These two dimensions define the major areas of uncertainty facing credit-union executives in the next decade. Based on these dimensions and following the steps outlined in Exhibit 4.10, four scenarios illustrated in Exhibit 4.11 can be developed.

Exhibit 4.11 Scenarios for the Credit-Union Industry

		Changes in the Playing Field	
		Minor	Major
Technological Change	Gradual	**Credit-Union Power 2005:** Both technology and the playing field have changed at a moderate pace, making this the most stable scenario. Even with moderate change in these areas, however, the changing basis of competition, new business models, human resource challenges, and industry dynamics are different enough to pose significant challenges for many financial-services companies.	**Wallet Wars 2005:** Prompted by free-market economics, the playing field is changing radically, enabling credit unions and other financial-services institutions to compete more intensely. At the same time, technical innovations have not developed as quickly as many observers and analysts had predicted.
	Radical	**Technocracy 2005:** The wide-scale adoption of the Internet by U.S. consumers has led to massive technological innovation for financial-services companies, increasing their range of distribution channels as well as their products, services, and geographic scope. Regulations and other changes in the playing field, however, have been slow to follow.	**Chameleon 2005:** Radical changes occurring in the playing field and in technology make this a highly tumultuous scenario for all credit unions. The nature of competition has evolved so much that banks and credit unions compete directly—under the same rules of the game. This situation has caused a wide-scale convergence of cultures among various financial-services providers, testing the boundaries of the traditional credit-union mission.

Source: Adapted from Credit Union Executives Society, 2005: Scenarios for Credit Unions, an Executive Report (Madison, WI: Credit Union Executives Society, 1999).

The process of developing scenarios and then conducting business according to the information that they reveal makes it easier to identify and challenge questionable assumptions. It also exposes areas of vulnerability (in a country, an industry, or a company), underscores the interplay of environmental factors and the impact of change, allows for robust planning and contingency preparation, and makes it possible to test and compare strategic options. Scenarios also help businesses manage information overload by focusing attention on trends and uncertainties with the greatest potential impact.

Once you've determined your target issue, scope, and time frame, you'll draw up a list of driving forces that's as complete as possible and organized into relevant categories (say, science/technology, political/economic, regulatory, consumer/social, industry/ market). As you proceed, be sure to identify *key* driving forces—the ones with the greatest potential to affect the industry, subindustry, or strategic group of interest.

Trends and Uncertainties   When analyzing the driving forces for change, be sure to distinguish between *trends* and *uncertainties*. Trends are forces for change whose direction—and sometimes timing—can be predicted. We can be reasonably confident, for example, in projecting the number of consumers in North America, Europe, and Japan who will be over age 65 in the year 2010. If businesses in your target industry serve these consumers, then the impact of this population growth will be significant; you may view it as a key trend. For other trends, you may know the direction but not the pace. China, for example, is experiencing a trend of economic growth, and a spate of foreign investments depends on the course of infrastructure development and consumer spending power in this enormous market. Unfortunately, the future pace of these changes is uncertain.

In contrast, uncertainties—forces for change whose direction and pace are largely unknown—are more important for your scenario. European consumers, for example, tend to distrust the biotechnology industry, and given the welter of competing forces at work—industry, academia, consumer groups, regulators—we can't predict whether they will be more or less receptive to biotechnology products in the future. Labeling regulations, for instance, may be either strengthened or relaxed in response to changing consumer opinion.

In some cases, you might want to consider the possibility of significant disruptions—steep changes that have an important and unalterable impact on the business environment. A major disaster—such as the attack on the World Trade Center—can spur regulatory and other legal reforms with major and lasting impact on certain technologies and competitive practices. The box entitled "How Would *You* Do That? 4.2" provides sample scenarios created for the credit-union industry and gives you an idea how scenario analysis could be applied to another industry setting. As you can see, the scenario analysis in this box identifies the entry of new competitors and the impact of technology as the two primary sources of uncertainty about the future.

SUMMARY

1. Explain the importance of the external context for strategy and firm performance. In order to understand the threats and opportunities facing an organization, you need a thorough understanding of its external context, including not only its industry, but the larger environment in which it operates. The proper analysis of the external context, together with the firm-level analysis you learned in Chapter 3 (e.g., VRINE, value chain), allow you to complete a rigorous analysis of a firm and its options. You could say that with these tools you can now perform a thorough and systematic (rather than intuitive) *SWOT analysis*; that is, an assessment of a firm's *s*trengths, *w*eaknesses, *o*pportunities, and *t*hreats.

2. Use PESTEL to identify the macro characteristics of the external context. PESTEL analysis and an understanding of the drivers of globalization can be used to characterize the macro characteristics of the firm's external environment. PESTEL is an acronym for the *p*olitical, *e*conomic, *s*ociocultural, *t*echnological, *e*nvironmental, and *l*egal contexts in which a firm operates. Managers can use PESTEL analysis to gain a better understanding of the opportunities and threats faced by the firm. By knowing the firm's opportunities and threats, managers can build a better vision of the future business landscape and identify how the firm may compete profitably. By examining the drivers of globalization, managers can identify how market, cost, governments, and competition work to favor the globalization of an industry.

3. Identify the major features of an industry and the forces that affect industry profitability. The major factors to be analyzed when examining an industry are rivalry, the power of suppliers, the power of buyers, the threat of substitutes, and the threat of new entrants. When suppliers and buyers have significant power, they tend to be able to negotiate away some of the profit that would otherwise be available to industry rivals. Thus, profits tend to be lower than average in industries that face high levels of supplier and buyer power. Likewise, as the threat of new entrants and the availability of substitutes increases, the ability of rivals in the industry to keep prices high is reduced. Rivalry within an industry decreases profitability. High levels of rivalry result in heavy emphasis on price-based competition. Rivalry is reduced when products are differentiated. Strategic-group analysis is used to gain a better understanding of the nature of rivalry. Whereas industry profits tend to be reduced when any of the five forces are strong, the presence of complementors results in the opposite; they increase the ability of firms to generate profits. Finally, an analysis of competitors' objectives, current strategies, assumptions, and resources and capabilities can help managers predict the future behaviors of their competitors.

4. Understand the dynamic characteristics of the external context. The various models and analytical tools presented can provide an excellent snapshot of a firm's external context. In some industries, such a snapshot view gives an accurate portrayal of what the business landscape will look like for the foreseeable future. Not only do the five forces of industry structure change, and very rapidly in some industries; other drivers of change in which managers must be attuned to include the stage and pace of transition in the industry life cycle and technological discontinuities.

5. Show how industry dynamics may redefine industries. In some cases, one industry becomes two or more distinct, but often related, industries. Industries may also divide when the market for a particular product becomes large enough that firms can economically justify dedicating a distribution channel to it. Whereas some changes lead to industry division, others result in new industry definitions that consolidate two or more separate industries into one. Industry convergence and division happen over time, and firms that identify such changes and initiate early changes have a better opportunity to create value.

6. Use scenario planning to predict the future structure of the external context. Scenario planning helps firms develop detailed and internally consistent pictures of a range of plausible outcomes as an industry evolves over time. It can be used to help formulate effective strategies. Scenarios are complex, dynamic, interactive stories told from a future perspective, making it easier to identify and challenge questionable assumptions. Scenario planning also exposes areas of vulnerability, underscores the interplay of environmental factors and the impact of change, allows for robust planning and contingency preparation, and makes it possible to test and compare strategic options.

7. Understand the external environment in your StratSim industry through PESTEL analysis and identify industry dynamics at play within your StratSim industry using the five forces model. Now that you understand PESTEL and industry analysis through the models and examples in the text, you will have the opportunity to experience them through StratSim. Several HWYDT exercises (below) have been designed expressly for this learning objective.

KEY TERMS

barrier to entry, 106	disruptive technology, 121	industry life cycle, 119	strategic group, 112
buyer power, 109	exit barriers, 107	key success factor (KSF), 102	supplier power, 107
commoditization, 119	five-forces model, 104	PESTEL analysis, 97	threat of new entry, 106
complementors, 111	globalization, 100	rivalry, 105	threat of substitutes, 109

REVIEW QUESTIONS

1. What constitutes the external context of strategy?

2. What are the five forces affecting industry structure?

3. What are complementors?

4. What is a key success factor (KSF)?

5. What are strategic groups?

6. What factors increase industry dynamics?

7. What is the industry life cycle?

8. What is a technological discontinuity?

9. How does globalization affect the external context of strategy?

10. What is industry redefinition?

11. What is scenario planning? When would you use it?

How Would you Do That?

1. The box entitled "How Would *You* Do That? 4.1" illustrates the five-forces model for the airline industry. Use the analysis there as an example and perform a five-forces analysis for one of the following industries: soft drinks, cable television, or cell-phone service providers. What are the one or two most important issues that arise in your analysis that managers in that industry must take into account when they revisit their strategies?

2. Using the scenario-planning example in the box entitled "How Would *You* Do That? 4.2" as a model, create a scenario that predicts the future of the airline industry. What are reasonable best-case scenarios? What does a pessimistic view look like? Are some competitors better prepared for the range of outcomes than others?

3. What do you believe are the key success factors (KSF) for competing in StratSim? Please provide a list of five KSFs for your industry. What will be your basis for monitoring and comparing these factors as the simulation progresses? Are there any KSFs where your firm appears vulnerable?

4. Perform a complete internal and external analysis for your StratSim firm. You may choose to use a SWOT style framework, but be sure to incorporate the VRINE and Value Chain frameworks for the internal analysis and the PESTEL and Five Forces framework for the external environment. Note that this analysis should only reflect issues that apply to the StratSim environment and not ones outside the scope of the simulation.

5. Scenario Planning in StratSim. Choose an important external driver that will impact your firm's performance and consider the range of possible outcomes and how those outcomes might impact your firm's performance. As an example, you might choose how GDP growth might impact the overall sales for your industry and how that might translate into an impact on your firm's sales. How then does the GDP growth impact your firm's profitability?

GROUP ACTIVITIES

1. Pick two of the industries listed in Exhibit 4.1, one on the high end of profitability and one on the low end. What are the boundaries of these industries? What are their market and geographic segments? Who are the key players? Draw up a five-forces model of each industry and compare and contrast their industry structure. Now shift your analysis to the dynamic five-forces model. What dimensions of the five-forces model are most likely to change in the near future?

Which are most likely to stay relatively stable? Answer these questions for both 5- and 10-year windows.

2. Develop a simple scenario for one of the industries you selected for Group Activity 1. What were the key dimensions of uncertainty (pick only two)? Did your findings in this exercise influence your responses to the questions in Group Activity 1? If so, in what ways? If you examined more than one segment within your focal industry, how did your scenarios differ from segment to segment?

ENDNOTES

1. J. C. Maxwell, *Beverage Digest Fact Book 2001* (Bedford Hills, NY: Beverage Digest Company, 2001); D. B. Yoffie, *Cola Wars Continue: Coke and Pepsi in the Twenty-First Century* (Cambridge, MA: Harvard Business School Press, 2002); J. C. Louis and H. Yazijian, *The Cola Wars* (New York: Everest House, 1980).

2. G. Yip, "Global Strategy in a World of Nations," *Sloan Management Review* 31:1 (1989), 29–40.

3. M. Porter, *Competition in Global Industries* (Boston: Harvard Business School Press, 1986); Yip, "Global Strategy in a World of Nations."

4. Porter, *Competition in Global Industries;* Yip, "Global Strategy in a World of Nations."

5. R. Amit and P. J. H. Schoemaker, "Strategic Assets and Organizational Rent," *Strategic Management Journal* 14 (1993), 33–46; J. A. Vasconcellos and D. C. Hambrick, "Key Success Factors: Test of a General Framework in the Mature Industrial-Product Sector," *Strategic Management Journal* 10 (1989), 367–382.

6. "A Fruit Revolution," *Convenience Store News* 41:4 (2005), 20; J. Cioletti, "Flavoring the Market," *Beverage World* 124:3 (2005), 6; B. Bobala, "Water Wars," March 10, 2003 (accessed July 15, 2005), www.fool.com/news/commentary/2003/commentary030310bb.htm.

7. M. Porter, *Competitive Strategy: Techniques for Analyzing Industries and Competitors* (New York: Free Press, 1980).

8. S. Leith, "Virgin Cola Returns—but More Quietly," *Atlanta Journal Constitution,* July 1, 2004, E1.

9. www.packersnews.com/archives/news/pack_10906648.shtml (accessed July 15, 2005).

10. A. Brandenburger and B. Nalebuff, *Co-Opetition* (New York: Currency Doubleday, 1996).

11. Much of this section is adapted from important studies in the field of game theory, and we'll return to the topic when we discuss strategic alliances and other cooperative strategies. At this point, we offer merely an overview. See A. Dixit and B. Nalebuff, *Thinking Strategically: The Competitive Edge in Business and Politics and Everyday Life* (New York: W. W. Norton, 1992); and A. Brandenburger and B. Nalebuff, *Co-Opetition.*

12. R. E. Caves and M. E. Porter, "From Entry Barriers to Mobility Barriers: Conjectural Decisions and Contrived Deterrence to New Competition," *Quarterly Journal of Economics* 91 (1977), 241–262; H. Daems and H. Thomas (eds.), *Strategic Groups, Strategic Moves and Performance* (New York: Pergamon, 1994); M. E. Gordon and G. R. Milne, "Selecting the Dimensions that Define Strategic Groups: A Novel Market-Driven Approach," *Journal of Managerial Issues* 11:2 (1999), 213–233; A. Nair and S. Kotha, "Does Group Membership Matter? Evidence from the Japanese Steel Industry," *Strategic Management Journal* 22:3 (2001), 221–235.

13. R. E. Caves and M. E. Porter, "From Entry Barriers to Mobility Barriers"; J. McGee and H. Thomas, "Strategic Groups: Theory, Research and Taxonomy," *Strategic Management Journal* 7 (1986), 141–160.

14. R. Wiggins and T. Ruefli, "Competitive Advantage: Temporal Dynamics and the Incidence and Persistence of Superior Economic Performance," *Organization Science* 13 (2002), 82–105.

15. L. Argote, *Organizational Learning: Creating, Retaining, and Transferring Knowledge* (Boston: Kluwer Academic Publishers, 1999); A. S. Miner and P. Haunschild, "Population Level Learning," *Research in Organizational Behavior* 17 (1995), 115–166.

16. D. Pringle, "Slower Growth Hits Cellphone Services Overseas in EU, Japan, Saturation Leads to Some Contraction; Looking Beyond Voice," *Wall Street Journal,* May 23, 2005, A1.

17. See G. Moore, *Crossing the Chasm* (New York: Harper Business Essentials, 2002); C. Shapiro and H. R. Varian, *Information Rules: A Strategic Guide to the Network Economy* (Boston: Harvard Business School Press, 1998).

18. N. Rosenberg, *Technology and American Economic Growth* (New York, Harper & Row, 1986); M. L. Tushman and P. Anderson, "Technological Discontinuities and Organizational Environments," *Administrative Science Quarterly* 31 (1986), 439–465.

19. W. P. Barnett, "The Organizational Ecology of a Technological System," *Administrative Science Quarterly* 35 (1990), 31–60; R. M. Henderson and K. B. Clark, "Architectural Innovation: The Reconfiguration of Existing Product Technologies and the Failure of Established Firms," *Administrative Science Quarterly* 35 (1990), 9–30.

20. Tushman and Anderson, "Technological Discontinuities and Organizational Environments."

21. Tushman and Anderson, "Technological Discontinuities and Organizational Environments."

22. C. M. Christensen, *The Innovator's Dilemma* (Cambridge, MA: Harvard Business Press, 1997).

23. Christensen, *The Innovator's Dilemma.*

24. Consolidation may result from increased concentration when bigger players in an industry absorb the functions of suppliers, substitutes, complements, or customers (a process under way in the global media and entertainment industries). By getting bigger, these firms broaden the definition of their operations, but successfully managing all the components of a broader operation is a separate matter. Concentration often results in division when players that have grown too big can no longer give adequate attention to some segment of their market or some facet of their operations. Division also occurs when, because of increased concentration, a new market emerges to attract large firms.

25. P. J. H. Schoemaker, "When and How to Use Scenario Planning," *Journal of Forecasting* 10 (1991), 549–564; P. J. H. Schoemaker and C. A. J. M. van der Heijden, "Integrating Scenarios into Strategic Planning at Royal Dutch/Shell," *Planning Review* 20:3 (1992), 41–46; P. J. H. Schoemaker, "Multiple Scenario Development: Its Conceptual and Behavioral Foundation," *Strategic Management Journal* 14 (1993), 193–213.

Creating Business Strategies

After studying this chapter, you should be able to:

1. Define *generic strategies* and explain how they relate to a firm's strategic position.

2. Describe the drivers of low-cost, differentiation, and focused strategic positions.

3. Identify and explain the risks associated with each generic strategic position.

4. Show how different strategic positions fit with various stages of the industry life cycle.

5. Evaluate the quality of your StratSim firm's strategy.

6. Understand the drivers of low-cost and differentiation strategies in StratSim.

7. Identify an appropriate generic strategy for your StratSim firm.

▶ **1976**
With a staff of five, Trek
begins making steel bikes in a
barn in Waterloo, Wisconsin.
It positions itself as a high-quality,
high-priced manufacturer,
distributing through independent
dealers only.

▶ **1982**
The first Trek mountain bike
hits the trail. Trek sponsors
its first bike race and further
diversifies its product line
by offering accessories
and clothing.

A TALE OF THREE WHEELS IN THE BICYCLE INDUSTRY

In 2004, over 18.3 million bicycles were sold in the United States.[1] According to industry trade reports, the total retail value of bikes, parts, and accessories was more than $5.7 billion. Who sold all of these bicycles and bike-related products? There are literally hundreds of bicycle manufacturers in the United States, but most are small, specialized firms. Pacific Cycle, which designs, markets, and imports a full range of bikes and recreation products under such familiar brand names as Schwinn, GT, Mongoose, Mongoose Pro, Pacific, InSTEP, Roadmaster, Flexible Flyer, Powerlite, Murray, and Dyno, sells more bicycles than any other company in North America. Its powerful brand portfolio serves virtually all consumer demographics, price categories, and product categories (e.g., children's, mountain, and racing bikes).

▶ **2002**
Trek diversifies further, launching Trek Travel for booking worldwide bike vacations.

▶ **2005**
Sponsored by Trek, Lance Armstrong wins his seventh straight Tour de France on a Trek Madone SSLX.

1995   2000

In fact, Pacific is one of the fastest-growing branded consumer-product companies in the United States. It has achieved its success by combining its aggressive acquisition of power brands with low-cost outsourcing, efficient supply-chain management, and multichannel retail distribution. Channels include leading mass-market retailers such as Wal-Mart, Target, and Toys "*R*" Us; sporting goods chains such as Dick's, The Sports Authority, and Gart Sports; and independent dealers serving local markets. The company's brands appeal to the full spectrum of demographics, price preferences, and image and usage criteria that are critical to targeting the key consumer segments served by each channel. This broad-based marketing strategy enables Pacific to provide retailers with one-stop shopping and to respond efficiently to changes in the marketplace. Pacific Cycle was recently acquired by Doral Inc., and now operates as an independent strategic business unit (SBU).

Another successful bike maker, Trek Bicycle, has revenues similar to those of Pacific Cycle. It was founded by partners Richard Burke and Bevill Hogg in 1976. With $25,000 in seed money, Burke and Hogg started building bikes by hand in a Wisconsin barn. From the beginning, they targeted upper-end users, and success came quickly. Today, customers pay top dollar for smooth suspensions, custom paint jobs, and innovations in racing geometry. With annual sales of about $400 million, Trek is now the country's number-one maker of high-quality bikes and was perhaps the first U.S. bike maker to overcome European resistance to American-made cycles by focusing on quality and innovation, which have long been company hallmarks. Trek introduced its first mountain bike line in 1983, the first bonded-aluminum road bike in 1985, and a carbon-fiber road bike in 1986.

Although most of the firm's growth has been fueled by internally developed products, Trek has also made a few strategic acquisitions, including Gary Fisher Mountain Bike and two mountain bike competitors (Bontrager and Klein) in 1995. Trek now makes various types of bicycles, including mountain, road, children's, recumbent, police, and BMX bikes. Internationally, Trek bikes are sold through wholly owned subsidiaries in 7 countries and through distributors in 65 others. Trek designs all of its bikes at its Wisconsin headquarters and manufactures a quarter of them in this country. Finally, sponsoring seven-time Tour de France winner Lance Armstrong has given the company tremendous exposure and the centerpiece for a marketing plan that, as one Trek executive puts it, can be summed up as "Lance, Lance, Lance."

Whereas Pacific Cycle and Trek represent the larger players in the U.S. market, Montague fits the profile of a boutique-style bike firm. Frustration prompted Harry Montague, a Washington, D.C., architect and inventor, to develop the Montague line of high-performance, travel-friendly bicycles: He was unable to find anything but small-wheeled folding bikes, and they were both uncomfortable and inefficient for serious cyclists who wanted to take their bikes in the car or on public transportation. After much trial and error, Montague succeeded in developing a full-size high-performance folding bicycle that he then custom-built and sold out of his garage for D.C.-area riders.

The business moved out of the garage when Harry's son David was required to draw up an extensive business plan for a course in entrepreneurship at the MIT Sloan School of Business. David designed a formal business plan around his father's bicycle, and as soon as David had passed the course, he and his father formed the Montague Corp. to design and produce full-size bicycles that sacrifice little in performance while providing convenience for a targeted market of customers. Today, Montague is the world's leading manufacturer of folding bikes. All Montague bikes fold into a compact size in less than 30 seconds without the use of tools. They have been sold to the military for tactical use and to several car manufacturers for promotional packaging with SUVs.

Pacific Cycle, Trek, and Montague are all in the same industry, but each pursues a very different strategy in an attempt to meet the needs of customers. In this chapter, you will be introduced to the basics of business strategy—the tools and models that will help you formulate coherent strategies for competing within an industry context. ■

AN INTRODUCTION TO BUSINESS STRATEGIES

In this chapter, we build on Chapters 3 and 4 by discussing ways in which firms formulate business strategies that capitalize on their resources and capabilities to exploit opportunities in their competitive environments. At the same time, we set the stage for Chapter 6, which explores strategy in dynamic contexts. As we saw in Chapter 1, *business strategy* refers to the choices that a firm makes about its competitive posture. These choices can be summarized by the *strategy diamond* and its *five elements of strategy*. For the diversified firm, business strategy is typically applied at the level of the strategic business unit (SBU). An SBU is an organizational subunit within a diversified corporation that is responsible for a specific business or group of related businesses. For instance, in the opening vignette you learned about Pacific Cycle, which is an SBU of Doral Inc. SBU strategy is similar to business strategy—but with one important exception: Because an SBU is an organizational unit within a larger firm, the SBU environment includes not only elements external to the firm but also elements of the parent firm. (We'll have more to say about SBUs in the chapters on corporate and global strategy because the choice of what value-chain operations and geographic and/or product markets to include in an SBU should flow from the overarching corporate strategy.)

As we saw in our opening vignette about three bicycle companies, there's more than one way to compete in an industry. Pacific Cycle, for example, markets a product for virtually every segment, offers a range of quality in its product mix, and keeps costs down by outsourcing all of its production to China and Taiwan. Trek, meanwhile, though also a large company with a broad product mix, focuses on specialized and innovative product attributes to target specific customer segments and one channel—independent bike distributors. Montague is an entirely different company, marketing a highly specialized product targeted at a narrow range of potential customers.

As a rule, competitive positions can be established in many different ways, and the task of finding the best configuration of positions is the subject of this chapter. We'll start by introducing a well-established framework for strategic positioning developed by Michael Porter and then describe the conditions under which particular strategic positions are viable. We'll also examine ways in which alternative strategic positions are compatible with

concept link

In Chapter 1, we explain that **business strategy** refers to the ways in which a firm will compete against present and future rivals *within a particular business*; the *five elements of strategy* refer to the choices that it makes in determining *how* to compete against its rivals.

To avoid head-to-head competition, Pacific Cycle positions itself differently than Trek. Pacific makes many different brands, selling them at various prices in numerous retail outlets. To keep costs down, it manufactures its bikes exclusively in countries where labor costs are low.

different stages of the industry life cycle. Finally, because a successful strategy must be consistent with both a firm's resources and the competitive environment, we'll conclude by describing a process for testing the quality of a strategy according to this criterion.

TYPES OF STRATEGIES—FINDING A POSITION THAT WORKS

strategic positioning Means by which managers situate a firm relative to its rivals

conceptlink

In Chapter 4, we identify **rivalry** as one of Porter's five forces of industry structure, define it as the intensity of competition in an industry, and explain that high degrees of rivalry are usually reflected in price competition.

Strategic positioning refers to the ways managers situate a firm relative to its rivals along important competitive dimensions. The strategic-positioning model that we present in this chapter is a classic framework in the field of strategic management—Michael Porter's *generic strategy model*. Recall that under the industry-structure model that we introduced in Chapter 4, the key force in an industry—indeed, the force around which all others revolve—is rivalry among the firms in the industry. The purpose of strategic positioning is to reduce the effects of rivalry and thereby improve profitability, and the generic strategies that derive from the strategic-positioning model are related to the industry-structure model: They help managers stake out a position for their firm relative to its rivals *in ways that reduce the effects of intense rivalry on profitability*. In this section, we'll introduce Porter's generic strategies.

Strategic Positioning and the Generic Strategy Model

The concept of strategic positioning is a useful starting point in dealing with issues deriving from the strategy diamond model that we explored in Chapter 1—namely, issues related to *arenas*, *differentiators*, and *economic logic*. Strategic position helps to answer basic questions about the arenas in which a firm will compete (specifically, questions about the breadth of geographic and product scope). An automobile manufacturer, for example, must decide whether to compete in all geographic markets and all product lines (say, everything from high-performance to economy-priced cars—as you might see when contrasting Porsche with Daimler-Chrysler).

This model also helps decision makers deal with questions about a firm's tactics for motivating customers to choose its products over those of competitors. Will customers buy from a firm because it offers the lowest-priced luxury sedan (such as the Buick Park Avenue), because it's known for its quality (say, Lexus), or because it offers the most valuable brand image (perhaps Mercedes Benz)? Likewise, the choice between these two criteria— low cost and differentiation—is critical to the issue of economic logic: The success of either choice depends on complementary decisions about how best to generate profit. For instance, Trek attempts to position its brands as possessing superior quality, and therefore warranting higher prices, through endorsements by industry superstars such as Lance Armstrong and exclusive distribution through independent bike dealers.

A firm's choice of position depends on two important factors: (1) firm resources and capabilities and (2) industry structure. Formulating a strategy means using tools such as those that we introduced in Chapters 3 and 4 to make critical decisions about how and where to compete—that is, how to position a company relative to its rivals. In addition, if a firm hopes to exploit opportunities while withstanding competitive threats from within its industry, its strategy should be built on its unique resources and capabilities.

Generic Strategies

In this section, we'll discuss one of the most durable concepts in the field of strategic management—Michael Porter's concept of the generic strategies by which firms develop defensible strategic positions. In particular, we'll explain the logic of four positions— *low-cost, differentiation, focused cost leadership,* and *focused differentiation*—and show how each can reduce the negative effects of industry rivalry.

Cost and Differentiation　In 1980, Michael Porter introduced an integrated theory of strategy based on principles of industrial organization (I/O) economics. Porter's model revised the concept of how firms achieve competitive advantage by going beyond the basic (and often wrong) notion that market share is the key to profitability. In part, Porter's theory considered the structure of an industry and its effect on the performance of firms within it (an idea that we introduced in Chapter 4). Porter also demonstrated the economic logic behind some prescriptions for choosing among viable means of gaining competitive advantage.[2] Porter's strategy model hinges on two dimensions: the potential source of strategic advantage and the breadth of the target market.

According to Porter, two key factors affect the economic logic (or the source) of competitive advantage. These alternative sources of advantage are having a lower cost structure than industry competitors and having a product or service that customers perceive as differentiated from other products in the industry—to the point that they will pay higher prices than what is charged for other products in the industry. In other words, a firm can gain a significant advantage over rivals in one of two ways:

■ It can produce an essentially equivalent product at a lower cost than its rivals.

■ It can produce a differentiated product and charge sufficiently higher prices to more than offset the added costs of differentiation.

We can use Porter's two dimensions—cost and differentiation—to develop a simple two-by-two matrix for visualizing alternative competitive positions; the alternative positions suggested by this model are what we mean by **generic strategies**. Exhibit 5.1 illustrates this model. Bear in mind that in order to be consistent with the overall model of strategy that we presented in Chapter 1 and avoid confusing Porter's categories with the more general concept of strategy, we'll refer to Porter's generic strategies as *strategic positions*. These strategic positions are not *strategies* in the way we define them using the strategy diamond. Rather, they are configurations of several elements of a firm's strategy.

Along the horizontal dimension of Exhibit 5.1, firms choose the underlying economic logic by which they intend to establish a competitive advantage—that is, whether to compete on differentiation or cost. *Differentiation* refers to a general condition of perceived product "uniqueness" that causes customers to be willing to pay premium prices. When are customers willing to pay more for a product? Generally, premium prices are paid when a firm is able to uniquely satisfy a customer's needs. This satisfaction could be along the dimensions of quality, image, speed, access, or other identifiable dimensions of perceived need. However, firms can gain advantage in other ways as well. As shown on Exhibit 5.1, firms may decide to seek higher returns and a competitive advantage by keeping costs lower than those of competitors.

Scope of Involvement　Firms also make choices about the arenas in which they'll compete when they decide how broadly they'll compete for customers—a decision known

generic strategy Strategic position designed to reduce the negative effects of rivalry, including *low-cost, differentiation, focused cost leadership, focused differentiation,* and *integrated positions*

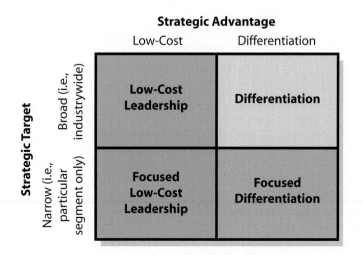

Exhibit 5.1 The Strategic Positioning Model

Source: Adapted from M. E. Porter, Competitive Strategy *(New York: The Free Press, 1980).*

as *scope of involvement.* In other words, firms make choices about which customers to pursue. Some firms compete broadly by trying to offer something for virtually everyone; others focus their efforts on narrower segments of the market. The vertical dimension in Exhibit 5.1 measures the scope of the market arenas in which a firm chooses to compete.

Four generic strategic positions result from the decisions measured by the model in Exhibit 5.1: *low-cost leadership, broad differentiation, focused (or niche) cost leadership,* and *focused (or niche) differentiation.* Let's look more closely at each of these positions.

Low-Cost Leadership   A strategic position that enables a firm to produce a good or offer a service while maintaining total costs that are lower than what it takes competitors to offer the same product or service is known as **low-cost leadership**. Not surprisingly, a firm that can produce substantially similar products at a lower cost has a significant competitive advantage. With a cost advantage, a firm can sell products for lower prices while still maintaining the same margins as rivals. In the process, of course, it will also gain market share. However, the same firm could keep its prices at market level and reap higher margins than competitors. In this case, it will accumulate surplus resources that it can either distribute to shareholders or use to finance future strategic initiatives. As a rule, however, because taking a low-cost position means sacrificing features or services, firms that stake out this position try to satisfy basic rather than highly specialized customer needs.

> **low-cost leadership** Strategic position based on producing a good or offering a service while maintaining total costs that are lower than what it takes competitors to offer the same product or service

The low-cost position works in many industries. In the bicycle industry, for instance, Pacific Cycle keeps manufacturing costs down by standardizing design and outsourcing production to low-cost labor markets. Unlike some low-cost leaders, Pacific also offers a wide array of products, many of which have strong brand equity, such as Schwinn and Mongoose—a strategic decision more often associated with a strategy of differentiation. Remember, however, that most of these brands came into Pacific's portfolio through acquisitions, and the company retained the brand names because they enjoy greater brand awareness than "Pacific Cycle." In the wine industry, Gallo Wines has achieved a low-cost leadership position by innovating cost-effective blending techniques, having lower costs due to scale of operations, developing efficiencies in the grape-procurement function, and generating scale economies in marketing and distribution.

In summary, with the low-cost position, firms attempt to deliver an acceptable product that satisfies basic needs at the lowest possible cost. In doing so, the firm attempts to create a sustainable cost gap over other firms. Successfully following this path results in above-industry-average profits. However, cost leaders must maintain parity or proximity in satisfying the basic needs of buyers. Doing so is a challenge, because it generally requires tradeoffs—eliminating some features or services in order to drive costs down.

Some well-known companies, including Wal-Mart, Southwest Airlines, and Home Depot, are successful low-cost leaders. Interestingly, each of these companies started out as a focused low-cost competitor but took up a more broad-based position as it grew.

Differentiation   If a firm markets products whose quality, reliability, or prestige is discernibly higher than its competitors', and if its customers are willing to pay for this uniqueness, the firm has a competitive advantage based on **differentiation**. Successful differentiation enables firms to do one of two things:

> **differentiation** Strategic position based on products or offers services with quality, reliability, or prestige that is discernibly higher than that of competitors and for which customers are willing to pay

- Set prices at the industry average (and gain market share because consumers will choose higher quality at the same price).
- Raise prices over those of competitors (and reap the benefits of higher margins).

Trek Bicycles, for example, is a broad-based differentiator: Although it offers products in numerous segments, its products boast high quality and demand price premiums over products from Pacific Cycle.

Coca-Cola and Pepsi—which spend billions to develop brand equity, sell in most markets, and strive to win customers through brand image—are also well-known differentiators. Or consider Mercedes Benz, perhaps the world's leading manufacturer of premium passenger cars. What differentiates Mercedes' products? A reputation for innovative engineering, safety, and comfort, along with product design aimed at buyers who will pay premium prices for the image that goes along with a Mercedes.[3] Interestingly, although most Americans regard Mercedes as a focused differentiator because only affluent customers can afford its products, Europeans have a different view. In Europe, Mercedes markets a wide line of products, ranging from the tiny SmartCar to more familiar luxury sedans.

In the motorcycle market, Honda, Yamaha, and Suzuki all have something for virtually every enthusiast. Honda's lineup, for instance, starts with the entry-level XR50R, which comes with semiautomatic gears to help youngsters learn off-road riding. Honda then proceeds to appeal to almost every other segment of the market with products ranging upward to the Gold Wing ST1300, a six-cylinder touring bike equipped with sophisticated sport-type suspension, antilock brakes, and luxury touring features.

A successful differentiation position requires that a firm satisfy a few basic criteria. First, it must uniquely satisfy one or more needs that are valued by buyers and do so in a manner superior to that available from most competitors. However, doing so will result in higher costs in some value-chain activities. Thus, the second requirement that must be satisfied is that customers must be willing to pay higher prices for the added points of differentiation. Consequently, companies successful at a differentiation position pick cost-effective forms of differentiation. The results are above-industry-above profits.

An example of a successful broad differentiator is Stouffers, the frozen-food company. Stouffers spends more on high-quality inputs than its competitors, it has developed a technology to make a superior sauce, and it offers innovative menus. Stouffers combines these features with high-quality packaging, the use of food brokers to get broad distribution, and advertising that creates the perception of quality. The price premium that Stouffers is able to generate exceeds the cost to improve frozen-food entrees above industry norms.

Focused Low-Cost Leadership

A strategic position that enables a firm to be a low-cost leader in a narrow segment of the market is known as **focused cost leadership**. JetBlue, a recent entry into the commercial-airline market, is a focused low-cost competitor that serves a small subset of commercial travelers who are price sensitive. Using a variation on Southwest Airline's early business model, JetBlue managed during its first few years of operation to keep its operating costs per airline seat mile lower than even Southwest's. It was the most profitable commercial U.S. airline in 2002 and 2003 and second behind only Southwest in 2004.

focused cost leadership Strategic position based on being a low-cost leader in a narrow market segment

Focused Differentiation

When unique products are targeted to relatively small segments, the positioning strategy is called **focused differentiation**. The greater the differentiation, the smaller the market segment to which a product will appeal: As quality is continually improved or luxury features added, fewer customers can afford the higher prices. In the bicycle industry, for example, Montague focuses on a small, specialized segment of the market that demands unique product features. You also may be familiar with Cannondale, another focused differentiator that produces high-end mountain bikes. Unfortunately for Cannondale, however, the firm sought to leverage its reputation for quality mountain bikes in the motocross motorcycle market and went bankrupt as a result. It found that the resources and capabilities required to compete in mountain bikes, such as sturdy, high-performance frames, were very different than those required for gas-engined bikes—namely high-performance engines and drive trains. Moreover, motorcycles are not typically sold by the same dealers that sell bikes.

focused differentiation Strategic position based on targeting products to relatively small segments

Likewise, Mercedes Benz imports into the United States only its most expensive top-of-the-line models in each product category. In the United States, therefore, Mercedes is a focused differentiator that markets only to the most affluent customers. Even more focused are such companies as Rolls-Royce and Ferrari. In the motorcycle industry, Harley-Davidson, which makes only larger models targeted at very specific segments of the market, is a more focused differentiator than Honda. Harley's lowest-priced motorcycle begins at about $6,500. Recently, other firms have entered this market space and have tried to out-focus Harley-Davidson. For instance, Orange County Choppers, which was made famous by the *American Chopper* TV series (see photo on page 138), sells only made-to-order

Harley-Davidson has successfully focused its business strategy on the large high-priced end of the motorcycle market. Other manufacturers, such as Orange County Choppers, have tried to muscle into Harley's well-defined market space with bikes such as the Fire Bike shown here.

integrated position Strategic position in which elements of one position support strong standing in another

motorcycles. Therefore, Orange County Choppers focuses on a very small segment of the overall motorcycle market.

Integrated Positions In reality, few firms are faced with such stark alternatives as being either a low-cost leader or a differentiator. Some firms are able to achieve an **integrated position**—one in which elements of one position support a strong standing in the other. Elements of a differentiating position can in fact be adopted by low-cost competitors. Many low-cost companies, for instance, develop strong brand images even though branding typically supports a differentiation strategy. Heavy reliance on branding enables McDonald's to position itself as a reliable, high-quality provider of low-cost fast food. Conversely, firms usually associated with differentiated products have succeeded in managing costs. Toyota, for example, keeps its costs below those of major competitors while maintaining extremely high levels of quality. (In particular, quality-improvement programs have proved valuable for both differentiation and cost-cutting efforts.)

Another example is IKEA Svenska AB, which manages to remain the world's largest home-furnishings retailer while specializing in stylish but inexpensive furniture. IKEA's success can be traced to its vast experience in the retail market, where it practices both product differentiation and cost leadership. IKEA outlets are essentially warehouses stacked with boxes of unassembled furniture. The company operates under a fairly unique premise: namely, that value-conscious buyers will perform some of the tasks that other retailers normally perform for them, such as transporting and assembling their own furniture. By transferring these functions to the customer, IKEA can drive costs down and, therefore, offer prices low enough to fit most budgets. Thus, IKEA targets a rather large segment of the market, ranging from young low- to middle-income families. At the same time, the company has established a highly differentiated image with its enormous selection of self-assembly home furnishings and fun in-store experiences.

Firms that have integrated low-cost and differentiation positions can be found in most industries. So can firms whose products don't seem to fall into either category. As Exhibit 5.2 shows, integrated—and enviable—positions have in fact been forged in the auto industry. Note, for instance, that both Honda and Hyundai generate better profit margins than Chevrolet. Chevrolet seems to be stuck in the middle. The hazards of this type of

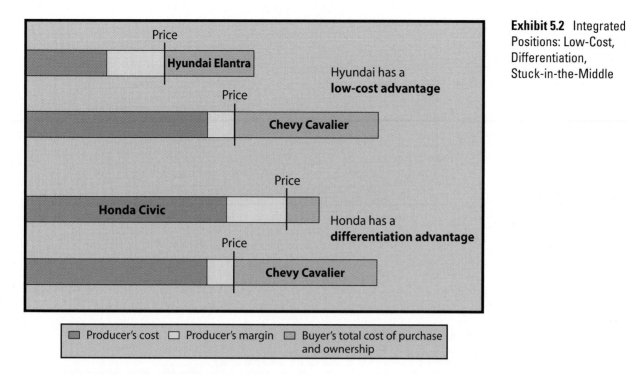

Producer's cost   Producer's margin   Buyer's total cost of purchase and ownership

Exhibit 5.2 Integrated Positions: Low-Cost, Differentiation, Stuck-in-the-Middle

straddling position between low cost and differentiation are reviewed later in the chapter. Honda enjoys better margins because it commands higher prices by delivering more consumer value, much of which derives from such intangibles as resale value, lower maintenance costs, and overall quality. Consequently, even though the initial price of the Chevy Cavalier is significantly lower, the Honda Civic is actually less expensive to own in the long run. So is the Hyundai Elantra, which boasts both lower total ownership costs and lower manufacturing costs. Although this example only compares one model from each of these three automakers for purposes of simplicity, the implications for strategic positions apply at the level of the firm's entire portfolio.

Generic Strategy and Firm Resources As we've seen, the appropriate generic strategy for any firm depends on two factors: (1) its resources and capabilities and (2) the condition of its industry environment. A firm with innovative capabilities, for example, will generally favor differentiation strategies. Why? Because the ability to make product improvements, whether incremental and radical, enables a firm to offer newer and more unique products directed at specific customer needs. Intel favors heavy investment in product innovation so that it can remain on the leading edge of new-product introductions in the microprocessor industry. This strategy enables the company to charge higher prices during the early stages of the product life cycle, generating increased cash flows that it can, in turn, invest in building its brand and further differentiating its products.

Alternatively, capabilities in large-scale manufacturing and distribution generally favor low-cost strategies. Cooper Industries, for example, has developed skills in consolidating companies in mature tool, hardware, or electrical-product industries, infusing them with modern manufacturing technology and increasing supplier power over critical customer segments. In particular, the ability to modernize manufacturing processes (the company calls it Cooperizing) gives the firm a cost advantage over many competitors.

The results of successful low-cost, differentiation, and integrated positions are illustrated in Exhibit 5.3. It is critical to remember that these successful positions are predicated on the effective implementation of the drivers of cost or differentiation advantage, or both. In the next section, we explore these drivers in detail.

conceptlink

In Chapter 3, we define a firm's **resources** as the inputs that it uses to create goods or services and its **capabilities** as its skill in using its resources.

Exhibit 5.3 The Interplay Between Cost and Differentiation

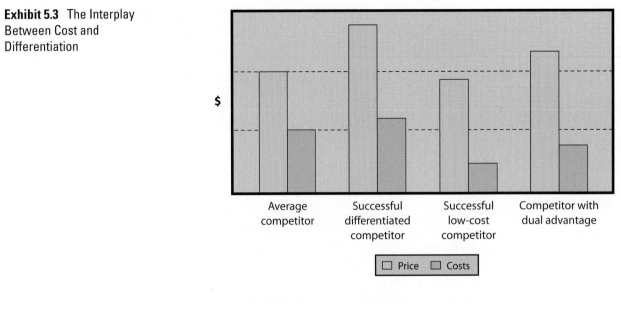

ECONOMIC DRIVERS OF STRATEGIC POSITIONING

concept link

In Chapter 1, we define its **economic logic** as the ways in which a firm plans to generate positive returns over and above its cost of capital; as such, it's crucial to the effort to assess the possibility of making an above-normal profit by competing in an industry.

Choices in strategic positioning are also influenced by economic logic. Thus in order to fully understand the logic behind different strategic positions, we need to identify the different economic drivers that encourage strategic positions and foster their success. In this section, we'll describe some of the key economic drivers of both low-cost and differentiation strategies. (Remember that because *focus* strategies are special variations on these two basic types of strategy, the same economic drivers apply to them.) In order to understand how firms manage to implement the strategies that produce the advantages that they enjoy, we need to understand economic drivers and how they function.

Drivers of Low-Cost Advantage

Firms have different production costs for several reasons. Some of the more common (and important) include economies of scale, learning, production technology, product design, and location advantages for sourcing inputs. In this section, we'll review some of the more important sources of potential cost advantage. A successful low-cost strategy means that a firm is proficient at exploiting some of these drivers. Conversely, of course, firms that are unable to leverage these cost drivers either need to acquire the capabilities and resources to do so or to reevaluate their prospects as low-cost leaders.

economy of scale Condition under which average total cost for a unit of production is lower at higher levels of output

Economies of Scale **Economies of scale** exist during a given period of time *if the average total cost for a unit of production is lower at higher levels of output.* To better understand the nature and importance of economies of scale, we need to review the various types of production costs:

- *Fixed costs* (such as rent and equipment) remain the same for different levels of production.
- *Variable costs* are the costs of variable inputs (such as raw materials and labor); they vary directly with output.
- *Marginal cost* is the cost of the last unit of production.
- *Total cost* is the sum of all production costs; it increases as output goes up.
- *Average cost* is the *mean* cost of total production during a given period (say, a year).

Economies of scale exist if *average costs* are lower at higher levels of production. Under what circumstances might it cost less to manufacture more products during one given time period than during another?

Economies of scale result from a variety of efficiencies, all related to higher volumes of production relative to a given asset base: spreading fixed costs over greater volume, specializing in a specific production process, practicing superior inventory management, exercising purchasing power, spending more effectively on advertising or R&D.

Economies of scale result primarily from the first reason—spreading fixed costs over greater levels of output. It stands to reason that within the feasible range of production at a given facility, increasing output will enable the firm to spread its fixed costs over greater levels of production. If, for example, R&D costs account for a significant portion of the firm's total cost, larger scale enables the firm to cut average cost by spreading R&D costs over more units of production.

In addition, greater scale often encourages the use of more sophisticated inventory-management systems. Some of these systems, though not cost-effective at lower volumes, bring significant rewards at sufficiently large scales of production. Audi, for instance, persuaded suppliers to locate operations in facilities adjacent to its newly centralized facilities in Ingoldstadt, Germany. In turn, the carmaker was able to implement just-in-time inventory techniques that didn't work when smaller-scale manufacturing operations were more widely dispersed.[4] Similarly, when numerous inputs are involved, the price depends, in part, on the volume purchased. That's why large buyers often have more leverage in negotiating price. Wal-Mart, for example, is renowned (even notorious) for exercising its buying power to hold down input costs.

If branding plays a key role in the firm's strategy, larger scale often provides a significant advertising advantage. In order to influence consumer decisions, advertising must first reach a certain "threshold" at which it creates awareness. If two firms of significantly different size allocate the same *proportion* of revenues to advertising, they'll achieve significantly different levels of awareness. Thus, large firms allocate more total dollars for advertising and reap the benefit of greater awareness. In addition, large firms can bargain for price discounts in various media that aren't extended to smaller accounts.

Diseconomies of Scale Do not, however, make the mistake of assuming that size automatically ensures economies of scale. In reality, almost all operations processes are subject to the **diseconomies of scale** that occur when average total cost *increases* at higher levels of output.

diseconomy of scale Condition under which average total costs per unit of production increases at higher levels of input

Diseconomies of scale can result from bureaucracy, high labor costs, and inefficient operations. Moreover, a firm may have economies of scale in some value-chain activities that result in diseconomies of scale on other dimensions. For instance, consider the world of institutional fund management. The 20 largest fund managers control over 40 percent of professionally managed money in the world. According to research by Mercer Oliver Wyman, a large consulting practice specializing in financial services, fund management is a very scale-sensitive business. A fund manager with a $10,000,000 portfolio incurs the same costs as a manager with a $100,000,000 portfolio. However, Mercer notes that although some expenses are lower in the large funds (due to scale economies), others must be larger, because the highest-performing firms in every segment of the industry are smaller boutique firms.[5]

Large-scale operations can also lead to inflexibility—and increased costs—in the face of changing needs.[6] This is what happened to General Motors in the early 1990s. After spending billions to complement its massive scale with an appropriate level of automation, GM discovered that its technological upgrade didn't allow it to switch platforms fast enough to respond to shifts in the market. Inflexibility in the face of changing consumer preferences and new-model introductions by competitors actually caused costs at GM's newly automated plants to go up, not down.

Minimum Efficient Scale How, then, can a firm achieve optimal performance? Ultimately, the objective is to find the scale necessary to achieve the lowest possible average cost. Let's examine this concept in a little more detail.

As we've just seen, costs may decline at some ranges of production but increase at others. This fact suggests that *total average cost* can be represented by a *U*-shaped curve that has a minimum point. The output level that delivers the lowest possible costs is the

Exhibit 5.4 Scale and Cost

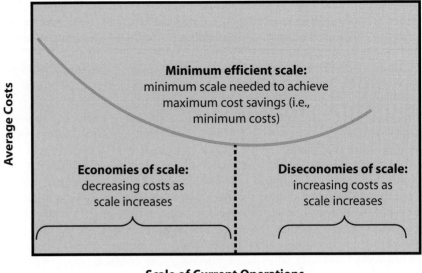

minimum efficient scale (MES)
The output level that delivers the lowest
total average cost

minimum efficient scale (MES). Often, firms operating below or above MES suffer from a cost disadvantage. Generally, there is a range of scale—or of output levels—at which costs will be minimized. MES is the smallest scale necessary to achieve maximum economies of scale. It's critical to decisions about a firm's scale of operations because it targets the level of production needed to enjoy all the benefits made possible by large scale. It also establishes the size that a new entrant must achieve in order to match the scale advantages enjoyed by incumbents. Exhibit 5.4 illustrates some possible relationships between economies of scale, diseconomies of scale, and minimum efficient scale. Although MES understandably varies by industry and market segment, the exhibit generally conveys the idea that managers must take into account economy-of-scale tradeoffs when making investments in service or production capacity.

MES and Technology Not surprisingly, MES is also a function of technology. Obviously, an industry may employ more than one type of technology. In the steel industry, for example, some plants—so-called minimills—use electric-arc furnaces, whereas old-line integrated steel companies continue to use blast-arc furnaces. Minimills are designed to make steel in a simple three-stage process that starts with scrap metal, whereas integrated steel manufacturing requires investments in equipment that start earlier in the value chain with iron ore and coal. Consequently, the scale requirements of the two technologies are quite different, and minimills can achieve MES at roughly one-tenth the scale required for efficient operation at an integrated mill.

With some technologies, MES is reached only at relatively low levels of production, and although there's no scale advantage at higher levels, neither is there any disadvantage. Some technologies result quite quickly in a disadvantage at a scale larger than MES, whereas still others support wide ranges of scale without generating any real cost differences.

The Learning Curve In addition to scale economies, other factors can contribute to lower operating costs. Two firms of the same size, for example, may have significantly different operating costs because one has progressed farther down the **learning curve**—in other words, it has excelled at the process of learning by doing. The basic principle holds that *incremental production costs decline at a constant rate as production experience is gained*; the steeper the learning curve, the more rapidly costs decline. This idea is attributed to T. P. Wright, who proposed a theory for basing cost estimates on the repetitive operations of airplane-assembly processes in 1936.[7] (In the 1970s, the Defense Department commissioned research to refine learning-curve mathematics so that it could make more precise cost estimates.) See the box entitled "How Would *You* Do That? 5.1" for more on the learning curve.

learning curve Incremental
production costs decline at a constant
rate as production experience is gained;
the steeper the learning curve, the more
rapidly costs decline

Before reading any farther, be sure that you understand the difference between economies of scale and the learning curve. Although both are related to the quantity produced, the underlying mechanisms are quite different. Economies of scale reflect the scale of the operation *during any given period of time*—the volume of current production. Cost decreases attributable to the learning curve reflect *the cumulative level of production since the production of the first unit.*

Putting the Learning Curve to Use   It is important to understand the relationship between experience and costs in a firm's use of technology for several reasons. For one, managers can make more accurate total-cost forecasts when they're preparing bids for large projects. In addition, taking the learning curve into consideration may enable managers to make more aggressive pricing decisions. Japanese motorcycle and automobile manufacturers, for example, considered the expected future costs savings associated with the learning curve when setting entry prices for the U.S. market. Although initial prices may actually have been below *current* production costs, they were set to reflect *future* cost estimates. The low prices also enabled the Japanese to make rapid gains in market share. Resulting higher volumes not only contributed to economies of scale, but also reduced costs due to learning. Later, Asian computer-chip manufacturers adopted the same strategy for entering the U.S. market.[8]

Multiunit Organizations and the Learning Curve   A related effect of the learning curve occurs when a multiunit organization transfers learning from one unit to another.[9] Franchise systems, for instance, can codify their knowledge about the most effective way to operate a store. Technically, therefore, each new franchise doesn't have to start from scratch. Rather, every unit benefits from corporate training programs that give new franchisees a head start at tackling the learning curve. Because units can share new knowledge about effective practices, multiunit firms can make faster progress in mastering learning curves than single-unit operations.

Other Sources of Cost Advantage   Other potential sources of cost advantage include *economies of scope, production technology,* and *product design.*

Economies of Scope   As the term suggests, *economies of scope* are similar to economies of scale. They refer, however, to potential cost savings associated with *multiproduct* production. When a firm produces two or more products, it has greater scope of operations than a firm that produces only one. If such a firm can share a resource among one or more of its products—thereby lowering the costs of each product—it benefits from **economies of scope**.[10] We discuss this concept more fully in Chapter 7 because it's fundamental to diversification as a corporate strategy. Economies of scope, however, are available not only to large diversified firms but also to small privately held enterprises that are just beginning to expand their product offerings.

economy of scope Condition under which lower total average costs result from sharing resources to produce more than one product or service

Here we offer a simple example to help you understand economies of scope.[11] The multipurpose table and furniture industry is made up of a fragmented group of about 60 major manufacturers who share a $1-billion market. One of these companies, Mity-Lite, was formed in 1987 by Gregory Wilson when he was in the church-furniture business. The company's original product line consisted of folding tables targeted at such institutional users as schools, churches, civic organizations, and hospitals. From the outset, Mity-Lite used a heat- and vacuum-thermoforming process to mold engineering-grade plastics, combining this process with durable folding-metal frames to build tables that are both much lighter and more durable than competing particle-board or plywood tables. As the company grew, it learned to implement a number of changes in both its manufacturing process and product designs—changes that have increased production volumes, improved quality, and lowered costs.

After a decade of successful market penetration, Mity-Lite had developed a reputation as a leading designer, manufacturer, and marketer of folding-leg tables. With excess capacity in his Orem, Utah, plant, Wilson began to study possible growth options. Because customers of folding-leg tables often buy folding or stacking chairs at the same time, Wilson saw at least one opportunity to expand into complementary products. He soon discovered that the same technology he used to form durable tables could be used to manufacture

How to Take the Learning Curve on Two Wheels

How can the learning curve actually help a company? To consider this question, let's review a problem faced by East Side Bikes, a hypothetical maker of custom cruiser bicycles. East Side's latest hit product is a bike with an amazing resemblance to a motor-cycle. The marketing manager for a high-end sporting goods retailer recently saw the bike at a trade show, fell in love with it, assured East Side that she can sell them in her com-pany's stores, and initiated negotia-tions for an initial order of 100 bikes. Of course, for such a large order she expects a good price. How can East Side take the principle of the learning curve into consideration in forecasting its cost and offering the most attractive price?

Because East Side has already made four prototypes, the firm knows that it took 30 hours to make the first bike, 27 hours for the second, and 24.30 hours for the last (fourth) bike made. (Fortunately, there were four prototypes; it's never wise to esti-mate trends with only two data points.) Using the concept of the learning curve, East Side can system-atically use historical data to esti-mate future costs. East Side can do this in several ways. (Bear in mind, by the way, that we could measure either in terms of costs or hours; for the sake of simplicity, we'll use hours throughout this exercise.)

One way to estimate future costs is simply to calculate projected values

Exhibit 5.5 The Time Value of Learning at East Side Bikes

Number of Bikes Produced	Hours per Bike
1st	30.00 actual
2nd	27.00 actual
4th	24.30 actual
8th	21.87 est.
16th	19.68 est.
32nd	17.71 est.
64th	15.92 est.
128th	14.34 est.

using some basic math. To do this, we need to know a fundamental rule for quantifying the learning curve: For every doubling of *cumulative* produc-tion levels, costs decline at a con-stant rate. In our example, cumulative production has reached four bikes. In other words, it's doubled twice—once from one to two and again from two to four. If we calculate the percent-ages for each doubling, we see that (conveniently enough) we have a 90-percent learning curve: The hours to make the second bike were 90 per-cent of the first, and the fourth was 90 percent of the second. Now we just repeat the process to estimate future costs: In other words, we take 90 percent of current production as our estimate for costs *once cumula-tive production doubles again*, repeat-ing the process until we've reached our target level of production (100

bikes). Using this quick and dirty method, we see that the time we'll need per bike falls to approximately 15 hours by the time we've reached 100 bikes. Our findings are summa-rized in Exhibit 5.5.

This procedure works fine for small batches, but it could become quite cumbersome for large production runs. In more complicated situations, we need the actual *learning-curve for-mula*. With this formula and a good calculator or spreadsheet, we can pro-ject costs for a specific estimated number of units rather than having to interpolate from a table of values that increase at doubling rates.

Here's the formula for estimating learning curves:

$$y = ax^{-b}$$

where *y* is the cost per unit for the *x*th unit produced; *a* is the cost of the first unit produced; x is the cumulative number of products produced (or desired level if the rate of learning, b, is already determined); and b is the *rate* at which costs are reduced every time cumulative production doubles (always a negative number calculated from other known quantities). Using this formula and a spreadsheet, we can project future costs for any level of production and thus make a more informed decision about our costs. Our new findings are summarized in Exhibit 5.6.

If you're math averse, you may prefer to resort to one of several aids. First, we could draw up a table in which we plug in the *rates* for several common learning curves (i.e., the figures needed to plug b into the previous formula). Then we can find our solutions by combining these rates with our spreadsheet capabilities, as shown in Exhibit 5.7.

If you want things even simpler, you could visit a NASA Web site that contains a "learning-curve calculator" at www.jsc.nasa.gov/bu2/learn.html. Using this handy device, you can plug in a few basic data and wait for it to solve the problem for you. (*Hint:* Use the Crawford version of the calculator, which corresponds to the current formulation used in business.)

Exhibit 5.6   The Learning Curve at East Side Bikes

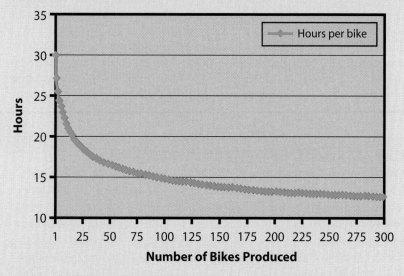

Exhibit 5.7   Spreadsheet for East Side Bikes

Learning Curve	80%	85%	90%	95%
Rate of Learning	−.322	−.234	−.152	−.074

chairs. Moreover, because expansion into chair production didn't require a new plant, the cost of the manufacturing facility could be shared in the production of both tables and chairs. These cost savings reflect economies of scope. From its small beginnings as a supplier of church furniture, Mity-Lite has grown an average of 35 percent per year and has become an international player in the institutional furniture industry.

Production Technology　Naturally, different production technologies entail different costs. Often, a new entrant who wants to compete against industry incumbents with significant scale and experience advantages tries to match or beat incumbents' costs by introducing a production technology that's subject to different economics. JetBlue, for instance, has the lowest operating costs of all major U.S. airlines, and the source of its successful strategy—its production technology—compares quite favorably with the technologies used by other airlines.

Similarly, Nucor Steel originally entered an industry that wasn't particularly attractive from a traditional point of view. Profits were low, capital intensity was high, and the bargaining power of buyers was strong (i.e., steel is a commodity, which means that buyers make purchase decisions primarily on price if all other factors are equal). In addition, most incumbents had the advantage of a century's worth of experience. Nucor, however, didn't use the same technology as its incumbent competitors. Rather than building an integrated mill with blast-arc furnaces, Nucor opted for the lower-cost electric-arc technology favored by minimills.[12]

Product Design　Similarly, product design can sometimes be altered to lower a firm's production costs.[13] When Canon, for example, decided to enter the photocopier industry, incumbents such as Xerox had formidable advantages in scale and experience. Canon, however, redesigned the photocopier so that it required fewer parts and allowed for simpler assembly. The new design dropped Canon's costs below those of Xerox and enabled the new entrant to gain significant market share at Xerox's expense.

Finally, different sourcing practices result in different cost structures. Some firms try to attain lower production costs by locating their operations in cheaper labor markets. Others outsource manufacturing altogether. Pacific Cycle, for instance, makes bikes for less than Trek, whose operations are in the United States, by outsourcing much of its production to China and Taiwan.

In Chapter 3, we define **outsourcing** as any *value-chain activity* performed for a company by people other than its full-time employees.

SimConnect

Creating a Low-Cost Advantage in StratSim

There are several drivers of cost advantage in StratSim, including economies of scale, learning curve effects, cost savings through product design, and investments in technology capabilities. Let's examine how each of these works within StratSim to help you decide if a low-cost strategy is an appropriate strategy for your firm, and, if so, how best to generate that advantage.

Economies of Scale　There are definite economies of scale present in the automobile industry and in StratSim as well. An obvious example would be use of existing capacity (a fixed cost). If two firms have the same capacity, the firm that operates at 90-percent capacity utilization will enjoy a cost advantage over a firm operating at 70-percent capacity utilization, presuming, of course, that each firm sells the vehicles that it produces and doesn't carry them in inventory. A second example is distribution. Distribution costs are generally fixed; so again, a firm that sells more vehicles per dealer enjoys a cost advantage where the fixed costs of the dealership network are spread over more vehicles. Also some fixed costs are included in the general and administrative expenses on the income statement, which are the same for all firms; so again, spreading these costs across more unit sales provides a relative advantage.

Learning Curve Effects　In StratSim, learning curve effects are present at both the product level and the class level. Therefore, all things being equal, a firm with higher market share with a particular product, or higher market share of a particular vehicle class will enjoy a cost advantage over those products or firms with lower unit market share.

Savings through Product Design It is important to recognize that the product design process has an impact on unit variable costs. Part of this is determined by the specifications of the product, with higher values increasing the unit costs, all things being equal. However, one of the major sources of lowering unit costs is provided through the upgrade process. When a vehicle is upgraded, along with creating the new product design, the engineers working on the product also attempt to find ways to lower the cost of the product without sacrificing quality. Your firm can calculate the impact of the cost savings of an upgrade by choosing to upgrade a product and making no changes to the design. Compare the base cost on the original ("previous") product design with the upgrade. This difference is the cost savings due to re-engineering the product design. Realize that you may both change the specifications and enjoy savings due to the upgrade process itself. In addition, products that share common design elements (e.g., HP of 120 – same engine, or safety of 3) also create cost savings by sharing common components across vehicles. Although these savings are minimal, it should be considered during the product design process.

Savings through Investment in Technology Capabilities Finally, a firm may invest in technology capabilities, which both allow your firm to create vehicles with higher specifications, but also lower costs on the existing vehicles. An estimate of the savings based on your current product portfolio and projected sales is provided on the technology capabilities input screen.

It is essential that your firm considers the effectiveness of using these cost savings techniques in the context of your overall strategy. Cost savings are a net positive whether it improves your profit margin or it is passed on to the customer in hopes of gaining more sales. However, remember that it is implementation of "smart" cost savings that is ultimately rewarded. Having the largest production capacity is only an effective cost savings if that capacity is used (and sold). Having a low-cost vehicle is only effective if consumers still want to purchase it. Thus, the successful manager is always looking for ways to lower costs, but keeps an eye on whether those cost savings are ultimately rewarded on the bottom line.

Drivers of Differentiation Advantages In order to sell products at premium prices, firms must make their uniqueness and value apparent to customers. In this section, we'll review the economic logic and some of the common drivers of a successful differentiation strategy. As a rule, differentiation involves one or more of the following product offerings: *premium brand image, customization, unique styling, speed, more convenient access*, and *unusually high quality*.

When Toyota introduced its premium Lexus line in 1989, its strategy was based on extensive market analysis and product-development efforts. Relying on its ability to manufacture high-quality automobiles, Toyota was confident that it could penetrate the highly profitable luxury-car segment. In fact, managers regarded the whole idea as quite logical, given the brand image already enjoyed by Toyota. Consequently, the company launched and developed an entirely new brand with a separate dealer network. High quality was a Lexus trademark from the beginning, with the new luxury car winning its first J.D. Power and Associates number-one ranking in the 1990 Initial Quality Study. Being named one of *Car & Driver*'s 10 best and the Motoring Press Association's Best Imported Car of the Year also bolstered the Lexus image.

Bear in mind, however, that although quality earned a slew of technical awards for Lexus, targeted marketing created something even more important—customer awareness. In practice, a differentiation strategy means that marketers understand how to *segment* the market in which they intend to compete—a process known as *market segmentation*. They must identify specific subgroups of buyers who have distinguishable needs, select one or more of these unique buyer needs, and satisfy them in ways that competitors don't or can't.

Curves International, for instance, saw a unique opportunity to segment the fitness-club industry by targeting women who desired a nonintimidating environment. Curves' equipment is different from that of competitors, not only because it's designed for women but because it uses hydraulic-resistance equipment that eliminates the need to worry about weight stacks. In addition, the Curves program features a convenient 30-minute exercise routine. Since its founding in 1992, Curves has opened more than 9,500 locations, and the company's success suggests that the segment it targeted was indeed overlooked or underserved by industry incumbents.

Creating Value and Promoting Willingness to Pay   The goal of differentiation is to be able to demand a price sufficient to do two things: (1) recoup the added costs of delivering the value-added feature and (2) generate enough profit to make the strategy worthwhile. The point of differentiation is to drive up the customer's **willingness to pay**—that is, to induce customers to pay more for the firm's products or services than a competitors'. The producer wants to drive a wedge between what customers are willing to pay and the costs of acquiring the resources needed to add value to the product. (Conversely, a low-cost strategy entails keeping costs down to compensate for customers' paying lower prices for undifferentiated products or services.)

willingness to pay Principle of differentiation strategy by which customers are willing to pay more for certain product features

SimConnect

Creating a Differentiation Advantage in StratSim

There are many drivers of differentiation advantage in StratSim, all of which cannot be discussed here, but some of the most important ones include product enhancements, service quality, and firm preference. Let's examine how each of these works within StratSim to help you decide if a differentiation strategy is an appropriate strategy for your firm, and, if so, how best to generate that advantage.

Product Enhancements   Probably the most obvious way to differentiate your firm from the competition is through continually enhancing your products and introducing new products to better meet unique customer needs. Thus, a firm that will differentiate through product development will likely open more development centers, introduce new products, and upgrade their current products more frequently.

Service Quality   In StratSim, service quality is measured through dealership ratings. Since the dealer is where the actual sale is made and all follow-up service and support is received, the experience at the dealership is an important source of competitive advantage. To improve your dealer ratings, consider how you can improve the gross/dealer value. This is basically the revenue the dealership has to operate their business. When their revenue per dealer is lower than the competition, they will likely have to cut some of the expenses that provide for a better quality experience at the dealership. In addition, you may want to consider investing in training and support for your dealership network.

Firm Preference   This measure attempts to capture consumers' overall preferred auto company. This is akin to firm reputation and brand equity in the real world. In effect, all things being equal, from which firm would customers prefer to purchase their new vehicle? This measure considers many different aspects of the firm, but it is one way to tell how successful your differentiation strategy is working. A low score on firm preference would tend to indicate that your firm is not providing anything special to consumers.

It is essential that your firm consider the effectiveness of using these differentiation techniques and measures in the context of your overall strategy. Differentiation should be used when it makes a difference to your target markets. Some potential customers would prefer a low-priced vehicle to a vehicle that provides additional features at a higher price. Thus, the successful manager is always looking for ways to better meet customer needs through the total product offering, but also balances that with whether the perceived value to the customer is greater than the cost of creating that value.

THREATS TO SUCCESSFUL COMPETITIVE POSITIONING

For a firm using any of the generic strategies that we've discussed in this chapter, success hinges on a number of factors. Does the firm have the right resources, such as those that may accrue from scale or learning, for implementing a low-cost strategy? Will the marketplace reward a differentiator? In some markets (those which, like steel, are more commodity-like), customers' purchase decisions are driven much more strongly by price than by product features, and in these cases there's not much that firms can do to justify higher prices. A summary of the common drivers of differentiation and low-cost advantage, along with the threats to those positions, is listed in Exhibit 5.8. Under most circumstances, a successful strategic position must satisfy two requirements: (1) It must be based on the firm's resources and capabilities, and (2) it must achieve some level of consistency with the conditions that prevail in the industry.

Threats to Low-Cost Positions

In terms of these two critical requirements, let's look first at the numerous threats facing firms aiming for a low-cost competitive position. First, the firm may face threats on the technological front. In particular, the resource that makes it possible for a firm to compete on the basis of cost—often a certain technology—can be imitated. Efficient production and process technologies can move from firm to firm by any number of means, such as consultants with clients throughout the industry and the movement of key personnel from company to company.

Granted, even though an imitator may acquire comparable technology, the original firm may still enjoy the benefits of greater experience and the learning curve. A more serious threat to low-cost competitors is the possibility that another firm may introduce a new technology—one which, like mini-mill technology in the steel industry, supports a different scale and a more efficient learning process. In such cases, even small latecomers can establish cost positions significantly lower than those of larger, more experienced low-cost leaders.

Second, low-cost leadership means offering an acceptable combination of price and quality. A real threat to an intended low-cost position is the failure to offer sufficient quality to satisfy buyers' basic needs. Over the past decade, for example, Kmart's experiments in low-cost positioning have been thwarted not only by Wal-Mart's ability to stake out an even lower-cost position, but by Kmart's own inability to offer a retail experience of comparable quality (customers complain of empty shelves, uninviting environments, and less helpful staff).

	Drivers	**Threats**
Low Cost	• Economies of scale • Learning • Economies of scope • Superior technology • Superior product design	• New technology • Inferior quality • Social, political, and economic risk of outsourcing
Differentiation	• Premium brand image • Customization • Unique styling • Speed • Convenient access • Unusually high quality	• Failing to increase buyers' willingness to pay higher prices • Underestimating costs of differentiation • Overfulfilling buyers' needs • Lower-cost imitation

Exhibit 5.8 Low Cost and Differentiation: Drivers and Threats

Recently, another serious threat has arisen to low-cost competitors in labor-intensive industries: increased public awareness of questionable labor practices in developing countries. Struggling to keep wage costs as low as possible, many companies (some unwittingly) have entered into agreements with suppliers who enforce excessive work hours, deny basic employee services, employ children, and violate what, at least in the United States, are considered acceptable working conditions. Watchdog groups regularly publicize such cases, and reforms push up costs.[14] Many multinational companies have established codes of ethical conduct for suppliers, but enforcing these standards—inspecting and auditing overseas suppliers—also increases costs. Managers must be certain that their foreign sourcing arrangements are in compliance with their corporate values.

Threats to Differentiation Positions

Needless to say, the intent to provide a differentiated product doesn't necessarily result in competitive advantage and enhanced profitability. A number of factors can sabotage a differentiation strategy. Obviously, a differentiating feature that buyers don't care about merely increases costs without increasing willingness to pay, which cuts into profit margins. Until recently, for example, Audi suffered from the fact that although its manufacturing costs were comparable to those of BMW and Mercedes, it couldn't get customers to pay comparable prices. In effect, Audi was either overfulfilling the needs of buyers who were in the market for well-made but more modestly priced cars or underfulfilling the needs of customers in the market for high-image, high-quality cars.

In addition, failing to understand the total costs entailed by differentiation can derail a differentiation position. The cost of differentiation has no direct effect on customers' willingness to pay, and in most industries, cost-plus pricing is not an option. Jaguar, for example, found itself in an apparently enviable position in the early 1980s: It had a highly differentiated product with good brand recognition and strong customer appeal, and unlike Audi's targeted customers, car buyers were willing to pay premium prices for Jaguars. Unfortunately, antiquated manufacturing processes had driven costs so high that, even with products selling in the top price range, the company lost money. Many of its operations weren't even automated, but ironically, Jaguar took pride in its traditional hands-on methods—in part because managers believed that brand recognition and customer loyalty were tied to an appreciation of the individualized manufacturing process. Ford purchased Jaguar in 1990 and, after studying the company's operations, revamped assembly plants in an effort to combine the best aspects of both traditional and modern methods. Ford, for instance, retained the practice of installing hand-sewn leather interiors and natural-wood inlays but significantly modernized the processes for assembling bodies and power trains.[15]

Two additional reasons differentiation can fail are overfulfillment and ease of imitation. When product features exceed buyer needs, the added costs to provide these unwanted features, coupled with customers' lack of willingness to pay for this differentiation, results in significantly lower margins. Finally, creating differentiation that competitors can emulate quickly or cheaply undermines any advantage that it might afford. Naturally, once competitors have matched a product's unique feature, it's no longer unique and will probably lose its ability to command premium prices. In some industries, patents provide short-term protection for innovative products. In others, companies must seek alternative means of protection. In the soft-drink industry, where products are easily imitated (they are, after all, simple combinations of water, sugar, color, and flavoring), Coke and Pepsi discourage imitation by exercising power of scale over suppliers and buyers and conducting aggressive marketing campaigns to sustain brand image.

Threats to Focus Positions

Although focused low-cost or focused differentiation positions are specialized cases of low-cost leadership and broad differentiation and thus subject to all the same threats as those just reviewed, they face one additional threat that deserves mention. Firms that implement focus positions face the threat of being out-focused by competitors. A firm relying on a focus strategy may lose its advantage by attempting to grow and consequently attempt to meet the needs of too many customers. If that happens, a competitor or new entrant may then more successfully target the needs of the original focused group of customers. As existing or new competitors identify new or previously unexploited needs of the segment, they may be in a better position to uniquely satisfy the needs of that segment. For instance, Harley-Davidson faces the threat that custom chopper shops will pull away customers because they can more uniquely satisfy the needs of a segment of Harley's market.

Threats to Integrated Positions

In his original analysis of generic strategic positions, Porter, arguing that they were mutually exclusive, warned against the temptation to straddle positions: Firms that try both to differentiate and to achieve a low-cost position will end up **straddling** two inconsistent positions.

All firms, Porter suggested, must make decisions about positioning their products and will consequently choose one strategy over the other. Developing a low-cost strategy means that a firm must forgo subsequent opportunities to enhance product uniqueness or quality (that is, to develop a position based on differentiation). In this respect, selected strategies and forgone opportunities must be regarded as tradeoffs. H&R Block, for example, can't enter the field of high-level estate and tax planning because such services require the kind of high-cost specialists that a low-cost competitor can't afford. Thus, Block trades off the advantages of high-margin services for the advantages of a low-cost tax-preparation business. By the same token, a "pure" differentiator trades off the cost-saving advantages of producing standardized products for the advantages of satisfying a demand for customized products.

Although many firms have succeeded in pursuing integrated strategies, it's still critical for managers to understand the tradeoffs they make when they opt for one position over the other. Virtually no firm can succeed in being all things to all customers. For one, firms need to know exactly what opportunities they're forgoing.

Second, knowing what tradeoffs can be made in an industry helps managers recognize what competitors can and can't do in attempts to juggle strategies. Why, for instance, can't United, American, and Delta lower their costs to match those of Southwest Airlines? Many of the specific practices by which Southwest maintains its lower-cost position entail tradeoffs that the other carriers can't make. United, Delta, and American don't have the option of flying just one type of aircraft, even if it would save on training and maintenance costs. Nor can they abandon their expensive hub facilities, which are integral to the logistics of their flight systems, even though the hub system and its accompanying gate fees are much more costly than Southwest's reliance on secondary airports and smaller destination cities.

STRATEGY AND FIT WITH INDUSTRY CONDITIONS

In Chapter 1, we introduced the strategy-diamond model of strategy formulation. Recall that an important input into this model is a firm's objectives. Earlier in the chapter we detailed generic strategies *by type*, but in order to show how the strategy-diamond and generic-strategy models are compatible, we need to remind ourselves that when managers decide on generic competitive positions, they aren't deciding on strategies themselves: Rather, they're stating *objectives* with respect to several elements of their overall strategy—indicating precisely how they intend the firm to deal with differentiators, economic logic, and certain aspects of arenas.

We know, too, that industry conditions have an important effect on strategy formulation. One way to illustrate this effect is to examine the threats and opportunities presented to a company during different phases of the industry life cycle. In this section, we'll treat each phase of the life cycle as if conditions are not likely to change in the short term. In other words, in order to show how alternative strategies function under different life-cycle conditions, we'll take advantage of the fact that industry analysis gives us a "snapshot" view of an industry at a particular point in its life cycle. In reality, of course, many industries are changing rapidly, and in Chapter 6, we'll turn our attention to strategies that take advantage of changes, such as the rapid and sometimes managed evolution of an industry from one stage in its life cycle to the next.

straddling Unsuccessful attempt to integrate both low-cost and differentation positions

concept link

In Chapter 2, we observe that most strategic positions involve *tradeoffs*—that deciding on one course of action generally eliminates other options.

concept link

We introduce the **industry life cycle** in Chapter 4, where we emphasize that the *evolution* of industries from emergence to maturity and even stagnation drives the strategies of the companies that compete in them.

Strategies for Different Industry Conditions

Industry conditions should inform strategic leaders and have an influence on the strategies their firms formulate. Of course, not all firms will respond similarly to different industry conditions, but conditions at different phases of an industry life cycle provide differential opportunities and constraints. Consequently, firms' strategies tend to vary across these different phases. Exhibit 5.9 summarizes some of the more common effects of the industry life cycle on the elements of firms' strategies.

Embryonic Stage During an industry's *embryonic* phase, when business models are unproven, no standardized technology has been established, capital needs generally outstrip the resources and capabilities of startups, and uncertainty is high. Early movers—those who succeed in establishing solid competitive positions during this stage—can set themselves up to be in a strong position during later phases of the industry life cycle.[16] Because primary demand is just being established and customers lack good information on

Exhibit 5.9 Life-Cycle Strategies

Phase of Industry Life Cycle	Arenas	Vehicles	Differentiators	Staging	Economic Logic
Embryonic	Staying local	Internal development Alliances to secure missing inputs or distribution access	Target basic needs, minimal differentiation	Tactics to gain early footholds	Prices tend to be high Costs are high; focus is on securing additional capital to fund growth phase
Growth	Penetrating adjacent markets	Alliances for cooperation Acquisitions in targeted markets	Increase efforts toward differentiation Low-cost leaders emerge through experience and scale advantages	Integrated positions require choice of focusing first on cost or differentiation	Margins can improve rapidly because of experience and scale Price premiums accrue to successful differentiators
Mature	Globalizing Diversifying	Mergers and acquisitions for consolidation	More stable positions emerge across competitors	Choices of international markets and new industry diversification need rational sequencing	Consolidation results in fewer competitors (favoring higher margins), but declining growth demands cost containment and rationalization of operations
Decline	Abandoning some arenas if decline is severe Focusing on segments that provide the most profitability	Acquisitions for diversifying Divestitures enable some competitors to exit and others to consolidate larger shares of the market	Fewer competitors result in less pressure for differentiation, but declining sales results in greater pressure for cost savings	Timing of exit from selected segments or businesses	Rationalizing cost

the relative quality of products, successful differentiation tactics during this phase include getting a strong foothold and building capacity to meet growing demand.

Growth Stage   As industries enter periods of rapid growth, incumbent firms increase market share by taking advantage of footholds established earlier. Rapid growth increases speed down the learning curve and presents leaders with an opportunity to establish low-cost positions that are difficult to imitate, at least in the short term. During this phase, however, technologies can change as new entrants learn from and improve on the work of early movers.

After introducing the Pilot, for example, Palm enjoyed an apparently formidable advantage in the PDA industry. The Palm Pilot was hailed as the most successful consumer-product launch in history, reaching sales of 2 million units within three years and surpassing the adoption rates of camcorders, color TVs, VCRs, and cell phones.[17] Although it considered itself primarily a hardware-device company, Palm developed its own operating system because it was dissatisfied with Microsoft's system for handheld devices. But as the PDA industry grew in size, it caught Microsoft's attention. Before long, Microsoft had renewed interest in its own operating system, and other new competitors, some of whom already had complementary relationships with Microsoft, entered the PDA-software industry.[18] There's obviously an advantage in moving early, gaining a foothold that supports quick growth, and reaping cost advantages by moving quickly along the learning curve, but it doesn't necessarily constitute an impenetrable competitive barrier. New technologies and changing industry competitive structure remain threats.[19]

During the growth phase of an industry, firms make important decisions about how they intend to grow: They determine the strategic vehicles that they'll use to implement their preferred strategies. High-tech companies, for example, may seek alliances with established firms in adjacent industries, similar to the embryonic stage, in order to fill in gaps in their own range of competencies. Such is the case in the biotechnology industry; virtually all of the pure biotech companies have established alliances with large pharmaceutical companies in order to access clinical-trial expertise and marketing capabilities.[20] During the growth stage, too, firms with desirable resources become attractive acquisition targets, both for incumbents wanting to grow rapidly and for firms in related industries seeking to enter the market.

Maturity Stage   As industries mature and growth slows, products become more familiar to the vast majority of potential customers. Product information is more widely available, and quality becomes a more important factor in consumer choice. A mature market, therefore, increases the ability of firms to reap premium prices from differentiation strategies.

Mature industries often undergo *consolidation*—the combination of competitors through merger or acquisition. Consolidation is often motivated by the twofold objective of exploiting economies of scale and increasing market power. The U.S. bicycle industry profiled through the examples of Pacific Cycle, Trek, and Montague, for instance, has experienced a virtual cascade of mergers and acquisitions for the better part of a decade. Although each new combination promises cost saving through greater economies of scale, evidence of significant savings remains inconclusive at best. Market power is a factor because many bicycle companies want to stay large enough to serve the needs of high-volume distribution channels such as Wal-Mart.

Decline Stage   In declining industries, products can take on the attributes of quasi commodities. Because price competition can be intense, containing costs is critical, and firms with low-cost positions have an advantage. Although customers don't entirely ignore differentiated products, declining sales discourage firms from investing in significant innovations.

During this stage, many firms consider the strategy of exiting the industry. Generally, the decision to exit means selling the company or certain divisions to competing firms. Because demand is declining, the industry probably suffers from overcapacity. Thus, reducing the number of competitors can enhance the profitability of those firms that remain. But this fact doesn't mean that exit signifies failure. In many cases, exit can be the best use of shareholders' resources.

A short case study about General Dynamics (GD) drawn from the defense industry demonstrates the potential benefits of exiting an industry during its decline stage.[21] GD was founded in 1899 as the Electric Boat Co. and a year later produced the first workable submarine, which it sold to the U.S. Navy. By the 1950s, GD was a full-fledged defense contractor, producing missiles, rockets, nuclear-powered submarines, and military aircraft. In the mid-1950s, due to the wide range of its defense-industry operations, the company changed its name to General Dynamics Corp. During the 1970s and 1980s, GD emerged as the only defense contractor to supply major systems to all branches of the U.S. military.

Despite many successful weapons programs, however, GD's profitability dropped during the late 1980s, largely because of changes in government procurement processes. In addition, the Cold War thawed rapidly in 1989 and 1990, with the Soviet withdrawal from Afghanistan, the fall of the Berlin Wall, and the collapse of Communist governments across Eastern Europe. Needless to say, the proliferation of arms treaties dampened the demand for weapons systems. GD was particularly hard hit because it was the least diversified of all defense contractors, with a full 87 percent of its revenue tied to defense-system sales.

In 1989, GD hired William Anders as chairman and CEO. His specific charge was to turn the floundering company around. Motivated by lucrative contracts that included generous incentives tied to stock-price performance, Anders and his top-management team set about implementing a radical new strategy. Anders' team made immediate changes, cutting capital spending to 20 percent of the level just two years earlier (saving $337 million). They lost over $1 billion in sales and slashed R&D spending targets by 50 percent. Spending cuts were followed by massive layoffs. Anders was quite public in his pronouncements that the defense industry suffered from overcapacity, too many competitors, and dwindling demand. He publicly urged the industry to consolidate.

Over a two-year period beginning in late 1991, GD sold seven defense businesses for more than $3 billion, emerging as a much smaller and more focused company. Revenues for the new GD were a mere 34 percent of levels of two years earlier, but exiting from so many markets enabled GD to eliminate 94 percent of its outstanding debt, repurchase over 13 million shares of stock, increase dividends by 140 percent, and issue special dividends totaling $50 per share. At the end of this massive downsizing and business-exit campaign, GD had returned $3.4 billion to shareholders and debt holders. Moreover, despite the massive reduction in size, GD's market capitalization increased from about $1 billion in January 1991 to almost $2.9 billion by the end of 1993. Shareholders who held their stock during the three-year restructuring campaign realized a return of over 550 percent.

General Dynamics was once the only defense contractor able to supply products to all branches of the military. After the Cold War ended, however, the company found many of the markets for its products in decline and exited a host of them.

Industry Conditions in StratSim

Although the automobile industry (North American, Western Europe, or Australia) would generally be considered a somewhat mature industry, you will find markets within StratSim in different stages of the industry life cycle. Consider, for instance, hybrids. In StratSim, none of these vehicles have been produced, so the market for hybrids would be considered in the embryonic stage. You may also find that as the simulation progresses, some markets offer higher growth opportunities, or that competitors are innovating more in particular vehicle classes that may be more characterized as being in a growth phase. Conversely, there may be little growth or innovation in some markets. Finally, if your instructor chooses to implement the international module, those markets may behave quite differently than the domestic industry. Remember that you and your competitors will have some impact on how markets grow, but that there are also underlying drivers of demand that are probably the main determinants of the life cycle stage.

TESTING THE QUALITY OF A STRATEGY

Now that you have command of an adequate repertory of strategy-formulation tools—namely, the strategy-diamond, VRINE, industry-structure, and the strategic-positioning models—you should be able to use them to test the quality of a firm's strategy. Clearly, developing a successful business strategy is a complex task. Although we've focused in this chapter on decisions regarding competitive position and strategic interactions, we must also stress that evaluating the effectiveness of a strategy requires that you apply all the tools and models that we've discussed in the first four chapters of this book. In this section, we'll lay out a simple five-step process that makes use of all of these tools and models to evaluate the quality of a firm's strategy.[22] These steps are summarized in Exhibit 5.10.

Does Your Strategy Exploit Your Firm's Resources and Capabilities?

Your first step is determining whether your strategy and competitive position exploit your firm's resources and capabilities. Low-cost strategic positions require manufacturing resources and capabilities that are likely to contribute to a cost advantage. For instance, Pacific Cycle is the lowest-cost bike distributor in the United States by virtue of its lean operations and the complete outsourcing of bike manufacturing to Taiwan and China. Likewise, a differentiation position depends on your ability to produce quality products and to project the necessary image of quality. In Trek's case, it has been careful to cultivate its high-performance image by sponsoring bike luminaries such as Lance Armstrong and selling only through the exclusive independent-dealer channel. When two firms follow similar strategies, you must determine whether you can use your resources to implement your strategy more economically than your competitors can. Finally, you need to be sure that you have the capital resources—both financial and human—necessary to pull off your strategy.

Does Your Strategy Fit with Current Industry Conditions?

Next, you must ask whether your strategy fits with the current conditions in your competitive environment. You need to know whether that environment is hostile, benign, or somewhere in between. Essentially, you want to be sure that you understand the profit *potential* of both your current position and the position toward which your strategy is taking you. Pacific Cycle viewed the big-box retailers and consolidation of the bike industry as opportunities for profitable growth. Ironically, Trek viewed the same environment with an eye toward shoring up relationships with independent bike dealers as a way to combat the influx of sales through low-cost, big-box retail channels. Thus, you need to determine whether your strategy aligns with the key success factors favored by your competitive environment.

Exhibit 5.10   Testing the Quality of Your Strategy

Key Evaluation Criteria	
1. Does your strategy exploit your key resources?	With your particular mix of resources, does this strategy give you an advantageous position relative to your competitors?
	Can you pursue this strategy more economically than your competitors?
	Do you have the capital and managerial talent to do all you plan to do?
	Are you spread too thin?
2. Does your strategy fit with current industry conditions?	Is there healthy profit potential where you're headed?
	Are you aligned with the key success factors of your industry?
3. Will your differentiators be sustainable?	Will competitors have difficulty imitating you?
	If imitation can't be foreclosed, does your strategy include a ceaseless regimen of innovation and opportunity creation to keep distance between you and the competition?
4. Are the elements of your strategy consistent and aligned with your strategic position?	Have you made choices of arenas, vehicles, differentiators, staging, and economic logic?
	Do they all fit and mutually reinforce each other?
5. Can your strategy be implemented?	Will your stakeholders allow you to pursue this strategy?
	Do you have the proper complement of implementation levers in place?
	Is the management team able and willing to lead the required changes?

Source: Adapted from D. C. Hambrick and J. W. Fredrickson, "Are You Sure You Have a Strategy?" Academy of Management Executive 15:4 (2001), 48–59.

Are Your Differentiators Sustainable?

If competitors can imitate your differentiators, can you protect your current relationship with your customers? Imitation can erode competitive advantage, but some forms of imitation can reinforce brand loyalty to individual firms. Frequent-flier programs, for example, are very easy to imitate, but customers who have accumulated many miles with one carrier are harder to steal than those who don't have very many miles. Ironically, then, imitation in this case actually serves to increase existing brand loyalty and, potentially, to benefit both firms. Frequent-flier programs put up barriers to customer mobility, and without some kind of barrier that increases the cost of switching brands, a firm with easily imitated differentiators will have to rely on a continual stream of innovative offerings in order to sustain revenues.

Are the Elements of Your Strategy Consistent and Aligned with Your Strategic Position?

Your next step is determining whether all of the elements of your strategy diamond are not only internally consistent but that they are also aligned with your strategic position, whether the one you occupy currently or the one toward which your strategy may direct you in the future. The challenge is to ensure that your choices of arenas, vehicles, differentiators, staging, and economic logic are mutually reinforcing and consistent with your objective, whether it's to be a low-cost leader, a differentiator, or a focused firm. For instance, to be poised for the growth phase, your strategy will need to accommodate rapid growth through the use of acquisitions or significant internal development of additional products and services. If you do not do so, your firm will be marginalized. This may be an acceptable outcome if the intended strategic position is one of focus. Alternatively, if your industry is approaching the end of the growth phase, have you implemented appropriate cost-containment measures that will be required when additional price competition increases? The key is to make clear and explicit links between the vision of the firm, your strategy, and industry conditions. When these factors are aligned, the likelihood of achieving your objectives is maximized. When one of these features is not in alignment with the others, lack of coherence almost always causes the firm to slip behind competitors.

Can Your Strategy Be Implemented?

It does no good to concoct a brilliant strategy within the safe confines of your office at headquarters if your firm can't implement it. To test whether your strategy can be implemented, you need to make sure that it's aligned with the appropriate implementation levers. For instance, do you have the appropriate people, the necessary systems and processes, and incentives that are congruent with your objectives? If not, can you make these modifications within the organization in time to execute the strategy? Do you have the sufficient managerial talent and interest to pursue the strategy? One of the biggest obstacles to firm growth is insufficient managerial resources (e.g., time, people, interests) to focus on the details of execution. As a startup, for instance, JetBlue has set aggressive objectives for financial returns, growth, and a focused low-cost leadership position. Among other things, executing this strategy will mean continually hiring new employees who fit the company culture—people who share the core values of the firm. Otherwise, it will be vulnerable to the sort of labor problems that have beset other low-cost airlines. The most successful firms routinely discuss the integration of strategy and leadership. For instance, all discussions of new strategic initiatives will include answers to the question of "who exactly will get this done?" If there is no clear answer to this question, or if those individuals are likely to be spread too thin as a consequence, even attractive plans should not be given a green light.

SimConnect

Testing the Quality of a Strategy Applied to StratSim

Does your strategy exploit your firm's resources and capabilities? Take an inventory of what your firm can accomplish in the areas of technology, product development, distribution, production, cash, etc. For instance, if you believe your firm has incredible technology capabilities, are those capabilities being utilized currently and will your strategy take advantage of those capabilities?

Does your strategy fit with current industry conditions? Be sure to consider how the industry is evolving. What are competitors likely to do? How will changes in the economic environment impact industry evolution? Are customer needs changing in a way that favors one type of strategy over another?

Are your differentiators sustainable? Can you maintain your current relative advantages or can your competitors easily imitate them? As an example, if you currently enjoy a distribution advantage, how long will it take a competitor to match the quality and/or coverage of your distribution network? Are there ways you can maintain that advantage even as your competitor attempts to imitate you?

Are the elements of your strategy consistent and aligned with your strategic position? Each firm in StratSim starts out with unique characteristics, some of which are better suited to particular strategies. Make sure you analyze your resources and capabilities (cost position, market position, technology capabilities, etc.) not only on their own, but more importantly, relative to the competition. Students often mistake what they wish were strengths for actual strengths relative to their competitors. Make sure you analyze this with an impartial eye.

Can your strategy be implemented? Once you've decided upon the right strategy, how will your team implement it? Who (specifically) will analyze complex research to improve your product development decisions? Who will make sure your financial structure is sound? Who will insure you have accurate product forecasts allowing your firm to set production and capacity accordingly? In other words, how will you organize yourselves as a team and how will you manage time (another essential resource)?

SUMMARY

1. Define *generic strategies* and explain how they relate to a firm's strategic position. Strategic positioning is the concept of how executives situate or locate their firm relative to rivals along important competitive dimensions. The strategic-positioning model—Porter's generic strategy model—is an enduring classic in the field of strategic management. Porter's strategy model uses two dimensions: the potential source of strategic advantage and the breadth of the strategic target market. The four generic strategies are low-cost leader, differentiation, focused low-cost, and focused differentiation.

2. Describe the drivers of low-cost, differentiation, and focused strategic positions. Low-cost leaders must have resources or capabilities that enable them to produce a product at a significantly lower cost than rivals. Successful low-cost leaders generally have superior economies of scale, are farther down the learning curve, or have superior production or process technologies than their rivals. However, to substantially reduce costs over rivals, low-cost leaders generally have to be willing to make tradeoffs—they cannot offer all the features, attributes, and quality that a successful differentiator can. Likewise, successful differentiators will normally have to accept higher costs than low-cost leaders. To make a differen-

tiation strategy pay off, firms must segment the market so that customer needs are well understood, products are designed to uniquely satisfy those needs, and the products offered drive up a customers' willingness to pay. Firms that attempt to straddle both positions generally do not perform well along either dimension. However, some firms have been successful at integrating basic features of both low-cost and differentiation. Those that do, typically perfect one set of economic drivers before trying to complement those with the seemingly inconsistent drivers associated with the other economic logic. A focused strategy is generally the application of a low-cost or differentiation approach to a narrowly defined arena.

3. Identify and explain the risks associated with each generic strategic position. Successful strategic positions are still vulnerable. Threats to low-cost leadership include not having the resources necessary to implement the position, having low-cost drivers imitated by firms with better products, and not having sufficient quality to attract buyers. Threats to a differentiation strategy include increasing costs significantly to differentiate a product only to misperceive customer preferences, excessive cost to provide the targeted differentiation, and differentiating in ways that are easily imitated. A firm relying on a focus strategy risks growing too large, trying to meet too many needs, and then being out-focused by a more specialized company. An integrated position runs the risk of unsuccessfully straddling the logic of seemingly inconsistent economic drivers, resulting in neither a low cost position nor a differentiated one.

4. Show how different strategic positions fit with various stages of the industry life cycle. During embryonic stages, primary demand is just beginning, and customers lack good information on the relative quality of products. Thus, building a strong foothold and the capacity to meet growing demand are more important than aggressively differentiating products. During growth stages, building on early footholds provides incumbents with an opportunity to gain market share and move down the learning curve and establish low-cost positions. Maturity stages bring lower levels of growth, and information is widely available to customers. Differentiation can reduce competitive threats and result in higher prices. During industry decline, price competition intensifies and cost containment becomes more important.

5. Evaluate the quality of your StratSim firm's strategy. The quality of a firm's strategy can be assessed by answering a few questions that can be answered by the basic tools of strategy, including the strategy diamond, the VRINE model, the industry structure model, and the strategic-positioning model. First, you must determine whether the strategy and competitive position exploit the firm's resources and capabilities. Strategic positions such as low-cost leadership

and differentiation have economic assumptions that cannot be satisfied in the absence of complementary resources and capabilities. Second, a quality strategy will also fit with the external environment—the current environment and the anticipated environment in dynamic contexts. Third, a firm's differentiators must be sustainable. Fourth, all of the elements of the strategy diamond must be internally consistent and aligned with the current or desired strategic position. Finally, a quality strategy is one that can be implemented by the firm. Brilliant plans are of little value if the firm is unable to execute them.

6. Understand the drivers of low-cost and differentiation strategies in StratSim. Among other factors, the chapter identifies economies of scale, learning curve effect, and savings through product design as key strategy drivers of a low-cost advantage in StratSim. With regard to differentiation, you have learned that product enhancements, service quality, and consumer preference are central StratSim drivers of a differentiation strategy and possible competitive advantage.

7. Identify an appropriate generic strategy for your StratSim firm. How will your firm compete? Through StratSim, you are making strategic choices based on your analysis of your firm's internal resources and capabilities, and its external environment. These choices add up to a unique constellation of value chain investments and drivers that support your intended StratSim strategy.

KEY TERMS

differentiation, 136	focused cost leadership, 137	learning curve, 142	straddling, 151
diseconomies of scale, 141	focused differentiation, 137	low-cost leadership, 136	strategic positioning, 134
economies of scale, 140	generic strategies, 135	minimum efficient scale	willingness to pay, 148
economies of scope, 143	integrated position, 138	(MES), 142	

REVIEW QUESTIONS

1. What do we mean by *generic strategies*?

2. What criteria must be met in order for differentiators and low-cost leaders to be successful?

3. What is the relationship between economies of scale and minimum efficient scale?

4. What are economies of scope?

5. How does the learning curve work?

6. What is market segmentation? What role does it play in strategic positioning?

7. What is willingness to pay? How does it relate to strategic positioning?

8. How does the industry life cycle affect business strategy?

9. What are the steps in testing the quality of a strategy?

How Would **you** Do That?

1. Let's revisit the learning curve and change some of the assumptions made in the box entitled "How Would *You* Do That? 5.1." Assume that the first bike took 100 hours, the second 85, and the fourth 72.25. What would the incremental "cost" in hours be for the 16th bike? For the 124th? For the 1,000th? Try to find these numbers using both the formula presented in the feature and the learning curve calculator located at www.jsc.nasa.gov/bu2/learn.html.

2. Based on the information in the box entitled "How Would *You* Do That? 5.1," assume that you have determined that established leaders have such an experience advantage that you'll never catch their cost position. Devise a realistic strategy for entering and competing against an established player that has a significant low-cost leadership position.

3. Based on your StratSim firm's current situation, find the single decision that would have the greatest impact on reducing your firm's expenses and would not significantly lower your revenues. Calculate the expected impact of that decision using the pro-forma analysis in StratSim or using your own assumptions. Should you make that decision this simulated year? Why or why not?

4. Of the firms competing in your industry, list the strategy that you believe each firm is using (low-cost, differentiation, focused). Which firm is most successfully implementing their strategy? Why?

GROUP ACTIVITIES

1. Review the opening vignette about the three bicycle manufacturers. Use the strategy diamond and the generic strategy model to describe the positioning strategy of each firm. Based on what you know about the bicycle industry, can you identify any underserved (or overserved) segments?

2. Go back to Exhibit 4.1 in Chapter 4. Identify low-cost leaders from two of these industries. What seem to be the drivers of their cost-leadership positioning strategies? Are they the same? If not, why?

ENDNOTES

1. Personal interview with Trek executives, fall 2004; "Trek Bicycle Corporation Hoover's Company In-Depth Records," *Hoover's,* www.hoovers.com (accessed September 28, 2005); S. Silcoff, "Dorel Buys Biggest U.S. Cycle Maker: Gains 27% of U.S. Market Share with US$310M Purchase of Schwinn, GT Brands," *Financial Post,* January 14, 2004, p.1; www.montagueco.com/aboutusourhistory.html (accessed October 20, 2005).

2. M. E. Porter, *Competitive Strategy* (New York: Free Press, 1980).

3. http://www.autointell.net (accessed July 15, 2005).

4. Personal interview with Audi senior management, May 2003.

5. S. Targett, "U.S. Companies Win at the Scale Game," *Financial Times,* February 16, 2004, p. 9.

6. R. Sanchez, "Strategic Flexibility in Product Competition," *Strategic Management Journal* 16 (1995), 135–149.

7. See S. S. Liao, "The Learning Curve: Wright's Model vs. Crawford's Model," *Issues in Accounting Education* 3 (1988), 302–315.

8. A. S. Grove, *Only the Paranoid Survey: How to Exploit the Crisis Points That Challenge Every Company* (New York: Currency, 1996).

9. E. D. Darr, L. Argote, and D. Epple, "The Acquisition, Transfer, and Depreciation of Knowledge in Service Organizations: Productivity in Franchises," *Management Science* 41 (1995), 1750–1762.

10. D. Teece, "Economies of Scope and the Scope of the Enterprise," *Journal of Economic Behavior and Organization* 1 (1980), 223–247.

11. Interview with Mity-Lite corporate officers, November 2004. See also www.mity-lite.com.

12. C. Christensen, *The Innovator's Dilemma* (New York: Harper Business Press, 2000).

13. C. K. Prahalad and G. Hamel, "The Core Competence of the Corporation," *Harvard Business Review* 68:3 (1990), 79–91.

14. See www.sweatshops.org/; www.uniteunion.org/sweatshops/sweatshop.html; and www.business-humanrights.org/Home.

15. Personal interview with Jaguar executives, June 2003.

16. D. C. Hambrick, I. A. MacMillan, and D. L. Day, "Strategic Attributes and Performance in the BCG Matrix: A PIMS-Based Analysis of Industrial Product Businesses," *Academy of Management Journal* 25 (1982), 510–531.

17. D. B. Yoffie and M. Kwak, "Mastering Strategic Movement at Palm," *Sloan Management Review* 43:1 (2001), 55–63.

18. Yoffie and Kwak, "Mastering Strategic Movement at Palm."

19. Hambrick, MacMillan, and Day, "Strategic Attributes and Performance in the BCG Matrix."

20. F. T. Rothaermel and D. L. Deeds, "Exploration and Exploitation Alliances in Biotechnology: A System of New Product Development," *Strategic Management Journal* 25:3 (2004), 201–221.

21. J. Dial and K. B. Murphy, "Incentives, Downsizing, and Value Creation at General Dynamics," *Journal of Financial Economics* 37 (1990), 261–314; company annual reports, hoovers.com (accessed September 28, 2005).

22. This section draws heavily on D. C. Hambrick and J. W. Fredrickson, "Are You Sure You Have a Strategy?" *Academy of Management Executive* 15:4 (2001), 48–59.

After studying this chapter, you should be able to:

1. Identify the challenges to sustainable competitive advantage in dynamic contexts.

2. Understand the fundamental dynamics of competition.

3. Evaluate the advantages and disadvantages of choosing a first-mover strategy.

4. Analyze and develop strategies for managing industry evolution.

5. Analyze and develop strategies for technological discontinuities.

6. Analyze and develop strategies for high-speed environmental change.

7. Explain the implications of a dynamic strategy for the strategy diamond and strategy implementation.

8. Understand and explain the dynamic contexts at work in StratSim.

9. Improve your ability to make decisions in StratSim taking into account the dynamic nature of the simulation.

▶ **2000**
College student Shawn Fanning taps out code for a digital file-sharing program that changes the music industry forever. Napster is born.

▶ **2002**
Napster underestimates the competitive and regulatory barriers it faces and goes bankrupt after being sued by the music industry. Software developer Roxio Inc. buys Napster a year later.

▶ **2003**
Apple Computer begins selling 99-cent songs over the Internet to enhance the sales of its popular iPod. A host of competitors emerge.

ROXIO AND THE RESURRECTION OF NAPSTER

When someone draws up a conclusive list of the software that made the Internet what it is, somewhere among e-mail and Web browsers there will be a spot for Napster.[1] Napster was really two pieces of software: freely available "client" software that ran on home computers, enabling individuals to copy music to their PCs and play it for free, and a central Napster-run server that dispensed information about music. When it arrived in late 1999, Napster showed how easily music could be distributed without a costly infrastructure (namely, recording-artist royalties and record stores). The timing was also right; as consumer preferences were shifting to entertainment-on-demand, big players such as Sony and Samsung were providing stylish, miniaturized portable music systems, and there was little in terms of clear legal precedent against music sharing. By facilitating music sharing, Napster sent ripples of

► 2004
Digital music generates more than $300 million in sales annually, drastically altering the competitive landscape for brick-and-mortar music retailers everywhere. Roxio resurrects the "Napster" name for its digital site.

► 2005
Fanning launches Snocap.com, a new service for the music industry that can identify songs illegally swapped online.

1995   2000

panic through the music industry, which depended on the traditional music-industry infrastructure to generate a considerable amount of revenue. In June 2002, after four years of legal battles with the Recording Industry Association of America (RIAA), which represents every major U.S. music label, Napster filed for bankruptcy. At the time, Napster had listed assets of $7.9 million and liabilities of more than $101 million.

Because of the crash in the value of most Internet stocks and the bankruptcy of firms like Napster, times were tough for pure-play Internet businesses. Only a few hardy rarities, such as Yahoo!, Google, and eBay, managed to stay alive and prosperous. In the same year, however, the online-music industry came roaring back. At the beginning of 2003, Apple Computer started selling songs over the Internet for 99 cents each, and within a year, players as diverse as Roxio, RealNetworks, Wal-Mart, Microsoft, Sony, Viacom, Yahoo!, BestBuy, and Amazon.com had entered the industry. In one week alone, five of these large companies entered or announced their intent to enter the music-download business. Rarely has technology had such a rapid, radical effect on an industry's existing business practices and distribution channels.

Among these new, remodeled, and reborn companies was Napster itself, which had been purchased by Roxio Inc. in 2003. Roxio itself had gone public in 2000 as a software-only firm specializing in the development and sale of CD-recording products to both original-equipment manufacturers (OEMs) of PCs and CD-recordable-drive manufacturers, integrators, and distributors. In preparation for the Napster launch, Roxio courted two tech-industry players once spurned by Napster—Microsoft and music producers. Why Microsoft? Roxio supplies the CD-burning software bundled with all new PCs operated by Microsoft XP. As for music producers, Roxio, unlike the original Napster, intended to keep them happy by abandoning the idea of free music sharing.

The question for Roxio was whether it would still be around in five years, after the online-music business had shaken out. It faced competition not only in its original software business, but in its new online-music business as well. Approaches to providing online music included the following:

- The *à la carte approach* (employed by Roxio and Apple's iTunes). For 79 cents to $1.20, customers can buy any number of individual tracks (or albums for $9.99 and up). After downloading music onto their hard drives, they can burn it onto CDs, copy it to portable music players, or stream it through home-entertainment centers.
- The *subscription model* (used by emusic). Customers pay a monthly fee to download a specified number of songs. For $9.99 a month, emusic lets customers download 40 songs (65 for $14.99) and use them any way they want.
- The *streaming model* (favored by RealNetwork's Rhapsody). Music lovers pay a monthly fee to listen to as many songs as they can stand and, for a little extra (usually under a dollar a track), download their favorites.

The uncertainty created by the availability of competing technological standards was heightened by the fact that the idea of online-music consumption had only just begun to catch on.

Going forward, Roxio aimed to compete by keeping its hand in the turbulent online-music business while keeping a firm grip on its position as the number-one seller of CD- and DVD-burning software. This strategy meant that the company had to maintain strong ties with Microsoft as well as with other tech-industry heavyweights, such as RealNetworks, and the music industry—an array of stakeholders who view Roxio as everything from a partner to competitor. Moreover, Roxio would also need to keep close tabs on firms that manufacture CD and DVD burner/players. Why? Because they may enter the software business as a means of differentiating increasingly commoditized hardware products.

Perhaps the most telling factor in this story of dynamic strategy in dynamic contexts is the sale of Roxio's software business to competitor Sonic Solutions in January 2004 and the subsequent renaming of the surviving online-music company to Napster. In May 2005, Yahoo! entered the online-music fray with a service priced at half that of Napster's—now that's a dynamic context! Today, Napster has adapted its distribution model to include a Napster Light, where you can download songs for 99 cents, and Napster To Go, which gives you unlimited downloads for $9.95 per month.

Perhaps the greatest testimony to the competitiveness and dynamism of this market space is Napster's profitability: From the date of its spinoff from Adaptec through 2005, Napster has never shown a profit. ■

STRATEGY AND DYNAMIC CONTEXTS

In this chapter, we build on Chapter 5 by showing you how firms can develop resource-based competitive advantages in the face of dynamic competition. Although the notion of the industry life cycle you studied in Chapter 5 suggests that strategy should always be dynamic, because it must be externally oriented to be effective, the dynamic competition we refer to here requires dynamic strategies by virtue of the rapid and sometimes unpredictable changes taking place in the firm's external environment. For most industries, certain features of the industry are dynamic. In some industries, these features are central to success in the largest and most lucrative parts of the industry. As you can see from our opening vignette about the online-music business, dynamic strategies still require firms to make coherent tradeoffs between the economic logic of low cost and differentiation as the primary factors in any strategy for getting customers to buy their products. Dynamic competition, however, challenges a firm to improve its game continuously, and maybe even figure out how to rewrite the rules of competition.

This challenge is what differentiates the relatively stable context of strategy explored in Chapter 5—even for strategies that address one stage of the industry life cycle—from the *dynamic* context of strategy. Moreover, successful dynamic strategies increasingly require the nearly seamless integration of formulation and implementation and tend to reward an appetite for experimentation and risk taking. This is why, after understanding what constitutes a dynamic context, you will also learn how to use dynamic-strategy tools such as the value curve and real-options analysis.

We start by identifying the specific ways in which dynamic contexts can undermine competitive advantage. Then we'll discuss the development of strategies designed to address competitive interactions and two other primary drivers of dynamism we identified in Chapter 4: industry evolution and technological discontinuities (Chapter 8 is devoted to global strategy and, as such, addresses globalization, the other driver of change identified in Chapter 4). An important theme in this section is the effect of *change drivers*—the conditions that make contexts dynamic. Remember, however, that because change is often rapid rather than gradual, we must focus on strategy under conditions of *high-speed change*. Finally, we conclude by applying the five-elements of the strategy diamond to strategies in dynamic contexts. When you're finished with this chapter, you should be able to formulate a strategy for managing the dynamic context and prepare a plan for implementing it.

THE CHALLENGES TO SUSTAINABLE COMPETITIVE ADVANTAGE

It's important to understand why dynamic conditions can undermine competitive advantage, whether with blinding speed or over an extended period of time. Indeed, as we saw in the opening vignette, even though it may seem that an industry has changed overnight, many of the seeds of that apparently dramatic change may have been sown and nourished over a fairly long period. For instance, changes in consumer preferences and portable music technologies evolved over an extended period of time. In addition, change often results from a combination of drivers, several of which you learned about in earlier chapters and which are reviewed further in this chapter.

Recall from earlier chapters that competitive advantage is developed when a firm can create value in ways that rivals cannot. And the likelihood of developing a competitive advantage is facilitated by possessing resources and capabilities that fulfill the VRINE criteria. Firms with VRINE resources and capabilities are much more likely to be able to create strategic positions of low cost and differentiation than firms that lack such resources and capabilities. Challenges to sustained competitive advantage include anything that threatens VRINE resources and capabilities. Consequently, we need to examine the types of change that make valuable resources and capabilities lose their value; that make valuable and rare resources and capabilities become common; that make valuable and rare resources and capabilities easy to imitate or substitute; and that weaken a firm's ability to exploit resources and capabilities that satisfy the value, rarity, inimitability, and nonsubstitutability criteria of the VRINE model.

In addition, formulating strategies either to protect against threats from or to exploit the opportunities associated with dynamic environments generally encompass special cases of finding new ways to generate a low-cost or differentiation advantage. Because dynamic markets move at a much faster pace than stable markets, strategies for dealing with dynamic markets involve special attention to the *arenas* and *staging* elements of the strategy diamond.

The three dimensions that cause dynamic contexts that we focus on are *competitive interactions, industry evolution,* and *technological disruptions.* These categories are interrelated and are intended to help you think about the different facets of a changing competitive landscape. The relative speed of changes in these categories further complicates strategy in dynamic contexts.

Competitive Interaction

Competitive interactions are composed of two related factors: the interactions between incumbents and the interactions of new entrants and incumbents. The interactions caused by new entrants are a particular source of dynamism when they use a new business model—that is, a strategy that varies significantly from those used by incumbents.

Industry Evolution

Rivalry and the nature of competition, as we pointed out in Chapter 4, often change as a function of industry evolution—from differentiation to cost, or vice versa. Because a successful low-cost strategy requires different resources and capabilities than a differentiation strategy, a change in the basis of competitive advantage will cause advantage to shift over time from firms with the obsolete resources and capabilities to those favored by industry conditions.

Technological Change

Technological change may foster similar shifts, especially when change is discontinuous, so that it does not sustain existing leaders' advantage. Additionally, technological change is particularly risky when it primarily affects business *processes.* The Progressive Direct online-insurance market is an example of this. Progressive bypasses traditional and costly insurance agents and relies instead on direct sales through the Internet. In doing so, Progressive is able to offer some of the lowest-priced insurance products on the market. And to ensure that customers shop with Progressive first, the company provides quotes for competitors' policies, and will even sell them instead if a consumer prefers that. Progressive makes money both ways, through the sale of its own policies and through the commissions it receives from the sale of competitors' policies. Discontinuities that affect *product* technology often favor differentiation strategies. In the moderate to high-end segment of the photo industry, for instance, the current technological shift from chemical film to digital photography gives firms like Sony an opportunity to establish a competitive stronghold based on their electronic-miniaturization capabilities in an industry that it might never have entered prior to the digital age. Similarly, Apple's pricey iPod portable music device takes advantage of the technological shift reviewed in the opening vignette on Napster.

Speed of Change

Over and above any particular change driver, the speed of change is a critical factor in keeping up with the basis of competition in an industry. Speed tends to compound the effects of every

Product-technology changes make for a dynamic marketplace. New digital technology quickly adopted by Sony gave it an advantage over Kodak, which was slow to react.

change driver, whether industry evolution, technological discontinuities, or other causes. As the pace of change increases, so, too, must a firm's ability to react swiftly to (and even anticipate) changes in the basis of competitive advantage. In extreme cases, a firm needs the ability to *lead* industry change.[2] *Reacting to change* means detecting and responding quickly to unexpected customer demands, new government regulations, or competitor's actions. *Anticipating change* means foreseeing the appearance of global markets, the development of new market segments, and emergence of the complementary or conflicting technologies.

Familiarity with the scenario-planning tool that we introduced in Chapter 4 should give you some insight into the factors that are critical in the strategic ability to anticipate change. Change leaders are consistently able to develop new technologies, products, and markets; raise industry standards and customer expectations; and increase the pace and frequency of product cycles. Because of these stiff requirements, few firms are able to maintain sustained competitive advantage in dynamic markets.

Strategy and Dynamic Contexts in StratSim

SimConnect

You may find it helpful to think of StratSim in three somewhat-overlapping stages. In stage 1, which comprises the initial years of the simulation experience, the focus is on managing the company you inherited while formulating a long-term strategy and investing in that long-term vision. The focus in stage 2 is on the formulation and implementation of your strategy and the discovery of whether your initial strategy is successful both in terms of the environment and competition. Here is where you can compare your *intended* versus your *emergent* strategy. Stage 2 blossoms after two or three simulated periods into the simulation, and peaks about year 5 as the initial strategies of all of the firms are revealed. Stage 3 then gives firms a chance to regroup or to build on their early success as they reflect on the performance of their initial strategy, consider the actions of their competitors, and recognize changes in the environment. It is in stages 2 and 3 that dynamic context truly begins in the simulation. Change is rapid and competitors adjust quickly as participants learn more about how to create advantages and what drives performance.

BUSINESS STRATEGY AND COMPETITIVE INTERACTION

Major actions taken by one firm are typically noticed by rivals. In fact, because some actions generate strong *re*actions, wise strategists try not only to anticipate them but to formulate strategies that will result in an optimal outcome from the process of action and reaction. In this section, we'll review some basic principles of competitive interaction and its implications for strategy formulation.

Strategy and Strategic Positioning in the Face of Competition

How do these principles complement the principles of strategic decision making that we've already discussed in prior chapters? We know that managers can use tools such as the strategy diamond, the VRINE model, and industry-structure analysis to formulate a strategy and hammer out a strategic position. We know, too, that the firm's strategy and strategic position should be consistent with its strengths and its ability to seize opportunities presented by its competitive environment. Finally, we know that strategic-positioning decisions are supported by a wealth of tactical decisions made to implement and reinforce the firm's strategy.

Now consider the possible effects of all this decision making in a context of interactive competition. Four underlying phases of competitive interaction are summarized in Exhibit 6.1. Let's say that a regional title-insurance company has developed a strategy designed to help it grow into a premier national company. That strategy will involve a sequence of activities: entry into adjacent regional markets, followed by increased focus on differentiators designed to build brand awareness, followed by more rapid expansion through acquisitions funded by an increasingly valuable stock price.[3] In its first phase, such an aggressive series of tactical moves may go unnoticed or ignored by competitors. Eventually, however, if customer reactions in phase 2 appear or are anticipated to be positive, then other firms will formulate responses to the first firm's competitive behavior, as shown in phase 3. In phase 4, competitors evaluate the results of their interactions, and the cycle may then recommence.

Competitive actions can generate a wide range of competitive responses.[4] *Competitive interaction theory* suggests that because competitive actions will generate reactions, a firm's managers should predict reactions to its actions and use that information to determine what would be the best course of action given competitors' likely reactions.[5] Competitive action can be initiated in phase 1 in essentially four ways: aggressiveness, complexity of the competitive-action repertoire, unpredictability, and tactics that delay the leaders' competi-

conceptlink

In Chapter 5, we emphasize that **strategic positioning** involves the ways in which a firm situates itself relative to its rivals, especially with regard to three factors of the *strategy-diamond model—arenas, differentiators,* and *economic logic.*

Exhibit 6.1 Phases of Competitive Interaction

Source: Adapted from K. G. Smith, W. J. Ferrier, and C. M. Grimm, "King of the Hill: Dethroning the Industry Leader," Academy of Management Executive 15:2 (2001), 59–70.

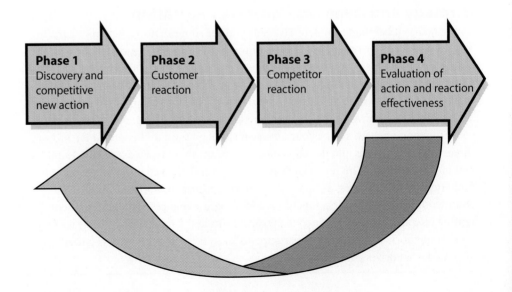

Phase 1
Discovery and competitive new action

Phase 2
Customer reaction

Phase 3
Competitor reaction

Phase 4
Evaluation of action and reaction effectiveness

tive reaction. The responses to those various actions have been shown to play out differently in terms of the competitive advantage of the challenger and the challenged.

With regard to competitive aggressiveness, strategy research has shown that a challenger can erode the leadership position of another firm by rapidly launching many assaults on the leader in a short period of time. Such interaction explains how Nike overtook Reebok's dominant sports-shoe position in the late 1980s and how, in 2005, SABMiller regained market-share-growth leadership from Anheuser Busch in the light beer segment. SABMiller did so through a combination of aggressive advertising that suggested that Anheuser Busch's beers lacked flavor and backed it up with consumer surveys saying that the SABMiller's beers had more and better taste.

Similarly, the more complexity and unpredictability inherent in these aggressive moves, the more likely the attacker will succeed in improving its market position. Complexity and unpredictability play to the attacker's advantage by confusing the industry leader and putting it on the defensive. As a result, the leader may also lose focus on the coherent execution of its strategy, as seen by the fragmentation of scarce resources to defending multiple competitive fronts. For example, Anheuser Busch was so thrown off by SABMiller's aggressive tactics that it responded by launching a new beer, Budweiser Select, and advertising it as a flavorful, high-quality beer. SABMiller turned around and pointed to the new product as further evidence that Anheuser Busch's products did not have taste.

Finally, to the extent that the challenger can engage in competitive moves that are difficult to respond to quickly or simply catch the leader unaware, the attacker can gain competitive market position. Strategy research has shown, for instance, that Nike's competitive success can be partially attributed to the fact that Nike initiated new competitive moves (e.g., promotions, new-product launches, endorsements) and responded to Reebok's actions much faster than Reebok responded to Nike's.[6] This same research has shown such tactics to hold true in industries ranging from telecommunications and personal computers to airlines and brewing.

When leading companies face new competitors who utilize new business models that are disruptive—strategies that are both different from and in conflict with those of incumbents—they face vexing dilemmas. Should they respond to these new entrants with disruptive strategies and, if so, how? These types of innovations essentially result in a possible change in the rules of competition within the industry. Such disruptions have several common characteristics. First, compared to incumbents, these firms typically emphasize different product attributes. Second, they generally start out as rather low-margin businesses. Third, they can grow into significant companies that take away market share. However, because of tradeoffs with value-chain activities that are essential to the incumbents, these new firms' business models cannot be imitated in short order by incumbents. Examples of these types of disruptive entrants are found in many industries, such as rental cars (Enterprise), retailing (Amazon.com), retail brokerage (E*Trade and Charles Schwab), steel (Nucor), and airlines (Southwest, JetBlue, and RyanAir). Devising appropriate strategies to deal with these types of competitive interactions is particularly difficult.

concept link

In Chapter 3, we define its **value chain** as a firm's collective capabilities, ranging from the conduct of simple tasks to the performance of complex processes, stressing that the ability to reconfigure value-chain activities in ways that are hard to duplicate can give a firm *tradeoff protection*.

Competitive Interactions in StratSim

It is essential in StratSim to anticipate competitive reactions to various strategies and tactics. It may be helpful to think of each tactical or strategic decision as having two dimensions. The first dimension is what your firm expects the outcome of a decision to be "ceteris paribus" or all things remaining the same. Examples of this level of thinking would be the expected impact of a 10-percent change in price on demand for your product based on current assumptions. The scenario planning tool that you learned about in Chapter 4 can further help you identify key areas of uncertainty and potential change. One can readily make these types of estimates using tools and research such as test markets, concept tests, and pro-forma analysis. In this context, decisions can be easily analyzed using NPV or ROI methodologies. If the investment is deemed to have an acceptable rate of return, the decision-maker will go forward with it. However, this is an incomplete analysis of the move because it ignores the second dimension of the impact of the decision, which is the dynamic nature of a decision. Strategically, this dimension may be more important, and is infinitely more difficult to quantify, which is what makes it more challenging to managers. How will the competition respond to this move? For instance, if the 10-percent change in price is matched by the competition, what advantage have you truly achieved? And once this price war has begun, are you committed to following it to the ultimate conclusion, which is the likely commoditization of the product category? It is this second dimension of the decision-making process that is often overlooked by managers and is one of the most important aspects of strategic thinking. Those who can take into consideration the competitive dynamic dimension of a decision are much more likely to be successful long term than those who make a series of short-term, reactive decisions.

Competitive Dynamics and the Positioning of Incumbents

Incumbents, such as Anheuser Busch, deserve special attention because they are increasingly viewed as Goliaths in the many David-and-Goliath competitive interactions unfolding around the world. In the mid-1990s, the front pages of the business press were littered with stories decrying the demise of the brick-and-mortar business and the rise of e-commerce and the dot-com. Inasmuch as most firms currently occupied real estate rather than cyberspace, the trend—or at least warnings about its repercussions—threatened most of them with extinction. Some, of course, did disappear, but most did not. As a matter of fact, the Internet phenomenon—and especially the breakneck speed with which it became a regular feature of the cultural landscape—underscored a number of strategies that incumbents can adopt to respond to rapid changes in the environment of an industry. As usual, the success of these strategies depends on a given firm's strengths and weaknesses. They are, however, particularly attractive to incumbent firms because they depend on—and can even reinforce—a firm's basic strengths. Each seeks a resource-based competitive advantage—that is, a position in which the exploitation of a resource makes that resource stronger and more resilient. Hopefully, the firm is organized per the VRINE framework to realize value from the stronger and more resilient resource.

Competitor-response strategies can be thought about in a number of different ways. Incumbent firms can respond to sources of industry dynamism through any of the following strategies: (1) containment, (2) neutralization, (3) shaping, (4) absorption, or (5) annulment. As shown in Exhibit 6.2, these responses typically vary in terms of the ease with which

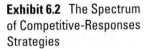

conceptlink

As we describe it in Chapter 3, the **VRINE model** holds that a firm with resources and capabilities that are valuable, rare, inimitable, non-substitutable, and exploitable will gain a competitive advantage.

Exhibit 6.2 The Spectrum of Competitive-Responses Strategies

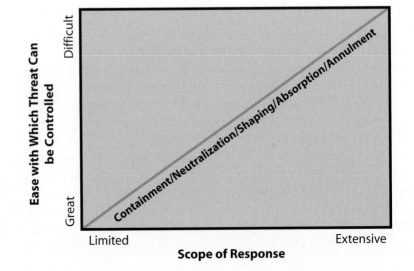

the external threat can be controlled and the corresponding level of action taken in response. We'll discuss and provide examples of each strategy in the following sections.

Containment   The containment strategy works well when the firm has identified the threat at an early stage. (You may detect facets of this strategy in the bundling or process-innovation strategies that we described in the context of industry evolution in Chapter 5.) Although firms sometimes select one of these strategies, they typically resort to a combination that aligns well with their particular resources and capabilities. American Airlines, for instance, can compete with Southwest not only by increasing the benefits of its frequent-flier program but by using its bargaining power to secure more exclusive airport gates (thus effectively raising Southwest's distribution costs at airports where it used to share gates with American).

Similarly, a large consumer-products company can release a copy-cat product that both leverages the new market created by a competitor and can be sold through its own existing channels. Consider, for example, the fact that retailers in industries from clothing to groceries typically charge *slotting fees*—fees that suppliers pay for access to retailers' shelf space. Because of this practice, any new product may bump an existing product from retail shelves, and if the one that gets bumped is a new entrant's only product, the containment strategy will have been highly effective.

Neutralization   If containment does not work, then leaders will try to neutralize the threat. Incumbents who pursue a neutralization strategy aggressively often succeed in short-circuiting the moves of innovators or new entrants even *before* they make them—or at least in forcing them to seek out the incumbent as a partner or acquirer. Microsoft, for example, is so aggressive at adding free software features to its popular Windows platform that new software firms routinely include partnership with Microsoft as part of their entry strategies.

A more common neutralization tactic, however, is the threat or use of legal action. (Because such action is often taken in concert with partners, we'll revisit it as an aspect of cooperative strategy in Chapter 8.) Recall from our opening case that one reason for Napster's initial downfall was legal action taken by the recording industry. In fact, the Recording Industry Association of America (RIAA) launched such a fierce legal attack on Napster that it forced even smaller Napster-like firms to stay out of the fray.[7] The German media giant Bertelsmann AG later acquired the Napster name when it realized that the Internet upstart was trying to engage in a legitimate music-sharing business. (When Bertelsmann couldn't turn a profit in the music-sharing business, Roxio was later able to acquire Napster and its assets for only $5 million.) Meanwhile, the RIAA also attempted to neutralize the Napster model by setting up an industrywide sharing standard, but this initiative collapsed when the major record labels squabbled about intellectual property rights, technology, and pricing.

Shaping   Sometimes, of course, it's simply not possible to contain or neutralize the growth of a new product, often due to antitrust laws. Moreover, in some cases, the new product may be attractive to the incumbent even if the incumbent can't gain full control of it. Today, for example, a state of peaceful coexistence prevails between the American Medical Association (AMA) and chiropractic medicine. For decades, however, the AMA had characterized chiropractors as quacks. Eventually, the AMA used regulators and educators as part of a strategy to *shape* the evolution of chiropractic practice until chiropractics transformed itself into a complement to conventional healthcare, as defined by the AMA.

Large firms can also use funding to pursue shaping strategies. Intel, for example, maintains its Intel Capital unit as one of the world's largest corporate venture programs for investing in the technology segment. The concept is fairly simple: Each investment is aimed at helping businesses that, if successful, will need Intel products to grow. In many ways, then, Intel is not only creating future markets for its own products but discouraging demand for competing products and technology and co-opting potential future competitors at the same time.

Absorption   The purpose of this strategy is to minimize the risks entailed by being either a first mover or an imitator. Sometimes, the approach is direct: The incumbent identifies and acquires the new entrant or establishes an alliance. In the late 1980s, for instance, Microsoft identified money-management software as a potentially attractive, high-growth market. It therefore entered into an agreement to acquire Intuit, the market leader, which offers such products as Quicken, QuickBooks, and TurboTax. Unfortunately, antitrust action forced Microsoft to abandon the purchase, and it resorted to a containment strategy—namely, by developing its own product, Microsoft Money (although Intuit's Quicken still has an 80-percent market share). If it's difficult to acquire the new entrant, the incumbent may also try to leverage a buyout by taking control over industry suppliers or distribution channels.

Annulment   Incumbents can annul the threat of new entrants by improving their own products. In many ways, for example, Kodak has so successfully improved the quality of film-based prints that they're superior to many digital-based alternatives. The annulment strategy, however, is less about quashing the competition than about making it irrelevant. Indeed, to excel at an annulment strategy a firm must often assume the role of first mover—a position that entails considerable risk. Kodak forestalled the advance of digital photography, but Kodak executives knew that in order to stay in the photo business, the company eventually had to shift to digital.[8] For this reason, firms usually resort to annulment only when the competition is otherwise unstoppable.

IBM provides another excellent example of a firm that annulled a competitive threat by sidestepping it.[9] In the early 1990s, IBM was faced with a flagging core business in PCs and minicomputers. Its first strategic shift catapulted IBM into second place behind Microsoft as a PC- and networking-software powerhouse. Its next move entrenched the company in the IT and Internet consulting markets, where it emerged as the largest firm among such competitors as Accenture. Next, IBM took on such companies as EDS to become the market leader in outsourcing IT and service solutions. Throughout this transition process, IBM leveraged its resources, capabilities, and dynamic capabilities in services and software. In many ways, IBM, though ostensibly on the defensive, was also wielding the tools of offensive strategy, effectively combining improvisation and experimentation with deft staging and pacing. As a result of this complex strategy, IBM not only emerged as a leader in information technology but, at the same time, avoided the commoditization pressures that affected PC firms such as HP-Compaq. Most recently, it has completely exited its core PC manufacturing business by spinning off this part of its operations to China-based Lenovo.

The Pitfalls of the Retaliatory Mindset

A word of warning about the five strategies covered in this section—and a good reason why you need to pay close attention to the sections that follow. Although they are certainly viable strategies for dynamic markets, many of the strategies are nonetheless purely defensive. If you rely on them exclusively, you'll soon stumble over an important pitfall of purely defensive strategizing: *Any firm that invests in resources and capabilities that support retaliation to the exclusion of innovation and change may only be prolonging its inevitable demise.*

Here's a good example. Ralston Purina was long considered one of the most efficient and competitively aggressive pet-food companies in the world. Every time a competitor made a move or a new entrant set foot in the market, Ralston responded with a twofold defensive strategy: undermining prices in the competitor's stronghold markets while simultaneously attacking its weaker markets. Although its defensive posture secured Ralston's market leadership for over 20 years, it also ensured that the company lagged behind the industry in terms of innovation. In 2003, Ralston sold out to Nestlé, whose constant attention to innovative products had positioned it to take over Ralston's slot as industry leader.

First Movers, Second Movers, and Fast Followers

Before further analyzing particular strategies, we must first understand the idea of *first-mover* and *second-mover* firms. Although the first- versus second-mover categories are related to the principles of competitive interaction that we discussed in Chapter 5, in this chapter, we focus on the relative magnitude of the firm's actions. Specifically, here we are talking about the introduction of a new product or service that defines or redefines a new

For more than 20 years, Ralston Purina fiercely—and successfully—defended its position as top dog in the pet-food industry. Unfortunately, the company put so much energy into its defensive strategy that it had little left for innovation. Ralston sold out to Nestlé in 2003.

market segment, whereas in Chapter 5, competitive interaction involved actions taken within a preexisting market segment. In particular, we need to know how each approach to technological discontinuities depends on a firm's resources and capabilities. The principle of dynamic strategies holds that firms consider their relative strengths when they determine whether to lead or to respond to change.

First movers are firms that choose to initiate a strategic action. This action may be the introduction of a new product or service or the development of a new process that improves quality, lowers price, or both. Consequently, you may see firms pursuing either differentiation or low-cost strategies here. **Second movers** are simply firms that aren't first movers, but their actions are important nonetheless.[10] A second mover, for instance, may simply imitate a first mover—that is, those aspects of its new product, service, or strategy that meet its needs—or it may introduce its own innovation.[11]

first mover Firm choosing to initiate a strategic action, whether the introduction of a new product or service or the development of a new process

second mover (often *fast follower*) Second significant company to move into a market, quickly following the first mover

First-Mover Strategy and the Industry Life Cycle
Being a second mover doesn't necessarily mean that a firm is a *late* mover; in fact, many effective second movers can legitimately be characterized as *fast followers*—even if the elapsed time between first and second moves is several years. Why isn't the lag necessarily detrimental? For one, new products don't always catch on right away. They may eventually generate rapid growth and huge sales increases, but this period—widely known as the **takeoff period**—starts, *on average*, at some point within six years of the new-product introduction.[12] Although the industry life cycle suggests that the drivers of industry demand evolve over time, it doesn't predict how *quickly* they'll evolve. Indeed, it may take some new products a decade or more to reach the growth stage, and only then will they attract competitors.

takeoff period Period during which a new product generates rapid growth and huge sales increases

By the same token, of course, *habitually* late movers will eventually fall by the wayside. Typically, survivors are either first movers or relatively fast followers. Late movers usually survive only if they're protected by government regulation, monopolistic or oligopolistic industry positions, or extensive cash reserves. Increasingly, however, competitive advantage results from the ability to manage change and harness the resources and capabilities consistent with first- or second-mover strategies.

The Pros and Cons of First-Mover Positioning
Intuitively, we tend to think of first movers as having a distinct advantage: After all, many races are won by the first contestant out of the starting blocks. The history of the Internet offers a wealth of first-mover success stories. The market dominance of Amazon.com, for instance, reflects a first-mover advantage—namely, the firm's ability to charge higher prices for books.

According to a recent study, a 1-percent price increase reduced Amazon.com sales by 0.5 percent; at BarnesandNoble.com, however, the same price hike cut sales by a relatively whopping 4 percent.[13]

However, if you take a close look at Exhibit 6.3, you'll see that first-movers don't always attain dominant positions. For instance, you are probably familiar with the Microsoft XBox, the Palm Pilot PDA, and the Boeing 747, but did you know that the first electronic games, PDA, and commercial jets were released by Atari, Apple (the Newton in 1993), and deHaviland, respectively? In some cases, a first-mover strategy can even be a liability, and in many others, the first mover isn't necessarily in a position to exploit the advantages of being first.

Exhibit 6.3   A Gallery of First Movers and Fast Followers

Product	Pioneer(s)	Imitators/Fast Followers	Comments
Automated teller machines (ATMs)	DeLaRue (1967) Docutel (1969)	Diebold (1971) IBM (1973) NCR (1974)	The first movers were small entrepreneurial upstarts that faced two types of competitors: (1) larger firms with experience selling to banks and (2) the computer giants. The first movers did not survive.
Ballpoint pens	Reynolds (1945) Eversharp (1946)	Parker (1954) Bic (1960)	The pioneers disappeared when the fad first ended in the late 1940s. Parker entered 8 years later. Bic entered last and sold pens as cheap disposables.
Commercial jets	deHaviland (1952)	Boeing (1958) Douglas (1958)	The pioneer rushed to market with a jet that crashed frequently. Boeing and Douglas (later known as McDonnel-Douglas) followed with safer, larger, and more powerful jets unsullied by tragic crashes.
Credit cards	Diners Club (1950)	Visa/Mastercard (1966) American Express (1968)	The first mover was undercapitalized in a business in which money is the key resource. American Express entered last with funds and name recognition from its traveler's check business.
Diet soda	Kirsch's No-Cal (1952) Royal Crown's Diet Rite Cola (1962)	Pepsi's Patio Cola (1963) Coke's Tab (1964) Diet Pepsi (1964) Diet Coke (1982)	The first mover could not match the distribution advantages of Coke and Pepsi. Nor did it have the money or marketing expertise needed for massive promotional campaigns.
Light beer	Rheingold's & Gablinger's (1968) Meister Brau Lite (1967)	Miller Lite (1975) Natural Light (1977) Coors Light (1978) Bud Light (1982)	The first movers entered 9 years before Miller and 16 years before Budweiser, but financial problems drove both out of business. Marketing and distribution determined the outcome. Costly legal battles, again requiring access to capital, were commonplace.
PC operating systems	CP/M (1974)	Microsoft DOS (1981) Microsoft Windows (1985)	The first mover set the early industry standard but did not upgrade for the IBM PC. Microsoft bought an imitative upgrade and became the new standard. Windows entered later and borrowed heavily from predecessors (and competitor Apple), then emerged as the leading interface.
Video games	Magnavox's Odyssey (1972) Atari's Pong (1972)	Nintendo (1985) Sega (1989) Microsoft (1998)	The market went from boom to bust to boom. The bust occurred when home computers seemed likely to make video games obsolete. Kids lost interest when games lacked challenge. Price competition ruled. Nintendo rekindled interest with better games and restored market order with managed competition. Microsoft entered with its Xbox when perceived gaming to be a possible component of its wired world.

Source: Adapted from S. Schnaars, Managing Imitation Strategies *(New York Free Press, 1994), 37–43.*

A first-mover advantage is valuable only under certain conditions:

- A firm achieves an absolute cost advantage in terms of scale or scope.
- A firm's image and reputation advantages are hard to imitate at a later date.
- First-time customers are locked into a firm's products or services because of preferences or design characteristics.
- The scale of a firm's first move makes imitation unlikely.[14]

First movers also bear significant risks, including the costs not only of designing, producing, and distributing new products, but of educating customers about them. Let's say, for example, that you're a midsized consumer-products company with a promising new product. When you stop to consider the immense power wielded by a certain member of your distribution channel—say, Wal-Mart—you'll recall how dependent you are on one giant retailer to help you attract a market large enough to make your product profitable. Meanwhile, certain second movers (say, Unilever or Procter & Gamble) may take the time to evaluate your new product and decide to compete with it only when it's developed some traction in the market (at some point during the takeoff period). Sometimes, a patient (and sufficiently powerful) second mover simply acquires the first mover; sometimes, a second mover introduces a similar product, perhaps of higher quality or with added features.

In short, first-mover advantages diminish—and fast-follower advantages increase—under a variety of conditions, including the following:

- Rapid technological advances enable a second mover to leapfrog a first mover's new product or service.
- The first mover's product or service strikes a positive chord but is flawed.
- The first mover lacks a key complement, such as channel access, that a fast follower possesses.
- The first mover's costs outweigh the benefits of its first-mover position. (Fast followers, for example, can often enter markets more cheaply because they don't face the initial costs incurred by the first mover.)

First Movers and Industry Complements An additional framework for assessing whether a firm should pursue a first-mover or fast-follower strategy incorporates the factor of *industry complements* (see Chapter 4). Exhibit 6.4, for example, provides a framework that explains why a number of notable first movers fared poorly despite apparently advantageous positions one would expect them to extract by virtue of being a first mover.

conceptlink

We define **complementors** in Chapter 4 as players who provide complementary rather than competing products, but we also emphasize a broader definition of *complementor* as any factor (such as an efficient distribution channel) that makes it more attractive for a firm to participate in an industry or segment. Here, the definition expands to include any asset that makes it more feasible to exploit an innovation or other opportunity.

Exhibit 6.4 Evaluating a Firm's First-Mover Dependencies on Industry Complements

Status of Complementary Assets

	Freely available or unimportant	Tightly held and important
Weak protection from imitation	It is difficult for anyone to make money: Industry incumbents may simply give new product or service away as part of its larger bundle of offerings	Value-creation opportunities favor the holder of complementary assets, who will probably pursue a fast-follower strategy
Strong protection from imitation	First mover can do well depending on the execution of its strategy	Value will go either to first mover or to party with the most bargaining power

Bases of First Mover Advantages

What's the moral of the lessons collected in Exhibit 6.4? Basically, they remind us that any firm contemplating a first-mover strategy should consider the inimitability of its new product, the switching costs holding together current customer relationships, and the strength of its complementary assets.[15] It should, for example, consider its distribution channels as important complementary assets. Industry key success factors are also complementary assets, as is access to capital.

Let's say, for instance, that a firm makes a critical breakthrough in cancer therapy. Before putting any product on the market, it will need to conduct a decade's worth of animal and clinical trials, and if it doesn't have hundreds of millions of dollars in the bank, it won't be able to pay for such extensive preliminary testing. New PC-software applications often depend on Microsoft because its operating system and bundled software constitute a whole set of complements—a product, a channel, and a potential competitor. As you can see from the illustrations in Exhibit 6.3, in the context of the framework summarized in Exhibit 6.4, first-movers tend to succeed if their initial advantages are unique and defensible *and* if they're in a position to exploit the complementary assets needed to bring a new product to market.

SimConnect

Hybrids Offer the Context for Analyzing First Mover Advantages

StratSim offers multiple opportunities for a firm to weigh the benefits of first mover versus fast follower strategies. Probably the most obvious example is the decision about whether to develop and launch hybrid vehicles or not. What are the potential benefits to being first to market versus a follower in hybrids? The drawbacks? Since hybrids require a three-year development cycle, can you afford to wait until the competition has launched a hybrid vehicle before beginning your own development? How does the hybrid opportunity compare with other opportunities?

STRATEGIES FOR MANAGING INDUSTRY EVOLUTION

conceptlink

In introducing the industry life cycle in Chapter 4, we emphasize the *evolution* of the industries in which companies compete. In Chapter 5, we explain the different evolutionary conditions of the **industry life cycle**—*embryonic, growth, maturity, decline*—that influence the dynamics of strategic opportunities and threats.

conceptlink

In Chapter 4, we explain that *scenario planning* is designed to provide an overview of specific trends and uncertainties and to outline a range of plausible strategic outcomes as an industry evolves over time.

conceptlink

In Chapter 4, we explain that **commoditization** is a common trend in the evolution of an **industry life cycle**.

Underlying competitive interaction, changes in rivalry, and first- versus second-mover strategies cause fundamental changes in an industry. Here we discuss strategies for industry evolution, followed by strategies for technological change. Because all industries evolve and mature, a firm's strategy must always anticipate the repercussions of change. As we saw in Chapter 5, for example, strategies may differ from one stage of the industry life cycle to another. The strategic management of industry evolution involves not only dealing with the industry life cycle but also strategies for changing arenas and strategies for responding to changes in a firm's environment. We saw in Chapter 4, for instance, that scenario planning can reveal the "trigger points" at which an industry is likely to undergo dramatic change. Moreover, a thorough understanding of industry evolution and its implications for strategy will help you better understand the three characteristics of the dynamic context that we introduced in the previous section—technological discontinuities, and speed of change. As noted in Chapter 4, globalization is a further complicating factor. Each of these facets also characterizes the larger evolutionary framework of an industry. One particular challenge associated with industry evolution that goes beyond the industry life cycle challenges outlined in Chapter 5 is the pressures of commoditization.

The Pressures of Commoditization

Managers must consider the pressure for change exerted by *commoditization*, which we defined in Chapter 4 as the process by which industrywide sales come to depend less on unique product features and more on price. As industry products become perceived as undifferentiated, the ability of firms to generate premium pricing diminishes. Consequently, differentiation strategies are vulnerable to the pressures of commoditization.

Research suggests that firms can choose from among four alternatives to deal with the pressures of commoditization.[16] The manager, however, must make difficult choices in terms of timing—for instance, if the firm changes its strategy too soon, it risks losing extra profits, but if it moves too late, it may never be able to regain the market lost to newcomers or incumbents who moved sooner. As you will see, two of these tactics anticipate commoditization, whereas the other two are typically more useful once it's clear that commoditization has set in. All four tactics have clear implications for four of the five elements in the strategy diamond—namely, arenas, differentiators, pacing, and economic logic.

Anticipating Commoditization Firms can take one of two approaches to deal with commoditization before it sets in. The first approach is a special case of differentiation. It is designed to protect an incumbent's ability to charge premium prices. The second approach is designed to reinforce a low-cost position. These two approaches are outlined in the following sections.

Value-in-Use Approach The first approach is a value-added, or "bundling," approach by which the firm increases service benefits while simultaneously either raising or holding prices. The value-in-use approach is a special case of differentiation. Note that if the increase in service, as a value-added feature, isn't valuable to customers, it simply raises the firm's cost base in the face of declining prices. Timken, a century-old bearing maker headquartered in North Carolina, provides a stellar example of this approach. Timken has actually increased profits on machined parts that most people would view as commodities because they're also available from numerous foreign competitors. Many of these competitors, however, market only a few simple products on the basis of price. In contrast, Timken bundles commodity-like roller bearings with additional key components in order to provide customers with products that exactly match their needs.[17]

Here's another example. Badger Meter Inc., a maker of water-flow meters, faced a flood of foreign competition and heavy domestic price competition in 2004. But instead of cutting prices in order to accommodate the global market, Badger chose to increase product quality, bundling the meters with state-of-the-art electronic radio-meter-reading technologies and targeting only markets willing to pay more for the significantly lower cost-of-use provided by bundled products.[18]

This strategy requires heavy investment in R&D—namely, the know-how necessary for combining parts that must otherwise be assembled by buyers. Critical to this innovative value proposition is a basic understanding of customers' product-acquisition, possession,

Badger Meter, Inc., a Milwaukee-based, water-meter manufacturer, faced a torrent of low-priced competitors in 2004. Instead of cutting its prices, Badger lowered the floodgates by successfully bundling its meters with state-of-the-art meter-reading products.

and usage costs. It's an approach that firms such as Timken and GE use to pass on higher quality, improved reliability, and lower costs to customers.

Process-Innovation Approach   The second approach to anticipating commoditization is *process innovation*. With this approach, the firm tries to lower its cost position so that it can further cut prices. These lower costs are generally found in process innovation, which enables the firm to reduce its own operating and service costs. One way firms do this is by eliminating services that others provide and finding alternative ways to substitute for those services.

Dell is perhaps the best example of a firm that uses this strategy. From the very start, Dell was able to offer the lowest-priced computers by buying and quickly assembling components for direct sale to knowledgeable customers. Dell carries little parts inventory and avoids obsolescent inventory by bypassing traditional distribution channels. It also has few returns because customers have designed their own end products. Perhaps more important, in pursuing this strategy, Dell also developed proprietary direct-sales processes that are now benchmarked by firms in industries ranging from automobiles to airline tickets.

Responding to Commoditization   More often than not, firms find themselves in the position of having to respond to pricing and other competitive pressures instead of driving them.

Market Focus   One approach to this situation is so-called *market focus*. This is a special case of a *focused-differentiation strategy*, which we described in Chapter 5. In this case, however, the firm transitions from serving a broad market to focusing on a selected subset of the market. It requires that the firm narrow, or focus, its customer base. It typically entails all of the following tactics:

- Maintaining or increasing service level (as in value-added strategy)
- Initially reducing the number of customers served
- Increasing prices (or at least avoiding further reductions)

Because this strategy usually emphasizes profits over sales growth, it generally results in a drop in market share. What is the value proposition? It permits the firm to target a small segment of the overall market that's willing to pay more for increased service. As with value-adding or bundling, however, the increased service must deliver value to the customer in the form of greater revenues (i.e., helping the customer sell more) or lower costs (i.e., lowering the total cost of use or ownership).

Although market-focus tactics work for firms in a variety of industries and situations, variations are most often pursued by companies that are in financial distress or in the process of restructuring. Thus, when retail chains Kmart and KB Toys laid out restructuring plans, they started by reducing the number of customers they served; in other words, they closed less-profitable stores. The message in both instances was the same: Given the firm's geographic location and customer relationships, some market segments or customer groupings were more attractive than were others.

Service Innovation   *Service innovation* is a tactic for achieving a cost advantage. It is especially challenging because it requires a firm to seek price competitiveness by eliminating services that were once bundled with its product. An intermediate move is often seen in commercial banking: The bank seeks to be price competitive in core products, such as bank loans, while tacking on fees for services that were once bundled with loans because they could be subsidized by higher interest rates and cash on hand. In other industries facing commoditization pressures, companies resort to similar incremental changes. Airlines, for example, may charge for food and extra baggage, hotels for cable TV and computer hookups. In an extreme case, a firm might remake itself from a high-price, high-service competitor into a low-cost, no-frills competitor. The fact that this strategy is rarely successful indicates how risky it is.

At the same time, however, we saw in Chapter 5 that it's quite difficult for a firm to be effective in multiple segments whose competitive requirements are diametrically opposed. Very rarely does a firm compete successfully in one segment as a focused differentiator and in another as a focused low-cost player. Strategies are most effective when firms leverage *unique, firm-specific resources and capabilities.* That's why the best response to industry commoditization is usually one of the following:

- Improve services and raise prices to serve a more narrowly defined market.
- Serve a larger market but lower costs and prices through process improvements.

Trying to do both doesn't generally work because it carries penalties similar to the stuck-in-the-middle situation described in Chapter 5.

The Forces of Commoditization in StratSim

SimConnect

In certain product classes the likelihood of commoditization is higher than others and you may find yourself trying to compete in this environment. First, how does one recognize that this process is underway? Generally, the forces of commoditization are present in a market in which competitors are lowering prices, margins are tightening, and product specifications converge. So how does one respond to this challenge? Just as outlined in the chapter, your firm has several options. One option is to stake out the low-cost position in the product class. Your success with this approach will be predicated on having higher market share (economies of scale and experience effects), lowering your cost position through upgrades and/or investment in technology capabilities (product and process engineering improvements), and carefully analyzing the cost/benefit trade-offs in the minds of the consumers to know which specifications to improve and which to cut for cost savings. A second option is to try to create a differentiation advantage through product development. This approach can be successful in markets where firms have not recognized the willingness of customers to pay more for certain enhancements. Of course, if your competitors match these enhancements, commoditization may occur at a higher level of expectations. However, it may be possible to stake out a differentiation advantage at a higher price if you can better meet the needs of a subset of customers. Third, by providing better service through dealership coverage and dealer ratings, one can attempt to offer a better product/service bundle where, though the product may be a commodity, the bundle is differentiated through the services offered. Finally, for all three options, recall that marketing (brand advertising and positioning, corporate preference and advertising) provides some measure of differentiation in the minds of consumers.

STRATEGIES FOR TECHNOLOGICAL CHANGES

Chapter 4 introduced you to the concept of *technological disruptions*, which can cause leading firms to fall by the wayside. A stylized version of how this process unfolds is depicted in Exhibit 6.5. The exhibit illustrates a truncated industry life cycle—sometimes called a double-S curve due to its interlocking industry life cycles. Industries do not have to fall into decline. Decline is often forestalled by the introduction of a new technology that propels the industry into another growth phase. A *technological discontinuity* is an innovation that dramatically advances an industry's price-versus-performance frontier; it generally triggers a period of ferment that is closed by the emergence of a dominant design. A period of incremental technical change then follows, which is, in turn, broken by the next technological discontinuity.[19] What is most striking about the diagram, however, is that different firms often operate on different curves. This means that a firm that excelled in the bottom left-hand curve of Exhibit 6.5 may be displaced by a new entrant that introduces the new curve in the upper right-hand corner of the diagram.

Keep in mind that *technology* is a very broad term. We tend to think of technology rather myopically, focusing only on pure technological innovations. However, the types of

concept link

In Chapter 4, we identify *technological discontinuities* as one of the key drivers of change in a firm's external context; we also observe that, as technologies which typically destroy incumbent technologies, **disruptive technologies** are usually introduced by new firms and should be distinguished from competency-sustaining technologies, which are often introduced by incumbents.

Exhibit 6.5 The Effect of
Technological Disruption

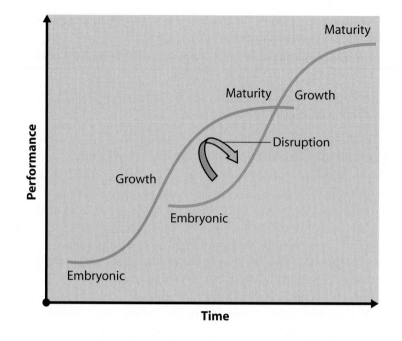

disruptions illustrated in Exhibit 6.5 may also be *process innovations* (such as Charles Schwab's migration to online trading), *application innovations* (such as GM's integration of Global Positioning Systems into vehicles through the OnStar system), and *business model innovations* (such as Amazon.com's move from online bookselling to becoming a logistics provider for countless retailers).[20]

If the new technology is introduced by an incumbent firm, it stands a good chance to continue its dominance. For instance, in the aircraft-manufacture business Boeing has long been an innovator in the development of new airframes and has persisted as a leading firm, though the technology of the most efficient design has changed numerous times. Some discontinuous technologies are introduced by new entrants, and because they change the face of the business landscape by altering who the leaders are, they are often referred to as *disruptive technologies.* When the new technology is developed by new entrants, incumbent firms face the very real possibility that they will be marginalized or eliminated. For instance, every leading firm in the minicomputer business was wiped out by firms that innovated and marketed the PC.

What can firms do to avoid or withstand a technological discontinuity? Research suggests that to withstand such technological changes, firms must either proactively create new opportunities for themselves or react defensively in ways to counteract the powerful forces of change. We reviewed these defensive strategies in the prior section. Here we review a few ways in which incumbents have been successful by creating new opportunities in response to dynamic markets or in anticipation of a changing market.

Creating New Markets

A strategy for dealing with and sometimes anticipating industry evolution or creating the technological discontinuities described in Exhibit 6.5 involves the creation of a new market segment. In this section, we will review the basic dimensions of new-market creation: high-end and low-end disruptions.

The Dimensions of New-Market Creation   Most companies have no trouble focusing on their existing rivals and actively trying to match or beat what their rivals have to offer customers. However, as a result of this focus on rivals' behaviors, strategies often converge. This convergence grows stronger the more conventional wisdom exists in the industry about how to compete. This type of convergence is often associated with incremental innovation. It will rarely result in breakthroughs that create new markets.

Creating new-market space, essentially the creation of a new value curve, requires a different approach and a different way of thinking about innovation. Instead of looking for the next incremental improvement, new markets are often created when managers create innovations that build on the best of the existing industry, import ideas from other industries, and eliminate some features that industry incumbents take for granted but which are not critical to key customers. This style of new-market creation has been shown to work in both fast-paced industries and those that are seemingly stagnant—both conditions that are ripe for significant changes. Fast-paced industries are dynamic by definition. Stagnant industries are often ripe for change—through new technologies that will send the industry on a new growth trajectory or through shakeout, which is a dynamic process but usually in a very negative sense for many incumbents.

The key to discovering a new-market space lies in asking four basic questions. These questions are illustrated in the Four Actions Framework shown in Exhibit 6.6. By answering these questions, you will be able to define a new value curve for an industry or at least a segment of an industry. First, what product or service attributes that rivals take for granted should be *reduced* well below the industry standard? Second, what factors should be *eliminated* that the industry has taken for granted? Third, what product or service attributes should be *raised* well above the industry standard? And fourth, are there any factors that the industry has never offered that should be *created*? By finding answers to these questions, managers could modify a firm's strategy either so that its products are further differentiated from competitors', so that its cost structure is driven significantly below that of competitors or, conceivably, both. In addition, by following this path, firms often generate net new customers; they grow the business by means other than stealing customers from competitors.

As a result of using the value-curve tool, firms can develop strategies that challenge and change the rules of competition. Research suggests that new value curves tend to fall into one of three categories: high-end disruptions, low-end disruptions, or hybrid.

High-End Disruption   A new-market disruption which significantly changes the industry value curve by disrupting the expectations of customers by vastly improving product performance is referred to as **high-end disruption**. High-end disruption often results in huge new markets in which new players unseat the largest incumbents. Incumbents can also use new-market disruption strategies. To do so, they need to shift competitive focus from head-to-head competition to the task of redefining the business model for at least a part of the existing market. A new-market-creation strategy, for example, may enable a firm to avoid the pitfalls of commoditization and evolution, but pursuing it doesn't necessarily mean that the same firm will become or even intends to become the industry leader. Cirque du Soleil significantly disrupted the circus industry by incorporating many features more common in Broadway theater than in traditional circuses, generating significant new growth and higher profits than any other traditional circus.

high-end disruption Strategy that may result in huge new markets in which new players redefine industry rules to unseat the largest incumbents

---

The key to discovering a new value curve lies in answering four basic questions.

Reduce
What factors should be reduced *well below* the industry standard?

Eliminate
What factors that the industry has taken for granted should be eliminated?

Creating new markets:
A new value curve

Create/Add
What factors that the industry has never offered should be created or added?

Raise
What factors should be raised *well above* the industry standard?

Exhibit 6.6   The Four-Actions Framework: The Key to the Value Curve

Source: Adapted from W. C. Kim and R. Mauborgne, "Blue Ocean Strategy," California Management Review *47:3 (2005), 105–121.*

Low-End Disruption   Recall the concept of *disruptive technologies*. Some disruptive technologies appear at the low end of industry offerings and are referred to as **low-end disruptions**. Incumbents tend to ignore such new entrants because they target the incumbents' least valuable customers. These low-end disruptions rarely offer features that satisfy the best customers in the industry. However, these low-end entrants often use such footholds as platforms to migrate into the more attractive space once their products or services improve. Indeed, by the time they do improve, these low-end disruptions often satisfy the needs of the center of the market better than incumbents' products do because incumbents have been busily making incremental improvements to satisfy their best clients' demands even while these improvements cause the firms to outshoot the needs of the center of the market. Southwest Airlines has been a very successful low-end disrupter, satisfying only the most basic travel needs and eliminating many services that had been taken for granted by established airlines.

Hybrid Disruption Strategies   As you might expect, most newcomers adopt some combination of new-market and low-end disruption strategies. Today, it may look as if Amazon.com has pursued a single-minded low-end disruption strategy, but along the way, it also has created some new markets, mainly by bringing more buyers into the market for books. Many Amazon customers buy in the quantities they do because of the information that the Amazon site makes available. The strategies of such companies as JetBlue, Charles Schwab, and the University of Phoenix are also hybrids of new-market and low-cost disruption strategies.[21] JetBlue's focused low-cost strategy, for instance, has been able to achieve the lowest-cost position in the industry by eliminating many services (a business model it borrowed from Southwest) but also adding services which increased customer loyalty. In addition, they targeted overpriced but underserved markets, thereby stimulating net new demand—both taking a portion of the existing market and creating a new market by attracting consumers who couldn't ordinarily afford air travel. Schwab pioneered discount brokerage as a new market but has since enticed legions of clients from full-service brokers such as Merrill-Lynch. The University of Phoenix is taking a strategic path much like the one blazed by Schwab.

The Value Curve

Now that we have described how firms create new-market space by being high-end, low-end, or hybrid disruptors, we'll describe the **value curve**, a convenient tool to help managers visualize how new disruptions might be targeted. The box entitled "How Would *You* Do That? 6.1" illustrates the application of this tool to the wine industry using [yellow tail]®.[22] The tool's purpose is to visually plot how major groups of firms are competing. This tends to reveal the underlying assumptions firms are making about the market and customers. The first step is to determine the existing key success factors as perceived by incumbents. List these factors along the horizontal axis. The vertical axis is used to rate the level of delivery of the major groups of firms. For instance, if room comfort were one of the key success factors that you had identified when evaluating the hotel industry, then you would rate establishments like Hyatt and Marriott much higher than hotels like Motel 6 and Best Western. The scale you use is not as important as the judgment you use in segregating different levels of products and services along the key success factors. Generally, you can plot firms by the central tendency of the major strategic groups, rather than each firm individually.

As you will recall from the earlier definition of strategic groups in Chapter 4, a strategic group is a cluster of firms that pursue similar strategies within an industry. For instance, even without plotting them you would assume that most of the major airlines would have very similar value curves and, therefore, constitute one strategic group. Plotting Southwest Airlines, as well as Southwest's imitators, such as JetBlue, or Ryanair in Europe, would probably reveal a strikingly different value curve. The next step is to plot the performance of each group on the key success factors identified. For each strategic group, you then draw the line that connects the points plotted on the graph—this is that group's value curve. It visually represents how those firms present their products to customers along key buying criteria. It conceptually represents the underlying logic incumbents use in positioning their products. Being able to visualize how competitors perform along these differentiators helps reveal the assumptions being made by the industry. It also helps you to determine which assumptions might be tested. Along these dimensions, question whether some levels of delivery on the key success factors can be reduced or eliminated; likewise, question whether some can be increased or whether new points of differentiation can be added.

A Shift in the Focus of Strategic Thinking Shifting focus from conventional head-to-head rivalry to creating new market space requires a different strategic mind-set. Some of the fundamental differences in assumptions between viewing strategy as head-to-head competition and thinking instead about creating new markets are summarized in Exhibit 6.7. Whereas the traditional view emphasizes actions and capabilities that are determined by competitors' moves, new-market creation emphasizes *actions and capabilities that eclipse the competition rather than meet it head on.* [yellow tail], this company discussed in the box entitled "How Would *You* Do That? 6.1," provides a nice example of such a strategy in dynamic contexts.

STRATEGIES FOR TURBULENT AND HYPERCOMPETITIVE MARKETS

You may already be wondering if anything could further complicate the job of drawing up a strategy that must deal—sequentially or simultaneously—with such factors as the industry life cycle and discontinuities. There is the dimension of *time*. Imagine, for example, that one or more of the change drivers that you have to deal with is moving extremely fast—so fast that you find yourself describing market conditions as turbulent or hypercompetitive. Such markets do exist: They're characterized by frequent, often bold, and typically dynamic moves on the part of competitors, and they seem to be beset by constant change and conditions of

Dimensions of Competition	Head-to-Head Competition	New-Market Creation
Industry	Emphasizes rivalry	Emphasizes substitutes across industries
Strategic group and industry segments	Emphasizes competitive position within group and segments	Looks across groups and segments
Buyers	Emphasizes better buyer service	Emphasizes redefinition of the buyer and buyer's preferences
Product and service offerings	Emphasizes product or service value and offerings within industry definition	Emphasizes complementary products and services within and across industries and segments
Business model	Emphasizes efficient operation of the model	Emphasizes rethinking of the industry business model
Time	Emphasizes adaptation and capabilities that support competitive retaliation	Emphasizes strategic intent—seeking to shape the external environment over time

Exhibit 6.7 Conventional Versus New-Market-Creation Strategic Mind-Sets

[yellow tail]® Creates a New Value Curve in the Wine Industry

Let's uncork an example of the value curve in action. With over $20 billion in annual revenues, the U.S. market is the largest contiguous wine market in the world. As a result, [yellow tail] eyed the U.S. wine market with great anticipation. However, the market is intensely competitive, and California wines command two-thirds of all U.S. wine sales. This intense competition is further fueled by the fact that wines are produced and imported from almost every continent on the planet, and new entrants increasingly sell their wines at very low prices.

The threat of new entrants to the wine industry is very high; suppliers (wine-grape growers) are powerful; wineries are concentrated (C8 is 75 percent); sales channels are powerful because of consolidation; consumers are powerful because of the breadth of choices; and substitutes (any beverage) are many. Moreover, complements, such as the *Wine Spectator* and wine experts such as Robert Parker, are also powerful, because they rank wines based on taste and price, potentially swaying channel and consumer purchases. These factors suggest that the industry is not very attractive to new entrants. In fact, an old saying in the wine industry is that if you want to make $5 million, you need to start with $40 million!

So what does this mean with regard to the value curve and dynamic strategy? If we map the wine industry based on the characteristics of the dominant players and those factors considered essential to success, we would produce a map similar to the one in Exhibit 6.8. Notice that Exhibit 6.8 captures the dominant strategic groups—wineries competing in the budget or high-price segments; while the third line portrays the unique position carved out by [yellow tail]. A new entrant could fight it out in the already hypercompetitive and overcapacity high-price or budget wine segments, or it could try to have a presence in both segments and use the resulting scale to its advantage. However, as you learned in Chapter 5, a straddling strategy is often a recipe for failure.

[yellow tail] arrived at this new value curve through a process of strategic steps taken over many years. It all began way back in the 1820s, when the first Casellas began crafting wine in Italy, moving to Australia in 1951 to pursue their hopes and dreams of a better life. After years of growing and selling grapes to local wineries in 1969, when the Casellas decided it was time to put their own winemaking skills to use, the Casella winery was born. A new generation of Casellas entered the family business in 1994 and embarked on an ambitious expansion to build a new winery with a vision of blending Old World heritage with New World technology. Today, Casella Wines is run by fifth and sixth generation Casella family members. In 2000, Casella Wines joined forces with another family-run company, W. J. Deutsch & Sons, to bring Casella wines and [yellow tail] to the United States.

You can use the value curve to see how [yellow tail] reconfigured the way it defined being a winery; offering wines at a moderate price; avoiding wine lingo;

»

encouraging impulse purchases with its catchy labels; and targeting only two high-demand wines, chardonnay and Shiraz. It also added new features that incumbents did not offer—easy drinking, ease of selection (again, only two varieties), and a spirit of fun and adventure. [yellow tail] used the four-actions framework to create a new value curve. It created alternatives instead of competing head-on with the major players. It converted noncustomers to customers by luring traditional beer and cocktail drinkers with its catchy labels and easy-drinking wines. Sold around $7 a bottle, the [yellow tail] Shiraz is the top-selling imported red wine in the U.S., while the [yellow tail] Merlot and Chardonnay are both number two in their respective categories. This year, the Australian brand could sell 8 million cases in the U.S.

Ultimately, the choice between new-market and low-end disruption strategies depends on a firm's resources and capabilities, and ability to then execute the chosen strategy. [yellow tail] conceived of a new way to approach the wine industry, but it did so with the knowledge that it possessed the resources and capabilities to do so.

Exhibit 6.8 A Value Curve for the U.S. Wine Industry

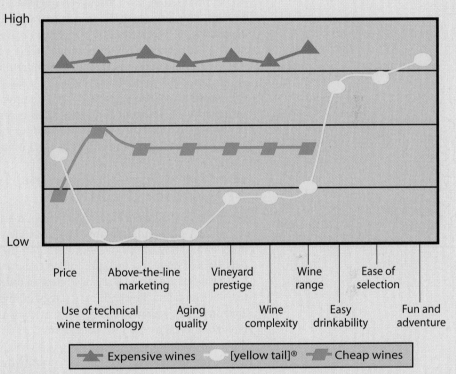

Source: Adapted from W. C. Kim and R. Mauborgne, "Blue Ocean Strategy," California Management Review 47:3 (2005), 105–121.

Sources: W. C. Kim and R. Mauborgne, "Blue Ocean Strategy," *California Management Review* 47:3 (2005), 105–121; Wine Institute, "Strong Sales Growth in 2004 for California Wine as Shipments Reached New High," April 5, 2005 (accessed July 12, 2005), www.wineinstitute.org; www.elitewine.com/site/index.php?lang=en&cat=news&art=159 (accessed July 12, 2005).

disequilibrium. What causes turbulence? It may be caused by short product life cycles, short product design cycles, new technologies, frequent unanticipated entry by outsiders, incumbent repositioning, and redefinitions of market boundaries as industries divide or merge.

It helps here to recount some recent examples of what might be considered turbulence, or at least hectic change. Bear in mind that, in reality, none of the usual disruptions is likely to cause overnight change in an industry. Often, however, firms perceive disruptions to be more traumatic than they are because they're finally surfacing after root causes have festered unheeded for years, maybe even decades. For instance, it took Microsoft 15 years to grow from a boutique software firm to the global operating-system monopolist with over $30 billion of cash on its balance sheet. Atari doubled its home-game business every year, growing from $50 million in sales in 1977 to $1.6 billion in sales in 1982. Similarly, Compaq Computer, prior to its merger with Hewlett-Packard, grew from zero revenues in 1985 to $1 billion in revenues in less than five years, overtaking IBM as the leader of the Intel-based PC market. Finally, Sony shipped 10 million CD-ROM players prior to 1992, shipped 10 million in the next 11 months, and then 10 million after that in the following five months.

In this section, we'll discuss strategies that may create rapid change, capitalize on it, or both. Any strategy that depends on rapid change requires that a firm's resources and capabilities support flexibility and responsiveness. In some cases, such strategies may prove extremely efficient, even though their outcomes aren't always positive. This situation may sound contradictory, but consider this fact: Firms that are leaders in turbulent and hypercompetitive markets are often like laboratories constantly conducting basic R&D activities. (We'll say more in Chapter 12 about new ventures and corporate *intrapreneuring.*) Although many of their experiments fail, the firms themselves succeed, either because their successes simply outnumber their failures or because the benefits of a few successes heavily outweigh the costs of numerous failures.

A Model for Competing in the Face of Hypercompetition

Competing in turbulent environments requires finesse in addressing the staging element of the strategy diamond. In many ways, strategies in this context require the regular deployment and testing of options—options with new growth initiatives, new businesses, and new ways of doing business. In this section, we review the findings of recent research on how firms manage the staging of strategy in order to succeed in turbulent or hypercompetitive environments. Research on strategy in this particularly dynamic context is typically anchored in so-called *systems, chaos,* or *complexity theories.* They're peppered with such biological terms as *self-organizing systems* and *co-adaptation,* and they're concerned with the same phenomenon—adaptation to a changing external environment in which change may be rapid and its direction uncertain.[23] By and large, they all share a basic premise: Firms need some degree of ability to thrive in chaotic environments in order to survive. In one study of several firms competing on the edge of chaos, researchers encountered the following three levels of activity, summarized by the curves in Exhibit 6.9:[24]

- Activities designed to test today's competitive strategy (defending today's business)
- Activities designed to lead to tomorrow's competitive strategy (drive growth in emerging businesses)
- Activities designed to influence the pacing and timing of change (seeding options for future new businesses and growth initiatives)

Improvisation and Simple Rules   The lower left-hand curve depicted in Exhibit 6.9 is the defense of existing businesses. Strategy in hypercompetitive contexts differs from that in more stable contexts in that the former is typically accomplished through managerial **improvisation**: managerial practices that contribute to a culture of frequent change dictated by a few **simple rules**. This view holds that when the business landscape was simple and relatively stable, companies could manage complex strategies. However, given the complexities that businesses in turbulent environments face, they need to simplify their strategies into a select set of cast-iron rules that define direction without confining it. The idea is borrowed from the practice of jazz musicians, who are, of course, masters of improvisation. Much of their music is sponta-

improvisation Managerial practices that contribute to a culture of frequent change, especially in turbulent or hypercompetitive contexts

simple rules Basic rules for guiding improvisation by defining strategy without confining it

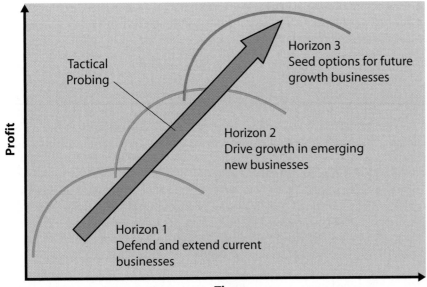

Exhibit 6.9 Creating Options for Future Competitive Advantage and Profitability

neous yet at the same time carefully organized around identifiable themes—simple rules—determined by the capacities and constraints of the instruments and musicians involved.

The range and diversity of musical outcomes is infinite, even though the practice of jazz improvisation acknowledges a few simple rules. Each player, for example, must know who the soloist is going to be, and the soloist must build off the work of other band members; players must expect occasional mishaps, and even learn to incorporate them into the performance. The simple rules typically involve autonomy, passion, risk tolerance, innovation, and listening. As with all good strategies, however, regardless of context, simple rules are not broad or vague (they require conscious tradeoffs). As we'll soon discuss, business strategies designed to accommodate experiments with processes, arenas, priorities, timing, and exit must also acknowledge a few simple rules.[25]

Sequencing Past and Future The middle and upper right-hand curves of Exhibit 6.9 represent activities focused on the future—the conditions toward which the change-oriented activities at the foundation of the strategy are aimed. At the same time, however, future products will embody indelible links to the past. In this model of business strategy, the bridge between past activities and future conditions is built on a substructure of experimentation and learning. For instance, S. C. Johnson found that one of its innovative home pesticide products in Europe could not pass U.S. regulatory hurdles, preventing its introduction in that country. However, through experimentation with its fragrances division, a key technology in the product was thought to be valuable and gave rise to the introduction of Glade PlugIns in 1993. S. C. Johnson effectively joined knowledge embedded in previously disconnected and geographically removed operating units (pesticides and fragrances divisions) to create an entirely new product category in the home air-freshener industry.

Successful new-business conditions are a reflection of those strategies that have been most successful. Ineffective strategies are jettisoned or marginalized as customers migrate toward firms with strategies that best meet their needs. Thus, managers use their understanding of the competitive environment to guide their selection and reconfiguration of portions of yesterday's business practices. Dell, for example, developed its direct-sales model for the consumer and small-business PC market, and when it entered the large-business computer-server market, it adapted its direct-sales model by providing onsite customer service. The model, however, had evolved: In this sector, while maintaining a very modest level of onsite staff for its largest corporate clients, most of Dell's consumer service is provided by a Web-based platform. With virtually a single stroke, Dell had changed the industry business model in a way that favored and further strengthened the model that had long been its fundamental source of competitive advantage. In other words, Dell's dynamic move forward into the server market was anchored in its past strengths in the PC market, and it has had a profound effect on the strategies of other firms as they've attempted to adapt to signals from the environment.

Tactical Probing   A striking feature of this model of dynamic strategy is the close relationship between tactical moves and strategy evolution. Simple rules enable the firm to excel in a given business, but they also give rise to experimentation that leads to options on future businesses—horizons 2 and 3 in Exhibit 6.9. Often, we don't think of the operating decisions that we call tactics as *strategic* activities because, in and of themselves, they're fairly inconsequential in affecting cost or competitive impact. In dynamic markets, however, many tactical moves can be used as low-cost "probes" for experimentation—testing the current strategy and suggesting future changes.

Tactics, in other words, can be both tools for competing today and experiments in new ways of competing tomorrow. Consider the case of discount broker Charles Schwab. When the company found itself being squeezed on one side by deep-discount Internet startups such as E*Trade and discount initiatives by full-service brokers such as Merrill Lynch on the other, it experimented with new ways of reinforcing customer relationships and identifying new markets. In particular, Schwab developed futures-trading programs, simplified its mutual-fund offerings, and launched Internet-based products and services. Some of these probes, of course, went nowhere (Schwab aborted a line of credit cards and a foray into online mortgages). But those that did succeed enabled Schwab both to further differentiate itself from bare-bones discounters and to gain ground in markets dominated by full-service brokers.

Setting Pace and Rhythm   Finally, as managers move from one horizon to another they must concern themselves with the speed and pace of change. You're already familiar with this aspect of strategy because you're familiar with the staging diamond of the five-elements strategy model. Many managers, however, fail to appreciate fully the role played by time and timing in formulating and executing strategy. Consider, for example, the various approaches to staging and pacing described in Exhibit 6.10. Obviously, attention to

conceptlink

In Chapter 1, we observe **staging**, as the *timing and pace* of strategic moves, entails the assessment of possible outcomes. In Chapter 4, emphasizing that industry analysis must reflect the evolution of industries *over time*, we underscore the importance of staging as a response to transitions in the **industry life cycle** and to **technological discontinuities**.

Exhibit 6.10 Staging and Pacing in the Real World

Source: S. Brown and K. Eisenhardt, Competing on the Edge: Strategy as Structured Chaos (Boston: Harvard Business School Press, 1998).

British Airways	"Five years is the maximum that you can go without refreshing the brand. . . We did it [relaunched Club Europe Service] because we wanted to stay ahead so that we could continue to win customers."
Emerson Electric	"In each of the last three years we've introduced more than 100 major new products, which is about 70 percent above our pace of the early 1990s. We plan to maintain this rate and, overall, have targeted increasing new products to [equal] 35 percent of total sales."
Intel	The inventor of Moore's Law stated that the power of the computer chip would double every 18 months. IBM builds a new manufacturing facility every nine months. "We build factories two years in advance of needing them, before we have the products to run in them, and before we know the industry is going to grow."
Gillette	Forty percent of Gillette's sales every five years must come from entirely new products (prior to its acquisition by P&G). Gillette raises prices at a pace set to match price increases in a basket of market goods (which includes items such as a newspaper, a candy bar, and a can of soda). Gillette prices are never raised faster than the price of the market basket.
3M	Thirty percent of sales must come from products that are fewer than four years old.

pacing and staging can prompt a company to think more seriously about the need for constant experimentation and probing. The concluding example of 3M may partially explain why that firm is consistently able to generate new and innovative products.

Staging and Pacing in StratSim

SimConnect

In stage one (typically years 1 to 4, though the stages overlap somewhat), since the focus is on managing your current portfolio, most of the outward competitive dynamics revolve around price, advertising, and minor upgrades. These decisions are more tactical in nature as incumbents wrestle with each other in the existing product classes. However, even with these more tactical decisions, your firm can get a glimpse into competitors' strategies. First is the position they inherited in the simulation. Are they a low-cost, high-volume provider or are they more positioned for a differentiation generic strategy? Second, what do their initial decisions indicate? Are they competing more on price, reducing costs, and driving volume or do the decisions indicate a desire to provide a more unique product that can command a higher price? Finally, firms should monitor long-term investments and prepare for the changes in the competitive landscape that occur in stage 2 (years 3 to 6). Which competitors are investing in R&D? Are the investments in overall firm capabilities or product development? Does the industry news indicate new product class introductions that will change the dynamics of this industry and challenge incumbents? How will your firm (as an incumbent or a new entrant) manage this change?

During stage 2 (typically years 3 to 6), each firm's initial strategy is revealed through new product launches, upgrades, cumulative investments, etc. This phase of the simulation is typically marked by fairly significant changes in market share, multiple new products, and many other indicators of the speed of change in the three dynamic contexts (competitive interaction, industry evolution, and technological disruptions). In some industries, only one or two firms will aggressively pursue new opportunities; in others, all will, and sometimes no firm does. It is important to recognize the intensity of the competitive rivalry within your simulated industry and manage your firm accordingly. In addition to recognizing the speed and intensity of change within your industry, your firm will also need to analyze how well your strategy is performing within that context. This analysis requires a cold, hard objective view of the world. No strategy is 100 percent effective. Some adjustments in execution or expectations will need to be made as the simulation progresses. However, unless your strategy is based on incorrect assumptions, it is typically unwise to completely redefine your strategy during the early stages of discovering whether the strategy itself will be successful.

Stage 3 (typically years 5 and on) is when the forces of industry evolution and competitive dynamics are fully revealed. Some of your firm's strategic bets will pay off and others, due to unanticipated changes in the environment, intense competition, or poorly executed decisions, will be less successful. Sometimes there are clear winners; other times multiple firms are successful. If your class is made up of multiple industries, comparing the evolution and profitability of these industries is extremely interesting. Though the underlying world is the same, the actions of the firms participating in that world can alter the landscape in very different ways. This is where the differences in the rates of change in the industry dynamics are most easily illustrated. But, just as is the case with managers in the "real world," your industry is what counts and you must adjust to the conditions that are present within your own dynamic context.

real-options analysis Process of maximizing the upside or limiting the downside of an investment opportunity by uncovering and quantifying the options and discussion points embedded within it

Putting a Value on Staging and Pacing

Just as strategy in dynamic contexts is understandably complex, so has the need to analyze the options that such complexity creates grown in importance. Although some of the analytical tools that can be used to analyze options are rather complex, it is valuable to have a general understanding of how they work. For instance, more firms are relying on such tools as **real-options analysis** to evaluate the substantive financial aspects of their dynamic strategies. Beyond the complex financial models that characterize real-options analysis, you should also see that a real-options mind-set provides managers with greater strategic flexibility in how they approach projects. Interestingly, firms that manage the timing aspect of their strategy well will also gain a better understanding of the internal rhythm by which they introduce new products. They realize that this rhythm must be synchronized not only with their own resources and capabilities but also with the needs and characteristics of key suppliers and customers.

The idea behind real options is to preserve flexibility so that the firm has an ability to be well positioned in the future when the competitive environment shifts. A perfectly positioned firm can become ill-positioned as the industry evolves, as new competitors emerge, and as technology makes current core competencies obsolete. By making small investments that preserve the option of taking a new course of action in the future, a firm can maintain its advantage. As an example, Intel invests heavily in internal R&D; however, it determined that it was unlikely to be the source of most innovations that could change how processing technology is used. Consequently, Intel made a conscious decision to invest in startups. By being a partial owner of the startups, Intel would have inside information on many new technologies being developed elsewhere. Intel has no obligation to increase its investment in these operations or to buy the products or internalize these innovations. However, by making these small investments, it has the option of doing so in the future.

Real-options analysis is based on the idea that strategic flexibility and adaptation are functions of experimentation and probing and, as such, should have implications for the way managers evaluate alternatives. Real options is a particularly useful tool for financially evaluating strategic alternatives because it recognizes not only that managers get valuable information after a new strategic initiative is launched, but that informed responses can make a big difference in the success of the new strategy. So, what are real options? Quite simply, a real option is *the opportunity (though by no means the obligation) to take action that will either maximize the upside or limit the downside of a capital investment.* The purpose of real-options analysis is to uncover and quantify an initiative's *embedded options* or critical decision points. Ironically, of course, the greater the uncertainty and flexibility in the project, the greater the potential value of having options in managing it. The traditional method of evaluating project performance involves the use of discounted cash flow (DCF) analysis; the most common is what is referred to as *net present value (NPV)*. NPV calculates the present value of a project by forecasting future cash flows and subtracting the initial investment. Some researchers now argue that NPV and DCF calculations should be viewed as a narrow subset of real options—one that's useful only in evaluating projects with little or no uncertainty and flexibility.

Increasingly, managers in industries characterized by large capital investments and high degrees of uncertainty and flexibility (such as oil and gas, mining, pharmaceuticals, and biotechnology) are beginning to think in terms of real options. These companies typically have plenty of the market and R&D data needed to make confident assumptions about uncertain outcomes. They also have the sort of engineering-oriented corporate culture that isn't averse to complex mathematical tools.

Although real-options analysis is not a cure-all for strategic uncertainty, the technique is getting much more attention not only in the fields of finance and strategic management but among other companies and industries as well. In addition to those industries cited earlier, the automotive, aerospace, consumer-goods, industrial-products, and high-tech industries are also interested in real-options analysis. Intel, for example, now trains finance employees in real-options valuation and has used the technique to analyze a number of capital projects. As a starting point, we suggest that you introduce yourself to real options by considering the following five categories:[26]

- *Waiting-to-invest options.* The value of waiting to build a factory until better market information comes along may exceed the value of immediate expansion.

- *Growth options.* An entry investment may create opportunities to pursue valuable follow-up projects.

- *Flexibility options.* Serving markets on two continents by building two plants instead of one gives a firm the option of switching production from one plant to the other as conditions dictate.

- *Exit (or abandonment) options.* The option to walk away from a project in response to new information increases its value.

- *Learning options.* An initial investment may generate further information about a market opportunity and may help to determine whether the firm should add more capacity.

An Example of Real Options at Work Here is an example of how a strategist might evaluate the investment in a potential new drug.[27] This example has aspects of all five of the real-options categories just mentioned—from *waiting to invest* to *learning*. One of the most dynamic industry contexts is in the biomedical sciences and the discovery of new drugs. When a pharmaceutical company starts to develop a new compound, it does not know if a new marketable drug will come out at the end of the project. However, opportunities and risks are tightly linked with each other, and this is specifically true for innovation investments. The higher the risk, the higher the possible return. We know this from most introductory financial-investments courses. The value of an investment can be exponentially increased if inherent risk can be limited. This is where so-called real options come into play. For the pharmaceutical firm, the "real" option generated through its innovation activities is the option to sell a "real" new product or service to the market in the future, after the development process has been successfully finished.

Let's get started. A pharmaceutical company developed a new drug that it wanted to take to market. The drug had to pass three clinical trials to test its efficacy before being reviewed by the FDA for final approval. Based on scientific evidence and academic research, the probabilities of passing each of the three phases were 75, 50, and 65 percent, respectively. The FDA approval probability, assuming the drug passed the trials, was 85 percent. The company estimated the costs of the entire trial-and-approval process to be $23 million.

Given all of this information about risks and costs, how can we use real-options valuation to determine if the company should proceed with the clinical trials? The equation, according to one possible application of real-options analysis, goes as follows: First, you create a decision tree incorporating all possible outcomes of future trials and all of management's decisions in each event. The NPV of each possible "end state" is calculated using the DCF model. Then, starting with the final year of the evaluation phase and working backward, assume that management chooses the highest NPV alternative at each decision point. This process clarifies whether it makes sense to abandon, repeat, or proceed should any of the trials fail.

Assuming you did the calculation correctly, it turned out to be optimal to reformulate if the first trial failed, repeat the second trial if it failed, and abandon the drug if the third trial failed. To calculate the NPV for the first trial, you eliminate the lower (unchosen) NPV scenarios to arrive at an adjusted NPV of $9.3 million (75% × 13.2 + 25% × −2.5).

If you were to evaluate this decision using the most common investment-analysis tool, DCF analysis, you would end up with an NPV of −$1.8 million. That calculation would have gone like this: First you would have calculated the overall probability of success (75% × 50% × 80% × 83% = 25%) and of failure (100% − 25% = 75%) and then the DCF value itself (25% × $62 million + 75% × −$23.1 million = −$1.8 million). The value of the decision-tree valuation, and of the real-options approach, is significantly higher because it recognizes the value of the real options present in the flexibility of management to choose at each decision point (in the event of failure in each respective phase) the remaining option that has the highest NPV.

In many cases, it is through a real-options mind-set, summarized in Exhibit 6.11, that firms also come to understand how this rhythm (i.e., timing and pacing of investments)

Exhibit 6.11 The Value
of Real Options

*Source: L.E.K. Consulting LLC,
Shareholder Value Added: Making
Real Decisions with Real Options
(accessed September 12, 2005),
www.lek.com/ideas/publications/sva
16.pdf.*

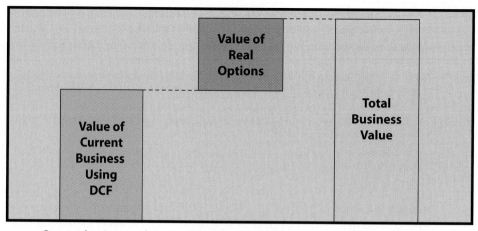

Current business value   +   Real-options value   =   Total business value

determines the pace of transitions from old to new markets, including the speed with which they exit the old ones. It's an important element of strategy to understand because firms often find it harder to drop old products than to launch new ones. Cisco Systems, for instance, has been successful in dynamic markets (especially telecommunications equipment) largely because of its ability to assess product life cycles, identify products that have no future, and then manage the exit strategy. Cisco continues to make money on products that it no longer produces by outsourcing both production and sales while retaining commissions on future sales.

FORMULATING AND IMPLEMENTING DYNAMIC STRATEGIES

In this final section we focus on the ways in which dynamic strategies should be reflected in your application of both the strategy diamond and the strategy-implementation models. The formulation and implementation facets of crafting strategy in dynamic contexts are brought together in the box entitled "How Would *You* Do That? 6.2," which focuses on the printing company R. R. Donnelley. (Because we devote Chapter 8 to a more detailed discussion of implementation levers and organizational structure, our remarks in this section will provide just a basic introduction.)

Focusing on Arenas and Staging

Let's look first at our model of strategy formulation, which is critical because it establishes a set of simple rules for describing the business and showing how it creates value. Of course, all five elements of strategy are important and must be managed in concert, but the *arenas* and *staging* diamonds are especially important. In addition to recognizing the need for dynamic capabilities, focusing on these facets of strategy is what differentiates a dynamic strategy from a strategy developed for more stable contexts.

The Role of Arenas   Arenas designate your choice of customers to be served and the products to be provided. In each section of this chapter on dynamic strategy—sections dealing with industry and product evolution, technological discontinuity, and turbulence—we've tried to emphasize that the strategist is always making important and reasoned choices about the firm's mix of customers, noncustomers, products, and services. The remaining four diamonds of strategy—vehicles, differentiators, staging, and economic logic, will tell the strategist whether the mix of arenas is consistent with what we called a *coherent* strategy in Chapter 2.

Moreover, the role of arenas in the firm's strategy will vary according to the factor of the dynamic environment being considered. In the context of *industry evolution*, for example, arenas must fit with a firm's resources, capabilities, and dynamic capabilities. With regard to *technological discontinuities*, the role of arenas, though overlapping with its role in low-end disruption strategies, was broadened to include noncustomers, particularly when the strategy is designed to create new markets. *Globalization,* introduced in Chapter 4, adds yet another dimension to the role of arenas: If a firm is going global, managers need to apply what they have learned about competing in one geographic arena to the task of competing in others. Finally, in dealing with *turbulent and hypercompetitive markets*, managers need to think of arenas as laboratories—sites in which to conduct experiments or launch probes into the possible future of the firm and its strategy.

The Role of Implementation Levers   In terms of strategy implementation, the previous discussion provides you with some perspective on the type of strategy that needs to be implemented. In applying any implementation framework, such as the five elements of strategy, the elements of the model must be balanced—in this case, a dynamic strategy should be reflected in organizational structures, systems, and processes that accommodate the strategic needs of firms in turbulent and hypercompetitive environments. One element of strategy formulation—staging—can also serve to bridge formulation and implementation because the staging component can specify how certain levers will be employed along the way.

Because accurate forecasting is quite difficult in dynamic contexts, scenario planning may be incorporated into the initial stage of the strategy. Scenario planning can be used to identify tipping points in the external environment that may signal when market demand or competitor characteristics are on the verge of significant change. Increasingly, real-options analysis (or at least some set of analytical tools to examine how time and experience may change the supply and demand characteristics of the target markets) should be included as well.

Finally, both the strategic leadership of senior management and the culture of the organization that they foster should reflect a commitment to reasoned risk taking, learning, and responding to change. Indeed, it's hard to promote core values that support the strategy implementation in dynamic contexts if top management doesn't practice and champion them. That's just one reason why we studied strategic leadership in such detail in Chapter 2.

Integrating Formulation and Implementation in Dynamic Contexts: The Case of R.R. Donnelley

R. R. Donnelley is one of the largest commercial printers in the world, reporting 2004 revenues of over $7 billion. Based on an analysis of the commercial print industry's five forces and its complements, you would conclude it is an unattractive industry, principally because it's characterized by extremely high fixed costs (large, expensive printing presses that need to run 24/7 to be profitable, excess industry production capacity, intensive rivalry, powerful customers). With the explosion of the Internet and digital and ink-jet print-on-demand technologies, multiple sophisticated substitutes and complements for traditional printed products and means of conveying information are available. So, in 2004 Donnelley's top-management team sought to redefine itself and its industry, embarking on a strategy to move beyond being a simple commercial printer to become an information-management company and a leader in marketing communications.

Recognizing that Donnelley faces a dynamic market and uncertain future, the following text describes how you might draw on what you have learned up to this point to propose a strategy for Donnelley that acts on its new company vision.

FORMULATION

Recall that our basic framework to formulate a strategy, or to analyze a firm's strategy, is the strategy diamond. Let's walk through the five elements of Donnelley's strategy.

- *Arenas*. Retain leadership position in providing information-management services to the burgeoning financial-services industry; focus new resource allocation on investments in proprietary-software development and

marketing-communications service offerings; use direct sales channels and leverage existing customer base; roll out marketing capabilities first in the United States, followed by Canada, Europe, Asia, and Latin America. We will focus on developing and leveraging core technologies based on proprietary-software and marketing-communications workflow. We will be the one-stop shopping source for our customers marketing-communications needs.

- *Vehicles*. We will focus on acquisitions to quickly gain the software development and marketing-communications skills, use internal development to push these skills through the organization, and build alliances with advertising agencies for sales and marketing of this marketing-communications solution.

- *Staging*. In the next 12 months, we will add a new corporate-level division responsible for the marketing-communications initiative, acquire the software and marketing companies for their expertise, and create a dialogue about the vision with our traditional print division managers so that we ≫

have a solid understanding of the new cross-divisional rules of engagement and opportunities. Within three years we will build market credibility, invest in more software and marketing-communications talent, and begin rolling out the vision and related marketing-communications offerings in non–U.S. geographic markets. We will also look at organic and acquisition growth opportunities to provide this solution beyond the financial-services industry (such as pharmaceutical firms and other heavily regulated industries). Alliances with advertising agencies and other creative firms will be sought out during this period. Within five years we will further push the global roll out of the vision and services and evaluate the potential divestiture of our traditional capital-intensive print assets.

• *Differentiators*. We will provide a single vendor solution focused in the area of marketing communications supported by world-class work-flow technologies and outsourcing capabilities. These differentiators will be offered in narrowly defined markets to ensure

customer intimacy, which allows us to show them how our services make our customers more efficient and more competitive.

• *Economic logic*. We will garner premium prices due to our comprehensive, unique, and industry-focused service offerings, proprietary-technologies and service capabilities, value-added consulting services, and customer intimacy.

IMPLEMENTATION

Our management team will allocate financial resources to the growth of the new division and the organizational changes required to align what we do in the firm with the new vision. Our team will invest its time in getting all divisions on board with the vision, see how their business fits the vision, and adjust the strategy so that division needs and capabilities are fully reflected. We also recognize that we will need to spend time building up a portfolio of acquisition targets and alliance partners and building relationships with those important future stakeholders in our vision and success.

To achieve this strategy we will reorganize, adapt systems and processes,

and change the incentive structure. As indicated in staging, we will establish a new corporate-level division that will be responsible for coordinating this strategy. The separate division will also make acquisition integration more effective and focus the objectives of future alliances. New systems and processes will emphasize working protocols across divisions to sell this Donnelley marketing-communications solution, provide seamless price quoting from a customer's perspective, and offer product development and consultative selling. Incentives will be redesigned to emphasize selling the full marketing-communications solution instead of individual pieces, such as printing. We will also reward, recruit, and promote individuals who move the one-firm concept forward.

Sources: Adapted from analysis of company's annual and 10-K reports, information provided throughout the company Web site at www.rrdonneley.com, and "For Digital Printers, the Profit Clock Just Ticks Away," *Printing News East*, July 22, 1996 (no author cited).

SUMMARY

1. Identify the challenges to sustainable competitive advantage in dynamic contexts. Dynamism can undermine competitive advantage—sometimes with blinding speed, but more typically over some extended period of time. Indeed, as noted in the opening vignette, although it may seem that the music industry has changed overnight, many of the seeds for that dramatic change were sown and nourished over an extended period of time. Technological discontinuities can alter the basis of competition and the requisite resources and capabilities for competitive advantage. The speed of change in an industry itself is a significant factor; it can either complement or compound the effects of industry evolution, technological discontinuities, and globalization.

2. Understand the fundamental dynamics of competition. Firms do not generate and implement strategies in a vacuum. Competitive interaction can be characterized by four phases, starting with the discovery by the focal firm of a new competitive action. The following two phases involve some combination of customer and competitor reaction. The final phase involves competitor interaction evaluation. Competitive interaction theory has shown that the way a competitor initiates these actions can determine its effectiveness. Actions that are aggressive, complex, unpredictable, and can delay a competitor's response usually result in the greatest competitive gains for the attacker. Specific tactics for hypercompetitive markets include containment, shaping, absorption, neutralization, and annulment.

3. Evaluate the advantages and disadvantages of choosing a first-mover strategy. First movers are firms that initiate a strategic action before rivals, such as the introduction of a new product or service or a new process that provides a traditional product or service of dramatically higher quality or at a lower price, or both. Second movers are relatively early movers (because they are still not last-movers), but delayed enough to learn from first movers. Effective second movers are sometimes referred to as *fast followers*. They are distinguished from late movers, whose tardiness penalizes them when the market grows. First movers do not always have an advantage because there are significant risks associated with being the first to introduce new products, services, and business models.

4. Analyze and develop strategies for managing industry evolution. Strategies may differ from one stage of the industry product life cycle to another. The strategic management of industry evolution involves these strategies, as well as the ability to *change* arenas and strategies along with changes in the environment. Using legal protections (e.g., patents, copyrights) is one way to protect a firm during industry evolution. Other value-added means of protecting a firm from commoditization include bundling strategies, process innovation, focused differentiation, and service innovation. A bundling strategy bundles increased service benefits with existing products (those valued by customers) while raising or maintaining firm prices. With process innovation, the firm seeks to lower prices through reductions in operating costs. A focused differentiation strategy in response to commoditization recognizes that to be able to extract premium prices, the firm must serve a narrower segment of the market. A service innovation approach attempts to increase margins by stripping away services that were formerly included with basic products.

5. Analyze and develop strategies for technological discontinuities. An approach for dealing with, and sometimes leading, technological discontinuities involves the creation of a high-end or low-end disruption. High-end disruptions generally result in the creation of a new market and require the introduction of new product or service features (and may even result in the elimination of some features) that are considered necessary by incumbent firms. Low-end disrupters offer products and services that lack many of the features taken for granted by incumbents, but the product still satisfies the basic needs of many customers. Being a disrupter is tricky, because new sales and customers come from niches that are not already being served or that are being served poorly by the largest firms. Over time, however, the "fringe" firms begin attracting the mainstream customers based on their combination of pricing and customer value added. Ultimately the choice of a new-market or low-end disruption strategy rests on where the firm believes its resources and capabilities lie. In the box entitled "How Would *You* Do That? 6.1" provides an example of value-curve mapping for [yellow tail] wines. Essentially, the firm must map the key differentiators in the industry (i.e., those items that drive willingness to pay) and then develop a strategy that makes the focal firm clearly distinct from its competitors and at the same time do so in a way that essentially creates a new market.

6. Analyze and develop strategies for high-speed environmental change. When one or more sets of industry change drivers are moving extremely fast, the market is often referred to as *turbulent* or *hypercompetitive*. Turbulent and hypercompetitive markets are in constant disequilibrium because of frequent, bold, and dynamic moves by competitors. Turbulence is a result of short product life cycles, short product design cycles, new product and business process technologies, frequent unanticipated entry by outsiders, incumbent repositioning, and redefinitions of market boundaries due to mergers and divestitures. Strategies for these environments require flexibility and rapid response capability.

7. Explain the implications of a dynamic strategy for the strategy diamond and strategy implementation. Vision is critical in that it serves as a set of simple rules that describe the business and how it creates value. The example from R. R. Donnelley in the box entitled "How Would *You* Do That? 6.2" shows how formulation and implementation can be woven together in a sophisticated manner to achieve Donnelley's new simple-rules vision. Although all five elements of strategy are important and must be managed in concert, the arenas and staging diamonds are perhaps most important in dynamic markets. And, like the five elements of strategy, a balance among the implementation levers is critical. These levers must accommodate environmental turbulence and hypercompetitive environments. The strategic flexibility demanded of these environments requires that organization structure and systems can be easily decoupled and recombined as circumstances change. Rigid bureaucracy is generally incompatible with turbulent environments. Strategic leadership must further support the firm's ability to identify the need for and undertake strategic change.

8. Understand and explain the dynamic contexts at work in StratSim.
You learned that the StratSim experience evolves over three somewhat overlapping stages. In stage 1 your team will likely focus on running the company you inherited, along with formulating your future strategy based on your resource base and competitive landscape. In stage 2 you have the opportunity to compare your intended strategy versus that which your company is actually realizing. In stage 3 you see firms more clearly staking out their commitments and at the same time the competitive environment is characterized by rapid change and dynamism.

9. Improve your ability to make decisions in StratSim taking into account the dynamic nature of the simulation.
While there are many facets of your StratSim experience that teach you about the dynamic nature of strategy, two are particularly salient. First, you will see the dynamics as a result of your strategic choices and the competitive responses of the other firms in your industry. Here you learn that competitive interaction is a function of what your firm does, and may be planning to do, and what other firms do in response, or plan to do in the future. Second, you will see how the use of pacing and staging will help you roll out your strategy, as well as give you some flexibility to adapt your strategy to emerging consumer preferences, other market opportunities, and competitors' moves.

KEY TERMS

first mover, 173
high-end disruption, 181
improvisation, 186

low-end disruption, 182
real-options analysis, 190

second mover, 173
simple rules, 186

takeoff period, 173
value curve, 182

REVIEW QUESTIONS

1. What are four sets of challenges to sustained competitive advantage outlined in this chapter?

2. What is the relationship between first and second movers?

3. What is industry commoditization? What are two strategies a firm may undertake to combat industry commoditization?

4. What is a new-market-creation strategy?

5. What is a low-end disruption strategy?

6. What are the three layers of activity that underlie strategies for turbulent and hypercompetitive markets?

7. What is the role of timing and pacing in strategies for turbulent and hypercompetitive markets?

8. How might you apply real-options analysis, financially and conceptually, in the context of strategies for turbulent and hypercompetitive markets?

9. What five defensive strategies might industry incumbents pursue in turbulent and hypercompetitive markets?

10. What are the implications of dynamic strategies for strategy formulation and implementation?

How Would you Do That?

1. Pick an industry and use the box entitled "How Would *You* Do That? 6.1" as a template to map its value curve. What are the key success factors that define industry participation? Does there appear to be more than one strategic group in this industry operating with different value curves? Can you come up with a new value curve that would change the industry?

2. Identify an industry that you believe is very dynamic and identify the drivers of that dynamism. Now pick a firm in that industry and formulate a strategy and basic implementation scheme to exploit its dynamic context. Use the R. R. Donnelley example presented in the box entitled "How Would *You* Do That? 6.2" as a template for your recommendations.

3. Choose an underserved vehicle class or customer in StratSim that you believe offers the most potential to your firm. Your analysis should include strategic fit, market potential and competitive dynamics. Create a plan for the initial launch (first mover to follower), and a five-year projection that includes likely competitor reactions. Be sure to include a list of the assumptions your plan uses, potential risks and how you would respond to those risks if they materialize.

GROUP ACTIVITIES

1. If you were the CEO of Napster (which started out as Roxio in the opening vignette), what material from this chapter would be most relevant to you? How would this material help you to formulate a strategy? What might key components of that strategy be? Now put yourself in Microsoft's shoes; would you see either Sonic Solutions or Napster as a threat? If so, what strategy would you formulate in response?

2. Review the list of first- and second-mover firms in Exhibit 6.3. What specific resources and capabilities do you think successful first movers must possess? What specific resources and capabilities do you think successful second movers and fast followers must possess? Do you think that a firm could be both a first mover and fast follower if it wanted to be?

3. Choose one of your vehicles that you believe faces the greatest risk of commoditization. What strategies and tactics can you employ to implement a differentiation advantage? What decisions could you employ to create a low-cost advantage? Which do you think would be more effective and why?

ENDNOTES

1. N. Wingfield and E. Smith, "With the Web Shaking Up Music, a Free-for-All in Online Songs," *Wall Street Journal,* November 19, 2003, A1; N. Wingfield and E. Smith, "Microsoft Plans to Sell Music over the Web," *Wall Street Journal,* November 17, 2003, A1; www.roxio.com (accessed June 28, 2005). "Napster Lives Again as Legal Distributor of Music on the Web," *The Wall Street Journal,* 25 February 2003, A10; N. Wingfield, "Roxio Agrees to Acquire Napster Assets," *The Wall Street Journal,* November 18, 2002, B4.

2. S. Brown and K. Eisenhardt, *Competing on the Edge* (Boston: Harvard Business School Press, 1998).

3. D. C. Hambrick and J. W. Fredrickson, "Are You Sure You Have a Strategy?" *Academy of Management Executive* 15:4 (2001), 48–59.

4. M. Chen, "Competitor Analysis and Interfirm Rivalry: Toward a Theoretical Integration," *Academy of Management Review* 21 (1996), 100–134; M. Chen and D. C. Hambrick, "Speed, Stealth, and Selective Attack: How Small Firms Differ from Large Firms in Competitive Behavior," *Academy of Management Journal* 38 (1995), 453–482.

5. A. M. Brandenburger and B. J. Nalebuff, *Co-Opetition* (New York: Currency Doubleday, 1996).

6. K. G. Smith, W. J. Ferrier, and C. M. Grimm, "King of the Hill: Dethroning the Industry Leader," *Academy of Management Executive* 15:2 (2001), 59–70.

7. www.riaa.org (accessed July 28, 2005).

8. www.kodak.com (accessed July 15, 2005).

9. R. D'Aveni, "The Empire Strikes Back: Counterrevolutionary Strategies for Industry Leaders," *Harvard Business Review* 80:11 (November 2002), 5–12.

10. M. E. Porter, *Competitive Strategy* (New York: Free Press, 1979), 232–233.

11. For a particularly rich discussion of these differences, see S. Schnaars, *Managing Imitation Strategies* (New York: Free Press, 1994), 12–14.

12. G. Tellis, S. Stremersch, and E. Yin, "The International Takeoff of New Products: Economics, Culture, and Country Innovativeness," *Marketing Science* 22:2 (2003), 161–187.

13. A. Goolsbee and J. Chevalier, "Price Competition Online: Amazon versus Barnes and Noble," *Quantitative Marketing and Economics* 1:2 (June, 2003), 203–222.

14. Schnaars, *Managing Imitation Strategies,* 37–43; J. Covin, D. Slevin, and M. Heeley, "Pioneers and Followers: Competitive Tactics, Environment, and Growth," *Journal of Business Venturing* 15:2 (1999), 175–210.

15. This framework is adapted from A. Afuah, *Innovation Management: Strategies, Implementation, and Profits,* 2nd ed. (New York: Oxford University Press, 2003). An earlier version appears in Schnaars, *Managing Imitation Strategies,* 12–14.

16. K. Rangan and G. Bowman, "Beating the Commodity Magnet," *Industrial Marketing Management* 21 (1992), 215–224; P. Kotler, "Managing Products through Their Product Life Cycle," in *Marketing Management: Planning, Implementation, and Control,* 7th ed. (Upper Saddle River, NJ: Prentice Hall, 1991), P. Kotler, "Product Life-Cycle Marketing Strategies," in *Mar-*

keting Management, 11th ed. (Upper Saddle River, NJ: Prentice Hall, 2003), 328–339.

17. C. Tejada, "The Allure of 'Bundling,'" *Wall Street Journal,* October 7, 2003, B1.

18. www.badgermeter.com (accessed July 15, 2005).

19. P. Anderson and M. L. Tushman, "Technological Discontinuities and Dominant Designs: A Cyclical Model of Technological Change," *Administrative Science Quarterly* 35 (1990), 604–633.

20. G. A. Moore, "Darwin and the Demon: Innovating within Established Enterprises" *Harvard Business Review* 82:7/8 (2004), 86–92.

21. These examples are drawn from an extensive and detailed list provided by C. Christensen and M. Raynor, The Innovator's Solution. Boston, MA: Harvard Business School Press (2003).

22. W. C. Kim and R. Mauborgne, "Value Innovation: The Strategic Logic of High Growth," *Harvard Business Review* 75:1 (1997), 102–113; Kim and Mauborgne, "Charting Your Company's Future," *Harvard Business Review* 80:6 (2002), 76–82.

23. See, for example, S. Kauffman, *At Home in the Universe: The Search for the Laws of Self-Organization and Complexity* (New York: Oxford University Press, 1995); M. Gell-Mann, *The Quark and the Jaguar* (New York: W. H. Freeman, 1994); J. Casti, *Complexification: Explaining a Paradoxical World through the Science of Surprise* (New York: HarperCollins, 1994); R. Lewin, *Complexity: Life at the Edge of Chaos* (New York: Macmillan, 1992).

24. Brown and Eisenhardt, *Competing on the Edge.*

25. K. Eisenhardt and D. Sull, "Strategy as Simple Rules," *Harvard Business Review* 79:1 (2001), 106–116.

26. M. Amram and N. Kulatilaka, *Real Options: Managing Strategic Investment in an Uncertain World* (New York: Oxford University Press, 1998); E. Teach, "Will Real Options Take Root? Why Companies Have Been Slow to Adopt the Valuation Technique," *CFO Magazine,* July 1, 2003, 73.

27. Example adapted from J. Daum, *The New Economy Analyst Report,* December 28, 2001.

Looking at International Strategies

After studying this chapter, you should be able to:

1. Define *international strategy* and identify its implications for the strategy diamond.

2. Understand why a firm would want to expand internationally and explain the relationship between international strategy and competitive advantage.

3. Describe different vehicles for international expansion.

4. Apply different international strategy configurations.

5. Outline the international strategy implications of the static and dynamic perspectives.

6. Explore exporting and importing options using StratSim.

► **Dell in the United States**
Michael Dell founds Dell in 1985, based on a strategy of selling PCs directly to individual U.S. consumers. By 2001, Dell ranks number one in global market share.

► **Dell in India**
To sell computers to individual consumers in India, Dell changes its strategy and begins distributing its products through Indian distributors.

1980   1985

DELL GOES TO CHINA

In 1999, Dell was the second-largest player in both the U.S. and worldwide PC markets.[1] However, Dell had a negligible presence in many regions of the world, most notably China, where it ranked a distant seventh in PC sales. Dell executives considered this lagging position to be problematic, given that computer-industry analysts were predicting that by 2002, China would become the second-largest PC market behind the United States. Consequently, Dell set ambitious China sales-growth targets in 1999, with a goal of achieving 10 percent of its global PC sales from China by 2002, which would amount to nearly 50 percent of PC sales for the entire Asian region.

For many U.S. companies, China is attractive simply due to its size, but it is also a competitive environment fraught with many hazards—and it can turn potential profits into a cash-flow black hole. Although

▶ **Dell in China**
To make headway in China, Dell first tapped a network of Chinese distributors, then sales through Chinese retailers, to sell PCs to individual consumers. In five years' time, Dell transforms itself from a market laggard to a market leader in China, and today uses product kiosks in China, just as it does in the United States, to let consumers look at the systems. If they decide to buy, they place their order online at the kiosk or call and order by phone later.

1995   2000

sourcing components and products from China has proven successful for many global firms, tapping the Chinese consumer market appears to be an entirely different matter. By 1999, for example, Motorola and Kodak had already sunk many millions of dollars into China hoping for large domestic market share and commensurate profits but instead were reeling from enormous and continuing losses. Dell's management was not ignorant of these warning signals but viewed the situation as "if we're not in what will soon be the second-biggest PC market in the world, then how can Dell possibly be a global player?"

The Dell-in-China situation showcases all five elements of strategy in action. It also shows how a firm must engage these elements flexibly and entrepreneurially to do business in markets different from their home markets. That is, internationalizing firms face challenges as to how to be global yet local at the same time and to what extent they should be global or local. China is a relatively new geographic arena for Dell. Within this country arena, Dell is targeting certain market segments, or sub-arenas; it is also using different channels as part of its market-segmentation strategy.

In terms of vehicles, and regardless of global location, Dell typically goes it alone in terms of assembly and distribution, entering into alliances only for its inputs and raw materials. A key facet of Dell's competitive advantage is distribution via its Dell Direct model—an online PC assembly and sales-on-demand powerhouse. In China, however, Dell initially formed alliances with independent distributors for the consumer market, a channel it had learned to exploit in its earlier entry into India. This was a risky move for Dell but also one that showed that management recognized that it had to be flexible and act in a locally sensitive fashion in approaching new geographic markets. Dell initially planned to use Chinese distributors, as it had in India, and then migrate sales over a five-year period to the typical kiosk-sales model it employs in other parts of the world, further allowing it to leverage its Dell Direct model. Dell was able to draw immediately on the model for the large multinational-firm market, with which it already had established customer relationships. It could also use the Dell Direct model for the government-users market. As in all of its other markets, Dell continued to exploit a performance-for-value differentiation strategy and leverage its unique Dell Direct service model to maintain its solid relationship with its corporate and government clients.

In terms of staging, Dell flipped its distribution model on its head. This is a third example of how the company flexibly adapted its historic strategic approach to enter into China. In the United States, Dell built up its Dell Direct model through the direct-to-consumer market; it entered the corporate-customer market once only after it had established a strong, profitable foothold with consumers. In China, however, the Dell Direct market was more commercially viable with corporate customers, who have both the cash and access to infrastructure to make the Dell Direct model work effectively. Although Dell initially worked through distributors in China for the consumer market, its staging plan was to migrate these consumers eventually to its Dell Direct model over a period of five years, which it did successfully.

Finally, Dell's economic logic is one of both scale and scope economies. It can leverage its size to gain the best terms and prices for the best technologies for the products it sells. It can use this cost advantage to compete in China and at the same time further enhance the Dell Direct model's footprint on the global computer market.

By the end of 2004, Dell reported that in just five years, it had become China's third-largest provider of computer systems and services. In 2004 alone, Dell's shipment growth in China was nearly 60 percent, four times that of the rest of the industry, and its revenues grew nearly 40 percent. China had become Dell's fourth-largest national market, and combined Asia Pacific–Japan operating income amounted to $313 million, 10 percent of its global income. Perhaps the icing on the cake came when IBM announced on December 9, 2004, the sale of its entire PC division to Lenovo, a Chinese multinational firm. This leaves Dell, Hewlett-Packard, and Lenovo as the world's top three PC makers. Industry analysts are placing their bets on wildly efficient Dell to broaden its lead, both globally and in China. Exhibit 7.1 presents some of the reasons why Motorola, Kodak, and IBM experienced difficulties in the China market, but it paints a rosier picture for astute firms such as Dell. So far, it appears that Dell's global strategy, and its flexible approach to entering countries like China, is paying off. ■

Exhibit 7.1 China: A Black Hole or a Diamond Mine?

Sources: Adapted from annual reports provided at www.walmart.com, www.ge.com, and Economist Unit White Paper, Coming of Age: Multinationals in China, June 2004.

If you read front-page stories from *Business Week*, the *Economist*, the *Financial Times*, *Forbes*, *Fortune*, or the *Wall Street Journal*, it almost seems to be accepted wisdom in the business world that the China accounts of almost all foreign firms are unprofitable. That is, it is difficult, if not impossible, to make a profit selling products to the business and consumer markets in China. Executives in multinational companies (MNCs) are easily dazzled by the prospect of selling to one billion consumers. For instance, think of how many pairs of shoes a 10-percent share of the Chinese market would represent to Nike!

However, many early entrants failed to give sufficient attention to the fact that only a small segment of the Chinese market was ready for expensive Western products. In addition, some firms encountered unexpected costs caused by corruption among local officials. Historically, this perception has not been far from the truth. It is not difficult to uncover a number of horror stories detailing the misadventures of foreign firms that have overestimated the size of the domestic Chinese market, underestimated the difficulties of accessing it, and ended up losing lots of money.

But beware of such urban legends. China has not been nearly the unmitigated disaster for foreign firms that such stories suggest. Many large Western companies have found the going tough, but the China operations of numerous companies have been hugely profitable. Although many MNCs have lost money trying to sell to the domestic market, they have made a great deal by using China as a sourcing and export base.

This aspect of foreign firms' business in China is often overlooked because it is difficult to record. The financial gains generated by cheap sourcing in China are impossible to document because they show up not as accounting items in their own right but rather in the profits MNCs make in their traditional markets in the United States and Europe. Similarly, that the export operations of foreign firms often show little or no profit is less a reflection of reality than of transfer pricing as foreign firms attempt to avoid capital controls and taxes in China.

It works like this. Imagine that a parent company in the United States receives an order from a European customer for 1,000 notebook computers at $700 each. Assume also that the computers cost $600 a unit. Typically, the parent company would subcontract its factory in China to produce this order and pay it $610 for each unit (foreign firms know that a factory operating at a loss would be suspicious and thus attract the unwanted attention of officials). This is the value of the export from China, although a change of invoice en route means it enters the United States at $700, which is the price the European customer pays directly to the parent company in the United States. In this way, the U.S. firm keeps most of the money offshore. So although official records may show that the China factory is making a profit of $10,000, in reality it has generated net earnings of 10 times that amount.

The money MNCs make from using China as a sourcing and exporting base may be difficult to trace, but it is far from negligible. Wal-Mart buys more than $12 billion in goods from China every year; Motorola's sourcing in the country totaled $2.8 billion in 2003; and GE plans to increase sourcing in China to $5 billion by 2005. Moreover, more than 50 percent of China's total exports—equivalent to $240 billion in 2003—are produced in foreign-invested factories. When trying to assess an MNC's overall performance in China, it makes less sense to ask how much money foreign firms have made *in* the country than how much they have made *from* it.

INTERNATIONAL STRATEGY

What is *international strategy?* When should managers consider such a strategy? In the narrowest sense, a firm's managers need only think about international strategy when they conduct some aspect of their business across national borders. Some international activities are designed to augment a firm's business strategy, such as sourcing key factors of production to cheaper labor markets (i.e., attempts to become more competitive within a core business). Other international activities represent key elements of the firm's corporate strategy (i.e., entering new businesses or new markets). Whether expanding internationally to reinforce a particular business's strategy or as part of a corporate strategy, international expansion is a form of diversification because the firm has chosen to operate in a different market. If your instructor has chosen to implement the international module in StratSim, you will experience international strategy related to vehicle choices about importing and exporting and other related facets of the strategy diamond.

Throughout this text, you have been exposed to many organizations, both those focused on one primary geographic region and others that are very global in their operating scope. For some organizations, a global mind-set pervades managerial thinking and is explicit in the firm's vision, mission, goals, objectives, and strategy. With other firms, international strategy may be very new. If this is the case, an international strategy must be carefully prepared for through staging and the other dimensions of the strategy diamond.

As shown in Exhibit 7.2, as of 2005, firms varied significantly in terms of their international presence. Papa John's, for instance, has a relatively miniscule dependence on non–U.S. markets for its revenues. However, even firms that are purely domestic must be attuned to international opportunities and threats. Competitors may emerge from parts of the globe where the firm does not conduct activities, and domestic competitors can radically change the home-market status quo through their international activities. For instance, Domino's Pizza derives 28 percent of its $4.2 billion in annual sales from non–U.S. markets, and these sales are spread over 50 countries.[2] By the end of this chapter, you will learn that keeping an eye on other firms' international activities is essential to avoid being blindsided by a new competitor or industry change.

The preventative cure for such myopia is a broad awareness of international strategy. We encourage you to internalize a broad perspective of international strategy as well. In the broadest sense, a firm needs to consider its international strategy when any single or potential competitor is not domestic or otherwise conducts business across borders. Increasingly, it is this latter context that makes it imperative that almost all firms think about the international dimensions of their business, even if they have no international operations whatsoever. Thus, a firm's **international strategy** is how it approaches the cross-border business

international strategy Process by which a firm approaches its cross-border activities and those of competitors and plans to approach them in the future

Exhibit 7.2 The International Presence of Selected MNCs

Company	Domestic Market	Products	Total Sales ($ millions)	Sales in Domestic Market %	Sales in Foreign Markets %
Nokia	Finland	Cell phones	37,031	1	99
Audi	Germany	Automobiles	29,378	32	68
Clarion	Japan	Audio equipment	1,540	52	48
Apple	U.S.	Computers, electronics	8,279	59	41
eBay	U.S.	Online auctions	2,165	65	35
Papa John's	U.S.	Pizza	917	96	4

Exhibit 7.3 International Strategy and the Five Elements of the Strategy Diamond

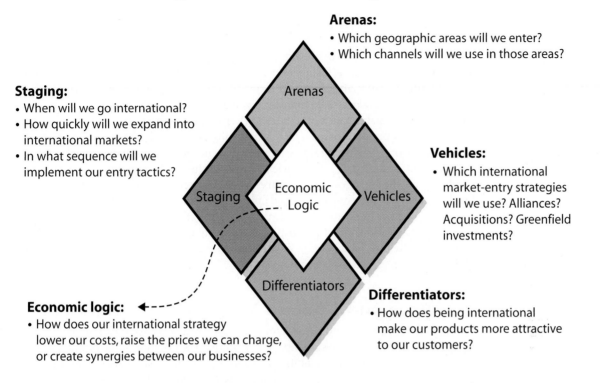

Arenas:
• Which geographic areas will we enter?
• Which channels will we use in those areas?

Staging:
• When will we go international?
• How quickly will we expand into international markets?
• In what sequence will we implement our entry tactics?

Vehicles:
• Which international market-entry strategies will we use? Alliances? Acquisitions? Greenfield investments?

Differentiators:
• How does being international make our products more attractive to our customers?

Economic logic:
• How does our international strategy lower our costs, raise the prices we can charge, or create synergies between our businesses?

activities of its own firm and competitors and how it contemplates doing so in the future. International strategy essentially reflects the choices a firm's executives make with respect to sourcing and selling its goods in foreign markets.

It probably comes as no surprise to you that all of the world's largest corporations are global as well. A simple review of the top-10 firms among *Fortune's* Global 500 provides you with a snapshot of these global behemoths each year, in terms of who is largest and who has the best global reputation. What may be surprising, however, is the increasing presence of arguably tiny firms that are global very early in their lives, such as Skype (which started in Sweden and went global in a year) and Logitech (which started in Switzerland and California and was global from inception).

As you work through this chapter, you will see how international strategy must be reflected in all facets of the strategy diamond. Exhibit 7.3 summarizes some of the key strategic questions that firms must answer, such as Dell did in the opening vignette, as they expand into international markets.

International Strategy in StratSim

SimConnect

If your instructor has enabled the international module in StratSim, you will have the opportunity to make a range of international strategy decisions related to the strategy diamond. For instance, exporting products and importing raw materials are vehicles for international strategy, and with the exporting avenue you will have the additional vehicle option of using an alliance for your exports. Arenas are important from the standpoint that you will choose geographic markets for exports and inputs based on your overall strategy, and their relative attractiveness. These international activities will need to contribute to your differentiation. Staging will be a key decision criterion as you weigh the timing of your exporting and importing moves. Finally, all these facets of your international strategy will be revealed in whether or not your strategy's economic logic makes sense—that is, are you profitable and beating your competitors?

INTERNATIONAL STRATEGY AND COMPETITIVE ADVANTAGE

Why expand internationally? Given the complexities and risks of managing business activities across borders, it is imperative to understand why any firm would take on the often significant costs of doing so in terms of time, dollars, and managerial attention. One reason is simply necessity. Increasingly, many experts in the field of strategic management view global expansion as necessary for just about every medium and large corporation. This opinion is based on a few basic observations: (1) that capital markets and employees favor fast-growing firms, and many domestic markets in developed countries are becoming saturated; (2) that efficiencies in all value-chain activities are linked across borders, and the linkages and pressures for efficiency continue to escalate; (3) that knowledge is not uniformly distributed around the world, and new ideas increasingly are coming from emerging economies; (4) that customers themselves are becoming global at both the organizational level in terms of the growth and proliferation of multinationals and at the individual level in terms of consumer preferences; and (5) that competitors are globalizing, even if your organization is not.[3]

The Pros and Cons of International Expansion

International expansion is no panacea for corporate-growth needs, and it is inherently hazardous even when it promises revenue opportunities. For instance, at the beginning of the 1990s, PepsiCo established an ambitious goal to triple its international sales from $1.5 billion to $5 billion within just five short years. PepsiCo aggressively pursued this growth, yet it failed to keep pace with the growth of international markets and actually lost ground to Coca-Cola. While Coke was reaping the benefits of the growth of soft drinks in international markets, Pepsi's international market share actually shrank.[4] Pepsi's experience demonstrates that simply participating in international markets does not equate to having a competitive advantage to exploit international opportunities. Indeed, if you consult *Fortune's* list of the largest global firms, you will typically find Wal-Mart at the top of that list. Yet, Wal-Mart's non–U.S. operations do very poorly in comparison to its domestic business. Global expansion can just as easily contribute to profitability as it can detract from it. The key is to align international expansion with the firm's strategy in a way to exploit and further develop firm resources and capabilities.[5] Ultimately, the benefits must outweigh the costs, and more often than not, questions about a firm's nondomestic profitability take years to answer. The opening vignette on Dell demonstrates the characteristics of such patience and the necessary alignment of the elements of strategy and the firm's resources and capabilities.

concept link

Among the criteria for **strategic coherence** that we propose in Chapter 2 is an overarching fit of various businesses such as those entered by international expansion under the corporate umbrella.

Liabilities of Newness and Foreignness   In addition to the possible benefits of international expansion, a firm incurs a number of costs when diversifying its business operations around the globe.[6] The costs of geographic diversification include the liabilities of newness and foreignness and governance and coordination costs. *Liability of newness* can be thought of as a disadvantage (cost disadvantage or other disadvantages) associated with being a new player in the market. For instance, a firm suffering from a liability of newness does not gain benefits from the learning curve. Likewise, *liability of foreignness* is the disadvantage a firm faces by not being a local player. This disadvantage may be cultural, in that the firm's managers do not understand local market conditions. It may also be political, such as when the firm does not understand local laws or have relationships in place to manage the local regulatory environment.

Firm managers contend with many challenges when establishing operations in a new country, including the logistics of purchasing and installing facilities, staffing, and establishing internal management systems and external business networks. Costs associated with establishing a new business can put a new foreign division in a disadvantageous position relative to local or more established foreign competitors. These types of disadvantages tend

concept link

We define the **learning curve** in Chapter 5 as the principle by which incremental production costs decline at a constant rate as production experience is gained.

to dissipate with time as the division gains local experience, which tends to diminish the negative influence of liability of newness and foreignness.

Costs Associated with Governance and Coordination Although these disadvantages of newness and foreignness typically decline over time, governance and coordination costs are disadvantages that tend to increase as international diversification increases. Some of the issues that increase governance and coordination costs include information distortion as it is transferred and translated across divisions. Coordination difficulties and possible misalignment between headquarters and divisional managers in international firms increases as international diversification increases, much as in highly diversified domestic firms. Because every country has a relatively unique business environment, the more country environments a firm must deal with, the greater the difficulty in coordination operations across these diverse environments.

Offsetting Costs and Benefits Thus, as shown in Exhibit 7.4, the costs associated with internationalization can offset the possible benefits of operating in multiple markets. The potential economic benefits of internationalization are modest at first, and then become quite significant before leveling off. These potential increases in revenue must of course be balanced with the costs of internationalization. Costs are significant in early efforts to internationalize. After a presence is established, economies of scale and scope kick in, and the incremental costs of further expansion are minimal. However, bureaucratic and management costs can spike at extreme levels of internationalization. This increase in costs is similar to the notion of diseconomies of scale introduced in earlier chapters. Consequently, research suggests that performance gains from internationalization, come not at the early stages but at moderate to high levels; however, at very high levels of internationalization, firms tend to suffer performance declines.[7] The key for managers is to find a way to exploit the possible advantages of economies of scale and scope, location, and learning without having them offset by the excessive costs of internationalization. This dynamic tension between the costs and benefits of internationalization is summarized in Exhibit 7.4. The tradeoff between costs and benefits of internationalization results in an S-curve relationship between internationalization and firm performance.

concept link

Recall our definition of a **diseconomies of scale** in Chapter 5 as the condition under which average total costs per unit of production increases at higher levels of output.

Key Factors in International Expansion

International strategy, particularly in the form of international expansion, can contribute to a firm's competitive advantage in a number of interrelated ways. The four most important aspects are *economies of scale and scope, location, multipoint competition,* and *learning.* Firms must understand the specific benefits in one or more of these areas if they are to say yes to international expansion plans.

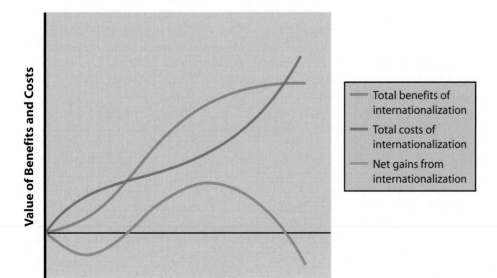

Level of Internationalization

Exhibit 7.4 The Benefits and Costs of Internationalization

Source: Lu, J. W. & P. W. Beamish, "International Diversification and Firm Performance: The S-Curve Hypothesis," Academy of Management Journal, *47 (2004), 598–609.*

Legend:
— Total benefits of internationalization
— Total costs of internationalization
— Net gains from internationalization

conceptlink

In Chapter 1, we explain the role of **economic logic** in the **strategy diamond** by describing it as the means by which a firm intends to generate positive returns over and above the cost of its capital. In Chapter 5, we show that the economic logic of an **economy of scope** revolves around cost savings associated with multiproduct production. In this chapter, we stress the strategy of lowering average costs by sharing resources on a global scale.

Global Economies of Scale and Scope   Referring back to the strategy diamond, international strategy affects a firm's economic logic through its implications for economies of scale and scope. Larger firms are not necessarily more efficient or more profitable, but in some industries, such as pharmaceuticals and aircraft manufacturing, the enormous costs of new-product development require that the firm be able to generate commensurate sales, and this increasingly requires firms to have a global presence.

For instance, R&D costs are skyrocketing in many industries. This requires that firms in those industries seek a larger revenue base, typically outside of their home countries. This relationship is demonstrated by strategy research showing that the performance benefits from R&D increase with a firm's degree of internationalization: Firms generate more profits out of their R&D investments if they are also highly global.[8] One reason for this is that there is a minimum threshold of R&D investment necessary to launch a new product. When the firm can amortize those costs across many markets, it can in effect lower its average cost per sale. It is interesting to note that, when graphed, the relationship between performance, R&D investment, and internationalization further demonstrates the S-curve relationship between internationalization and firm performance discussed earlier in this chapter. Such economies of scale can also be realized for intangibles, such as a firm's brand, much as CitiGroup, McDonald's, and Coca-Cola leverage their brands in practically every country in the world.

Scale and Operating Efficiency   The larger scale that accompanies global expansion only creates competitive advantage if the firm translates scale into operating efficiency. As you learned in Chapter 5, cost savings are not axiomatic with larger scale. Larger scale must be managed to avoid diseconomies of scale. As with economies of scale in general, the potential scale economies from global expansion include spreading fixed costs and increasing purchasing power.[9] Attempts to gain scale advantages must be focused on resources and activities that are scale sensitive, and it means that these resources and activities must be concentrated in just a few locations.[10] However, if these resources and activities are concentrated in a few locations, they can become isolated from key markets, which may lead to delayed responses to market changes.

Economies of Global Scope   A specialized form of scope economies is available to firms as they expand globally. Recall that scope economies were defined as the ability to lower average costs by sharing a resource across different products. The example of MITY Enterprises reviewed in an earlier chapter was that of a firm that manufactures heavy-duty plastic and metal tables for institutional users (e.g., schools, churches). MITY Enterprises is able to use excess capacity in its manufacturing facility to produce chairs. By sharing this resource, MITY's average cost for tables and chairs is reduced. Numerous scope economies are similarly available to firms that expand globally. For example, CitiGroup, McDonald's, and Coca-Cola profit from scope economies to the extent that the different country markets share the benefits of brand equity that these firms have built up over time. The opening vignette on Dell, too, provides several examples of scope as well as scale economies across different geographic and customer markets, starting with its ability to take advantage of its brand; its capability to leverage its Dell Direct sales model and related Internet sales and support technologies; its experience and relationships with distributors in India and then China; and its different geographic units' ability to pool their purchasing power for key components, such as CPUs, from powerful suppliers like Intel.

Consider how a supplier to McDonald's could exploit economies of global scope, which in turn provide it with economies of scale in production and other related value-chain activities. McDonald's needs the same ketchup products in Europe and South America as it does in the United States. A vendor with sufficient global scope to satisfy McDonald's worldwide demand for ketchup would be an attractive sourcing alternative to McDonald's compared with sourcing this supply from numerous local suppliers.[11] In this case, global scope gives a supplier an opportunity to generate revenue that it would be unable to generate in the absence of global scope. Of course, McDonald's global scope also gives it access to more suppliers from around the globe, including local suppliers in many markets. Local suppliers may also have some advantages over global players in terms of being able to provide more immediate service and greater knowledge of local business practices. Thus, firms like McDonald's are in the enviable position of being able to source

Huge international chains, such as McDonald's, are able to achieve economies of scope, thereby lowering the costs of inputs they purchase both globally and in local markets.

the lowest cost inputs and use lower local prices and service levels to force global suppliers to keep prices down and service levels high.

Attempts to gain economies of scope also face numerous hazards as well. Although economies of scope are possible as resources are shared across markets, strategy must still be executed at the national level.[12] In cases such as China, the United States, and Europe, where the "nation" is actually composed of distinctly different subgeographic markets (cantons in China, states in the U.S., and countries in Europe), successful execution at the local level is further complicated. This can easily lead to tension between the need to identify and satisfy the local client contact and the aim of lowering costs by sharing resources and having actions coordinated across markets.

Location National and regional geographic location has an impact on competitive advantage as well, because of its implications for input costs, competitors, demand conditions, and complements. A basic five-forces industry analysis can be used to determine the importance of a given location. The analysis of industry structure should include such features as barriers to entry, new entrants, substitutes, and existing competitors, both domestic and international. Related and supporting industries that are forward and backward in the value chain, as well as true complements, also need to be identified.

With such an analysis in hand, the value chain and five-forces analysis can be geographically segmented to consider how and why rivalry may play out differently in different locales. In terms of customer, for instance, an analysis of consumption trends among the top 25 countries in the global soft-drink industry shows that India and China exhibit fairly steady growth. A firm's managers can thus assess the desirability of investing in one market versus another, the competitive consequences of such an investment, and the value-chain activities needed to locate in which regions. For instance, India and China may be prime locations to launch new growth initiatives for large players like Coca-Cola and Pepsi. Such an analysis should show how the firm's strategy has connected the dots, so to speak, in terms of linking resources, capabilities, and locations.

Arbitrage Opportunities Beyond the five-forces and value-chain assessment, location differences also present an opportunity for arbitrage. Arbitrage represents the age-old practice of buying something in one market and selling it in another market where it garners a higher price. Historically, the value added in such arbitrage was simply tracking down a desirable commodity, such as spice, tea, or silk, from a faraway land, and transporting it to a market that would pay a premium for it. Companies can improve performance and potentially build competitive advantage by optimizing the location of their value-chain activities. Significant cost differences for different types of value-chain activities exist around the globe. A firm that can optimize the intercountry cost differences better than its rivals will have a cost advantage. The caveat here is that arbitrage opportunities may be fleeting in that once identified and lacking entry barriers, competitors can quickly realize them as well. Therefore, a firm that relies on arbitrage as a core part of its competitive strategy must possess greater capabilities in continually identifying new arbitrage opportunities as well as in increasing entry barriers for competitors trying to follow it.

The CAGE Framework   Generally, the greater the distance covered and the greater the value differences between the disconnected markets, the greater the profit potential arising from arbitrage. However, greater distance also tends to be accompanied by greater entry costs and risks. Although most people tend to think of distance in geographic terms, in the area of international strategy distance can also be viewed in terms of culture, administrative heritage, and economics. As summarized in Exhibit 7.5, this broader **CAGE framework**—**C**ulture, **A**dministrative, **G**eographic, and **E**conomic—provides you with another way of thinking about location and the opportunities and concomitant risks associated with global arbitrage.[13] CAGE-related risks would be most relevant in industries in which language or

CAGE framework Tool that considers the dimensions of culture, administration, geography, and economics to assess the distance created by global expansion

Exhibit 7.5   The Cage Distance Framework: Opportunities for Global Arbitrage

Cultural Distance	Administrative Distance	Geographic Distance	Economic Distance
Attributes Creating Distance			
Different languages Different ethnicities; lack of connective ethnic or social networks Different religions Different social norms	Absence of colonial ties Absence of shared monetary or political association Political hostility Government policies Institutional weakness	Physical remoteness Lack of a common border Lack of sea or river access Size of country Weak transportation or communication links Differences in climates	Differences in consumer incomes Differences in costs and quality of: • natural resources • financial resources • human resources • infrastructure • intermediate inputs • information or knowledge
Industries or Products Affected by Distance			
Products have high linguistic content (TV) Products affect cultural or national identity of consumers (foods) Product features vary in terms of size (cars), standards (electrical appliances), or packaging Products carry country-specific quality associations (wines)	Government involvement is high in industries that are: • producers of staple goods (electricity) • producers of other "entitlements" (drugs) • large employers (farming) • large suppliers to government (mass transportation) • national champions (aerospace) • vital to national security (telecom) • exploiters of natural resources (oil, mining) • subject to high sunk costs (infrastructure)	Products have a low value-of-weight or bulk ratio (cement) Products are fragile or perishable (glass, fruit) Communications and connectivity are important (financial services) Local supervision and operational requirements are high (many services)	Nature of demand varies with income level (cars) Economies of standardization or scale are important (mobile phones) Labor and other factor cost differences are salient (garments) Distribution or business systems are different (insurance) Companies need to be responsive and agile (home appliances)

Source: Recreated from www.business-standard.com/general/pdf/113004_01.pdf.

cultural identity are important factors, the government views the products as staples or as essential to national security, or income or input costs are key determinants of product demand or cost.

Application of the CAGE framework requires managers to identify attractive locations based on raw material costs, access to markets or consumers, or other key decision criteria. For instance, a firm may be most interested in markets with high consumer buying power, so it uses per capita income as the first sorting cue. This would result in some type of ranking. For example, one researcher examined the fast-food industry and found that based on per capita income, countries such as Germany and Japan would be the most attractive markets for the expansion of a North American-based fast-food company. However, when the analysis was adjusted for distance using the CAGE framework, the revised results showed that Mexico ranked as the second-most-attractive market for international expansion, far ahead of Germany and Japan.[14]

Any international expansion strategy would still need to be backed up by the specific resources and capabilities possessed by the firm, regardless of how rosy the picture painted by the CAGE analysis. Think of international expansion as a movement along a continuum from known markets to less-known markets; a firm can move to more CAGE-proximate neighbors before venturing into markets that are portrayed as very different from a CAGE-framework perspective.

The opening vignette on Dell further demonstrates the usefulness of the CAGE framework. As you saw in the case of Dell, the vehicles it used to enter China were just as important in its China strategy as the choice of geographic arena it entered. For Dell's corporate clients in China, a CAGE framework would reveal relatively little distance on all four dimensions, even geographic, given the fact that many PC components are sourced from China. However, for the consumer segment, the distance is rather great, particularly on the dimensions of culture, administration, and economics. One outcome here could have been Dell's avoidance of the consumer market altogether. However, Dell opted to choose an alliance with distributors whose knowledge base and capabilities enabled it to better bridge the CAGE-framework distances until it was in a position to engage its Dell Direct model with consumers (staging and pacing).

So what have we learned by using CAGE in the context of Dell, and international expansion more generally? You should now see that the CAGE framework can be used to address the questions of where to expand internationally (which arena) and how to expand (by which vehicle). It can also help you map out the staging and pacing of your strategic international expansion moves so as to maximize the strategy's anchoring in the firm's VRINE-based resources and capabilities.

Multipoint Competition   Chapter 6 introduced the advantages firms can develop through multimarket competition. When the firm competes in multiple international markets, as a special kind of multimarket tactic, the stronghold assault becomes available. *Stronghold assault* refers to the competitive actions a firm takes in another firm's key markets, particularly when the attacking firm has little presence in that market. In the case of international strategy, stronghold assault refers to attacks on the geographic markets that are most important to a competitor's profitability and cash flow. A classic example of international stronghold assault is provided by the actions of French tire manufacturer Michelin and the U.S. tire company Goodyear in the 1970s.[15] Early on, both firms had negligible market presence in each other's respective domestic markets (Europe and the United States). Michelin became aware of Goodyear's intent to expand its presence in Europe, so it started selling its tires in the United States at or below its actual cost. Although these sales were a miniscule part of Michelin's overall sales, Michelin's sales tactic forced Goodyear to drop its prices in the United States, and hence lower the profitability of its largest market.

As discussed in Chapter 6, such multimarket competitive tactics often initially benefit customers at the expense of competitors until a new market equilibrium is reached. Moreover, Michelin's low-price ploy earned it a larger share of the U.S. market, such that

conceptlink

We introduce the **VRINE model** in Chapter 3 as a five-pronged test for determining the extent to which a firm's **resources** and **capabilities** will contribute to competitive advantage: value, rarity, inimitability, nonsubstitutability, and exploitability.

the lost profits in the United States began to take a toll on Michelin's overall profitability. In addition, nothing prevented Goodyear from doing the same thing in Michelin's home markets, further eroding both firms' profitability. Eventually, both firms ended up in the international courts charging each other with "dumping"—selling goods below cost in a foreign country.

Even today, stronghold assault is a motivation for global investment, but as the Michelin case highlights, it must be used with care and is typically not sustainable. Therefore, firms that employ this tactic should also have strategies in the staging component that take into account when and how the firm will shift from price competition to more sustainable bases of competition. For this reason, stronghold assault is used not only to underprice a competitor's products in its home market but also to simply eliminate the competitor's home market monopoly. Just as with the Cola Wars, the Michelin–Goodyear war left the industry landscape forever changed, and both firms had to adjust their strategies to survive in the new industry structure that resulted.

Learning and Knowledge Sharing   Learning is very important to the success of a firm's international strategy for a variety of reasons. At the very least, a firm with operations that cross borders must learn how to cope with different institutional, legal, and cultural environments. For the most successful firms, international expansion is used as a vehicle for innovation, improving existing products in existing markets, or coming up with new ideas for new markets. It is one thing to use such tools as the five-forces, value-chain, and CAGE frameworks to identify profit or arbitrage opportunities, for instance, but it is quite another thing to exploit them successfully and profitably. For instance, Michelin initially shipped products to the United States and didn't care whether it made money on them because it viewed any losses as insignificant. But eventually that tactic caused the U.S. market to grow in importance as part of the French tire maker's overall global sales, and it had to reckon with making this part of its business profitable or admit defeat and abandon the U.S. market—one of the auto industry's largest and most profitable markets.

Similarly, Dell first used Chinese distributors in serving the consumer segment in China, but this is a much less profitable vehicle and differentiator than its core distribution and sales engine—the Dell Direct model. Dell's goal was to migrate from its Chinese distributors and eventually learn enough about the Chinese marketplace to use its direct-sales vehicle, which can be accessed through kiosks placed in busy foot-traffic locations.

Like the product-diversified firm, the geographic-diversified firm must somehow learn how to ensure that the benefits of being international outweigh the added costs of the infrastructure necessary to support its nondomestic operations.

Learning and local adaptation appear to be particularly difficult for U.S. firms, even when they are very big firms that already have an international presence. For instance, with nearly a half-billion dollars in annual sales, Lincoln Electric completed its largest acquisition ever in 1991—the $70-million purchase of Germany's Messer Gresheim, a manufacturer of welding equipment, which was Lincoln's core business.[16] Although Lincoln maintained the bulk of its business in the United States, it had over 40 years of marketing and manufacturing experience in Canada, Australia, and France. Moreover, the company was in the process of aggressively ramping up manufacturing and sales operations in Japan, Venezuela, Brazil, the Netherlands, Norway, and the U.K. With the acquisition of Gresheim, as with the other newly established international operations, Lincoln's management simply assumed that it could transplant its manufacturing approach, aggressive compensation and incentive systems (Lincoln pays employees only for what they produce), and culture—the three key success factors in the U.S. business—to the newly obtained German and other foreign operations. Within a year, the European operations were in disarray; losses were mounting in Japan and Latin America; and Lincoln reported a quarterly consolidated loss of $12 million—the first quarterly consolidated loss in the company's 97-year history.

Although Lincoln eventually recovered from the brink of disaster and ruin, it only did so after top management recognized and took steps to remedy the harsh reality that it had insufficient international experience, a dearth of experience in and knowledge about running a globally dispersed organization, and no understanding of how to manage foreign operations and foreign cultures. Part of its salvation involved scaling back many of the foreign operations it had acquired, giving the firm breathing room to develop its international operating and managerial capabilities. As a consequence of its learning from its failures abroad, Lincoln is now a global success story, as summarized in excerpts from its 2003 annual report shown in Exhibit 7.6.

Learning, Knowledge, Transfer, and Innovation Beyond the rather obvious aspects of learning shown in the Lincoln Electric case, a firm that has operations in different countries has the opportunity to increase innovation and transfer knowledge from one geographic market to another. For example, SC Johnson's European operations learned about a product that involved the combination of household pesticides and a simple plug-in device. In Europe, this product was sold in stores to consumers who needed a cheap and efficient deterrent for mosquitoes and other annoying insects. SC Johnson demonstrated its ability to learn from its European operation by transferring the technology to its fragrance division in the United States, thus giving rise to a whole new category of airfresheners called Glade Plug-ins.[17]

A second facet of this form of learning is to locate a firm or a particular aspect of its operations in a part of the world where competition is the fiercest. So, for example, a U.S.

Exhibit 7.6 How Lincoln Electric (Eventually) Achieved Global Success

Source: Annual Report, 2003.

To Our Shareholders: Our carefully planned, ongoing strategy to expand Lincoln Electric's global footprint while growing market share, improving profitability, maximizing cash flow, and enhancing shareholder value continued on course in 2003. As the clear worldwide leader in the arc welding industry, our Company is truly in the strongest position of its long and successful history. Despite overcapacity in our industry and tough competition as companies fought for a shrinking volume of orders, we were able to persevere in 2003 and take advantage of opportunities in the global markets.

Net income for 2003 was $54.5 million, or $1.31 per diluted share. Net sales were $1.04 billion. Cash flow from operations in 2003 was a very strong $95.7 million and was significantly affected by voluntary funding of $40 million to the Company's U.S. pension plans. This was $20 million more funding than in 2002. Without the incremental pension funding, cash flow was $115.7 million. Both our sales and our profitability in 2003 were approximately split between our U.S. and non-U.S. businesses, excluding our nonconsolidated joint ventures in Turkey and China.

Today: Lincoln Electric is the world's largest designer and manufacturer of arc welding and cutting products. Growing global demand from the energy and construction sectors is fueling growth in pipeline and other infrastructure projects that require welding products. The Company's major end markets include metal forming and fabrication; pipeline, building, bridge, and power facility construction; transportation and defense industries; equipment manufacturers in construction, farming, and mining; retail resellers; and the rental market.

> **At Lincoln Electric, our corporate vision is to continue to be the undisputed world leader in sales, technology, profitability and enhanced shareholder value in the arc welding industry.**

automaker might locate a product facility in Japan. Ironically, although one goal of such a move is actually to compete on Japan's own turf against incumbents Toyota and Honda, the learning objective would be to try to emulate and learn from Japan's auto manufacturers' leading-edge production practices and transfer that advanced knowledge to the U.S. company's plants in other parts of the world, such as the United States, Canada, and Mexico. Similarly, because France and Italy are leaders in the high-fashion industry, companies such as DuPont and W. L. Gore & Associates, which aim to compete with leading-edge fabrics such as Lycra and Gore-Tex, place high value on those countries as production and marketing locations because of the learning opportunities about future customer preferences (e.g., touch, feel, color, etc.). In this view, the strategically most important markets will be those which feature not only intrinsic market attractiveness but an opportunity to learn and innovate in ways that can improve the organization's operations, products, and services around the globe.[18]

Sharing Knowledge Across Business Units   Finally, large multinationals can exploit opportunities for inter-business-unit collaboration, which results in valuable knowledge sharing.[19] Sharing knowledge across business units has several tangible benefits. First, it enables firms to transfer best practices across national and business-unit boundaries. Because these best practices are proprietary—and probably tailored to the idiosyncrasies of the firm—they are more likely to result in competitive advantage than borrowing best practices from other firms. Why? Because all competitors have access to that information as well.

An example of this type of knowledge sharing is illustrated by a case study of BP PLC. A U.S. business unit that operates service stations was looking for novel ways to reduce costs in BP convenience stores. A manager borrowed ideas from colleagues in the Netherlands and the U.K. about how to reduce working-capital requirements. Copying these practices and implementing them in the United States resulted in a 20-percent reduction in working capital.

Sharing knowledge across business units can also uncover revenue-enhancement opportunities. The country manager of GlaxoSmithKline in the Philippines found a new drug therapy for tuberculosis in the company's R&D lab in India. Although this therapy was not widely known within the company because it represented a very small slice of the multinational firm's business, it represented a huge market opportunity in the Philippines and other developing countries, where tuberculosis is more widespread than it is in Europe and the United States.

ENTRY VEHICLES INTO FOREIGN COUNTRIES

The strategy diamond says that a critical element of a firm's strategy is how it enters new markets. With international strategy, these new markets just happen to be in different countries, with different laws, infrastructure, cultures, and consumer preferences. The various entry mechanisms are referred to as *vehicles of strategy.* Consequently, a critical element of international expansion is determining which vehicles to use to enter new global markets. The first choice that managers must make is whether they will enter a foreign country with a vehicle that requires the firm to put some, or even considerable, capital at risk. As shown in Exhibit 7.7, firms can choose among a variety of nonequity and equity vehicles for entering a foreign country.

The second choice that managers must make is the form of the vehicle. Typically, each form offers differing levels of ownership control and local presence. Although firms can expand internationally in a number of different ways, we present them to you under three overarching foreign-country entry vehicles: *exporting, contractual agreements and alliances,* and *foreign direct investment (FDI),* either through the acquisition of a company or simply starting one from scratch. At the end of this section, we will briefly discuss the use of importing as a foreign-country entry vehicle; it is somewhat of a stealth form of internationalization.

Exhibit 7.7 Choice of Entry Modes

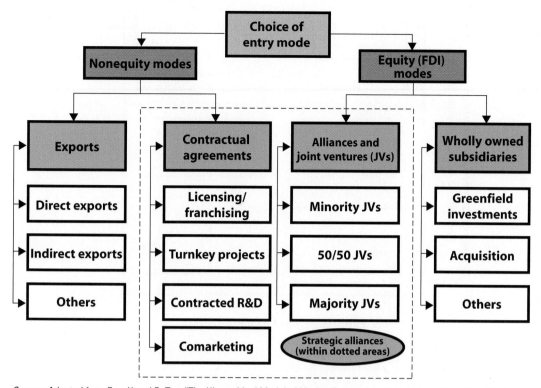

Source: Adapted from Pan, Y. and D. Tse, "The Hierarchical Model of Market Entry Modes," Journal of International Business Studies, 31 (2000), 535–554.

Foreign-country entry has been viewed historically as a staged process. Like the industry life cycle, the internationalization life cycle starts with a firm importing some of its raw materials or finished product for resale at home, followed perhaps by exporting products or raw materials abroad, and lastly ending in some type of partial or full ownership of plant, equipment, or other more extensive physical presence in a foreign country. These stages could be accomplished using vehicles ranging from simple contracts for purchases or sales on a transaction basis, through alliances, and perhaps even via mergers or wholesale acquisitions. Lincoln Electric, which was discussed in the previous section, offers an example of international growth through acquisition.

Over time, research has suggested that although some firms do follow such stages, they are better viewed as being more descriptive than predictive. Specifically, some firms follow the stages, starting with importing through foreign direct investment, whereas others jump right to the direct investment stage as their first internationalization effort.[20] It is also helpful to note that the different entry vehicles have differing degrees of risk and control. For instance, a company that is only exporting its products abroad is typically risking only payment for the product and, perhaps its reputation if the product is not serviced well in the foreign locale. This also shows how little control the exporter has over the downstream activities once it has shipped the product. Although the exporter may have some legal or distribution agreement with local firms, this is very little control compared to ownership of local factories or distribution or partial ownership through some form of alliance. In this section, we will walk you through these alternative entry vehicles. Examples of firms following them and the basic tradeoffs among them are summarized in Exhibit 7.8.

Exporting

Exporting is exactly the opposite of importing; it can take the form of selling production or service inputs or actual products and services abroad. With the advent of the Internet

exporting Foreign-country entry vehicle in which a firm uses an intermediary to perform most foreign marketing functions

Exhibit 7.8 Vehicles for Entering Foreign Markets

Source: Examples drawn from A. Gupta, and V. Govindarajan, "Managing Global Expansion: A Conceptual Framework," Business Horizons, *March/April 2002, 45–54.*

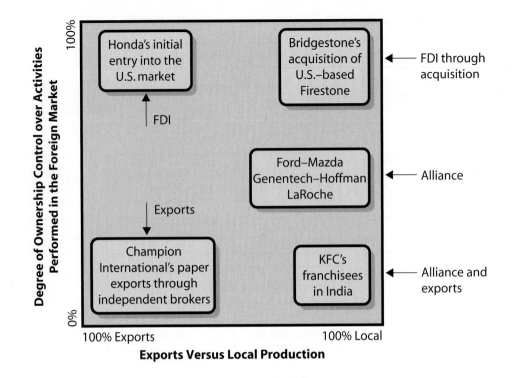

and electronic banking, the physical entry barriers to becoming an exporter are lower than ever before. Although the importer is ultimately responsible for the issues relating to customs, packaging, and other trade requirements, the exporting firm will generally only be successful to the extent that it can deliver a product or service that meets customers' needs.

Costs of Exporting   Exporting is a popular internationalization vehicle with small firms because the costs of entering new markets are relatively minimal with this vehicle. Exporters generally use local representatives or distributors to sell their products in new international markets. The main costs associated with exporting are transportation and meeting the packaging and ingredient requirements of the target country. Consequently, exporting is most common to international markets that are relatively close to the domestic market or to markets in which competitors and substitutes for the firm's products are not readily available. A large percentage of the born-global firms discussed later in the chapter used exporting as a vehicle to go global quickly.[21]

Licensing and Franchising   Exporting can take the form of shipping a product overseas and leaving marketing and distribution up to a foreign customer. It can also take the form of licensing or franchising, turnkey projects, R&D contracts, and comarketing. Due to some of the characteristics of these latter vehicles, as shown in Exhibit 7.7, such contractual arrangements are often considered a form of strategic alliance. Licensing and franchising provide a case in point. When a firm licenses its products or technologies in another country, it transfers the risk of actually implementing market entry to another firm, which pays the licensor a fee for the right to use its name in the local country. Franchising in a foreign country works similarly to franchising in a domestic market. A firm receives a sign-up fee and ongoing franchise royalties in exchange for teaching the franchisee how to open and operate the franchisor's business in the local market.

The risk, of course, to the licensor or franchisor is that the licensee or franchisee will violate the terms of the agreement, either to the detriment of the product or service itself, by refusing to pay agreed-upon fees or royalties or simply selling a copy of the product or service under another name (that is essentially stealing the intellectual property entirely). The primary risks to the franchisee or licensee are that the product or service will not perform as promised or that the licensor or franchisor will do something that diminishes the market attractiveness of the product or service.

Turnkey Projects, R&D Contracts, and Comarketing The latter three forms, turnkey projects, R&D contracts, and comarketing, are specialized contractual agreements whereby a firm agrees to build a factory, conduct a specific R&D project, or comarket or cobrand a product such that the contracting firm has used it as a foreign-market entry vehicle. For example, the Norwegian firm Kvaerner A/S contracts to build paper mills and deep-sea oil rigs for Brazilian paper and petroleum companies; the German firm Bayer AG contracts a large R&D project to the U.S. firm Millennium pharmaceuticals with the work undertaken in both firm's respective countries; McDonald's in Japan packages its kids meals with characters that are familiar to Japanese children based on characters like Pokémon or Hello Kitty that are popular at the time.

Alliances

Alliances are another common foreign-market entry vehicle. Because we devote an entire chapter to alliances later in the text, here we simply explain why alliances are so commonly used for international expansion. Often, alliances are chosen because of government regulations. For example, only recently did the Chinese government allow non-Chinese ownership of companies in China. As a result, firms could only enter China through various partnerships. Alliances may also be used as an international-strategy vehicle due to management's lack of familiarity with the local culture or institutions or because the complexity of operating internationally requires the firm to focus on the activities it does best and to outsource the rest. Some combination of these three factors—regulations, market familiarity, or operational complexity—typically explain why alliances are so often used by firms competing internationally. The box entitled "How Would *You* Do That? 7.1" provides an example of how the British retailer Laura Ashley responded to one of these motivations for an international alliance—the simplification of global operating complexity—and how it chose its ultimate alliance partner.

Foreign Direct Investment

Foreign direct investment (FDI), as the term implies, is an international entry strategy whereby a firm makes a financial investment in a foreign market to facilitate the startup of a new venture. FDI tends to be the most expensive international entry tactic because it requires the greatest commitment of a firm's time and resources. FDI can be implemented in several ways, such as through acquisitions or through a so-called greenfield alliance—the startup of a foreign entity from scratch. This latter form of FDI is called **greenfield investment**. In the previous section, we reviewed how alliances can be a vehicle to foreign market entry. Many alliances do involve equity investment, and when they do in the context of foreign market entry, it is a special case of greenfield investment. For instance, Daimler-Chrysler and BMW each invested $250 million to start a new engine factory in Curitiba, Brazil.

foreign direct investment (FDI) Foreign-country entry vehicle by which a firm commits to the direct ownership of a foreign subsidiary or division

greenfield investment Form of FDI in which a firm starts a new foreign business from the ground up

Acquisitions and Equity Alliances Because greenfield investment usually involves the greatest risk, expense, and time, many firms pursue FDI through acquisitions or alliances. Acquisitions provide the firm with rapid entry because the firm purchases existing businesses that are already staffed and successfully operating. For instance, when the battery-maker Rayovac entered Brazil in 2005, it did so by purchasing Microlite, the dominant battery maker in Brazil. Similarly, South African Breweries purchased Miller Brewing in 2002 to gain an instant presence and production capacity in one of the largest beer markets in the world, the United States.

Finding a Global Partner to Deliver the Goods

In the early 1990s, U.S. executive Jim Maxmin was brought in as CEO to turn around Laura Ashley, Ltd., the flagging and bloated British fashion retailer. At the time, Laura Ashley was vertically integrated, with operations spanning design, manufacturing, distribution, and retail sales. It had 481 retail shops located around the world, primarily in North America (185 shops), the United Kingdom (184 shops), and Europe (65 shops). Revenues in 1992 were $261 million,

and the firm had experienced three year's of declining sales and cumulative annual losses totaling nearly $30 million.

Maxmin's objective was to focus Laura Ashley's strategy on what the firm did best—namely, design and retail functions. Product quality had steadily declined, leaving production as a question mark, and Ashley's distribution system, as measured by its in-stock performance, was in shambles. This meant that the firm would need to fix or outsource production and distribution in some way that allowed the firm to maintain its quality in these areas and ultimately return the venerable firm to its historic profitability. Making the issues all the more complex was the fact that Laura Ashley's retail presence was international, so that any solution would need to coordinate products not only among the firm's distribution warehouses in the United Kingdom, Holland, New Jersey, California, Canada, Paris, and Australia but among its retail stores in those same parts of the world.

Maxmin viewed an alliance with a strong international distribution company as one solution because it would allow Laura Ashley to focus on the product and the customer (design, production, and retail) and free it from owning and managing the distribution infrastructure. To develop a strategic alliance, Maxmin would need to find a partner who would agree to collaborate to achieve mutually

agreed-upon goals and with whom Laura Ashley could pool key value-chain resources and capabilities. To ensure that an alliance would have some chance of succeeding, Maxmin identified three fundamental criteria that would need to be satisfied by its future partner:

1. *Complementary needs and competencies:* Laura Ashley would target partners who were dedicated to the distribution business, who had international expertise and capabilities, and who needed international partners like Laura Ashley to help them grow.

2. *Similar management styles and operating systems:* Under Maxmin, Laura Ashley had adopted the simple strategic vision of "simplify, focus, act" as a way to guide turnaround efforts. Maxmin was looking for a partner with a similar orientation. In addition, Laura Ashley had a very poor information-technology infrastructure, and it would need this to be first class for it to survive. Thus, Maxmin was also looking for a distribution partner that would allow Ashley to upgrade its operating systems to a world-class standard.

3. *Divergent strategic objectives:* Maxmin did not want a partner who wanted to be, or might evolve into, a potential competitor. This ruled out using the distribution capabilities of one »

of its suppliers or partnering with another retailer that had strong distribution capabilities and infrastructure, such as Wal-Mart.

So with whom did Maxmin ally with? FedEx ("when you absolutely positively have to get it there overnight"). Even though FedEx was large at the time, with nearly $8 billion in revenues, the Laura Ashley relationship was still relatively substantial and gave FedEx further dedicated business worldwide. At the same time, FedEx offered Ashley both immediate world-class distribution capability and a longer-term opportunity to learn about global logistics from one of the best logistics firms on the planet. In Maxmin's terms, "The alliance is not about trucks and sheds. Logistics gives the organization an opportunity to achieve competitive advantage by focusing on its core competencies."

An alliance is not a panacea for a firm's ills nor is it a substitute for strategy. What this means for Laura Ashley in practical terms is that the firm must now identify what competencies are truly "core," in the sense that they differentiate Laura Ashley's business operations and offerings from those of competitors. It's one thing for Maxmin to say "we are going to focus on our core competencies"; it's another thing to execute this somewhat ambiguous statement profitably. By aligning the remaining facets of the strategy diamond with

this new strategy vehicle, Laura Ashley stands a chance of delivering the good to shareholders and other key stakeholders.

At the same time, relationships between alliance partners evolve over time, such that one partner may increase its relative power in the relationship and begin to exploit its partner, in the form of passing on higher costs. Though it is unlikely that Laura Ashley will be able to diversify profitably into a logistics company like FedEx, Laura Ashley may become so dependent upon FedEx that it can leave the relationship only by doing irreparable damage to its strategy, a future viability. A related risk is that Laura Ashley may lose touch with some of its customers as a result of this new outsourced distribution arrangement. If this diluted touch somehow also dilutes the firm's unique ability to link insights into customer taste and preferences with the design capabilities that differentiate it, then the FedEx arrangement may simply prolong and then contribute to the eventual demise of Laura Ashley. You would want to accommodate both these risks through the staging facet of the strategy diamond, along with a regular review of the fit among the other four facets.

Sources: K. Rankine, "Getting Lost, and Found, in the Translation: Former Laura Ashley Boss Jim Maxmin Has a New Book, a New Theory and His Own Language," *The*

Daily Telegraph (London), September 20, 2003, 34; F. Schwadel, "Laura Ashley Taps Newcomer to Bring Profit Back in Vogue," *Wall Street Journal* (Europe), July 18, 1991, 3; R. Hobson, "Eliminate Unnecessary Cost and Structure: Logistics Focus," *The Times* (London), November 8, 1993, 11.

South African Breweries, the maker of Castle Lager, successfully entered one of the largest beer markets in the world—the United States—by acquiring Miller Brewing Company in 2002. The combined corporation is known as SABMiller.

After its horrendous experiences with rapid international expansion, Lincoln Electric amended its corporate policy on FDI: It now engages only in FDI through alliances with local players in order to maximize the knowledge needed about local market conditions, both in terms of production and market demand. Sometimes alliances are dictated by the necessity to have a certain proportion of local content in a product, such as a car or motorcycle, in order to sell the product into a nonlocal market. Brazil and China are two examples of countries that have stringent local-content laws. Minimum efficient scale is another explanation for the use of alliances as an FDI foreign-entry tactic.

For example, the Daimler-Chrysler and BMW alliance mentioned earlier was necessary because neither company could justify the volume of production needed by the new plant to justify it economically. Therefore, the two firms joined forces to form Tritec, a state-of-the art automotive engine factory that supplies parts for BMW's Mini Cooper assembly plant in the United Kingdom and DaimlerChyrsler's PT Cruiser assembly plants in Mexico, the United States, and South Africa.[22]

SimConnect

Exporting Options in StratSim

The first issue to address in exporting is to decide which markets are most attractive for investment. This will typically be a more complex decision than choosing from new domestic business opportunities due to the added complexity of international PESTEL analysis and the choice of mode of entry. Thus, market attractiveness analysis must be considered in the context of PESTEL analysis and potential strategic partners.

In StratSim, two export options are available. The first is direct export via an alliance with an international partner. This is the quickest way to enter a market, but the terms with a potential partner must be negotiated, and generally a firm has less control over how the exported product is ultimately sold to the customer. The second option is through greenfield investment in a wholly owned foreign distribution network. This typically is more expensive and time consuming, but does allow your firm more control and consumer interaction in the foreign market.

Importing and International Strategy

importing Internationalization strategy by which a firm brings a good, service, or capital into the home country from abroad

In many ways, **importing** is a stealth form of internationalization because firms will often claim they have no international operations and yet directly or indirectly base their production or services on inputs obtained from outside their home country. Firms that engage in importing must be knowledgeable about customs requirements and informed about compliance with customs regulations, entry of goods, invoices, classification and value, determination and assessment of duty, special requirements, fraud, marketing, trade finance and insurance, and foreign trade zones. Importing can take many forms, from the sourcing of components, machinery, and raw materials to the purchase of finished goods for domestic resale to outsourcing production or services to nondomestic providers.

Outsourcing and Offshoring This latter activity, international outsourcing, has taken on the most visible role in business and corporate strategy in recent years. International outsourcing is not a new phenomenon. For instance, Nike has been designing shoes and other apparel for decades and manufacturing them abroad. Similarly, Pacific Cycle does not make a single Schwinn or Mongoose bicycle in the United States but instead imports them from Taiwanese and Chinese manufacturers. It just seems that international outsourcing is new because of the increasingly rapid pace with which businesses are sourcing services, components, and raw materials from developing countries such as China, Brazil, and India.

Information technologies (IT), such as telecommunications and the widespread diffusion of the Internet, have provided the impetus for the international outsourcing of services as well as factors of production. Such *business process outsourcing (BPO)* is the delegation of one or more IT-intensive business processes to an external nondomestic provider which, in turn, owns, administers, and manages the selected process based on defined and measurable performance criteria. Sometimes this is referred to as *offshoring* because the business processes (including production/manufacturing) are outsourced to a lower-cost location, usually overseas. Offshoring refers to taking advantage of lower-cost labor in another country. Although outsourced processes are handed off to third-party vendors, offshored processes may be handed off to third-party vendors or remain in-house. This definition of offshoring includes organizations that build dedicated captive centers of their own in remote, lower-cost locations. The many U.S. firms that have established *maquiladoras* (assembly plants) in Mexico are examples of offshoring without outsourcing.

Firms in such service and IT-intensive industries as insurance, banking, pharmaceuticals, telecommunications, automobiles, and airlines seem to be the early adopters of BPO. Of the industries just mentioned, insurance and banking are able to generate savings purely because of the large proportion of processes they can outsource, such as claim processing, loan processing, and client servicing through call centers. Among those countries housing BPO operations, India appears to be experiencing the most dramatic growth for services that require English-language skills and education. BPO operations have been growing 70 percent a year and are now a $1.6 billion industry, employing approximately 100,000 people. In India alone, BPO has to grow only 27 percent annually until 2008 to deliver $17 billion in revenues and employ a million people.[23]

More generally, foreign outsourcing and offshoring locations tend to be defined by how automated a production process or service can be made, the relative labor costs, and the transportation costs involved. When transportation costs and automation are both high, then the knowledge-worker component of the location calculation becomes less important. You can see how you might employ the CAGE framework to evaluate potential outsourcing locations. However, in some cases firms invest in both plant and equipment and the training and development of the local workforce. Brazil is but one case in point, with examples from Ford, BMW, Daimler-Benz, and Cargill. Each of these multinational organizations is making significant investments in the educational infrastructure of this significant emerging economy.[24]

SimConnect

Importing Options in StratSim

StratSim provides two options of sourcing foreign-manufactured vehicles. The first is direct import where your firm would negotiate with a foreign manufacturer to import one of their vehicles for domestic sale. Thus, once a domestic market opportunity has been identified, importing may offer advantages over designing one's own vehicle from scratch—typically in the areas of speed to market and cost. The second import option is sourcing production of one's own vehicle in a foreign location. This may provide your firm with access to lower labor costs, or other unique sources of advantage. Sourcing of production may also serve as either a first step of market entry or as a follow-up once success in a foreign market has been achieved and local production would provide an advantage over exporting.

INTERNATIONAL STRATEGY CONFIGURATIONS

How a firm becomes involved in international markets, which appears to be increasingly important, if not obligatory, for many if not all firms, differs from how it configures the interactions between headquarters and country operations. It is important to note that international-strategy configuration is as much about strategy formulation as it is about implementation, because management is making choices about which value-chain components to centralize, where to centralize those operations geographically, and the degree to which those decentralized and centralized value-chain activities will be managed and coordinated. Remember, too, that strategy helps a firm manage important tradeoffs that differentiate it and its products from competitors.

Resolving the Tension Between Local Preferences and Global Standards   In this section, we discuss the underlying tensions created between a firm's attempts to be responsive to the local needs of diverse sets of customers and yet remain globally efficient. Meeting the ideal tradeoff between customizing for local needs and achieving cost efficiencies requires further tradeoffs with respect to the firm's value chain regarding which activities will be standardized and which will be locally tailored. These are the central tradeoffs a firm must wrestle with in designing and managing its international strategy.

Globalizing firms must reconcile the natural tension that exists between local preferences and global standards. The domination of local preferences over the search for global efficiencies, left unchecked, often leads to what strategy researchers describe as *national fragmentation*.[25] In addition, local adaptation of products and services is significantly more expensive than relying on global standards. Consequently, attempting to achieve high levels of local responsiveness will almost always lead to higher cost structure.[26] A product that is uniform across markets is highly efficient to produce because the firm can simply design a factory of the most efficient size in a location that most efficiently balances the costs of inputs with the transportation costs of getting outputs to the desired markets. If this product has the same brand around the world, then marketing and promotion efforts are similarly focused on that single brand. However, even products like Coca-Cola, which appear to be ubiquitous, have different flavorings, packaging, and promotion constraints in each market. Some of these constraints are a function of local regulatory pressures; others reflect underlying differences in consumers' tastes. Just as important, other constraints are a function of the competitive norms that have prevailed in the industry, either globally or locally. The variations of international strategy configuration that we cover in this section are summarized in Exhibit 7.9.

We will also speak briefly about born-global firms in this section because more and more organizations appear to have operations that span national borders early in their existence. As you will see, born-global firms employ an amalgam of exporting and FDI, but do so much more rapidly than firms have in the past. In the strategy diamond, exporting and FDI would be considered vehicles, and the timing and sequencing of the usage would be viewed in the context of staging. Each of these vehicles provides a firm and its management with experience and knowledge about cross-border business practices.

Multinational Configuration

Each of the configurations identified in Exhibit 7.9 presents tradeoffs between global efficiency and local responsiveness. Recognize that these configurations are "pure forms" and that, in reality, most firms' international configurations vary slightly or significantly from those shown in Exhibit 7.9. By definition, strategy must be internally consistent and externally oriented. However, management must make judgments as to what an external orientation means in terms of how the strategy takes competitive pressures and consumer preferences into account. At the same time, management must also make judgments about the firm's internal resources and capabilities to support a particular international-strategy configuration. This explains why firms with seemingly very different international-strategy configurations can coexist in the same industry.

Exhibit 7.9 International Strategy Configurations, Global Efficiency, and Resource Requirements

	Relatively Few Opportunities to Gain Global Efficiencies	Many Opportunities to Gain Global Efficiencies
Relatively High Local Responsiveness	**Multinational Configuration** Build flexibility to respond to national differences through strong, resourceful, entrepreneurial, and somewhat independent national or regional operations. Requires decentralized and relatively self-sufficient units. **Example:** MTV initially adopted an international configuration (using only American programming in foreign markets) but then changed its strategy to a multinational one. It now tailors its Western European programming to each market, offering eight channels, each in a different language.	**Transnational Configuration** Develop global efficiency, flexibility, and worldwide learning. Requires dispersed, interdependent, and specialized capabilities simultaneously. **Example:** Nestlé has taken steps to move in this direction, starting first with what might be described as a multinational configuration. Today, Nestlé aims to evolve from a decentralized, profit-center configuration to one that operates as a single, global company. Firms like Nestlé have taken lessons from leading consulting firms such as McKinsey and Company, which are globally dispersed but have a hard-driving, one-firm culture at their core.
Relatively Low Local Responsiveness	**International Configuration** Exploit parent-company knowledge and capabilities through worldwide diffusion, local marketing, and adaptation. The most valuable resources and capabilities are centralized; others, such as local marketing and distribution, are decentralized. **Example:** When Wal-Mart initially set up its operations in Brazil, it used its U.S. stores as a model for international expansion.	**Global Configuration** Build cost advantages through centralized, global-scale operations. Requires centralized and globally scaled resources and capabilities. **Example:** Companies such as Merck and Hewlett-Packard give particular subsidiaries a worldwide mandate to leverage and disseminate their unique capabilities and specialized knowledge worldwide.

Source: C. Bartlett, S. Ghoshal, and J. Birkenshaw, Transnational Management *(New York: Irwin, 2004).*

When Lincoln Electric first embarked on becoming a global firm, it had relatively independent operations in many markets around the world. It used its strongest national positions to **cross-subsidize** market-share battles or growth initiatives in other countries. Such an approach is typically referred to as a **multinational configuration** because the firm is essentially a portfolio of geographically removed business units that have devoted most of their resources and capabilities to maximizing local responsiveness and uniqueness. Firms which, like Lincoln Electric, employ a multinational configuration have the objective to develop a global presence but may or may not use the same brand names in each market or consolidate their buying power or distribution capabilities.

cross-subsidizing Practice by which a firm uses profits from one aspect of a product, service, or region to support other aspects of competitive activity

multinational configuration Strategy by which a firm is essentially a portfolio of geographically removed business units that have devoted most of their resources and capabilities to maximizing local responsiveness and uniqueness

International Configuration

international configuration The firm leverages key resources and capabilities by centralizing them to achieve economies of scale, but it decentralizes others, such as marketing, so that some activities can be somewhat localized

Another configuration, sometimes simply referred to as an **international configuration,** centralizes some resources, such as global brand and distribution capabilities, in order to achieve costs savings, but decentralizes others, such as marketing in order to achieve some level of localization. This strategy is common among firms that have created something in their home market that they wish to replicate in foreign markets, allowing them the economies of scale and scope necessary to create and exploit innovations on a worldwide basis. Heavy R&D companies such as Intel and Pfizer fit this mold: Even though the products that they produce are relatively standardized around the world, local marketing and distribution channels differ.

Global Configuration

global configuration Strategy by which a firm sacrifices local responsiveness for the lower costs associated with global efficiency

A pure **global configuration** focuses only on global efficiency. A global configuration is one that makes a tradeoff between local responsiveness and the lower costs associated with global efficiency. With this configuration, production and sourcing decisions are designed to achieve the greatest economies of scale. Firms following this configuration potentially sacrifice the higher prices that follow customization, but they are counting on the likelihood that their products or services will meet enough needs to be demanded without finely tuned customization. Firms in commodity industries such as steel and copper, such as BHP-Billeton, fall into this category. Because end-customers make purchase decisions based on price alone, the firm is organized to realize the lowest possible production costs.

Transnational Configuration

transnational configuration Strategy in which a firm tries to capitalize on both local responsiveness and global efficiency

The final international-strategy configuration that we discuss, the **transnational configuration,** is one that attempts to capitalize on both local responsiveness and global efficiency. When successfully implemented, this approach enables firms to achieve global economies of scale, cross-subsidization across markets, and the ability to engage in retaliatory and responsive competition across markets. This configuration is available to companies with high degrees of internationalization. However, as with any other strategic tradeoff, it is extremely difficult to find the balance between cost efficiencies and the ability to customize to local tastes and standards. McDonald's is often used as an example of a firm that fits this configuration because it uses its purchasing power to get the best prices on the global commodities it uses for inputs yet tries to tailor its menu offerings to fit local tastes and cultural preferences.

Born-Global Firms

One reason that global strategy—and the four international strategy configurations—will become an increasingly important topic is the fact that more and more firms, even very small ones, have operations that bridge national borders very soon after their founding. Perhaps appropriate for the Internet age, this new breed of firms that emerged in the 1990s is being dubbed "born global" because their operations often span the globe early in their existence. A common characteristic of such firms is that their offerings complement the products or capabilities of other global players, take advantage of global IT infrastructure, or otherwise tap into a demand for a product or service that at its core is somewhat uniform across national geographic markets. Although many firms may fall into this category by virtue of their products, the operations and customers of born-global firms do actually span the globe. Born-global firms position themselves globally, exploiting a combination of exporting and FDI.

Logitech, the computer-mouse and peripherals company, is perhaps one of the best early examples of a successful born-global firm.[27] It was founded by two Italians and a Swiss, with operations and R&D initially split between California and Switzerland. Logitech's primary focus was on the PC mouse, and it rapidly expanded production to Ireland and Taiwan. With its stylish and ergonomic products, Logitech had captured 30 percent of the global mouse business by 1989, garnering the startup a healthy $140 million in revenues. Today, Logitech is an industry leader in the design and manufacture of computer-peripheral devices. It has manufacturing facilities in Asia and offices in major cities in North America, Europe, and Asia Pacific and employs more than 6,000 people worldwide.[28]

Skype is one of the most recent born-global firms, and you may already have it on your laptop or home computer, taking advantage of its free Internet phone technology (*voice-over-IP*, or *VOIP*).[29] At any point in time, millions of users are logged in to Skype, and the program and service have made such a strong impression that the phrase "skype me" has replaced "give me a call" in some circles. Initially founded in Sweden as Tele2, Skype is now headquartered in Luxembourg, with offices in London and Tallinn, Estonia. It received significant venture-capital funding from some of the largest venture-capital firms in the world, and was recently acquired by eBay. Skype was founded by the inventors of Kazaa, one of the most popular Internet file-sharing software programs in the world. Both Logitech and Skype exhibit a number of characteristics required for successful global startups.

How to Succeed as a Global Startup   Successful global startups must complete two phases. In the first phase, managers ask, "Should my firm be a global startup?" If they can answer yes to all or most of the follow-up questions entailed by phase 1, then they need to be sure that they can quickly build the resources and capabilities identified in phase 2. Research has shown that those firms unable to connect the dots in phase 2 were forced to cease operations after short, albeit sometimes lively, adventures.[30]

During phase 1—*and before moving on to phase 2*—managers should consider questions that will help them determine whether the firm should be a global startup:

- Does the firm need human resources from other countries in order to succeed?
- Does the firm need financial capital from other countries in order to succeed?
- If the firm goes global, will target customers prefer its services over those of competitors?
- Can the firm put an international system in place more quickly than domestic competitors?
- Does the firm need global scale and scope to justify the financial and human capital investment in the venture?
- Will a purely domestic focus now make it harder for the firm to go global in the future?

If the answer to all or most of these questions is yes, managers can commit to moving the firm into phase 2 and put together the tools they will need to move the firm into the global market:

- Strong management team with international experience
- Broad and deep international network among suppliers, customers, and complements
- Preemptive marketing or technology that will provide first-mover advantage with customers and lock out competitors from key suppliers and complements
- Strong intangible assets (both Logitech and Skype have style, hipness, and mindshare via their brands)
- Ability to keep customers locked in by linking new products and services to the core business, while constantly innovating the core product or service
- Close worldwide coordination and communication among business units, suppliers, complements, and customers

So why do we introduce the concept of global startups at this point in the text? One reason is because of their increasing prevalence, which is driven, in part, by globalizing consumer preferences, mobile consumers, large global firms, and the pervasiveness of the Internet and its effects. The second reason, which should become clear after reading the next section, is that dynamic contexts typically give rise to the need for firms to strive for a global presence and to understand global markets early in their evolution.

INTERNATIONAL STRATEGY IN STABLE AND DYNAMIC CONTEXTS

A recent McKinsey study suggests that the creativity which some companies have located in emerging economies, and which have resulted in inexpensive but high-quality products, will now compel incumbents to go down the same road.[31] This assertion gets at the heart—the question of urgency and timing—of how international strategy is approached in relatively stable versus dynamic contexts. Moreover, it also suggests that industries that might have been considered relatively stable will increasingly take on dynamic characteristics as a result of global competition. In many ways, what you have learned so far about business and corporate strategies in dynamic contexts is equally applicable in purely domestic and already globalizing organizations. The key difference, however—a difference that we hope is apparent after reading this chapter—is that cross-border business adds another level of complexity to both strategy formulation and execution and, that unfortunately, such complexity may be unavoidable for firms in dynamic contexts.

Global Context and Industry Life Cycle

Recall from earlier chapters that we differentiated between external- and internal-based views of strategy. The internal view emphasizes resources, capabilities, and activities as the source of competitive advantage, whereas the external view draws attention to how firms need to adapt or modify their competitive positions and strategies to the external environment to position themselves in a manner conducive to superior returns. These views have implications for the dynamic nature of international strategic action as well. Taking the external perspective, for instance, typically draws managerial attention to the dynamic nature of the industry life cycle and how that drives decisions to internationalize. Specifically, as an industry matures, the international implications of industry structure—and therefore strategic choices and firm behavior—should change in fundamental ways.[32]

conceptlink

In Chapter 6, we defined **first movers** as firms that choose to initiate a strategic action. We also pointed out that the benefits of first-mover strategy are subject to conditions in the **industry life cycle**. In Chapter 1, we noted that the need for early wins was one factor in driving **staging**—i.e., timing—decisions.

First-Mover Advantage   In the introductory stage of an industry's life cycle, the external perspective would expect firms to engage in few exports, largely because the market for the industry's products is still highly uncertain and there are few accepted quality, service, or technological standards. As you will see, the length of this stage may vary significantly by country. Firms should begin to export during the growth stage of industry life cycle because new entrants enter the market and compete for existing customers. Early movers in the domestic market then have an opportunity to be early movers in foreign markets as well and to continue growth even as domestic competition heats up. As the industry matures, exports gain even more steam in the face of domestic market saturation, and firms start producing products abroad to satisfy foreign demand and to search for global efficiencies. Industry shakeout and consolidation also tend to follow industry maturity, and consolidation through acquisitions leads to a few large global companies.

Staging and Geographic Markets   Similarly, when discussing international strategy from an external perspective, the fact that geographic markets differ in many legal, cultural, and institutional ways—differences which, in turn, are likely to have implications for product demand—must also be taken into account. Indeed, demand characteristics of geographic markets have been shown to evolve at different rates. For example, the time from new-product introduction to the growth stage (sometimes called market takeoff) in Portugal may occur after a longer period of time than the same transition in Denmark. Indeed, although the average period of time between a new-product or -service introduction and market takeoff is 6 years, a new product takes only about 4 years to take off in Denmark, Norway, and Sweden, compared to 9 years in Greece and Portugal (the U.S. averages 5.3 years).[33]

Role of Arenas in Global Strategies   Identification of arenas ensures that the most critical national markets are identified and brought into the plan. Similarly, even with thoughtful treatment of staging and arenas, structures, systems, and processes must be in complete alignment with the firm's vision and global intent. A firm that strives to execute the most complex global strategy—the transnational strategy—must have enormous investments in its ability to coordinate and integrate activities around the globe, complemented by customer characteristics that enable such a global strategy to create true value.

Resources and Global Strategy   The resource-based perspective has important implications for international strategy in dynamic contexts as well. It is here, too, that the questions of staging and geographic arenas from the strategy diamond model are critically important to effective international strategies. From the resource-based perspective, staging is important because the firm's global resources and capabilities do not materialize overnight. Lincoln Electric's experience is a case in point here. Lincoln's pace of international expansion exceeded its organizational capabilities to integrate foreign acquisitions, let alone manage them once they were integrated. Lincoln also attempted to internationalize almost exclusively through acquisitions. However, research on foreign expansion reveals that the firms most successful at internationalizing combine greenfield investments with acquisitions and alliances.[34] Simply expanding through greenfield investment can lead to inertia and lack of learning. Acquisitions help broaden a firm's knowledge base. However, exclusive reliance on acquisitions is not only costly but makes knowledge transfer and learning more difficult. Firms that balance greenfield investments and acquisitions seem to transfer more knowledge and create more value than firms that rely on either process exclusively.

Capabilities and Global Strategy One of the fundamental ideas of having a dynamic view of strategy is to continuously build and renew firm capabilities. Many born-global firms fall into this dynamic-context category nearly from inception. By continuously evolving its stock of resources and capabilities, a firm maximizes its chances of adapting to changing environmental conditions. Thus, when a firm decides to enter a particular new foreign market, it must also embark on developing the resources necessary to make that market-entry decision a success. At the same time, what it learns in those new geographic markets should be evaluated for application or adaptation to existing market positions.

In addition, as a firm internationalizes and becomes more dependent on a particular foreign location, the need for high-level capabilities to perform the local activities increases commensurately.[35] For instance, as Ikea expands around the globe, its ability to understand local furniture markets increases. However, these needs are greatest in markets where it faces the most exposure; Ikea's early missteps in the United States have been attributed to lack of market intelligence.[36] This leads us to our closing section on global strategy in dynamic contexts.

Developing a Mind-Set for Global Dynamic Competitiveness

Given the emphasis on the importance of leadership skills throughout this text, it should come as no surprise that what may make or break the effectiveness of a firm's international strategy is the internationally related capabilities and global mind-set of the firm's executives, particularly in dynamic markets. Moreover, such capabilities and mind-set may enable one firm to change a once relatively stable competitive context into a dynamic and vibrant one. In the box entitled "How Would *You* Do That? 7.2," international strategy researchers have identified four particularly effective tactics that organizations can use to develop global leaders.

Global Perspective The global mind-set has two distinct but related dimensions. The first dimension is something that strategy researchers simply refer to as global perspective.[37] Executives with a global perspective require a combination of specific knowledge and skills. In terms of knowledge, executives with a global mind-set have an appreciation for the fact that countries and their peoples differ culturally, socioeconomically, and sociopolitically, view those differences as potential opportunities as opposed to threats, and can link such differences to necessary adaptations in business operations. In addition, they also recognize that the management processes guiding those business operations must also be adapted to cultural, socioeconomic, and sociopolitical differences.

It is this latter aspect of knowledge that leads to the international-skills aspect of global perspective. In this instance, skills are the experience gained from *acculturation*—living in other cultures for extended periods of time as an expatriate. It also refers to the leadership skills necessary for managing a culturally diverse managerial team and world-wide workforce. The end result of this combination of knowledge and skills is that the firm is able to build strong relationships within the organization across geographies and with customers in different geographic locations.

Tactics for Developing Globally Minded Executives

A study of top-management teams across Asian, European, and North American firms identified four particularly effective tactics for developing global leaders. Although these tactics may seem obvious, they are not universally utilized, evidenced by the striking fact that even in multinationals, fewer than 15 percent of executives have substantive international experience. The researchers identified the following four tactics:

- *Travel*. This tactic aims to put managers in the middle of foreign cultures so that they can learn first-hand about people, schools, economy, political system, markets, and so on. It is important that such travel be unfettered as much as possible by the filters created by private drivers and fancy hotels. The executives who gain the most experience from international travel actually spend time with end consumers and local suppliers so that they see with their own eyes what opportunities and challenges may lie ahead. More firms are beginning to use "inpatriates"—foreign-country nationals who are integrated into the host company's corporate headquarters as a means to further knowledge transfer.

- *Teams*. This tactic involves the formation of teams composed of members from different cultures. Although part of the objective of such teams is to tailor solutions for particular country environments, an important by-product of this tactic is that the team members gain experience working with people from countries other than their own. The firms that have been most effective at exploiting this type of global acculturation have done so by taking three steps: (1) making sure a manager has been a member of a multicultural team before assuming a leadership position; (2) ensuring that the first multicultural-team experience is within one function, such as finance or marketing, before that member is introduced to a cross-functional, multicultural team; and (3) seeing to it that all members are provided prior and ongoing training in cross-cultural communication, team dynamics, and conflict resolution.

- *Training*. Although training was mentioned as an important component of the team-development tactic, it can also, if properly orchestrated, be a tactic in and of itself to gain a global mind-set and to build a within-firm global network. First, program participants should be drawn from geographically diverse units. Second, the training can foster intercultural understanding and cooperation by focusing on broad topics such as vision, strategy, change management, and interunit cooperative business initiatives, as well as specifically addressing cross-cultural communication, multicultural-team dynamics, and conflict resolution.

- *Transfers*. The most effective—though most expensive—tactic for developing global leaders is the actual transfer of individuals to foreign assignments. Such expatriate assignments tend to be the most effective because they typically force individuals to become immersed in the local culture. Expatriate assignments are the most expensive because the compensation packages often include doubling of the base salary, buying or paying for rent on the local housing, and providing for the feeding and education of the expatriate's family members. In practice, it is also expensive because many expatriates return sooner than expected, » often because their family members have trouble adjusting to the new country setting or because they leave the company altogether perhaps due to some aspect of the expatriate assignment, perhaps due to their being hired away by a local competitor. Firms that exploit this tactic most effectively take the following steps: (1) explicitly considering how the person and firm will use that person's experience in the future; (2) factoring in the person's family and how he or she will handle the move; (3) providing the training identified in the team and training tactics mentioned earlier; (4) furnishing a high-level home country mentor so the expatriate always has ties to headquarters; and (5) clearly spelling out the repatriation timeframe and possible career paths once the assignment is complete. These last two steps are key, because even 25 percent of the expatriates who have *successfully completed* an overseas assignment leave the firm after one year!

So if travel, teams, training, and transfers are the appropriate tactics for developing globally minded executives, where would you introduce this into the formulation and implementation aspects of your strategy? Well, if your firm is in a competitive field where it must grow or acquire global executive competencies quickly, then it would need to quickly recruit or promote individuals with the requisite global skills into the top management team. As you saw with Lincoln Electric, if a firm does not involve key decision makers with international management experience and skills in the formulation process, its international strategy may lead it into rocky waters. Depending on how critical these skills are for the firm's strategy and future success, you would need to integrate them in some way into the staging facet of the strategy diamond, and then leverage one or more of the tactics that were identified in this feature.

As we have demonstrated throughout this chapter, and have summarized in Exhibit 7.3, you also would need a clear vision about how an expansive global strategic posture is reflected in all five facets of the strategy diamond. From a personal standpoint, you may be interested in the two following related data points. First, large-sample strategic management studies have shown that firms perform better when their CEO and top executives have the global skills that complement their international strategy. Second, those studies also show that the executives themselves receive higher pay in those firms that can leverage their global experience. So not only is interna-tional experience fun to obtain, it also appears you can take it to the bank.

Sources: Adapted from H. Gregersen, A. Morrison, and J. Black, "Developing Leaders for the Global Frontier," *Sloan Management Review* 40:1 (1998), 21–32; J. Black, H. Gregersen, M. Mendenhall, and L. Stroh, *Globalizing People Through International Assignments* (Boston: Addison-Wesley, 1998); M. Harvey and M. Novicevic, "The Influences of Inpatriation Practices on the Strategic Orientation of a Global Organization," *International Journal of Management* 17:3 (2000), 362–372. M. A. Carpenter and W.G. Sanders, "The Effects of Top Management Team Pay and Firm Internationalization on MNC Performance," *Journal of Management* 30:4 (2004), 509–528; M. A. Carpenter, W. G. Sanders, and H. Gregersen, "Bundling Human Capital with Organizational Context: The Impact of International Assignment Experience on Multinational Firm Performance and CEO Pay," *Academy of Management Journal* 44:3 (2001), 493–512.

Research has found that firms which internationalize via a mixture of strategies, acquisitions, alliances, and greenfield investments tend to be more successful. Lincoln Electric, based in Cleveland, Ohio, discovered this firsthand. After initially relying primarily on acquisitions to grow overseas, Lincoln Electric determined that, to be successful, individual acquisitions had to be part of an integrated global strategy that also used joint ventures and greenfield startups. The result was the global industry leader we see today with 26 manufacturing locations in 18 countries.

Learning on a Worldwide Scale In many ways, the second dimension of a global mind-set requires the first dimension as a foundation. The second dimension is the capacity to learn from participation in one geographic market and transfer that knowledge to other operations elsewhere in the world. This means that the firm not only has globally savvy executives, but that these executives form an effective network of communication throughout the organization on a worldwide scale. You can tell that a firm and its managers possess this second dimension when the firm is routinely able to take knowledge gained in one market and apply it elsewhere, as was demonstrated in the case of SC Johnson's transfer of a plug-in household insect repellent product from Europe to the development of a new category of air-freshener products in the United States—Glade PlugIns.

Such learning also means that executives recognize how failure in one market can help the firm overcome failure in another. Lincoln Electric's failure with its unique incentive scheme in Germany taught it to introduce and experiment with an incentive structure in its Mexican operation on a gradual, bottom-up basis. As a result, the entire Mexican production operation has been transformed: The firm's executives recognized that failure in Germany could be used to develop a staging strategy for growth—and, ultimately, dramatic success—in its Mexican operation. Ironically, the more quickly a firm is able to cycle such knowledge throughout the firm, the less likely it is to stretch its managerial capabilities too thin over its expanding global empire.[38]

Obviously, the development of a global mind-set is more easily said than done. Our hope is that, given the fact there are very few industries or markets untouched by global competition (just look around your classroom for instance and you will likely see at least one person from another country), you will take it upon yourself to start investing in your own global mind-set.

SUMMARY

1. Define *international strategy* and identify its implications for the strategy diamond. A firm's international strategy is how it approaches the cross-border business activities of its own firm and competitors and how it contemplates doing so in the future. International strategy essentially reflects the choices a firm's executives make with respect to sourcing and selling its goods in foreign markets. A firm's international activities affect both its business strategy and its corporate strategy. Each component of the strategy diamond may be affected by international activities.

2. Understand why a firm would want to expand internationally and explain the relationship between international strategy and competitive advantage. Firms often expand internationally to fuel growth; however, international expansion does not guarantee profitable growth and should be pursued to help a firm build or exploit a competitive advantage. International expansion can exploit four principle drivers of competitive advantage: economies of scale and scope, location, multipoint competition, and learning. However, these benefits can be offset by the costs of international expansion, such as the liabilities of newness and foreignness and governance and coordination costs.

3. Describe different vehicles for international expansion. Foreign-country entry vehicles include exporting, alliances, and foreign direct investment (FDI). Exporters generally use local representatives or distributors to sell their products in new international markets. Two specialized forms of exporting are licensing and franchising. Alliances involve partnering with another firm to enter a foreign market or undertake an aspect of the value chain in that market. FDI can facilitate entry into a new foreign market and can be accomplished by greenfield investment or acquisition. Although importing is not technically a form of international expansion, it does provide firms with knowledge, experience, and relationships on which future international expansion choices and activities can be based.

4. Apply different international strategy configurations. The different forms that international strategies may take are driven by tradeoffs in attempts to customize for local needs and to pursue global cost efficiencies. The multinational configuration seeks to achieve high levels of local responsiveness while downplaying the search for global efficiencies. The international configuration seeks relatively few global efficiencies and markets relatively standard products across different markets. The global configuration seeks to exploit global economies and efficiencies and accepts less local customer responsiveness (i.e., more standardized products). The transnational configuration attempts to simultaneously achieve global efficiencies and a high degree of local product specialization.

5. Outline the international strategy implications of the stable and dynamic perspectives. Cross-border business adds another level of complexity to both strategy formulation and execution, and unfortunately such complexity may be unavoidable for firms in dynamic contexts. As products mature, firms' international strategies evolve, often moving from little global involvement during the introductory phase to high degrees of internationalization in mature markets. Resources need to be renewed more rapidly in dynamic markets. Thus, when a firm enters a new foreign market, it must also embark on developing the resources necessary to make that market-entry decision a success. In addition, what is learned in new markets can be leveraged for application in existing markets. Obviously, these objectives can be best achieved when managers with an international mind-set are in place.

6. Explore exporting and importing options using StratSim. If your instructor has enabled the international module in StratSim you will have a number of important decisions to make regarding your international strategy. Exporting and importing are two vehicles that you can employ, and each of these can take different forms. Your choices will need to be in alignment with the other four facets of the strategy diamond so that your overarching economic logic makes sense, as revealed by your relative profitability and attainment of your other balanced scorecard objectives.

KEY TERMS

REVIEW QUESTIONS

1. What is meant by *international strategy*?

2. Which aspects of the strategy diamond are related to international strategy?

3. What are the four most important ways a firm's international strategy can be related to its competitive advantage?

4. What three foreign-country entry vehicles are emphasized in this chapter?

5. What is typically the most cost- and time-intensive entry vehicle?

6. What are the four international strategy configurations discussed in this chapter?

7. On what two dimensions do the four international strategy configurations differ?

8. What does the external perspective tell you about international strategy in dynamic contexts?

9. What does the resource-and-capabilities-based perspective tell you about international strategy in dynamic contexts?

10. What role do managers play in effective international strategies, particularly in dynamic contexts?

How Would **you** Do That?

1. Refer to the box entitled "How Would *You* Do That? 7.1." What sources of information can management draw upon to identify the ideal international alliance partner? What risks is Laura Ashley taking when it becomes so dependent on one firm, such as FedEx? What can Laura Ashley do to reduce its dependence on FedEx?

2. The box entitled "How Would *You* Do That? 7.2" maps out what an organization can do to develop managers with a global mind-set. Many experts argue that a business student must have a global mind-set to be competitive in the human-capital marketplace. Your assignment is to design a learning program for yourself that would advance your global mind-set through an internship. What is the learning purpose of your internship? What are your specific global learning objectives? What experiences would contribute to meeting those objectives? What firms would you target for this mission, and what resources would you engage to approach them? Now, approach a firm and take action on your global mind-set agenda!

3. Analyze each of the foreign markets in StratSim. Which offers the best opportunities for export for your firm and why? Which foreign firm would be your first choice for partner? Would it be likely that your competitors would come to the same conclusion? Why would your firm be the best choice for this partner?

GROUP ACTIVITIES

1. Why have firms typically followed an international strategy path that started with importing or exporting, followed by alliances, and then FDI? What risks do born-global firms face in trying to do all of these at once? What resources and capabilities must they possess to do all of these effectively at once?

2. Are all Internet firms global by definition? What opportunities and barriers does the Internet present to firm internationalization?

ENDNOTES

1. P. Ng, "Dell: Selling Directly, Globally" (Hong Kong: Centre for Asian Business Cases, 2000); N. Chowdury, "Dell Cracks China," *Fortune,* June 21, 1999, 120; D. Chi, L. Manlu, D. Downing, and A. Tung, "Kodak in China" (France-China: INSEAD/CEIBS, 2000); "Telecom Tremors," *Business Week,* October 16, 2000, p. 68; Dell Annual Report, 2004, www.dell.com; W. M. Bulkeley, E. Ramstad and K. Linebaugh, " IBM, Lenovo Plan Joint PC Venture," *Wall Street Journal,* December 7, 2004, A3.

2. www.dominos.com.

3. The imperatives are summarized in A. Gupta and V. Govindarajan, "Managing Global Expansion: A Conceptual Framework," *Business Horizons* 43:2 (2000), 45–54.

4. R. Tomkins, "Battered PepsiCo Licks Its Wounds," *The Financial Times,* May 30, 1997, 26.

5. A. K. Gupta and V. Govindarajan, "Converting Global Presence into Global Competitive Advantage," *Academy of Management Executive* 15 (2001), 45–56.

6. J. W. Lu and P. W. Beamish, "International Diversification and Firm Performance: The S-Curve Hypothesis," *Academy of Management Journal* 47 (2004), 598–609.

7. Lu and Beamish, "International Diversification and Firm Performance."

8. Lu and Beamish, "International Diversification and Firm Performance."

9. A. D. Chandler, *Scale and Scope: The Dynamics of Industrial Capitalism* (Cambridge, MA: Harvard University Press, 1990).

10. Gupta and Govindarajan, "Converting Global Presence into Global Competitive Advantage."

11. Gupta and Govindarajan, "Converting Global Presence into Global Competitive Advantage."

12. Gupta and Govindarajan, "Converting Global Presence into Global Competitive Advantage."

13. P. Ghemawat, "The Forgotten Strategy," *Harvard Business Review* 81:11 (2003), 76–84.

14. P. Ghemawat, "Distance Still Matters," *Harvard Business Review* 79:8 (2001), 1–11.

15. K. Ito and E. L. Rose, "Foreign Direct Investment Location Strategies in the Tire Industry," *Journal of International Business Studies* 33:3 (2002), 593–602.

16. This anecdote is based on an interview with Lincoln Electric's chairman emeritus in D. Hastings, "Lincoln Electric's Harsh Lessons from International Expansion," *Harvard Business Review* 77:3 (1999), 163–174.

17. Based on information from a personal interview with Sam Johnson.

18. Adapted from A. Gupta and V. Govindarajan, "Managing Global Expansion: A Conceptual Framework," *Business Horizons* 43:2 (2000), 45–54.

19. The points in this paragraph draw heavily on the work of M. T. Hansen and N. Nohria, "See How to Build a Collaborative Advantage," *Sloan Management Review* Fall (2004), 22–30.

20. J. Johanson and J. Vahlne, "The Internationalization Process of the Firm," *Journal of International Business Studies* 8 (1977), 23–32; F. Weidersheim-Paul, H. Olson, and L. Welch, "Pre-Export Activity: The First Step in Internationalization," *Journal of International Business Studies* 9 (1978), 47–58; A. Millington and B. Bayliss, "The Process of Internationalization: UK Companies in the EC," *Management International Review* 30 (1990), 151–161; B. Oviatt and P.

McDougall, "Toward a Theory of International New Ventures," *Journal of International Business Studies* 25 (1994), 45–64.

21. O. Moen, "The Born Globals: A New Generation of Small European Exporters," *International Marketing Review* 19 (2002), 156–175.

22. www.tritecmotors.com.br.

23. Gupta and Govindarajan, "Managing Global Expansion."

24. www.fordfound.org, www.tritecmotors.com.br, and www.cargill.com.br.

25. G. Hamel and C. K. Prahalad, "Do You Really Have a Global Strategy?" *Harvard Business Review* 63:4 (1985), 139–148.

26. Gupta and Govindarajan, "Converting Global Presence into Global Competitive Advantage."

27. B. Oviatt and P. McDougall, "Global Start-Ups: Entrepreneurs on a Worldwide Stage," *Academy of Management Executive* 9:2 (1995), 30–44.

28. www.logitech.com.

29. www.skype.com.

30. Summarized from Oviatt and McDougall, "Global Start-Ups."

31. J. S. Brown and J. Hagel, "Innovation Blowback: Disruptive Management Practices from Asia," *McKinsey Quarterly,* January (2005).

32. M. Porter, *Competitive Advantage* (New York: Free Press, 1998).

33. G. Tellis, S. Stremersch, and E. Yin. 2003. "The International Takeoff of New Products: Economics, Culture and Country Innovativeness," *Marketing Science* 22:2 (2003), 161–187.

34. F. Vermeulen and H. Barkema, "Learning Through Acquisitions," *Academy of Management Journal* 44 (2001), 457–476; M. A. Hitt, M. T. Dacin, E. Levitas, and J. Arregle, "Partner Selection in Emerging and Developed Market Contexts: Resource-Based and Organizational Learning Perspectives," *Academy of Management Journal* 43 (2000), 449–467.

35. Gupta and Govindarajan, "Converting Global Presence into Global Competitive Advantage."

36. "Furnishing the World," *The Economist,* November 19, 1994, 79–80.

37. B. Kedia and A. Mukherji, "Global Managers: Developing a Mindset for Global Competitiveness," *Journal of World Business* 34:3 (1999), 230–251.

38. Gupta and Govindarajan, "Managing Global Expansion."

Implementation in Dynamic Contexts

After studying this chapter, you should be able to:

1. Understand the interdependence between strategy formulation and implementation.

2. Demonstrate how to use organizational structure as a strategy implementation lever.

3. Understand the use of systems and processes as strategy implementation levers.

4. Identify the roles of people and rewards as implementation levers.

5. Explain the dual roles that strategic leadership plays in strategy implementation.

6. Understand how global and dynamic contexts affect the use of implementation levers.

7. Be able to discuss and use strategy implementation levers in the context of StratSim.

► **1957**
Bill Gore, a scientist for DuPont, suggests using polytetrafluoroethylene (commonly known as Teflon) to insulate wires and cable. However, DuPont isn't interested. In 1958, Gore and his wife, Vieve, begin the New Year by starting their own business based on Bill's idea in the basement of their Delaware home.

► **1969**
Bob Gore discovers a way to stretch Teflon into a rainproof, insulated fabric, which becomes known as GORE-TEX®. Cable produced by Gore goes to the moon with astronauts Edwin Aldrin, Jr. and Neil Armstrong.

W. L. GORE & ASSOCIATES: WEAVING THE FABRIC OF ORGANIZATIONAL CULTURE

Perhaps best known for its GORE-TEX® fabrics, W. L. Gore & Associates makes fabrics, as well as electronic, industrial, and medical products.[1] Founded in 1958 by Wilbert (Bill) L. Gore, the company has been around for 48 years, thanks to a fortuitous early discovery, tireless entrepreneurship, and dedicated employees who continue to pursue the creation of value through innovation.

In 1941, Bill Gore, then a scientist at DuPont, began researching and developing plastics, polymers, and resins, helping to develop, among other products, a synthetic substance known as Teflon®. Gore left DuPont in 1958 to start a business for Teflon-type products, and the company's original product line consisted of Teflon-insulated

▶ **1970s and 1980s**
W. L. Gore & Associates develops the GORE-TEX® material into a wide array of products, including filters, fabrics for outerwear, and fiber for space suits.

▶ **2004**
Fast Company magazine names W. L. Gore & Associates the most innovative company in America. W. L. Gore & Associates, which produces a wide array of products ranging from guitar strings to medical supplies, employs approximately 7,400 people in 45 locations around the world—not bad for a company that began in a home basement.

1995   2000

electronic wires and cables. Today, the privately held company boasts 7,400 employees around the world and $1.84 billion in annual sales. The majority of its stock is owned by the Gore family, with the remainder held by employees.

But back to Teflon, an extremely versatile polymer known as PTFE (polytetrafluoroethylene, or CF_2CF_2). Bill Gore had set out to develop applications for PTFE that didn't interest DuPont, but it was his son Bob, who had a doctorate in chemistry, who hit the product-development jackpot. In 1969, he discovered a way to stretch Teflon at the microscopic level, creating a membrane with holes large enough to release body heat and moisture but small enough to deflect raindrops. In 1976, Gore received a patent for the GORE-TEX material, which proved to have applications in such diverse products as space suits, outerwear, filters, and artificial arteries, and the company soon experienced explosive growth.

By the 1980s, GORE-TEX fabric had become the company's core product. Eventually, of course, Gore's patent expired, opening the door to a host of competitors. Although the company retains patents on several subsequent products and processes, in some cases it's eschewed the patent route, suspecting that patents often supply competitors with blueprints on how to innovate around unique technologies. Instead, in some cases it protects proprietary knowledge within the company. Gore thus relies on highly secretive manufacturing processes to which employees have access only on a strict need-to-know basis. Outsiders are barred from certain sections of Gore facilities, and many internal personnel have never witnessed key processes in operation.

In 1975, Gore entered the medical-products industry with a GORE-TEX-based graft designed to replace human arteries. In the late 1990s, the company developed a filter system that converts carcinogenic by-products of industrial combustion into water and harmless chemicals. Today, Gore's diverse product line includes ELIXIR® guitar strings, fiber for GLIDE® dental floss, GORE-TEX and WINDSTOPPER® fabrics, and numerous highly specialized medical products.

Gore is guided by four core values:

- Employees should be treated fairly, and they should extend the same fairness to everyone with whom they come in contact.
- Employees are free to encourage and help colleagues grow in knowledge, skill, and scope of responsibilities.
- Employees can choose the projects to which they commit themselves.
- Employees should consult with each other before committing to any action that could affect the reputation of the company.

From the outset, Bill Gore wanted a unique company culture that fostered innovation, and in this respect, Gore is in fact much different from most companies. For instance, there are no official bosses and very few job titles. Employees are called "associates," and when they're hired, new associates are assigned to "sponsors" within their functional areas. Sponsors mentor new associates and instill a healthy attitude toward commitment, and as associates' commitments change, they may choose new sponsors. Gore's philosophy revolves around the principle that growth is fueled by innovation and that innovation is fostered by a culture based on commitment and experimentation.

Because of the desire to maintain a distinct and deeply shared culture, hiring new associates is a critical process that includes multiple interviews with other employees as well as with HR specialists. Because there are no official bosses, the company lacks a formal hierarchy and does not have rigid channels of communication. Without titles, associates aren't locked into specific tasks. They're encouraged to take on new project commitments and to communicate freely with anyone who can help them develop those commitments. Gore refers to its organizational structure as "the lattice."

Depending on the requirements of the task or project at hand, every associate is potentially connected with every other associate, and leaders are associates who are followed by other associates. Salary is based on peer feedback on the contributions made by teammates, and committees composed of leaders from each functional area determine salary structure. Salaries ultimately depend on an associate's contributions to the success of a given business rather than technical expertise alone.

Most companies of Gore's size and success have gone through IPOs so that the founders can cash out their equity and raise capital to fuel growth. Gore, however, has resisted the lure of the IPO, not because the Gore family isn't interested in earnings, but because they don't want to sacrifice innovation and long-term prosperity to the pressure of capital markets to demonstrate short-term earnings performance. ■

INTERDEPENDENCE OF STRATEGY FORMULATION AND IMPLEMENTATION

By now, you should have a very good idea of what makes a good strategy: Good strategies enable an organization to achieve its objectives. You've also learned how to describe and evaluate business and corporate strategy formulation according to the strategy diamond. You know that *strategy formulation* is *deciding what to do* and that *strategy implementation* is the process of *executing what you've planned to do.*[2] You understand that neither formulation nor implementation can succeed without the other, and you're aware that the most successful firms often adjust strategies and execution according to feedback from the implementation process itself. That's why the processes of formulation and implementation are iterative and interdependent, with the objective being a consistent and coherent set of strategy elements and implementation levers. As Exhibit 8.1 reminds us, the overarching model of strategy hinges on the integral relationship among *formulation* (the process of aligning the five elements of the strategy diamond), *implementation levers*, and *strategic leadership*. In this chapter, we'll focus on issues concerning strategy implementation—specifically, implementation levers and the aspects of strategic leadership that facilitate successful implementation.

When a firm is experiencing difficulties, it's always good to ask three questions:

- Is the strategy flawed?
- Is the implementation of the strategy flawed?
- Are both the strategy and implementation flawed?

It shouldn't come as any surprise that, more often than not, implementation problems are the source of performance problems.[3] Obviously, no strategy can be effective if its implementation isn't. By the same token, although we tend to attribute success to effective strategies, some of the most stellar performers achieve competitive advantage because of *how* they execute their strategies.

conceptlink

In Chapter 2, we define **strategic leadership** as the task of managing an overall enterprise and influencing organizational outcomes. We explain that strategic leaders are equally responsible for **strategy formulation** and **implementation**, and in Chapter 1, we stressed the two critical roles played by leaders in implementation: (1) deciding on **resource allocations** and (2) developing **stakeholder** support.

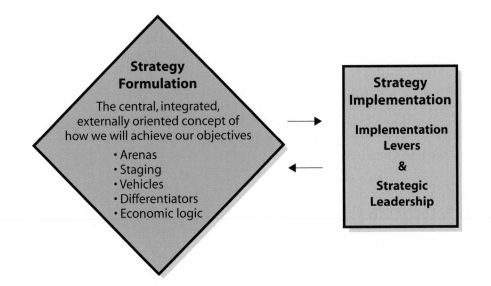

Exhibit 8.1 Formulation and Implementation

Strategy Formulation

The central, integrated, externally oriented concept of how we will achieve our objectives

- Arenas
- Staging
- Vehicles
- Differentiators
- Economic logic

Strategy Implementation

Implementation Levers

&

Strategic Leadership

A Model Company

The opening vignette on Gore describes a company whose strategy implementation integrates all of the key elements of the overarching implementation model outlined in Exhibit 8.1 (and indeed, it hits on all the points of the more detailed implementation framework we will review later in the chapter):

- Gore's implementation levers function in unison to support a focused strategy of growth through innovative new products.

- The lack of formal titles, hierarchy, and bureaucracy reflect a flat organizational structure that facilitates both the flow of information and quick decision making (though this presents a challenge to coordination and rapid change at an organizational level).

- Systems are in place to identify new-product opportunities, to ensure that they have product champions, and to reward employees for their contributions to both product lines and the company's overall profitability.

- Because the selection and retention of people, in terms of both necessary skills and personal fit with the organization, are a critical factor in Gore's success, these functions are rigorously managed. Attention to human resources also reinforces a deep culture that values leading-edge innovation, and top management reiterates the importance of the firm's "core values."

- Gore operates in both international and dynamic contexts. It competes in areas of leading-edge technology in different markets around the globe. Because of this, it limits the size of its facilities to about 200 people or fewer, reinforcing operating flexibility and responsiveness to local conditions.

- Finally, Gore's product-line strategy provides an excellent example of the iterative nature of implementation and formulation. For example, its strategy to enter the dental-floss market under the Glide brand reflects the confluence of the firm's valuable resources and its unique array of implementation levers. A new manager was able to assume accountability for this previously unknown product based on Gore's Teflon technology, launch the product in a small town using word-of-mouth advertising, and grow the product's share of market from 0 to 22 percent in just 8 years.[4] Just as important were the allocation of strategic resources and the effective communication of the strategy itself to key stakeholders.

By the end of this chapter, you should be able to identify the implementation levers and strategic-leadership functions that drive successful strategies. You should be able to identify levers that are in need of repair and propose a plan for using certain levers to implement a strategy more effectively.

The Knowing-Doing Gap

Let's go back to a couple of admonitions that we cited in Chapter 1:

- "A strategy . . . is only as good as its execution."[5]
- "The important decisions, the decisions that really matter, are strategic. . . . [But] more important and more difficult is to make effective the course of action decided upon."[6]

These principles apply to our focus in this chapter as well: By and large, firms find it much more difficult to implement good ideas than to generate new ideas and knowledge. A recent study, for instance, found that 46 percent of large companies surveyed regarded themselves as good or excellent at generating new knowledge; only 14 percent of the same firms reported having launched new products based on the application of new knowledge.[7] This difference between what firms *know* and what they *do* has been dubbed the **knowing-doing gap**.[8] Let's look a little more closely at this phenomenon.

knowing-doing gap Phenomenon whereby firms tend to be better at generating new knowledge than at creating new products based on that knowledge

What Causes the Knowing-Doing Gap?   One explanation of the knowing-doing gap is the fact that the strategy-formulation process itself isn't shared with those stakeholders, including lower-level managers, who will be integral in rolling out the strategy. Other observers argue that, even if all the right stakeholders are included in the strategy-formulation process, management often fails either to determine whether the proper implementation levers are in place or to take appropriate strategic-leadership actions.

SimConnect

The Knowing-Doing Gap in StratSim

The knowing-doing phenomenon is present in StratSim as well. Doing in StratSim is somewhat simpler than in real life, yet there are still obstacles to overcome. Poor execution in StratSim can run the gamut from something as simple as running out of time to enter decisions, to failing to understand exactly how to translate a strategic directive such as "be first to market in a particular vehicle class and gain a leadership position to achieve a low cost advantage" into the set of decisions that need to be made. Most of the knowing-doing gap can be bridged through solid team organization, good communication, time management, pre-simulation preparation, and operating as a learning organization. This final point is especially important in a dynamic setting, such as a simulation. You can be assured that not everything will go as planned as your intended strategy morphs into realized and emergent strategies. Your firm will likely make mistakes or misinterpret information, the environment will change, and the competition will constantly challenge you. Therefore, learning from these challenges and adjusting your tactics (and possibly your strategy) based on what you've learned is an essential part of bridging the knowing-doing gap. Blaming others, wishing things would go as planned, and other non-learning behavior will only serve to make the gap larger going forward.

Obstacles, External and Internal Some experts believe that strategy-implementation failures result from management's inability to assess potential implementation obstacles. Some obstacles reside in the external environment. Prior to its merger with Hewlett-Packard, for example, Compaq's attempts to mimic Dell's direct-sales model met with stiff resistance from its existing retail base, including such outlets as CompUSA and Best Buy. Of course, obstacles also exist inside the firm—a fact that we've already touched on by emphasizing the importance of assessing existing resources, implementation levers, and management-action plans. In diversified firms, the parent company itself may be an internal obstacle, particularly if one business unit is proposing a strategy that puts it in direct competition with another.

The Impact of Culture One of the most critical, and yet most overlooked, internal implementation obstacles is a firm's *culture*. Culture sometimes presents management with a persistent challenge: It's both difficult and time consuming to change, and it can be a source of competitive advantage.[9] **Culture** consists of the core organizational values that are widely held and shared by organizational members (including employees, managers, and owners). Recent studies have found evidence confirming the theory that firms with strong shared values are better at implementing strategies and achieving higher levels of performance than firms with weaker values. Across industries, for example, firms with strong cultures generally achieve higher average levels of return on investment, net income growth, and change in share price.[10] In addition, firms with strong cultures seem to be less variable in their performance outcomes.[11] Finally, these positive effects of shared values on performance appear to be even stronger in highly competitive markets.[12] Why? Perhaps because effective strategy implementation is even more important in highly competitive industries, where there's less room for error.

culture Core organizational values widely held and shared by an organization's members

Sometimes, company culture reflects the values of the CEO and other top managers, whereas at others leaders steward and protect existing values. Shared values are typically few in number, deeply embedded in the organization, give meaning and identity to the firm's members, and state the purpose of the firm's work. The shared values of Gore may be one of the reasons why it thrives despite having a structure that seems too chaotic for a firm of its size. Gore's values can be summed up as fairness, freedom, commitment, and consultation. Associates, for instance, are expected to treat one another fairly. They're given the freedom to grow in knowledge, skill, and scope of responsibility. Gore expects associates to spend 10 percent of their time tinkering with new ideas and to demonstrate commitment to their chosen projects. Finally, although everyone is empowered to make decisions, any management decision that may affect the firm's image or performance must be run past other associates.

In short, a firm's strategy must be consistent with its shared values if it's to be implemented successfully. Thus, it's crucial that strategists understand what's really important to members of the organization. First, of course, they need to ask whether employees have any shared values. If the answer is no, top management may have to spend some time developing and communicating a core set of values and getting organizational members to buy into them.

concept link

In discussing threats to rational decision making in Chapter 2, we explain some of the biases that can lead to such flawed judgments. In Chapter 10, we detailed the threat of **managerialism**—the tendency of managers to make decisions based on personal rather than stakeholder interests—to the process of implementing mergers and acquisitions.

Mismatches Not surprisingly, mismatches between strategy and implementation levers or between strategy and strategic-leadership actions are easy to recognize in hindsight. Of course, they're much more difficult to catch in real time. Executives who are responsible for formulating strategy are often prone to making overly optimistic projections and downplaying the obstacles to execution. Consider, for instance, the number of hardware and software firms that have attempted to become IT-solution providers by adding a consulting arm to their existing business. Most have failed, usually because they lacked the organization to execute the strategy.[13] SAP provides a good example of this.

As a provider of ERP software, SAP grew quickly at first because of demand for its unique product. In its zeal for growth, however, the firm neglected to focus on structure, employee retention, and balance between rewards for sales and rewards for profitability. SAP eventually recovered (as you will see in the box entitled "How Would *You* Do That? 8.1"), but only after a new CEO dramatically revamped the firm's infrastructure, cost controls, and human resource policies.[14]

As the SAP example in the "How Would *You* Do That?" box shows, implementation levers tend to be interrelated, which means that a change in one will probably require a change in all or some of the others. We'll deal with further examples of these interrelationships in the following sections, but at this point, we suggest that you use the following statement to guide you in your study of the material in this chapter:

> [T]he strategist will not be able to nail down every action step when the strategy is first crafted, nor should this even be attempted. However, he or she must have the ability to look ahead at the major implementation obstacles and ask, "Is this strategy workable? Can I make it happen?"[15]

By the end of this chapter, you'll be able not only to answer questions such as these, but offer recommendations for employing implementation levers and taking strategic-leadership actions. These two facets of strategy implementation—levers and leadership—are summarized in Exhibit 8.2.

Exhibit 8.2 Key Facets of Strategy Implementation

Implementation Levers
- Organizational structure
- Systems and processes
- People and rewards

Intended Strategy

Realized & Emergent Strategies

Strategic Leadership
- Making lever and resource allocation decisions
- Communicating the strategy to stakeholders

Picking Up the Pieces at SAP

The enterprise software company SAP dodged a bullet, but just barely. It did so not by overhauling its strategy but rather by dramatically changing its leadership and implementation approach. We will focus on SAP America, one of the largest subsidiaries of the German firm SAP, because it characterizes much of what took place globally in this firm. From 1992 through most of 1996, SAP America's revenues grew at an astounding triple-digit annual rate, from $49 million to an annualized $818 million. The number of employees over that same period grew from 284 to 1,621. This rapid growth was spurred by two things. First, SAP had what many U.S. multinationals perceived to be the best ERP product on the market. The product was highly profitable due to its relatively standardized design and high market demand. Second, SAP was a fairly decentralized organization, with functional emphasis primarily in sales and on an incentive system that rewarded sales and sales growth. Career paths were unclear and focused on regions, but because the compensation was so lucrative, employees could earn huge salaries based on sales and then jump ship to a firm where their career and mobility might be more clearly laid out. As a result, SAP America was built for speed (though not efficiency), and its rocket-like sales growth reflected the levers and leadership that were in place.

Coming into late 1995, however, the rocket seemed to be running out of fuel. The combination of growing competition from the likes of Oracle and Siebel systems, market saturation, and a lack of organizational accountability that was a by-product of the growth focus was beginning to undermine SAP's profitability, customer service, and reputation. SAP Germany's kick in the pants to SAP America started with the promotion of then-CFO Kevin McKay to the position of CEO (and the departure of the old CEO, Paul Wahl, to competitor Siebel Systems). McKay moved quickly to increase cultural sensitivity to costs and cost management, implement an administrative structure to bolster the organization's overall professionalism, and formalize human resource policies.

This latter step took the form of hiring an HR director (no one had held that role at SAP America before, despite all of the hiring that had gone on) who put a formal HR system in place. These decisions were complemented by increased R&D funding to explore the Internet applications of SAP software, a platform that the software giant had ignored up to that point. At the same time, McKay subtly shifted SAP's strategy from one of pure growth through new accounts to account "farming"—an increased focus on garnering a greater share of each existing customer's IS business needs, coupled with the modification of the firm's reward system to reward such behaviors.

While these changes caused many people to leave SAP, this loss was more than offset by the hiring of new executives and workers who bought into the new organizational arrangements and SAP's vision. By 2000, the firm had successfully launched a Web-based version of its software, called MySAP, and regained its position of industry leadership.

Sources: SAP Annual General Shareholders' Meeting, Mannheim, Germany, May 3, 1997; SAP 1997–2003 Financial Reports (accessed on July 15, 2005), www.sap.com/company/investor/reports/pastfinancials/index.epx; Harvard Business School Case 9-397-067, SAP America, December 3, 1996; N. Boudette, "How a German Software Titan Missed the Internet Revolution," *Wall Street Journal,* January 18, 2000, A1.

IMPLEMENTATION LEVERS

implementation levers
Mechanisms used by strategic leaders to help execute a firm's strategy

concept link

Recall that we introduced and described the three main categories into which **implementation levers** could be divided back in Chapter 1: (1) organizational structure; (2) systems and processes; and (3) people and rewards.

organizational structure
Relatively stable arrangement of responsibilities, tasks, and people within an organization

We have been using the term *implementation lever* without providing a precise definition. Before we explore the concept in detail, therefore, it may be useful to make clear that **implementation levers** are mechanisms that a strategic leaders has at his or her disposal to help execute a strategy. Although anything that enables an executive to get leverage to execute change can be considered an implementation lever, we categorize the major levers as *structure, systems and processes,* and *people and rewards.* In this section, we will go into some depth on each of these.

Structure

Because structure is the implementation lever that usually gets the most attention in an organization, we'll start with it. Alfred Chandler's classic research on the interdependence of strategy and structure based on studies of General Motors, DuPont, and Sears raised the topic to prominence in the 1960s.[16] Today, practically every issue of the *Wall Street Journal* announces that some firm is busy "restructuring" or reporting decreased earnings due to "restructuring charges." Most firms develop *organizational charts*, which are static representations of their structure. But what is *structure* itself? We'll define **organizational structure** as the relatively stable arrangement and division of responsibilities, tasks, and people within an organization. Organizations are composed of people who are assigned to certain divisions and who perform certain delegated and specialized tasks. The *structure* of an *organization*, therefore, is the framework that management has devised to divide tasks, deploy resources, and coordinate departments.[17] Structure provides a way for information to flow efficiently from the people and departments who generate it to those who need it. Structure also spells out *decision rights*—policies that tell individuals who's responsible for generating particular information and who's authorized to act on it.

Control and Coordination   Briefly, structure includes a firm's authority hierarchy, its organizational units and divisions, and its mechanisms for coordinating internal activities. Organizational structure performs two essential functions:

- It ensures control.
- It coordinates information, decisions, and the activities of employees at all levels.

As both functions become more complex, firms generally modify their structure accordingly. Structure should be consistent with the firm's strategy. The more diversified the firm, the more the structure that will have to be designed to accommodate coordination. After all, if a firm is participating in related businesses, it is probably trying to exploit synergies—a task that, as we saw in our chapters on corporate and international strategy, often requires sharing information and resources across product or geographic divisions. Conversely, the more focused the firm is on a single business (or even on each of multiple unrelated businesses), the more its structure should be designed to emphasize control. As we'll see, the popular means of organizing firm structure include the *functional, multidivisional, matrix,* and *network* forms.[18]

Traditionally, both scholars and managers have thought of structure as being determined by a firm's strategy,[19] and in most cases, this assumption is valid. We'll soon see, however, that structure can result in new or modified strategies. In fact, the way in which tasks are delegated and resources deployed can produce rather dramatic changes in a firm's strategy.

With respect to structure, a key question is whether the firm's current structure facilitates the implementation of its strategy and provides the information it needs to revise its existing strategy. At all times, a firm's structure should seek a balance between the control needed to achieve efficiency and unity of direction and the delegation of authority required to make timely decisions in a competitive environment. Let's examine two cases in which new structure resulted directly in changes in strategy.

How Structure Influences Strategy (I)   After developing an innovative process for economically producing industrial gas onsite at customers' factories, the French firm Air

Liquide (translated as *liquid air*) began locating personnel at client sites. This restructuring gave employees at customer sites more decision-making autonomy. Before long, on-site employees discovered a host of new services that Air Liquide could offer its clients, such as handling hazardous materials, troubleshooting quality-control systems, and managing inventory. The result, of course, was a wealth of new business opportunities—most of which offered higher margins than the company's core gas production and distribution business. Such services now account for 25 percent of Air Liquide's revenues, as opposed to just 7 percent before the restructuring.[20]

How Structure Influences Strategy (II)   Part of this next story was presented in the opening vignette to Chapter 6 on dynamic strategies. In the early 1980s, Intel derived more than 90 percent of its revenue from the manufacture of memory chips. A feature of its organizational structure is credited with being the key to its transformation into a maker of PC microprocessors in a span of less than two years. Although they appear similar, the capabilities underlying effective competition in memory versus microprocessors differ. Originally, Intel's structure permitted production managers to make production decisions based on a set of established rules. Among other things, these rules stipulated that managers allocate production capacity based on margins per square inch of silicon wafer. In response to this requirement, production managers started shifting manufacturing capacity from memory chips to microprocessors (previously just a small side business), because the margins were much greater. Interestingly, this shift wasn't dictated or orchestrated by senior management. In fact, Intel's senior management didn't ratify the decision to become a microprocessor manufacturer until well after microprocessors had come to account for about 90 percent of company-wide output.[21]

Forms of Organizational Structure

In this section, we'll review four basic forms of organizational structure: *functional, multi-divisional, matrix,* and *network.* We also briefly describe partnerships and franchises. Consider these structures to be "pure" forms. In reality, they're just basic models on which many variations have been played. Later in the chapter, we'll show how they've been modified to accommodate global and dynamic contexts.

Functional Structure   A **functional structure** organizes its activities according to the specific functions that a company performs. As shown in Exhibit 8.3, common units include finance, sales and marketing, production, and R&D. From a practical standpoint, any of the functions in a firm's value chain can be organized as a unit in a functional structure.

> **functional structure** Form of organization revolving around specific value-chain functions

Functional structures tend to work best in smaller firms and those with few products or services. Platypus Technologies, for instance, is a small nanotechnology firm with 30 employees,[22] most of whom are R&D scientists working in the lab. Obviously, however, Platypus also has small departments dedicated to finance, marketing, and human resources.

Functional organization helps managers of smaller firms improve efficiency and quality by fostering professionalism in the performance of specialized tasks. Bear in mind, however, that as firms grow and become more complex (perhaps by venturing into multiple lines), a functional form can become downright dysfunctional. Often, problems arise if

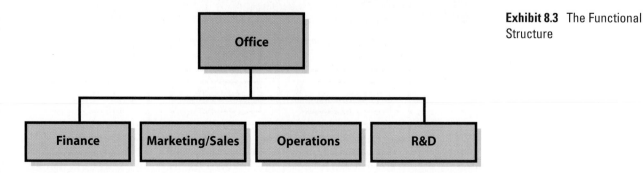

Exhibit 8.3 The Functional Structure

Functional structures tend to work best in smaller firms, such as Platypus Technologies, LLC, a Wisconsin nanotechnology firm, which employs about 30 people.

each functional unit begins to focus too narrowly on its own goals and operations, thus losing sight not only of other functional activities but of customer needs and corporate objectives. This phenomenon has given rise to the term *functional silos.*

The functional organizational model may also exacerbate problems in multiproduct, multimarket firms. Expansion, whether into product or geographic markets, can become problematic if the strategy that's appropriate in one market doesn't work very well in another. The types of products, for example, that enjoy dominant domestic share may not meet the needs of foreign consumers. Similarly, a firm involved in two different product markets may find that the same competitive methods don't work equally well in both or that different markets call for different sales channels. When a functional structure is used in contexts characterized by varying market demands and sales characteristics, functionally structured organizations may be sluggish in responding to changing customer demands and in accessing potential new customers.

multidivisional structure Form of organization in which divisions are organized around product or geographic markets and are often self-sufficient in terms of functional expertise

Multidivisional Structure   One solution to the problems of managing activities in multiple markets is the **multidivisional structure**, illustrated in Exhibit 8.4. Divisions can be organized around geographic markets, products, or groups of related businesses, with division heads being responsible for the strategy of a coherent group of businesses or

Exhibit 8.4 Typical Multidivisional Organization

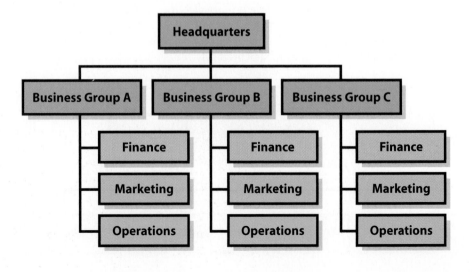

markets. Such strategic specialization means that strategic decisions are more likely to be appropriate and timely. It also enables firms to design compensation systems that reward performance at the business-unit, versus functional, level.

One of the first companies to adopt a multidivisional structure, GM is mostly organized according to product divisions (GM Trucks, Chevrolet, Buick, Cadillac, Saturn, and so forth). Each division maintains a finance function, a marketing function, and so on. Multidivisional structure makes it possible to implement division-specific incentives and performance-accountability standards, and because each division has ready access to key resources, multidivisional structure also fosters speedier reactions to opportunities and challenges.

Multidivisional structure is also effective in coordinating diverse economic activities. Headquarters, for example, plans, coordinates, and evaluates all operating divisions, allocating the personnel, facilities, funds, and other resources needed to execute divisional strategies. Divisional managers, meanwhile, are in charge of most of the functions revolving around major product lines and, as such, are typically responsible for divisional financial performance.

For instance, Emageon, a 225-employee provider of advanced visualization tools to hospitals and other medical organizations, has two divisions.[23] One offers electronic hardware, and its sales force works with executives who are responsible for IT decisions at target customers. The second division specializes in software for x-rays and CAT scans, and because physicians usually make the software-purchase recommendations, Emageon's software sales force focuses on them. Together, the two divisions provide a complete solution for firms in Emageon's target industry, and as it so happens, each can cross-sell the other's products.

Of course, multidivisional structure is not without drawbacks. It can, for instance, foster undesirable competition between divisions. Emageon doesn't have this problem, but it's not hard to see how GM's higher-end Buicks bump up against its lower-priced Cadillacs.

In addition, when each division is functionally self-contained, there may be costly duplications of staff functions that could be handled more efficiently under some other form of organization. Finally, coordination across divisions can be difficult if cooperation is in the best interests of one division but not those of another.

Matrix Structure The matrix structure, which is represented in Exhibit 8.5, is a hybrid between the functional and multidivisional structures. A **matrix structure** is designed to take advantage of the benefits of both basic forms—namely, functional specialization and divisional autonomy. As you can see in Exhibit 8.5, two reporting channels exist simultaneously. In our hypothetical company, for instance, there are functional divisions for finance and marketing, but personnel from both divisions are assigned to specific product or geographic divisions. A finance specialist, therefore, reports simultaneously to a finance executive and an executive in one or another of the product or geographic divisions.

The Swiss–Swedish technology giant Asea Brown Boveri (ABB) furnishes perhaps the most dramatic example of the matrix structure in action. In the early 1990s, the firm was composed of more than 900 matrix units. Any structure that sets up so many dual loci of authority is going to have problems with conflicts over authority and accountability. At ABB, however, managers in one matrix unit rarely exercise direct authority over their counterparts in other units. (Dealings between units, therefore, often depend on managers' skills in the arts of negotiation and persuasion.) Moreover, the matrix provides flexibility by making it possible to organize teams around specific projects, products, or markets.

The utility of a matrix structure increases when the pressures facing a firm are unpredictable and require both high degrees of control and extensive coordination of resources. Many firms find it difficult to implement the matrix structure because it calls for high levels of resource sharing across divisions; in fact, it's generally feasible only when strong culture and shared values support cross-division collaboration. As it turns out, even though ABB enjoyed a strong culture, the company eventually realized that coordinating 900 matrix units was far too complex. Massive restructuring began in early 2000, and today, though still operating under a matrix structure, ABB has reduced the number of its operating units by about half.

conceptlink

In Chapter 5, we defined a *strategic business unit (SBU)* as an organizational subunit within a diversified corporation that's responsible for a specific business or group of related businesses; we emphasized that the SBU environment includes both elements *external to* the firm and elements of the parent firm.

matrix structure Form of organization in which specialists from functional departments are assigned to work for one or more product or geographic units

Exhibit 8.5   Hypothetical Matrix Structure

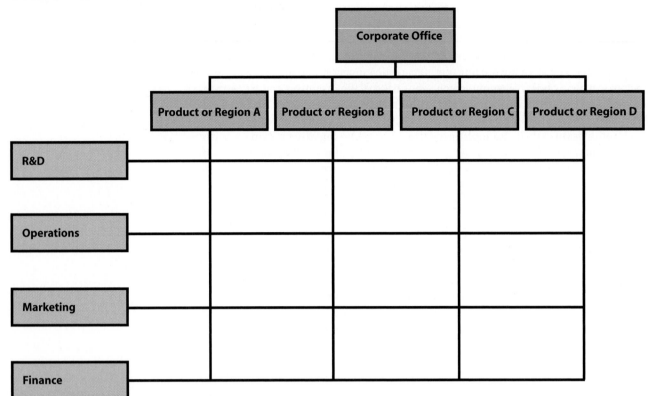

Source: E. Prewitt, "GM's Matrix Reloads," CIO, September 1, 2003.

network structure Form of organization in which small, semiautonomous, and potentially temporary groups are brought together for specific purposes

Network Structure   A more recent development in organization design, the **network structure** consists of small, semi-autonomous, and potentially temporary groups that are brought together for specific purposes—a team, for example, that's been assembled to work on a new-product idea. A network structure also includes external linkages with such groups as suppliers and customers. Authority is based on the control of resources, knowledge, and expertise, rather than on hierarchical rank, and because it's highly flexible, a firm can reconfigure staff and resources rapidly enough to exploit rich but fleeting bubbles of opportunity. Drawbacks include the potential for confusion and ambiguity.

Gore's "lattice" organization is a special (and extreme) version of a network structure. Although difficult to diagram here, imagine what an organizational structure would look like for Gore, with its approximately 7,400 associates working in more than 45 plants and sales locations worldwide. Sales and customer-service sites are located in Argentina, Australia, Austria, Brazil, China, Finland, France, Germany, Greece, Hong Kong, India, Italy, Japan, Korea, Malaysia, the Netherlands, New Zealand, Poland, Russia, Scotland, Singapore, Spain, Sweden, Taiwan, and the United States. Manufacturing operations are clustered in the United States, Germany, Scotland, Japan, and China. Gore separates its products into 10 categories: aerospace, automotive, chemical processing, computers/ telecommunications/electronics, energy, environment, industrial/manufacturing, medical/ healthcare, military, and textiles. As is the typical network organization, Gore employees work in small teams and are encouraged to participate in direct one-on-one communication with other Gore associates, customers, and suppliers.

Partnerships and Franchises   Before leaving this section, we should mention two additional forms of organization structure—the professional partnership and the franchise system. Although both are as much forms of legal ownership as they are organizational structures, they offer a few unique structural characteristics that can be brought to bear on persistent organizational problems. In addition, because both are common fixtures on the business landscape, it's important that you understand their role in the national economy.

Professional Partnerships In several industries, the professional partnership is the structural form of choice. In a professional partnership, the company is organized as a group of partners who own shares or units in the company. Generally, the partners vote on a managing partner who will act as a supervisor, but this person serves at their pleasure. Consequently, a senior partner has significant authority and prestige but perhaps not nearly the power that a CEO of a large firm has over subordinates. Partnerships are pyramid-shaped structures, with each partner having a number of associates (of various levels). Industries in which the partnership form is common include the legal offices, accounting firms, consulting firms, advertising agencies, and real estate companies. Until recently, investment-banking firms were structured as partnerships, but most have converted to publicly held corporations. The management structure of investment-banking firms has remained relatively the same, but the change to a corporate form has enabled firms to increase their capitalization.

Franchise Structure The franchise system not only transfers ownership of local facilities to a franchisee, it likewise shifts all local management responsibility to the franchisee. One purpose of using a franchise model is that it enables a firm to grow rapidly because much of the capital costs are picked up by the franchisees. However, the franchise model fundamentally changes the organizational structure of the firm. A franchisee assumes all management responsibility for individual business locations. For the right to the franchisor's business model and brand name, the franchisee pays a royalty percentage and other fees to the franchisor.

Systems and Processes

When asked to think about the systems and processes needed to manage an organization, people usually mention information systems (IS). In reality, an IS is just one type of vital system. Systems and processes make it possible to manage budgeting, quality control, planning, distribution, and resource allocation in complex contemporary organizations.

In Chapter 2, we pointed out that ambitious vision and mission statements don't automatically translate into higher levels of financial performance.[24] Conversely, of course, a myopic focus on financial-accounting results, such as return on equity or return on sales, may cause managers to lose sight of long-term strategic initiatives and divert their attention from other key stakeholders.[25] For this reason, many firms are developing performance-measurement and management systems that enable them to balance the need to report short-term financial returns with the need to pursue longer-term (and often intangible) objectives. Various approaches can be used to gauge the success with which implementation levers are aligned with strategic objectives; the most common term for these performance-management systems is the *balanced scorecard.*

The Balanced Scorecard The **balanced scorecard** has evolved into what might just as well be called a *strategy scorecard.* It's a strategic management support system devised to help managers measure vision and strategy against business- and operating-unit-level performance along several critical dimensions.[26]

The balanced-scorecard approach teaches three fundamental lessons:

- Translate strategy into tangible and intangible performance metrics (recall the summary of financial and nonfinancial performance measures summarized in Exhibit 2.8 of Chapter 2).
- Use a *strategy map* to align metrics with strategy.
- Make strategy a continuous and dynamic process.[27]

Let's look a little more closely at each of these principles.

Relying on a Range of Metrics Managers should pay attention to a variety of performance metrics, not just to short-term financial-performance indicators. Granted, financial performance is the easiest metric to apply, but other indicators are just as critical in diagnosing and maintaining the long-term health of an organization. The balanced scorecard prevents managers from relying solely on short-term financial or other outcome measures and forces them to focus instead on those measures, both tangible and intangible, that are relevant to the elements of value being delivered to key stakeholders.

balanced scorecard Strategic management support system for measuring vision and strategy against business- and operating-unit-level performance

Exhibit 8.6 Translating Vision and Strategy in Action Through the Balanced Scorecard System

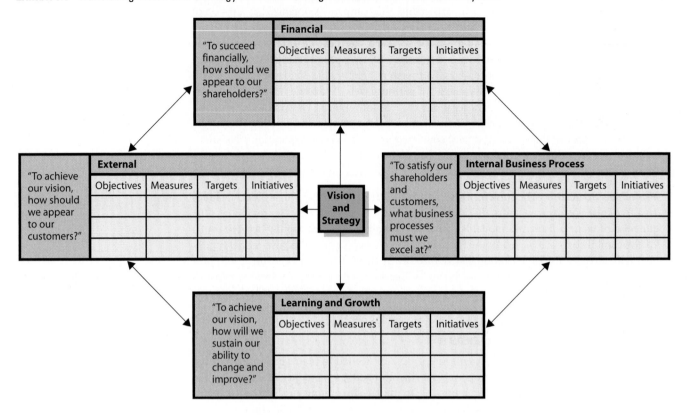

Leading proponents of this approach advise managers to consider four perspectives on performance: *financial, customer, internal business process*, and *learning and growth*:

- The *financial perspective* involves strategy for growth, profitability, and risk when viewed from the shareholder's or owner's perspective.
- The *external-relations perspective* pertains to strategy for creating value and differentiation from the perspective of the customer.
- The *internal-business-process perspective* reflects strategic priorities among processes according to their contributions to customer and shareholder satisfaction.
- The *learning-and-growth perspective* focuses on the organization's priorities for fostering change, innovation, and growth.

Exhibit 8.6 illustrates the links among these four perspectives and a firm's vision and strategy. It can also serve as a worksheet for identifying a performance metric, its target level, and the specific initiatives aimed at achieving the target. Recall that the overarching strategic management process introduced in Chapter 1 flows from vision to goals and objectives and then to the strategy diamond, which sets out how those goals and objectives are to be achieved. You can think of the balanced scorecard as an elaborate summary of the goals and objectives in the strategic management process. Essentially, management must distill tangible and intangible strategic objectives for each area down into specific measures that will be used to gauge those objectives. Targets are then set for those measures and initiatives that are launched to reach the desired targets. Ideally, these measures will have leading, pacing, and lagging characteristics such that management can tell if they are moving forward, how well and quickly they are doing so, and when initiatives are drawing to a successful conclusion.

Developing a Strategy Map   Exhibit 8.6 shows how managers can begin the strategy-mapping process. The next, and most critical, step of the process is to develop a *strategy map* wherein managers link all performance metrics to the firm's strategy. Many managers begin mapping systems and processes by diagramming activities across the four perspectives that we've already developed: (1) financial, (2), external relations (3) internal business processes, and (4) learning and growth.

Exhibit 8.7 The Balanced Scorecard in the Context of a Strategy Map

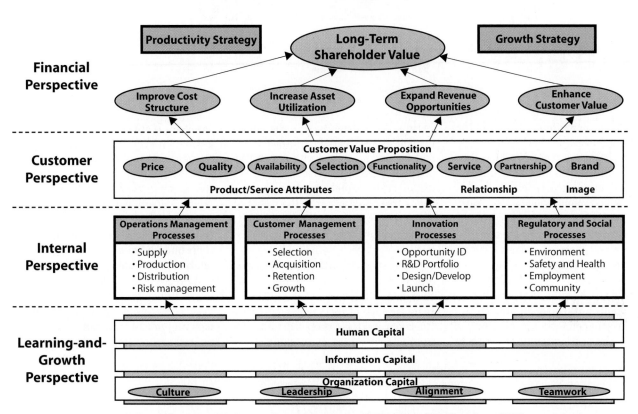

Sources: *Adapted from R. Kaplan and D. Norton. The Strategy-Focused Organization, Boston:* Harvard Business Press *(2001);*
www.valuebasedmanagement.net/methods_strategy_maps_strategic_communication.html.

An example of this cause-and-effect approach to strategy mapping is shown in
Exhibit 8.7. The strategy map states objectives—in terms of business processes, cycle time,
productivity, and other important internal processes—to guide key activities. When mapping learning-and-growth objectives, managers should indicate what must be done—in
terms of people and product and process development—if learning-and-growth processes
are to be developed and sustained.

The two remaining perspectives—external relations and financial—state objectives
that reflect the desired outcomes. How, for instance, does the firm want customers, partners, and other external stakeholders to perceive it? How will planned activities ultimately
translate into financial results and economic value? As the box entitled "How Would *You*
Do That? 8.2" demonstrates, a balance scorecard can smooth the process of strategy implementation. Linking objectives in this way helps managers articulate causality between
objectives—a key factor in linking strategy to relevant performance measures.[28]

Making Strategy a Continuous and Dynamic Process To ensure that a strategy remains
continuous and dynamic, managers must succeed at two tasks:

■ Disseminating the key features of a strategy and stipulating responsibilities for executing it throughout the organization
■ Linking the strategy with the financial budget

In one important sense, the balanced scorecard can serve as a tool for communicating
vision, mission, and strategy throughout an organization—a theme to which we'll return
later in the chapter when we discuss the roles of strategic leadership in strategy implementation. Employees who've participated in developing and revising a balanced scorecard
should have a fairly in-depth understanding of a firm's strategy and of the ways in which

Developing a Balanced Scorecard for the NUWC

Exhibit 8.8 shows the first steps in the mapping process at the U.S. Naval Undersea Warfare Center (NUWC), the Navy's full-spectrum research, testing, and engineering center for submarines, autonomous underwater systems, and weapons systems associated with undersea warfare. As a result of the strategic-mapping process, which involved communication among managers in all parts and levels of the organization in addition to external stakeholders, three organizational themes emerged—innovation, affordability, and putting the customer first.

In turn, these themes led to the development of a system of performance metrics that is aligned with the clearly articulated strategic direction of NUWC. (This example, by the way, shows that the concept of the balanced scorecard can be applied to both non-profit and for-profit organizations.)

The next step (for NUWC or any other organization) is to develop objectives, measures, targets, and initiatives for each of the key perspectives. These perspectives should then be used to develop the overarching strat-

egy map. If there are inconsistencies between pieces in the map, then the relevant stakeholders can use this information as an opportunity to refine the implementation of the strategy, including revision of the objectives, measures, targets, and initiatives. Because the perspectives and their underlying objectives are related to strategic priorities, the system goes well beyond a mere listing of things to do or key performance indicators. By means of the mapping process, all metrics are related to strategic objectives.

Exhibit 8.8 Balanced Scorecard Development at the Naval Undersea Warfare Center (NUWC)

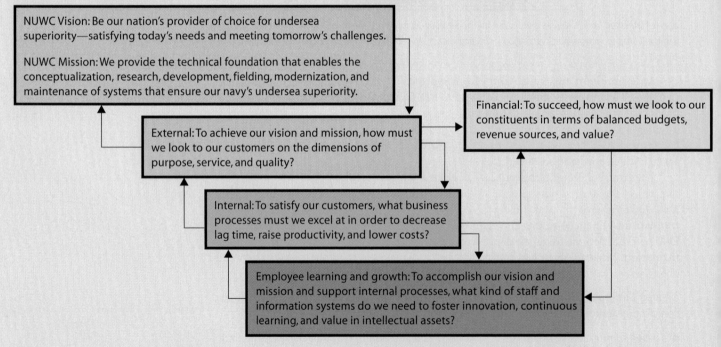

Source: Adapted from G. Harrigan and R. Miller, "Managing Change Through an Aligned and Cascading Balanced Scorecard," Perform 2:2 (2003), 20–26.

underlying maps come together to support it. During the process, they should also develop a good sense of whether the organization's culture will support the strategy. Finally, beyond simple communication, the dissemination process can foster broader support for the strategy among stakeholders, improve understanding of how the balanced scorecard works to ensure that the strategy is effectively implemented, and furnish a mechanism for receiving feedback.

To be sure, in the form of operational budgets, the process of financial budgeting not only provides a feedback tool, but also helps to determine resource allocation. However, operational budgets impose a form of outcome control that, by its very nature, tends to constrain managers and hamper investment in new capabilities and products.

In contrast, a *strategic* budget focuses on identifying and acquiring new customers, new capabilities, new operations, and new products. The balanced scorecard is important in determining the mix and amount of spending in the strategic budget, and the relationship between strategic priorities and the scorecard is further reinforced when compensation is tied to financial and nonfinancial measures. Microsoft, for instance, now ties the compensation of its top 600 officers to customer-satisfaction scores, a critical nonfinancial performance measure in the company's balanced scorecard.[29]

SimConnect

Balanced Scorecard in StratSim

A common error in StratSim is to focus solely on "bottom line" performance measures. Though the ultimate goal may be to have the highest stock price or net income, often a team that focuses on those measures in the short term may miss the long-term steps necessary to reach that objective in years 7 to 10. One of the most effective ways to guard against this short-term tendency is to create a balanced scorecard approach to tracking performance that includes other measures such as dealer ratings, share of target markets, technological leadership, or forecasting accuracy. The purpose of using these other measures is to help guard against decisions such as cutting costs to improve short-term profitability at the expense of good implementation of your long-term strategy.

People and Rewards

This subset of implementation levers draws attention to the importance of people and the rewards that can be used to align their energies and actions with the organization's objectives. We'll treat people and rewards together because inappropriate incentives and controls can frustrate the efforts of even the best people. Let's go back to our earlier example of the impact of inadequate compensation policies on SAP's strategy. One problem was that the company's compensation system rewarded people for generating new sales regardless of whether SAP product packages were priced to yield a profit for the firm. In terms of sales, the firm grew quickly, but SAP eventually realized that, over time, many of its customer relationships were costing it more money than it was making.

People   Employees are sometimes called a firm's *human capital* in order to distinguish them from fixed assets and financial capital. Individually, people are a critical component in strategy formulation and implementation. Collectively, people comprise the firm's culture, and such culture contributes strongly to a firm's dynamic capabilities and competitive advantage. Barclay's Global Investors (BGI) provides a good case in point of how a firm's culture of action orientation and self-reliance can and must be aggressively nurtured and protected:

> One of the things we discovered was that there are certain basic things—values, vision, the culture of the firm—that are not up for discussion. You can discuss it in the sense of explaining it and understanding it, but it's not something that is going to be changed. It's important for people to understand that. When you become part of BGI, this is what you are signing up for. And quite frankly, we've still got a small hard-core group of our managing directors that still are questioning it. So we are at the point of saying to them, "Well, maybe it's best that you go someplace else, because these things aren't up for discussion."[30]

As we've indicated on several occasions, a strategy will succeed only if a firm has the right people with the right experience and competencies. As the BGI example demonstrates, this also includes people who share and steward the corporate culture. Thus, recruitment, selection, and training with an eye to competencies and values are critical to strategy implementation. In a recent study, management researcher Jim Collins examined 11 firms that went from good to excellent performance and sustained it over a 15-year period. He then compared these firms with peer companies that had similar prestudy performance but never reached the level of great performance. In all 11 cases of good-to-great companies, making sure they had the right people working was a major priority for CEOs early in their tenures. Collins reports that many executives believe the people lever to be the most crucial to the successful implementation of strategy. Successful CEOs, according to Collins, "attended to people first [and] strategy second. They got the right people on the bus, moved the wrong people off, ushered the right people to the right seats—and then they figured out where to drive it."[31] In BGI's case, for example, management's clarity on the requisite values and principles each employee should hold enabled managers to identify quickly those individuals who fit the desired BGI culture.

So how do people influence firm performance? In many organizations, of course, the skills of their people make it possible for them to do what they do best.[32] That's why the VRINE framework regards such expertise as an important part of a firm's bundle of strategic capabilities. Some consultants and scholars think that these bundles of skills, all the way down to the level of those possessed by teams and even specific individuals, are the key factor in a firm's long-term viability and its ability to innovate new products.[33] People decisions are critical to performance because decisions about which and how many people to employ hinge on the desire either to improve efficiency or generate new revenues.[34]

Because human resources are generally a firm's largest operating cost, many managers focus on reducing this cost. Moreover, the stock market tends to react positively to downsizing.[35] Ironically, however, research shows that although downsizing results in a short-term stock-price improvement, it's often followed by productivity declines that can take several years to correct.[36] These results are consistent with research showing that when a firm's HR policies focus on enhancing its human capital, there are positive effects on several dimensions of operational performance (such as employee productivity, machine efficiency, and the alignment of product and service capabilities with customers' needs).[37]

The continued success of highly profitable growth companies results largely from skill in recruiting people who fit the organization, adhere to its values, and work toward common goals. Both JetBlue and Southwest Airlines, for example, expend considerable effort

concept link

We introduce the **VRINE model** of **resources**, **capabilities**, and **competitive advantage** in Chapter 3, where we suggest that human capital can be a source of advantage, especially when it contributes to **causal ambiguity**—complex conditions within an organization that competitors find it hard to imitate. In Chapter 6, we characterize threats to sustained competitive advantage anything that threatens VRINE resources and capabilities.

Many companies focus on staffing cuts because employees represent their largest expense. Although Wall Street usually reacts positively to such moves, firms that downsize often experience long-term performance declines.

making sure that new hires will fit the firm. When hiring new sales and marketing talent, W. L. Gore not only puts prospects through a series of rigorous, behavior-oriented interviews, but usually hires associates from outside the industry. The reason? Gore worries that people from within the industry have picked up habits that aren't consistent with Gore's ways of doing things. John Spencer, who designed an innovative marketing plan for Gore's Glide dental floss, was a former U.S. Navy midshipman and nuclear-submarine engineer—hardly qualifications for getting dental floss to market.

Regardless of the specifics of the strategy, at the end of the day, success depends on hiring the right people and developing and training them in ways that support a firm's strategy. Competitive advantage, therefore, is inextricably bound up in a firm's human capital.[38] Unfortunately, many firms don't seem to appreciate fully the role of people in developing and sustaining a competitive advantage. One study found that only 50 percent of managers in firms today believe that human capital matters; only about half of those actually launch human-resource initiatives, and only about half of those stick to those initiatives.[39] Not surprisingly, the remaining one-eighth includes such world-class companies as Southwest Airlines, General Electric, and Microsoft. According to the authors of another recent study, few leaders seem to understand that their "most important asset walks out the door every night."[40]

The importance of having the right people is accentuated in human-capital-intensive industries. If, for instance, a key resource in a firm's industry is access to oil fields, it doesn't have the same concern about resources as a firm whose key resource is access to scientific knowledge. Oil fields can't quit and jump to a competitor, demand higher wages, reject authority, lose motivation, or become dissatisfied with management and coworkers.[41] Consequently, firms in human-capital-intensive industries must develop strategies to reduce the risk of losing the human capital. Besides fostering job satisfaction, companies can develop firm-specific knowledge that's less transferable to other firms. Profit-sharing initiatives encourage valuable people to stay with an employer because they have a stake in any value that they help to create. Adjusting organization structure to eliminate authoritative and mechanistic processes and to accommodate more egalitarian and participative models reduces turnover.[42]

Rewards   Although rewards are technically the function of a system, we discuss them in this section because of their obvious relationship to people. An old management adage is *you get what you measure*. In reality, however, this proposition may need to be altered slightly: In the real workplace, it seems that what gets done is that which is rewarded.[43] Some experts grant that although organizational culture may be difficult to change, **reward systems**, which determine the compensation and promotion of an organization's employees, express and reinforce the values and expectations embedded in its culture.[44] Thus, any strategist who wants to get things done must think and act flexibly with regard to compensation and align rewards not only with strategy, but also with other implementation levers.

reward system Bases on which employees are compensated and promoted

The Components of the Reward System   Reward systems have two components:

- Performance evaluation and feedback
- Compensation, which can consist of salary, bonuses, stock, stock options, promotions, and even such perquisites as cars and coveted office spaces

Single-business firms usually have one reward system, although the compensation component will probably vary by functional area. Salespeople, for instance, will have incentives based on sales growth, particularly profitable sales growth, whereas employees in production and procurement will have incentives based on quality, cost control, and customer service. Again, rewards are designed to encourage achievement of the organization's strategic objectives, and neither rewards nor penalties apply to performance that's unrelated to those objectives.

Rewards as a Form of Control   Like structure, systems, and processes, rewards also serve as a form of control. Rewards necessarily require that performance and behavior targets be stipulated, but their control function can take one of two forms: outcome controls or behavioral controls.

outcome controls Practice of tying rewards to narrowly defined financial criteria

behavioral controls Practice of tying rewards to criteria other than simply financial performance, such as those broadly identified in the balanced scorecard

Outcome Controls   **Outcome controls** monitor and reward individuals and groups based on whether a measurable goal has been achieved. Such controls are generally preferable when just one or two performance measures (say, return on investment or return on assets) are good gauges of a business's health. Outcome controls are effective when there's little external interference between managerial decision making and business performance. It also helps if little or no coordination with other business units is required, because each unit's people will be seeking to maximize their performance on the targeted measure. Because of this, outcome controls often provide a disincentive for cross-unit collaboration.

Behavioral Controls   **Behavioral controls** involve the direct evaluation of managerial decision making, not of the results of managerial decisions. Behavioral controls tie rewards to a broader range of criteria, such as those identified in the balanced scorecard. Behavioral controls and commensurate rewards are typically more appropriate when many external and internal factors can affect the relationship between a manager's decisions and organizational performance. They're also appropriate when managers must coordinate resources and capabilities across different business units.

Compensation in the Diversified Firm   Although diversified firms may rely on a single reward system for all business units, reward systems usually vary in order to reflect both overall corporate strategy and the competitive environment and strategy of each business unit. A diversified company like GE, which owns several unrelated businesses, achieves the best results by linking the pay of division managers to the performance of the units that they manage. On the business-unit level, therefore, outcome-based controls and reward systems are aligned with both corporate strategy and organization structure.

However, in a diversified firm that expects divisions to share resources and otherwise cross-subsidize each other, the same sort of compensation would provide *disincentives* for resource sharing. Division managers who are paid solely on the basis of business-unit performance, for instance, might reasonably conclude that it's not in their best interest to subsidize other divisions because doing so may jeopardize their own units' performance and, therefore, their pay.

Conversely, a diversified firm that's trying to generate synergies across business units can increase the likelihood of desired outcomes by linking unit managers' rewards to actual decisions and other balanced-scorecard criteria rather than to individual unit performance.[45] To encourage managers to recognize their own stakes in organizational prospects, rewards often include stock-based incentives or bonuses based on firmwide performance.

To further illustrate how reward systems can affect strategy implementation, let's consider the ways in which incentive systems can impact the realization of postmerger synergies. Many mergers are driven by the belief that two companies can generate net new revenue if they're combined in one firm. But what if compensation systems don't reward employees for sharing knowledge and resources? Obviously, synergies probably won't materialize. Mergers between commercial and investment banks, for instance, are often hampered by incongruent incentive systems.[46] Key employees of commercial banks are typically rewarded for managing relationships, whereas investment bankers are rewarded for doing deals. Paying bankers to do deals is generally at odds with the need for commercial banks to minimize risk and retain customers. Alternatively, investment bankers generally earn bigger bonuses on larger and higher-risk deals.

STRATEGIC LEADERSHIP AND STRATEGY IMPLEMENTATION

Strategic leadership plays two critical roles in successful strategy implementation. We're going to highlight them here so that you can incorporate them into your assessment of a strategy's feasibility and include them in your implementation plans. Specifically, strategic leadership is responsible for:

- Making substantive implementation lever and resource-allocation decisions
- Communicating the strategy to key stakeholders

Let's take a closer look at both of these roles.

Decisions About Levers

We hope that it is obvious to you that the choices about which levers to employ and when to employ them do not appear out of thin air as a result of executive action (and sometimes inaction or neglect). The examples you have seen in this chapter, and in other parts of the text, have emphasized the importance of aligning strategy with the appropriate implementation levers. For instance, the executives at Gore are very careful to preserve the organization's deep culture of innovation and the unique levers that reinforce this culture and, ultimately, the firm's strategy and competitive advantage. New ventures by Gore, such as the successful Glide dental floss product, are also launched with all of these key supporting implementation levers in place.

Like strategy-formulation decisions, decisions about levers involve important trade-offs regarding what the firm will and will not do. Misalignment between the levers and the strategy can arise because management has made poor choices about which levers to employ, is employing too simple or too complex a repertoire of levers for the given situation, or the organization or its competitive environment has changed such that the levers need to be changed but have not been. For example, a firm that is small, experiencing the growth stage of its respective arena, and facing little direct competition may be well served by a functional structure, relatively little bureaucracy, and an incentive system that emphasizes growth and innovation. However, as the firm grows, its operations typically become more complex, including diversification into new product and geographic markets. Similarly, it is likely that it will face growing competition and cost pressures. Top management should probably be in the process of changing the implementation levers to favor some form of multibusiness or matrix structure and a compensation system that rewards financial accountability and not just growth. Absent such important management choices about which levers to employ, the firm may lose its once-strong competitive foothold.

Decisions About Resource Allocation

A good strategy guides managers in making decisions about the allocation of resources. Again, a good strategy tells managers what the firm should and shouldn't be doing, and thus helps them decide on important tradeoffs—an extremely important function because an organization that tries to be all things to all people by investing equally in every value-chain activity is doomed to mediocrity at best. Top managers must allocate resources in ways that are consistent with the firm's strategy and make the tradeoffs that this entails. Unfortunately, internal interests—whether political, self-serving, or misguided—can sabotage effective resource-allocation decisions and undermine even well-crafted strategies.

Both the misallocation of resources and the failure to make hard investment choices often result from a firm basing its resource allocation on that of its competitors. As a result, not only does the firm become less distinctive from a competitive standpoint, but many of the key players in an industry start to look like clones of one another.

Let's look at the ways in which different carriers in the airline industry manage—and don't manage—certain tradeoffs.[47] Exhibit 8.9 summarizes the key areas in which commercial airlines make strategic resource-allocation decisions (if you look back at the example of [yellow tail] wine in Chapter 6, you will see a similar picture of the importance of resource-allocation tradeoff choices in the wine industry). As you can see, in the airline industry, the key resource-allocation choices are numerous and range from price for tickets to frequent departure times. Recall that these lines are not meant to depict trends but rather the different patterns of resource-allocation choices made by the respective parties. What's striking is the fact that most major airlines seem to be mimicking each other's resource-allocation decisions. Two exceptions are Southwest and JetBlue, which, as you

conceptlink

We point out in Chapter 2 that strategic leaders must master the art of the *tradeoff*. The decision to take one course of action usually eliminates other options. In Chapter 3, we discuss the concept of *tradeoff protection*. Because every tradeoff contributes to a system of interdependent value-chain activities, competitors—who have already invested in their own **value-chain** tradeoffs—may find it hard to imitate those of their rivals.

Exhibit 8.9 Resource Allocation Decisions in the Airline Industry

Source: Adapted from W. C. Kim and R. Mauborgne, "Charting Your Company's Future," Harvard Business Review *80:6 (2002), 76–82.*

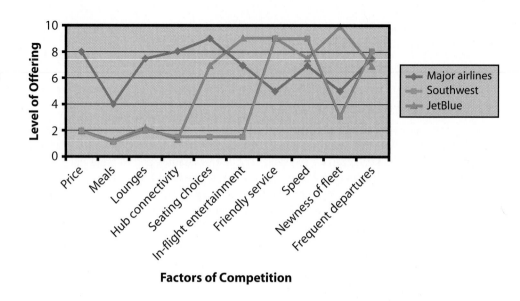

can tell from their resource-allocation decisions, are following decidedly different strategies. Some have even suggested that for Southwest, with its extensive network of short routes and frequent departures, the greatest competition actually comes from customers' automobiles! JetBlue's management committed itself to allocation decisions that would support the airline's overarching strategy, even when tempted with less expensive options. As a low-cost airline, for instance, JetBlue decided that it needed a modern fleet of new, fuel-efficient aircraft. Used aircraft would have been significantly cheaper (but only in the short run), and management could have rationalized the savings of precious startup capital. Such a shortcut, however, would have been inconsistent with the specific low-cost economic logic of the firm's strategy.

The point to be made here—and which we've made throughout this book—is that competitive advantage goes to those firms who develop unique advantages. Most of the time, such firms develop unique advantages because they make independent resource-allocation decisions instead of mimicking those of everybody else in the industry. Remember, too, that resources and capabilities—especially those that are likely to distinguish a firm from its competitors—are usually scarce. Scarcity takes many forms; a firm, for example, may have a team of brilliant researchers who can only work on so many projects for so many hours in a week. Managers, therefore, must revisit their strategy diamond and make at least two difficult decisions when allocating the firm's resources and capabilities: (1) what to direct at each arena and (2) what to direct to each differentiator.

SimConnect

Resource Allocation in StratSim

StratSim does not dictate to you either (a) what to invest in or (b) how much to spend in those areas. This freedom can either be viewed as a great benefit (you may choose your own path) or as a frustration (why don't we have more direction!?!). If you are frustrated by this lack of direction, remember that a big part of strategy is deciding priorities for your firm, allocating resources to those priorities, and potentially finding the resources necessary to fund your priorities at the appropriate level. If your frustration level is very high, this might also be a good time for you and your team members to compare and talk about your tolerance for ambiguity scores from the Chapter 2 survey. For some issues, there are tools that can help with this decision process. For example, the test market tool can help your firm decide on whether a product should have more or less advertising or promotional support. However, even though this information provides insight into the sensitivity of these expenditures, all things being equal, it does not take into account the dynamic nature of strategy such as how a competitor's changes in decisions will impact the results. The pro-forma analysis is another helpful tool for your firm to use, but again, it is only as good as the assumptions that you provide regarding sales forecasts. However, it definitely can help you analyze the economic logic of your decisions. You may also look to some of the multitude of resource allocation grids that have been designed to help with the allocation question, but at the end of the day, these too are simplifications of a complex reality and not a substitute for your team's strategic thought process. Remember that resource allocation is ultimately about creating a unique, sustainable competitive advantage. If it were easy to do, everyone would do it the same way, and no one would be able to gain that advantage. The VRINE framework tells us why this should play out as it does in the simulation (and in real businesses). Therefore, your firm will need to exercise judgment based on your knowledge, experience, and analysis; have faith in the decisions you make; monitor your progress; and make adjustments as necessary. Refer back to the Business Strategy Diamond that consists of the arenas, vehicles, differentiators, staging, and economic logic of your strategy. We teach with this framework for a reason—these topics should be the focus of your group discussions.

Communicating with Key Stakeholders About Strategy

From the outset, we've emphasized the interdependence of strategy formulation and implementation. In many ways, because suppliers, customers, and an organization's own managers will ultimately contribute to the strategy's success or failure, the process of communicating with stakeholders about strategy begins in the strategy formulation process itself. It is, therefore, a strategic-leadership function.

In performing this strategic-leadership role, managers must evaluate both the need and the necessary tactics for persuasively communicating a strategy in four different directions: *upward*, *downward*, *across*, and *outward*.[48]

Communicating Upward Increasingly, firms rely on bottom-up innovation processes that encourage and empower middle-level and division managers to take ownership of strategy formulation and propose new strategies. Such is particularly the case at highly diversified firms, but even fairly focused firms such as W. L. Gore endorse bottom-up processes. Communicating upward means that someone or some group has championed the strategy internally and has succeeded in convincing top management of its merits and feasibility.

Communicating Downward Communicating downward means enlisting the support of the people who'll be needed to implement the strategy. Too often, managers undertake this task only after a strategy has been set in stone, thereby running the risk of undermining both the strategy and any culture of trust and cooperation that may have existed previously. Starting on the communication process early is the best way to identify and surmount obstacles, and it usually ensures that a management team is working with a common purpose and intensity that will be important when it's time to implement the strategy.

Communicating Across and Outward The need to communicate across and outward reflects the fact that implementation of a strategy will probably require cooperation from other units of the firm (*across*) and from key external stakeholders, such as material and capital providers, complementors, and customers (*outward*). Internally, for example, the strategy may call for raw materials or services to be provided by another subsidiary; perhaps it depends on sales leads from other units. Recall, for instance, our earlier example of Emageon. Emageon couldn't get hospitals to adopt the leading-edge visualization software that was produced and sold by one subsidiary until its hardware division started cross-selling the software as well. This internal coordination required a champion from the software side to convince managers on the hardware side of the need and benefits of working together.

concept link

In Chapter 2, we explain in detail the role of *stakeholder analysis* as a **strategic-leadership** function.

IBM's ThinkPad, launched in the early 1990s, was an unexpected hit. However, IBM couldn't produce ThinkPads fast enough to keep up with demand, so potential sales suffered.

External constituencies play a comparable role, and a strategy must similarly be communicated to them. Managers can use stakeholder analysis to identify these key players and determine whether suppliers, customers, complementors, and relevant regulatory agencies support the firm's strategy. In the early 1990s, for instance, when IBM first launched its ThinkPad, the product was an unexpected hit with customers. The launch, however, was so successful that IBM's key component suppliers couldn't keep up with IBM's demand, thus costing the company sales on what should have been an even more profitable rollout.

The Three C's of Strategy Communication   Just as communicating the strategy to stakeholders is a key factor in successful strategy implementation, so, too, is having the right people in place to communicate it. As one researcher puts it, "The strategy champion must have three C's—contacts, cultural understanding, and credibility."[49]

Contacts   Contacts are key because implementing a strategy—particularly one that's dynamic and innovative—often entails some back-channel maneuvering. 3M's Post-it notes, for instance, made it to market only because an enterprising manager convinced internal people to supply clerical and other support staff with experimental versions of the product as a means of demonstrating that there was actually a market. Within Gore, its lattice structure fosters contacts among thousands of employees around the globe. Externally, Gore's introduction of Glide through word-of-mouth advertising directed at a small, local drug-store chain and dentists' offices is another example of successful back-channel tactics.

Cultural Understanding   Cultural understanding refers to the fact that the people communicating the strategy need to have a rich familiarity with the organization's culture, policies, and procedures. In an earlier example on BGI, you saw how culture provides a screen for recruitment, retention, and promotion. It may also provide strategy communicators with insights into internal and external network dependencies that may not be obvious but that nonetheless will be essential to the effort to sell across and outward.

Credibility   Needless to say, it helps if strategy communicators are respected by management, peers, and staff, all of whom expect them to present ideas with a good chance of success. Credibility is based on perceptions of trustworthiness, reliability, and integrity. Yet studies indicate that many employees just don't believe or trust their organizational leaders. According to Bruce Katcher, president of Discovery Surveys, a Massachusetts–based firm specializing in employee-opinion and customer-satisfaction surveys and focus groups, just 53 percent "of employees believe the information they receive from senior management."[50] He bases the figure on a review of the company's database of 30,000 respondents from 44 international companies. Closing the credibility gap can be helped by developing regular— at least annual—processes to gauge real employee perceptions about their managers' level of leadership as well as other issues, including morale, obstacles to higher performance, pet peeves, or key irritants. Managers must then pay attention to the findings and demonstrate real commitment to act on them. When actions speak louder than words, employees will have more reason to trust those above them.

IMPLEMENTATION LEVERS IN GLOBAL FIRMS AND DYNAMIC CONTEXTS

As we've observed throughout this text, firms are increasingly facing challenges that are both global and dynamic in nature. In this section, we'll show how implementation levers can be adapted to these particularly important contingencies. We'll also link strategy implementation explicitly to strategy formulation through the staging component of the strategy diamond model.

Implementation Solutions for Global Firms

As you learned in Chapter 7, two critical needs confront firms in implementing global strategies: the need for *efficiency* and the need for *local responsiveness*.[51] In this section, we want to stress their role in terms of implementation levers and their function in executing globalization strategies. Paralleling the strategy research on global strategy, research has found that firms deeply involved in international business adopt one of four structural forms in the effort to manage the tension between the need for efficiency and the need for local responsiveness.[52] As we'll see, most of these forms place more emphasis on one or the other of these two competing forces and build on the general understanding of structure you have amassed thus far from this chapter. These four structural solutions accommodate the four international-strategy configurations discussed in Chapter 7: multinational, international, global, and transnational. Each configuration is characterized by different structures, systems, and processes.

Structure for Multinational Configurations
This structural solution resembles a decentralized federation, much like the relationship between the U.S. federal government and the 50 state governments. Assets and resources are decentralized, and foreign offices are given the authority to respond to local needs when they differ from those of the home market. Control and coordination are managed primarily through the interactions of home-office corporate executives and overseas executives, who are usually home-country managers who've been dispatched to run foreign offices.

From the perspective of top management, the corporation is a portfolio of relatively independent businesses located around the globe. SAP, for example, adhered to this model for much of the 1990s, until it determined that it fostered costly duplications of effort across markets and inadequate coordination among units across borders. Indeed, because SAP's customers were global firms with better coordination and integration than SAP itself, many of them managed to get SAP to compete against itself for new system sales. Nestlé, for instance, would get bids from SAP U.S. and SAP U.K. without informing either party that they were actually bidding against one another.

Structure for International Configurations
The structure supporting an international strategy reveals an organization that is a coordinated group of federations over which more administrative control is exerted by home-country headquarters. For reasons of both efficiency and strategy, firms like SAP typically evolve into this structure. SAP itself, for example, adopted it at the end of the 1990s when it realized that its customers were taking advantage of its multinational structure.

Under this model, although resources, assets, and responsibilities are delegated to foreign offices, additional control—usually in the form of more formal management systems, such as centralized planning and budgeting—is exercised centrally. This control facilitates global account management, so that services provided to global clients can be made uniform in terms of quality and price. As a rule, top management regards overseas operations as appendages to the domestic firm. Local units, therefore, are highly dependent on home-office coordination of resource allocation, knowledge sharing, and decision approval.

Structure for Global Configurations   Ideally, firms adopting a global configuration have a structure that is based on the centralization of assets, resources, and responsibilities. Foreign offices are used to access customers, but demand is filled by centralized production. This form of organization was pioneered by firms such as Ford, which exported standardized products around the globe, and was popular among Japanese companies undertaking globalization in the 1970s and 1980s. The global configuration affords much less autonomy to foreign offices or subsidiaries than either the multinational or international models. Operational control is tight and most decisions centralized. Top management views foreign operations as pipelines for distributing products to a global, but homogeneous, marketplace.

Structure for Transnational Configurations   Each of the three preceding organizational models responds in a different strategic fashion to the challenge of balancing the two fundamental demands of managing across borders. The global configuration, for example, is clearly designed to achieve maximum efficiencies, largely through scale economies derived from centralized production. Because decisions and resources are controlled locally, the multinational form is well suited to respond to local needs. The international model attempts to meet local needs while retaining central control. The transnational model is designed to accommodate both demands.

The structure for transnational configurations (or *transnationals*, for short) was designed to achieve not only efficiency and local responsiveness but innovation as well. Its structural characteristics enable firms—at least those that are able to manage it—to achieve multidimensional strategic objectives. The key functions in this multidimensional strategy are *dispersion*, *specialization*, and *interdependence*. Resources and capabilities are dispersed to local units, and a networked control system is designed to achieve both coordination and cooperation. Because geographically dispersed organizational units are strategically interdependent, large flows of products, resources, and personnel, as well as value-chain activities, are channeled through the structure. To some extent, McDonald's, which features both standard and locally tailored menu items at outlets around the globe, depends on this structure. The structure fits with McDonald's transnational strategy and affords the global food company greater flexibility in adapting to local tastes while enabling it at the same time to exploit the global economies of scale that it enjoys by virtue of its size and geographic breadth.

People and Rewards Solutions in Global Firms   As firms expand globally, they face the critical issue of how to find and reward managers. On the one hand, using local managers can enhance a firm's understanding of local markets. On the other hand, using home-country managers strengthens the relationship between the foreign subsidiary and the parent company.

Naturally, operating subsidiaries in culturally distant locations gives rise to a great deal of uncertainty. Research suggests that a company's policy for finding and rewarding foreign managerial staff can have a significant bearing on its performance. For instance, multinationals that use overseas management positions as a training ground for future executives of the parent significantly outperform those that allow senior managers to ascend to the top ranks without spending time in overseas posts.[53]

The performance of foreign subsidiaries may be affected when parent-country nationals, or expatriates, are sent to manage them. When multinationals have subsidiaries in culturally distant locations (as opposed to those that are just geographically distant), costs and risks increase because of a so-called *information-asymmetry* problem: Onsite overseas information may not be readily available to the parent company.[54] When a multinational relies more on parent-country nationals than local managers, the information-asymmetry problem gradually diminishes: As subsidiaries gain experience in conducting transactions with home-country nationals, there's less need for deploying expatriates. Indeed, research shows that when a multinational firm staffs a culturally distant foreign subsidiary with parent-country managers, it improves subsidiary performance, largely because it's easier to exercise cultural control and enhances the transfer of firm-specific resources from the parent to the subsidiary.[55]

Apparently, however, this positive effect decreases over time because host-country nationals not only acquire knowledge and skills from expatriate managers, but also adopt the shared values of the parent company. Not surprisingly, given the high cost of managing an expatriate workforce (not to mention the high percentage of expatriate failure), reliance on expatriates is declining.

Implementation Levers in Dynamic Contexts

We observed early in this text that, because competitive pressures are compounded in dynamic, "high-velocity" industries, companies' strategies necessarily grow more complex. Moreover, the difficulties in *implementing* strategies in such industries are an order of magnitude more challenging than those of implementing strategies in relatively stable industries. As we've also seen, the task is becoming even more complex and difficult because dynamic markets are increasingly becoming global markets as well. Consider, for instance, the threat to a firm in a global industry that needs to develop or adopt a radically new technology in order to survive industry evolution. In Chapter 6 we described a special problem known as the innovator's dilemma—a situation where new entrants innovate in low-end, unattractive segments of the market that leaders tend to overlook because margins are apparently lower there, only to have those new entrants migrate into the more profitable segments with lower cost structures and increasingly popular products.[56] Firms have developed several structural adaptations to deal with the problems of implementing strategies in dynamic contexts, and in this section, we'll examine two of the most effective adaptations: the *ambidextrous organization* and the use of *patching* among diversified firms.

The Ambidextrous Organization   Even a firm that's successful at executing a strategy can face a problem as its industry becomes well established: In particular, it's difficult to retain market leadership when a new disruptive technology (product or process) is pioneered and introduced by another firm. The incumbent also faces a disadvantage because it invests in order to sustain an advantage, not (like the new entrant) to destroy one.

Incremental Change Versus Radical Innovation: Revisiting the Innovator's Dilemma
This is the essence of the innovator's dilemma, and despite leaders who are perfectly capable of recognizing the problem, it often persists because of structural deficiencies among many organizations. When, for example, one division of a leading incumbent tries to pioneer its own version of disruptive technology, the rest of the organization may resist. Why? Perhaps because the status quo is perceived to be in the best interests of managers and employees. Or perhaps submerged but strong facets of the organizational culture favor the continued influence of large established divisions.

Granted, many firms are skilled at introducing refinements into their current product lines. Usually such organizations don't resist moderate innovation because it's perceived as a means of sustaining or improving current competitive positions. At the same time, however, the same firms may face monumental obstacles when they try to introduce *radical* changes or offer products that require disruptive technologies. In that case, of course, they're faced with a paradoxical problem: To flourish in the long run, they must exploit existing advantages and explore innovations that will probably alter the industry significantly in the future. In other words, if a firm wants to sustain long-term competitiveness in a dynamic context (and most, of course, do), it must learn to integrate both incremental changes and radical innovations.

The **ambidextrous structure** is one response to this problem.[57] In fact, the idea evolved from studies of how firms dealt with the problem of simultaneously integrating two types of innovations:

concept link

Such a situation, as we observe in Chapter 6, reflects a "turbulent" or "hypercompetitive" market—one characterized by frequent, bold, dynamic moves on the part of competitors, especially new entrants. We also explain the importance of understanding **implementation levers** in such *dynamic contexts*. Recall, too, from Chapter 4 the distinction between *discontinuous* and incremental changes and the discussion of why *new entrants* in a market often initiate the former.

ambidextrous structure
Organizational structure for dynamic contexts in which project teams are organized as structurally independent units and encouraged to develop their own structures, systems, and processes

■ *Incremental innovations* are those that make small improvements in existing products and operations and that are aimed at existing customers.

■ *Discontinuous innovations* are those that make radical advances that may alter the basis of competition in an industry and that are aimed at new customers.[58]

Four Structures for Handling Innovation   Researchers identified four basic forms of organization among the companies studied:

■ A functional form in which innovation efforts are completely integrated into an existing organization structure.

■ A cross-functional or matrix-style form in which groups of people from established organizational divisions are formed to work outside the functional hierarchy.

■ A form in which teams or units, though nominally independent and working outside the established hierarchy, are limited in their independence and relatively unsupported by the organizational hierarchy.

■ An "ambidextrous" form in which project teams focusing on radical improvements are organized as structurally independent units and encouraged to develop their own structures, systems, and processes. As you can see in Exhibit 8.10, these semiautonomous units may be integrated into the organizational hierarchy only at the senior-management level.

Exhibit 8.10   The Ambidextrous Organization

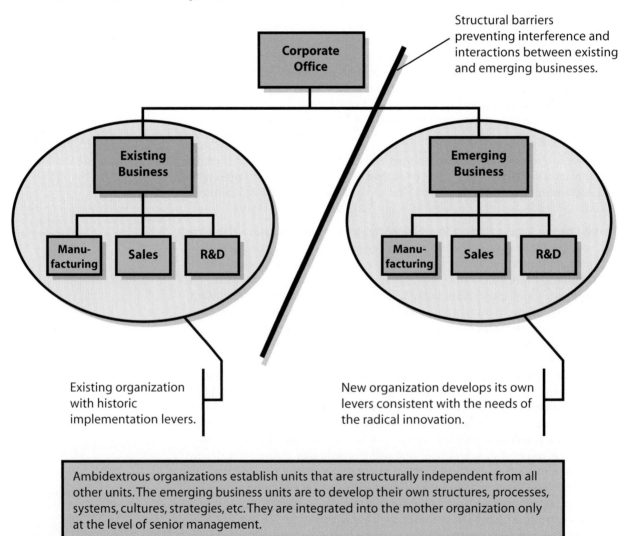

Source: Adapted from C. A. O'Reilly and M. L. Tushman, "The Ambidextrous Organization," Harvard Business Review 82:4 (2004), 74–81.

Researchers found that the ambidextrous structure was quite effective in facilitating the integration of radical innovations; 93 percent of radical innovations were launched by firms characterized as ambidextrous. Firms that pursued radical innovation through autonomous units bound to the organizational hierarchy only through senior management had very high success rates for launching new products or operations. Conversely, firms trying to achieve radical innovation within the existing corporate hierarchy found that their efforts were often stymied. Finally, the ambidextrous form also fostered innovations that were initiated under some other organizational form and only later moved into an ambidextrous structure.

Among other things, these findings reveal just how difficult it is for firms to compete in dynamic industry environments that require not only constant incremental innovations, but periodic radical innovations as well. The "ambidextrous" allows for the simultaneous maintenance of the status quo (incremental business improvements made through conventional organizational units) and proactive preparation for future industry-wide alterations (radical innovation made through units that are unencumbered by existing organizational practices and allowed to implement strategies consistent with the requirements of competitive conditions).

Diversified Firms in Dynamic Markets: Patching   A multidivisional firm operating in diverse product markets can create new synergies by actively managing the structure of its corporate portfolio through a process known as *patching*. **Patching** is the process of regularly remapping businesses in accordance with changing market conditions and restitching them into new internal business structures.[59] It can mean combining, splitting, or transferring units or exiting businesses or adding new ones. Patching is particularly effective in dynamic markets because it enables managers to exploit the best business opportunities while bypassing less promising ones. However, as you can imagine, patching is very complex to manage and requires a culture and workforce that is action oriented and flexible, such as the one described at BGI.

patching Process of remapping businesses in accordance with changing market conditions and restitching them into new internal business structures

Here's an example of patching at work. Originally, Hewlett-Packard's laser-printing business was a small startup operation with only modest growth expectations. Shortly after launch, however, sales climbed to 10 times the expected level (100,000 units per month instead of the forecasted 10,000). As new applications for related technologies, such as the ink-jet printer, emerged, management stripped them away from the laser-printer business and patched them onto other business units. This technique of patching units not only allowed managers in the laser-printer unit to focus on their core growth business but ensconced the ink-jet business in a unit where it could get the support it needed to get off the ground, develop into a growth business, and become a major source of cash flow. In this case, patching required the transfer not only of a business but of related resources and personnel as well.

With patching, therefore, structure is intentionally altered so that managers can better maintain focus on core and growth businesses while seeding and protecting new opportunities. Because it requires managers to view organizational structure as flexible and contingent, they tend not to fret about getting a new structure exactly right. In addition, although patching is a proactive tool, it usually involves relatively small and incremental changes. Change, however, is ongoing, as managers constantly search for new combinations. To make patching work, firms need to adjust internal systems so that when a business is detached from one division and restitched elsewhere, company-wide systems don't require extensive modification. Compensation systems, for instance, need to be fairly consistent across organizational borders.

Finally, we should note some key differences between patching and the ambidextrous organizational structure. Patching is a tool that helps diversified firms operate in multiple product or geographic markets. It doesn't involve radical technologies, but rather leverages either existing businesses or new but related businesses. It works when systems are consistent across the organization. In contrast, the ambidextrous organization is designed to enable radically new businesses to develop unencumbered by existing structures and processes.

Linking Strategy Implementation to Staging

Before wrapping up this chapter, we'd like to underscore the relationship between implementation levers and a specific facet of strategy formulation. Recall that the staging element of the strategy diamond refers to the timing and pacing of strategic moves. Staging decisions typically depend on available resources—resources that include structures, systems and processes, and people and rewards. From the opening vignette on Gore, you gained some insight into how the firm coupled a unique resource base—its knowledge and intellectual property relating to Teflon—with the implementation levers necessary to launch new and highly innovative ventures. Thus, management of the implementation process should anticipate the staging objectives of the strategy.

More generally, it would be a rare case in which a change in strategy did not have implications for implementation. Consider, for instance, a firm that's considering expansion into foreign markets. It can achieve this strategic goal through a variety of vehicles, including exporting, alliances or acquisitions, and the establishment of foreign offices from which to conduct value-chain activities. If international staging is an explicit component of the firm's strategy, then managers must start modifying other implementation levers. In other words, they must determine whether the firm has the appropriate structure, systems, human capital, expertise, and culture to support its evolution into a global competitor. If, for example, the vehicle of choice calls for alliances or acquisitions, then the related skills and capabilities must be acquired as well. If the vehicle is exporting, the firm will need to acquire people who understand customer demands and distribution channels in foreign markets.

SUMMARY

1. Understand the interdependence between strategy formulation and implementation. Strategy formulation and implementation are interrelated. The introductory section of the chapter showed you the various ways in which formulation and implementation are interrelated and provided you with an overarching model for thinking about how to translate an abstract strategy into concrete action. You also learned that the relationship between formulation and implementation is not necessarily a linear one. In some cases, the iterative evolution of strategy is advantageous and desirable. The section closed with a discussion of why implementation efforts can and often do fail. Organizational culture can be one barrier to (or facilitator of) effective strategy execution and strategic change.

2. Demonstrate how to use organizational structure as a strategy implementation lever. Organizational structure exists to perform two essential functions within the organization: ensuring control and coordinating the efforts of managers and employees. As control and coordination become more difficult, firms generally modify their structure to improve control and coordination. Popular forms of organizing firm structure include the functional, divisional, matrix, and network forms. The structure

chosen should be consistent with the firm's strategy. For instance, the more diversified the firm, the more the structure will need to accommodate coordination. The more focused the firm is in a single business, or in several unrelated businesses, the more the structure should emphasize control.

3. Design systems and processes as strategy implementation levers. Formal processes and procedures used by a firm should support the execution of strategy. Information systems are the most common systems, but all systems should be considered for their alignment with strategy (and other implementation levers). For instance, management control, performance and rewards, budgeting, quality, planning, distribution, client management, and resource allocation are all managed by systems. Systems can affect what people pay attention to and what information they have access to.

4. Understand the roles of people and rewards as implementation levers. For a strategy to succeed, a firm needs the right people with the right experiences and competencies. As a result, recruitment, selection, and training are critical to strategy implementation. Because human resources, or staffing issues, are often large sources of operating costs, too much focus may be placed on reducing the staffing costs. Investments in human resource systems have positive effects on multiple dimensions of firm performance. The importance of people is even more important in high-human-capital industries. Rewards are an important implementation lever. They reflect the degree to which a firm employs outcome versus behavioral controls. Rewards are composed of both performance evaluation and feedback and incentives, such as compensation and promotion. Ultimately, rewards enable the firm to get the right people to do the right things for the firm, such that it can achieve its goals and objectives.

5. Explain the dual roles that strategic leadership plays in strategy implementation. This section showed you that strategy implementation is much more than simply putting the right levers into place. The levers are important, but they must also be complemented by strategic-leadership actions. The two actions we emphasized were decisions about resource allocation and levers and communicating the strategy to stakeholders. The resources and capabilities that differentiate a firm from its competitors are by definition scarce. Strategic leadership shows its mettle by making difficult tradeoffs in terms of the levers chosen and where and where not to deploy scarce resources. Communicating the strategy to stakeholders requires that managers promote and get strategic buy-in from top management, lower-level workers, other key organizational units, and external stakeholders, such as suppliers, customers, and complementors.

6. Understand how global and dynamic contexts affect the use of implementation levers.

As a firm becomes more global, it faces contradictory needs for efficiency and local responsiveness. Depending on the primacy of these two demands, four structural solutions are available: multinational, international, global, and transnational. The solution for transnationals is the most complex; transnationals attempt to simultaneously achieve global efficiency and maximum local responsiveness. As in global contexts, coordination and control are made more difficult in dynamic contexts. In addition, being able to protect potentially radical innovations can be accommodated through the ambidextrous structure. Diversified firms in high-velocity environments can increase the likelihood of synergies by using patching techniques, which essentially assumes that the organizational structure is flexible and allows for the constant reconfiguration of business units. This enables managers to remain focused on high-volume businesses by placing high-potential-growth businesses in units that can better exploit these opportunities. This section closed by showing you how to link formulation and implementation through the staging component of the strategy diamond.

7. Be able to discuss and use strategy implementation levers in the context of StratSim. To be effective in StratSim, you must be able to connect the dots between strategy formulation and implementation in a highly dynamic fashion. As you experience StratSim, you will have the opportunity to regularly discuss and evaluate how much of your firm's performance is a consequence of a good strategy, good execution, or the combination of both.

KEY TERMS

ambidextrous structure, 261
balanced scorecard, 247
behavioral controls, 254
culture, 239

functional structure, 243
implementation levers, 242
knowing-doing gap, 238
matrix structure, 245

multidivisional structure, 244
network structure, 246
organizational structure, 242
outcome controls, 254

patching, 263
reward system, 253

REVIEW QUESTIONS

1. What is strategy implementation?

2. How are formulation and implementation related?

3. What are the basic forms of organizational structure? When is each appropriate?

4. What are some common systems and processes that are relevant to strategy implementation?

5. How are people relevant to strategy formulation and implementation?

6. How can rewards affect strategy?

7. What are the roles of strategic leadership in successful strategy implementation?

8. How does globalization affect organization structure?

9. What are organizational solutions to the problems caused by dynamic environments?

10. What component of the strategy diamond maps most closely to issues related to strategy implementation?

How Would you Do That?

1. In the box entitled "How Would *You* Do That? 8.1," you learned how SAP America responded to performance problems primarily through changes in strategy implementation. Find one or two firms that were once high flyers but that have recently fallen on hard times. Are these hard times primarily a function of a flawed strategy, flawed strategy implementation, or both? Using SAP as an example, what changes would you suggest in terms of implementation?

2. The example of the NUWC in the box entitled "How Would *You* Do That? 8.2" demonstrated the strategy-mapping process and how to develop a balanced scorecard. Review Exhibits 8.7 and 8.8 and generate suggestions for specific objectives, measures, targets, and initiatives that would complete NUWC's use of the scorecard. If you prefer using the scorecard with a for-profit firm then apply the framework from scratch to a firm of your choosing.

3. Choose an aspect of your firm's strategy in StratSim that has not been as successful as you planned or hoped and determine why the shortfall occurred. Was it due to flawed strategy? If so, what assumptions did you make that were not valid? If it was due to flawed execution, what could your firm do to improve its execution going forward? Did an altered, emergent strategy flow from this process?

GROUP ACTIVITIES

1. Apply the concepts of strategy formulation and implementation to your college experience. What was your objective in going to college? When did your strategy for achieving this objective emerge? Has it ever changed? How would you adapt the implementation levers and strategic leadership roles to evaluate how well you have implemented your strategy? What is your overall personal evaluation?

2. Refer to the opening case on Gore. Assume that, for reasons of estate planning, the Gore family (75 percent owners of the company) decided to take the company public through an IPO. What would be the effect on the firm's strategy and implementation practices if this were to happen? What, if anything, would need to change?

3. Choose the two products in StratSim that contribute the most to your gross margin and compare the impact of a cost reduction upgrade on each (that is, an upgrade with no changes, but that reduces the unit cost of the product). Assume that only one of these projects could be implemented (perhaps due to a limitation on development centers). Which one has the greatest positive impact on your business? Show your work and assumptions. Now compare that project with an equivalent investment in technology. Which is preferable? Which comparision was easier to perform and why?

ENDNOTES

1. www.gore.com/en_xx/aboutus/timeline/index.html (accessed November 16, 2005); D. Anfuso, "Gore Values Shape W. L. Gore's Innovative Culture," *Workforce* 78:3 (1999), 48–53; www.hoovers.com.

2. K. R. Andrews, *The Concept of Corporate Strategy* (Homewood, IL: Irwin, 1987); *The Strategy Execution Imperative: Leading Practices for Implementing Strategic Initiatives* (Corporate Executive Board, 2001); C. M. Christensen, "Making Strategy: Learning by Doing," *Harvard Business Review* 75:6 (1997), 141–156.

3. D. Hambrick and A. Cannella, "Strategy Implementation as Substance and Selling," *Academy of Management Executive* 3:4 (1989), 278–285.

4. P. C. Judge, "How Will Your Company Adapt?" *Fast Company* 128 (2001); S. Ellison, "P&G Is to Buy Glide Dental Floss, A Popular Brand," *Wall Street Journal*, September 17, 2003, A19.

5. M. Porter, "Know Your Place: How to Assess the Attractiveness of Your Industry and Your Company's Position in It," *Inc.*, September 1991, 90.

6. P. F. Drucker, *The Practice of Management* (New York: HarperCollins, 1954), 352–353.

7. R. Ruggles, "The State of the Notion: Knowledge Management in Practice," *California Management Review* 40 (1998), 82–83.

8. J. Pfeffer and R. I. Sutton, *The Knowing-Doing Gap* (Boston: Harvard Business School Press, 2000).

9. J. R. Kotter and J. L. Heskett, *Corporate Culture and Performance* (New York: Free Press, 1992); C. A. O'Reilly and J. A. Chatman, "Culture as Social Control: Corporations, Culture and Commitment," in B. M. Staw and L. L. Cummings, eds., *Research in Organizational Behavior* 18 (Greenwich, CT: JAI

Press, 1996), 157–200; J. B. Sønrensen, "The Strength of Corporate Culture and the Reliability of Firm Performance," *Administrative Science Quarterly* 47 (2002), 70–91.

10. Kotter and Heskett, *Corporate Culture and Performance.*

11. Sønrensen, "The Strength of Corporate Culture and the Reliability of Firm Performance."

12. R. S. Burt, S. M. Gabbay, G. Holt, and P. Moran, "Contingent Organization as a Network Theory: The Culture Performance Contingency Function," *Acta Sociologica* 37 (1994), 345–370; Sønrensen, "The Strength of Corporate Culture and the Reliability of Firm Performance."

13. A. Slywotzky and D. Nadler, "The Strategy Is the Structure," *Harvard Business Review* 82:2 (2004), 16.

14. SAP Harvard Business School Case, SAP America 9-397-067, December 3, 1996.

15. Hambrick and Cannella, "Strategy Implementation as Substance and Selling," 278.

16. A. Chandler, *Strategy and Structure* (Cambridge, MA: MIT Press, 1962).

17. R. L. Daft, *Management*, 6th ed. (New York: Southwestern, 2003).

18. L. G. Hrebiniak and W. Joyce, *Implementing Strategy* (New York: MacMillan, 1984).

19. Chandler, *Strategy and Structure.*

20. Slywotzky and Nadler, "The Strategy Is the Structure," 16.

21. R. A. Burgelman, "Fading Memories: A Process Theory of Strategic Business Exit in Dynamic Environments," *Administrative Science Quarterly* 39 (1994), 24–56.

22. www.platypustech.com (accessed July 15, 2005).

23. www.emageon.com (accessed July 15, 2005).

24. C. K. Bart and M. C. Baetz, "The Relationship Between Mission Statements and Firm Performance: An Exploratory Study," *Journal of Management Studies* 35:6 (1998), 823–853.

25. W. G. Sanders and M. A. Carpenter, "Strategic Satisficing? A Behavioral-Agency Perspective on Stock Repurchase Announcements," *Academy of Management Journal* 46 (2003), 160–178.

26. G. Reilly and R. Reilly, "Using a Measure Network to Understand and Deliver Value," *Journal of Cost Management* 14:6 (2000), 5–14; R. Kaplan and D. Norton, *The Strategy-Focused Organization* (Watertown, MA: Harvard Business School Press, 2001).

27. "The Balanced Scorecard's Lessons for Managers," *Harvard Management Update*, October 2000, 4–5.

28. R. Simons, *Levers of Control: How Managers Use Innovative Control Systems* (Boston: Harvard Business School Press, 1995); M. J. Epstein and J. F. Manzoni, "The Balanced Scorecard & Tableau de Bord: A Global Perspective on Translating Strategy into Action," INSEAD Working Paper 97/63/AC/SM (1997).

29. E. Schonfeld, "Baby Bills," *Business 2.0* 4:9 (2003), 76–84.

30. Quote from BGI's head of human resources, Garret Bouton, in J. Pfeffer and R. I. Sutton, *The Knowing-Doing Gap*, 227.

31. J. Collins, "Level 5 Leadership," *Harvard Business Review* July–August (2001), 66–76.

32. J. Bradach, *Organizational Alignment: The 7-S Model* (Boston: Harvard Business School Publishing, 1996).

33. C. K. Prahalad and G. Hamel, "The Core Competence of the Corporation," *Harvard Business Review* 79:1 (1990), 1–14; R. Nelson and S. Winter, *An Evolutionary Theory of Economic Change* (Cambridge, MA: Harvard University Press, 1982); D. J. Teece, G. Pisano, and A. Shuen, "Dynamic Capabilities and Strategic Management," *Strategic Management Journal* 18 (1997), 509–534; K. M. Eisenhardt and J. A. Martin, "Dynamic Capabilities: What Are They?" *Strategic Management Journal* 21 (2000), 1105–1121.

34. B. Becker and B. Gerhart, "The Impact of Human Resource Management on Organizational Performance: Progress and Prospects," *Academy of Management Journal* 39 (1996), 779–802.

35. W. N. Davidson III, D. L. Worrell, and J. B. Fox, "Early Retirement Programs and Firm Performance," *Academy of Management Journal* 39 (1996), 970–985.

36. C. Chadwick, L. W. Hunter, and S. M. Walston, "The Effects of Downsizing Practices on Hospital Performance," *Strategic Management Journal* 25:5 (2004), 405–428.

37. M. A. Youndt, S. A. Snell, J. W. Dean Jr., and D. P. Lepak, "Human Resource Management, Manufacturing Strategy, and Firm Performance," *Academy of Management Journal* 39 (1996), 836–866.

38. See J. B. Barney and P. M. Wright, "On Becoming a Strategic Partner: The Role of Human Resources in Gaining Competitive Advantage," *Human Resource Management* 37 (1998), 31–46; J. Pfeffer, *Competitive Advantage Through People* (Boston: Harvard Business School Press, 1994).

39. J. Pfeffer, *The Human Equation* (Boston: Harvard Business School Press, 1998).

40. F. Luthans and C. M. Yousseff, "Human, Social, and Now Positive Psychological Capital Management: Investing in People for Competitive Advantage," *Organization Dynamics* 33:2 (2004), 143–160.

41. R. W. Coff, "Human Assets and Management Dilemmas: Coping with Hazards on the Road to Resource-Based Theory," *Academy of Management Review* 22 (1997), 374–402.

42. See Coff, "Human Assets and Management Dilemmas."

43. B. Gerhart and S. Rynes, *Compensation* (Beverly Hills, CA: Sage Publications, 2003).

44. J. Kerr and J. Slocum, "Managing Corporate Culture Through Reward Systems," *Academy of Management Executive* 1:2 (1987), 99–108.

45. C. W. L. Hill, M. A. Hitt, and R. E. Hoskisson, "Cooperative Versus Competitive Structures in Related and Unrelated Diversified Firms," *Organization Science* 3 (1992), 501–521.

46. CIBC Corporate and Investment Banking (A). Harvard Business School Publishing, 1999.

47. Adapted from W. C. Kim and R. Mauborgne, "Charting Your Company's Future," *Harvard Business Review* 80:6 (2002), 76–82.

48. Hambrick and Cannella, "Strategy Implementation as Substance and Selling," 278–285.

49. N. Wreden, "Executive Champions: The Vital Link Between Strategy Formulation and Implementation," *Harvard Management Update* 7:9 (2002), 3–5.

50. www.clemmer.net/excerpts/pf_credibility.html (accessed October 25, 2005).

51. The information in this section draws heavily upon the work of Christopher Bartlett and Sumantra Ghoshal, *Managing Across Borders: The Transnational Solution* (Boston: Harvard Business School Press, 1989).

52. Bartlett and Ghoshal, *Managing Across Borders.*

53. M. A. Carpenter, W. G. Sanders, and H. B. Gregersen, "Bundling Human Capital with Organizational Context: The Impact of International Assignment Experience on Multinational Firm Performance and CEO Pay," *Academy of Management Journal* 44 (2001), 493–511.

54. Y. Gong, "Subsidiary Staffing in Multinational Enterprises: Agency, Resources, and Performance," *Academy of Management Journal* 46 (2003), 728–739.

55. Gong, "Subsidiary Staffing in Multinational Enterprises."

56. C. Christensen, *The Innovator's Dilemma* (Boston: Harvard Business School Press, 1997).

57. C. A. O'Reilly and M. L. Tushman, "The Ambidextrous Organization," *Harvard Business Review* 82:4 (May–June 2004), 74–81.

58. For details of this study, see O'Reilly and Tushman, "The Ambidextrous Organization."

59. This section draws heavily on K. M. Eisenhardt and S. L. Brown, "Patching: Restitching Business Portfolios in Dynamic Markets," *Harvard Business Review* 77:3 (1999), 72–82.

Glossary

acquisition Strategy by which one firm acquires another through stock purchase or exchange.

acquisition premium Difference between current market value of a target firm and purchase price paid to induce its shareholders to turn its control over to new owners.

agency problem Separation of its ownership from managerial control of a firm.

agent Party, such as a manager, who acts on behalf of another party.

ambidextrous structure Organizational structure for dynamic contexts in which project teams are organized as structurally independent units and encouraged to develop their own structures, systems, and processes.

arena Area (product, service, distribution channel, geographic markets, technology, etc.) in which a firm participates.

balanced scorecard Strategic management support system for measuring vision and strategy against business- and operating-unit-level performance.

barrier to entry Condition under which it is more difficult to join or compete in an industry.

behavioral controls Practice of tying rewards to criteria other than simply financial performance, such as those broadly identified in the balanced scorecard.

board of directors Group of individuals that formally represents the firm's shareholders and oversees the work of top executives.

bootstrapping Process of finding creative ways to support a startup business financially until it turns profitable.

business strategy Strategy for competing against rivals within a particular industry.

buyer power Degree to which firms in the buying industry are able to dictate terms on purchase agreements which extract some of the profit that would otherwise go to competitors in the focal industry.

CAGE framework Tool that considers the dimensions of culture, administration, geography, and economics to assess the distance created by global expansion.

capabilities A firm's skill at using its resources to create goods and services; combination of

procedures and expertise on which a firm relies to produce goods and services.

causal ambiguity Condition whereby the difficulty of identifying or understanding a resource or capability makes it valuable, rare, and inimitable.

codes of governance Ideal governance standards formulated by regulatory, market, and government institutions.

coevolution Process by which diversification causes two or more interdependent businesses to adapt not only to their environment, but to each other.

commoditization Process during industry evolution by which sales eventually come to depend less on unique product features and more on price.

competitive advantage A firm's ability to create *value* in a way that its rivals cannot.

complementor Firm in one industry that provides products or services which tend to increase sales in another industry.

conglomerate Corporation consisting of many companies in different businesses or industries.

consortia Association of several companies and/or governments for some definite strategic purpose.

co-opetition Situation in which firms are simultaneously competitors in one market and collaborators in another.

core competence Capability which is central to a firm's main business operations and which allow it to generate new products and services.

corporate governance The system by which owners of firms direct and control the affairs of the firm.

corporate new venturing New-venture creation by established firms.

corporate renewal Outcome of successful strategic change in the context of an established business.

corporate strategy Strategy for guiding a firm's entry and exit from different businesses, for determining how a parent company adds value to and manages its portfolio of businesses, and for creating value through diversification.

cross-subsidizing Practice by which a firm uses profits from one aspect of a product, service, or region to support other aspects of competitive activity.

culture Core organizational values widely held and shared by an organization's members.

differentiation Strategic position based on products or offers services with quality, reliability, or prestige that is discernibly higher than that of competitors and for which customers are willing to pay.

differentiator Feature or attribute of a company's product or service (e.g., image, customization, technical superiority, price, quality and reliability) that helps it beat its competitors in the marketplace.

diseconomies of scope Condition under which the joint output of two or more products within a single firm results in increased average costs.

diseconomy of scale Condition under which average total costs per unit of production increases at higher levels of input.

disruptive technology Breakthrough product- or process-related technology that destroys the competencies of incumbent firms in an industry.

distinctive competence Capability that sets a firm apart from other firms; something that a firm can do which competitors cannot.

diversification Degree to which a firm conducts business in more than one arena.

divestiture Strategy whereby a company sells off a business or division.

dominant logic Way in which managers view the firm's competitive activities and make corporate resource-allocation decisions.

due diligence Initial pre-closing screening, analysis, and negotiations for an acquisition.

dynamic capabilities A firm's ability to modify, reconfigure, and upgrade resources and capabilities in order to strategically respond to or generate environmental changes.

economic logic Means by which a firm will earn a profit by implementing a strategy.

economy of scale Condition under which average total cost for a unit of production is lower at higher levels of output.

economy of scope Condition under which lower total average costs result from sharing resources to produce more than one product or service.

entrepreneurial process Integration of opportunity recognition, key resources and capabilities, and an entrepreneur and entrepreneurial team to create a new venture.

entrepreneurship Recognition of opportunities and the use of resources and capabilities to implement innovative ideas for new ventures.

equity alliance Alliance in which one or more partners assumes a greater ownership interest in either the alliance or another partner.

escalation of commitment Decision-making bias under which people are willing to commit additional resources to a failing course of action.

ethnocentrism Belief in the superiority of one's own ethnic group or, more broadly, the conviction that one's own national, group, or cultural characteristics are "normal."

exit barriers Barriers that impose a high cost on the abandonment of a market or product.

exporting Foreign-country entry vehicle in which a firm uses an intermediary to perform most foreign marketing functions.

first mover Firm choosing to initiate a strategic action, whether the introduction of a new product or service or the development of a new process.

five-forces model Framework for evaluating industry structure according to the effects of rivalry, threat of entry, supplier power, buyer power, and the threat of substitutes.

focused cost leadership Strategic position based on being a low-cost leader in a narrow market segment.

focused differentiation Strategic position based on targeting products to relatively small segments.

foreign direct investment (FDI) Foreign-country entry vehicle by which a firm commits to the direct ownership of a foreign subsidiary or division.

functional structure Form of organization revolving around specific value-chain functions.

general resources Resource that can be exploited across a wide range of activities.

generic strategies Strategic position designed to reduce the effects of rivalry, including *low-cost, differentiation, focused cost leadership,* *focused differentiation,* and *integrated positions.*

geographic roll-up Strategy whereby a firm acquires many other firms in the same industry segment but in different geographic arenas in an attempt to create significant scale and scope advantages.

geographic scope Breadth and diversity of geographic arenas in which a firm operates.

global configuration Strategy by which a firm sacrifices local responsiveness for the lower costs associated with global efficiency.

globalization Evolution of distinct geographic product markets into a state of globally interdependent product markets.

goals and objectives Combination of a broad indication of organizational intentions (*goals*) and specific, measurable steps (*objectives*) for reaching them.

greenfield investment Form of FDI in which a firm starts a new foreign business from the ground up.

high-end disruption Strategy that may result in huge new markets in which new players redefine industry rules to unseat the largest incumbents.

horizontal alliance Alliance involving a focal firm and another firm in the same industry.

horizontal scope Extent to which a firm participates in related market segments or industries outside its existing value-chain activities.

hubris Exaggerated self-confidence that can result in managers' overestimating the value of a potential acquisition, having unrealistic assumptions about the ability to create synergies, and a willingness to pay too much for a transaction.

illusion of control Decision-making bias under which people believe that they're in greater control of a situation than rational analysis would support.

illusion of favorability Decision-making bias under which people tend to give themselves more credit for their successes and take less responsibility for their failures.

illusion of optimism Decision-making bias that leads people to underestimate the prospect of negative future events while overestimating the prospect of positive outcomes.

implementation levers Mechanisms used by strategic leaders to help execute a firm's strategy.

importing Internationalization strategy by which a firm brings a good, service, or capital into the home country from abroad.

improvisation Managerial practices that contribute to a culture of frequent change, especially in turbulent or hypercompetitive contexts.

incentive alignment Use of incentives to align managerial self-interest with shareholders'.

industry life cycle Pattern of evolution followed by an industry inception to current and future states.

initial public offering (IPO) First sale of a company's stock to the public market.

institutional investors Pension or mutual fund that manages large sums of money for third-party investors.

integrated position Strategic position in which elements of one position suport strong standing in another.

international configuration The firm leverages key resources and capabilities by centralizing them to achieve economies of scale, but it decentralizes others, such as marketing, so that some activities can be somewhat localized.

international strategy Process by which a firm approaches its cross-border activities and those of competitors and plans to approach them in the future.

intrinsic value Present value of a company's future cash flows from existing assets and businesses.

joint venture Alliance in which two firms make equity investments in a third legal entity.

key success factor (KSF) Key asset or requisite skill that all firms in an industry must possess in order to be a viable competitor.

knowing-doing gap Phenomenon whereby firms tend to be better at generating new knowledge than at creating new products based on that knowledge.

learning curve Incremental production costs decline at a constant rate as production experience is gained; the steeper the learning curve, the more rapidly costs decline.

Level 5 Hierarchy Model of leadership skills calling for a wide range of abilities, some of which are hierarchical in nature.

long-term incentive plans Incentive plan tying future bonus payouts to defined accounting-return targets over a three- to five-year period.

low-cost leadership Strategic position based on producing a good or offering a service while maintaining total costs that are lower than what it takes competitors to offer the same product or service.

low-end disruption Strategy that appears at the low end of industry offerings, targeting the least desirable of incumbents' customers.

managerialism Tendency of managers to make decisions based on personal self-interest rather than the best interests of shareholders.

market for corporate control Phenomenon by which the possibility that corporate control can be shifted to competitors or other buyers encourages management to operate a firm effectively and ethically.

market value Current market capitalization of a firm.

matrix structure Form of organization in which specialists from functional departments are assigned to work for one or more product or geographic units.

merger Consolidation or combination of two or more firms.

minimum efficient scale (MES) The output level that delivers the lowest total average cost.

mission Declaration of what a firm is and what it stands for—its fundamental values and purpose.

monitoring Functioning of the board in exercising its legal and fiduciary responsibility to oversee executives' behavior and performance and to take action when it's necessary to replace management.

multidivisional structure Form of organization in which divisions are organized around product or geographic markets and are often self-sufficient in terms of functional expertise.

multinational configuration Strategy by which a firm is essentially a portfolio of geographically removed business units that have devoted most of their resources and capabilities to maximizing local responsiveness and uniqueness.

network structure Form of organization in which small, semiautonomous, and potentially temporary groups are brought together for specific purposes.

new-venture creation Entrepreneurship and the creation of a new business from scratch.

nonequity alliance Alliance that involves neither the assumption of equity interest nor the creation of separate organizations.

organizational structure Relatively stable arrangement of responsibilities, tasks, and people within an organization.

outcome controls Practice of tying rewards to narrowly defined financial criteria.

outsourcing Activity performed for a company by people other than its full-time employees.

overconfidence bias Decision-making bias under which people tend to place erroneously high levels of confidence in their own knowledge or abilities.

patching Process of remapping businesses in accordance with changing market conditions and restitches them into new internal business structures.

PESTEL analysis Tool for assessing the political, economic, sociocultural, technological, environmental, and legal contexts in which a firm operates.

portfolio planning Practice of mapping diversified businesses or products based on their relative strengths and market attractiveness.

principal Party, such as a shareholder, who hires an agent to act on his or her behalf.

profit pool Analytical tool that enables managers to calculate profits at various points along an industry value chain.

purchase price Final price actually paid to the target firm's shareholders of an acquired company.

real-options analysis Process of maximizing the upside or limiting the downside of an investment opportunity by uncovering and quantifying the options and discussion points embedded within it.

related diversification Form of diversification in which the business units operated by a firm are highly related.

relational quality Principle identifying four key elements (initial conditions, negotiation process, reciprocal experiences, outside behavior) in establishing and maintaining interorganizational trust.

resources Inputs used by firms to create products and services.

reward system Bases on which employees are compensated and promoted.

rivalry Intensity of competition within an industry.

road show Series of presentations in which top management promotes an IPO to interested investors and analysts.

S-1 statement Legal document outlining a firm's financial position in preparation for an initial public stock offering.

second mover (often *fast follower*) Second significant company to move into a market, quickly following the first mover.

self-serving fairness bias Decision-making bias under which people believe that they're fair and want to act in ways that are perceived as fair and just.

serial acquirers Company that engages in frequent acquisitions.

simple rules Basic rules for guiding improvisation by defining strategy without confining it.

specialized resources Resource with a narrow range of applicability.

staging Timing and pace of strategic moves.

stakeholder Individual or group with an interest in an organization's ability to deliver intended results and maintain the viability of its products and services.

stereotyping Relying on a conventional or formulaic conception of another group based on some common characteristic.

stock options Incentive device giving an employee the right to buy a share of company stock at a later date for a predetermined price.

straddling Unsuccessful attempt to integrate both low-cost and differentiation positions.

strategic alliance Relationship in which two or more firms combine resources and capabilities in order to enhance the competitive advantage of all parties.

strategic change Significant changes in resource allocation choices, in the business and implementation activities that align the firm's strategy with its vision, or in its vision.

strategic coherence Symmetric coalignment of the five elements of the firm's strategy, the congruence of functional-area policies with these elements, and the overarching fit of various businesses under the corporate umbrella.

strategic group Subset of firms which, because of similar strategies, resources, and capabilities, compete against each other more intensely than with other firms in an industry.

strategic leadership Task of managing an overall enterprise and influencing key organizational outcomes.

strategic management Process by which a firm incorporates the tools and frameworks for developing and implementing a strategy.

strategic positioning Means by which managers situate a firm relative to its rivals.

strategic purpose Simplified, widely shared mental model of the organization and its future, including anticipated changes in its environment.

strategy Central, integrated, externally focused concept of how the firm will achieve its objectives.

strategy formulation Process of developing a strategy.

strategy implementation Process of executing a strategy.

succession planning Process of managing a well-planned and well-executed transition from one CEO to the next with positive outcomes for all key stakeholders.

superordinate goal Overarching reference point for a host of hierarchical subgoals.

supplier power Degree to which firms in the supply industry are able to dictate terms to contracts and thereby extract some of the profit that would otherwise be available to competitors in the focal industry.

synergy Condition under which the combined benefits of activities in two or more arenas are greater than the simple sum of those benefits.

synergy value Difference between the combined values of the target and the acquiring firm after the transaction and the sum of the values of the two firms taken independently.

takeoff period Period during which a new product generates rapid growth and huge sales increases.

threat of new entry Degree to which new competitors can enter an industry and intensify rivalry.

threat of substitutes Degree to which products of one industry can satisfy the same demand as those of another.

transnational configuration Strategy in which a firm tries to capitalize on both local responsiveness and global efficiency.

unrelated diversification Form of diversification in which the business units that a firm operates are highly dissimilar.

value chain Total of primary and support value-adding activities by which a firm produces, distributes, and markets a product.

value curve A graphical depiction of how a firm and major groups of its competitors are competing across its industry's factors of completion.

value-net model Map of a firm's existing and potential exchange relationships.

vehicle Means for entering new arenas (e.g., through acquisitions, alliances, internal development, etc.).

vertical alliance Alliance involving a focal firm and a supplier or customer.

vertical integration Diversification into upstream and/or downstream industries.

vertical scope The extent to which a firm is vertically integrated.

vision Simple statement or understanding of what the firm will be in the future.

VRINE model Analytical framework suggesting that a firm with resources and capabilities which are valuable, rare, inimitable, non-substitutable, and exploitable will gain a competitive advantage.

willingness to pay Principle of differentiation strategy by which customers are willing to pay more for certain product features.

winner's curse Situation in which a winning M&A bidder must live with the consequences of paying too much for the target.

Name Index

Organization/Product Index

Subject Index

Photo Credits

CHAPTER 1

2, Getty Images, Inc.–Liaison/Gilles Mingasson
2, Getty Images Inc.–Hulton Archive Photos/Peter Keegan
3, AP Wide World Photos
11, Rolls-Royce International Limited
14, AP Wide World Photos
19, AP Wide World Photos

CHAPTER 2

28, Getty Images/Time Life Pictures
28, AP Wide World Photos
29, Courtesy of Xerox
29, AP Wide World Photos/Doug Kanter
29, Courtesy of Xerox
33, AP Wide World Photos
53, AP Wide World Photos

CHAPTER 3

64, AP Wide World Photos
64, Intel Corporation Pressroom Photo Archives
65, Corbis/SABA Press Photos, Inc./Shepard Sherbell
65, AP Wide World Photos
76, PhotoEdit/Felicia Martinez
78, Michael L. Abramson Photography
86, Getty Images, Inc.–Liaison/Pam Francis

CHAPTER 4

92, Corbis/Sygma
92, AP Wide World Photos
92, AP Wide World Photos
93, Getty Images, Inc.–Liaison/Alex Wong
93, AP Wide World Photos
101, Getty Images, Inc.–Agence France Presse/Pascal Pavani
108, Index Stock Imagery, Inc.

CHAPTER 5

130, Courtesy of Trek Bicycle Corp.
130, Courtesy of Trek Bicycle Corp.
131, AP Wide World Photos
131, Courtesy of Trek Bicycle Corp.
133, Corbis/Sygma/Jacques Langevin
138, Getty Images/Matthew Peyton
154, NewsCom/Kamenko Pajic

CHAPTER 6

162, AP Wide World Photos/Dan Loh
162, AP Wide World Photos
162, NewsCom/Jeff Christensen
163, Getty Images, Inc.–Agence France Presse/Robyn Beck
163, Getty Images, Inc.–Liaison/Chris Hondros
167, Getty Images, Inc.–Agence France Presse/Yoshikazu Tsuno
173, Myrleen Ferguson Cate
177, Badger Meter, Inc.

CHAPTER 7

200, AP Wide World Photos
200, Getty Images, Inc.–Agence France Presse/Prakash Singh
201, Landov LLC/Kyodo/Tai Qisen
209, AP Wide World Photos
220, SABMiller plc
230, Courtesy of Lincoln Electric Co.

CHAPTER 8

234, Photo Researchers, Inc./Courtesy of NASA
234, W. L. Gore & Associates, Inc.
235, W. L. Gore & Associates, Inc./Ace Kavoli
235, AP Wide World Photos
244, Courtesy of Platypus Technologies, LLC
252, Getty Images Inc.–Stone Allstock/Doug Armand
258, AP Wide World Photo